Books By Robert Coles

CHILDREN OF CRISIS I: A STUDY OF COURAGE AND FEAR

STILL HUNGRY IN AMERICA

THE IMAGE IS YOU

UPROOTED CHILDREN

WAGES OF NEGLECT (WITH MARIA PIERS)

DRUGS AND YOUTH (WITH JOSEPH BRENNER AND DERMOT MEAGHER)

ERIK H. ERIKSON: THE GROWTH OF HIS WORK

THE MIDDLE AMERICANS (WITH JON ERIKSON)

THE GEOGRAPHY OF FAITH (WITH DANIEL BERRIGAN)

MIGRANTS, SHARECROPPERS, MOUNTAINEERS (VOLUME II OF CHILDREN OF C

THE SOUTH GOES NORTH (VOLUME III OF CHILDREN OF CRISIS)

FAREWELL TO THE SOUTH

A SPECTACLE UNTO THE WORLD: THE CATHOLIC WORKER MOVEMENT (WIT
    ERIKSON)

THE OLD ONES OF NEW MEXICO (WITH ALEX HARRIS)

THE BUSES ROLL (WITH CAROL BALDWIN)

THE DARKNESS AND THE LIGHT (WITH DORIS ULMANN)

IRONY IN THE MIND'S LIFE: ESSAYS ON NOVELS BY JAMES AGEE, ELIZABETH E
    AND GEORGE ELIOT

WILLIAM CARLOS WILLIAMS: THE KNACK OF SURVIVAL IN AMERICA

THE MIND'S FATE: WAYS OF SEEING PSYCHIATRY AND PSYCHOANALYSIS

ESKIMOS, CHICANOS, INDIANS (VOLUME IV OF CHILDREN OF CRISIS)

PRIVILEGED ONES: THE WELL-OFF AND THE RICH IN AMERICA (VOLUME
    CHILDREN OF CRISIS)

A FESTERING SWEETNESS (POEMS)

THE LAST AND FIRST ESKIMOS (WITH ALEX HARRIS)

WOMEN OF CRISIS: LIVES OF STRUGGLE AND HOPE (WITH JANE COLES)

WALKER PERCY: AN AMERICAN SEARCH

For Children

DEAD END SCHOOL

THE GRASS PIPE

SAVING FACE

RIDING FREE

HEADSPARKS

ESKIMOS, CHICANOS, INDIANS

ESKIMOS, CHICANOS, INDIANS

Volume IV of *Children of Crisis*

ROBERT COLES, M.D.

with illustrations

LITTLE, BROWN AND COMPANY
BOSTON · TORONTO · LONDON

"Listening in October" by John Haines.
Copyright © 1963 by John Haines. Reprinted from *Winter News* by permission of Wesleyan University Press.

LIBRARY OF CONGRESS CATALOGING IN PUBLICATION DATA

Coles, Robert.
    Eskimos, Chicanos, Indians.

    (His Children of crisis; v. 4)

    Bibliography: p.
    Includes index.
        1. Eskimos—Alaska—Children. 2. Indians of
North America—Children. 3. Mexican American
children. 4. Eskimos—Alaska—Social conditions.
5. Indians of North America—Social conditions.
6. Mexican Americans—Social conditions.
I. Title.
HC110.P6C56   vol. 4   [E99.E7]   309.1'73'092s   77-21430
ISBN 0-316-15162-9   [309.1'73'092]

10 9 8 7 6 5 4 3 2

MV

*Published simultaneously in Canada
by Little, Brown & Company (Canada) Limited*

PRINTED IN THE UNITED STATES OF AMERICA

*In memory of Robert Francis Kennedy
and to the Eskimo children, Chicano children, and
Indian children of the United States of America*

Who hath believed our report? and to whom is the arm of the Lord revealed?

For he shall grow up before him as a tender plant, and as a root out of a dry ground: he hath no form nor comeliness; and when we shall see him, there is no beauty that we should desire Him.

He is despised and rejected of men; a man of sorrows, and acquainted with grief: and we hid as it were our faces from him; he was despised, and we esteemed him not.

Surely he hath borne our griefs, and carried our sorrows: yet we did esteem him stricken, smitten of God, and afflicted.

But he was wounded for our transgressions, he was bruised for our iniquities: the chastisement of our peace was upon him; and with his stripes we are healed.

All we like sheep have gone astray; we have turned every one to his own way; and the Lord hath laid on him the iniquity of us all.

He was oppressed, and he was afflicted, yet he opened not his mouth: he is brought as a lamb to the slaughter, and as a sheep before her shearers is dumb, so he openeth not his mouth.

He was taken from prison and from judgment: and who shall declare his generation? For he was cut off out of the land of the living: for the transgression of my people was he stricken.

Isaiah, 53:1–8

FOREWORD

WHEN I was writing the forewords to the second and third volumes of *Children of Crisis*, I made mention of the Spanish-speaking children of Texas and New Mexico I was already working with, the Indian children I had begun to see, and the Eskimo children I hoped soon to meet. Those two volumes were published at the same time because they take up, really, two sides of a coin — the way rural poor children, black and white, of the South and Appalachia grow up and the way ghetto children, so often brought from the South and Appalachia to our northern cities by desperate parents, also try to make sense of the world. I didn't sit down and write Volume II of the series and then, when done, begin Volume III. I would write one section of the second volume (on share-croppers, for instance) and then write a section of the third volume that had to do with children born to sharecropping parents who had moved into an urban ghetto. I was constantly crisscrossing, trying to use whatever knowledge I had ac-quired in the rural South or up in the mountains of Appalachia to understand the children who live in cities like Chicago, Cleveland, Detroit. For many urban children their parents' experiences as migrant farm workers, sharecroppers, or Ap-palachian mountaineers got fitted into a crowded slum tenement, with no earth, never mind grass, crops, trees, or hills, in sight. And increasingly, blacks in our northern cities, or the Appalachian whites who have ventured to some of them, have begun to return "home" — for good, as opposed to the traditional holiday and vacation journeys "back." Enough have been doing so to make for a historical reversal of sorts — and a reminder of what might have been spared this nation had terribly adverse social, economic, and political forces been challenged head-on and denied their fateful power over the lives of millions of hard-pressed American families.

I mentioned in Volume II of *Children of Crisis* that an increasing number of the migrants who work in the so-called eastern stream (a Public Health Service expression that refers to travel along the Atlantic seaboard, from Florida to Maine and back) have in recent years become Spanish-speaking people who have come east from the Rio Grande Valley of Texas for work, as opposed to the Midwest or the Pacific Northwest. (A substantial number of Puerto Rican people also have become involved in migrant work in states like New Jersey, New York, Connecticut, and Massachusetts.) Once migrants in the southern states were the region's former sharecroppers and tenant farmers; now about a third of those migrants are Spanish-speaking, come east from Texas (and before that Mexico) in search of work, money, a better chance for survival.

Their leaders, fighting hard for unions to represent thousands of poorly paid and extremely vulnerable working men, women, and children, call themselves, call all the Spanish-speaking people they work with and on behalf of, Chicanos. Many of the people themselves say they are "from Mexico" or "from Texas." (How chary they are of simply referring to themselves as Americans, even when they have been born on our side of the Rio Grande!) Often in the past they have been called Mexican-Americans or, alas, an assortment of crude, vulgar names by white people and, upon occasion, by their own kind — as happens among all groups subject to prejudice and exploitation. I have decided to refer to them in this book as Chicanos; for one thing, I feel close to and emphatically side with the efforts of Cesar Chavez and others to bring farm workers into the labor movement; and besides, the term *Chicano* is a strong one — increasingly the preferred one among the particular people I have come to know longest, in Florida and Texas. I have to add, however, that the word *Chicano* does not at all enjoy the favor of the old Spanish-speaking people (Hispano-Americans) I came to know in New Mexico, while working with Pueblo Indian children. (I have discussed the matter of who calls whom what in *The Old Ones of New Mexico.*)

It was in southern Florida that I began visiting Chicano families — part of my work with the state's large farm worker population, much of it made up of migrants who spend most of their time in the Lake Okeechobee region but go north annually, come May or June, and return in September or October. At first I was going to include a chapter or two about Chicano children in Volume II of *Children of Crisis,* in the section dealing with migrants. But I began to see over the years that there were significant social and cultural distinctions between the Chicanos and the blacks. The sustained impact of those distinctions upon children required more than a qualification or two, even of chapter length.

In 1968, at which time I had spent a decade doing the kind of work I was then writing up for Volumes II and III of *Children of Crisis,* my wife and I made a critical decision. I had first come to know Senator Robert F. Kennedy in 1965 when I testified before him and others about the problems of our cities. I came to know him much better in 1967 when he showed a strong and influential interest in the hunger and malnutrition a group of us physicians had documented in Mississippi. In my book *Still Hungry in America,* which came out in 1969 and, like this one, is dedicated to Robert Kennedy, I tried to describe how the children of America's poor grow up. Chicano boys and girls were among those children I knew and had testified about. By the middle 1960s Robert Kennedy had made clear his support of Cesar Chavez and his great interest in helping Eskimo, Chicano, and Indian children, as well as the black and Appalachian children he had taken pains to visit and stand up for. One day in early 1968, as we talked about the impoverished, hungry, and often enough sick young people we both had seen in the delta of Mississippi and in various hollows of Appalachia, he suddenly turned to me (he could concentrate upon one the most relentless, unflinching, penetrating of stares) and asked me: "What about the Chicano children, and Indian children and Eskimo children of this country? How do we make things better for them?"

He had no answers to his questions; he knew full well how hard it was going to be for anyone, even a person as powerful and influential as himself, even himself as President of the United States, to change many of this nation's priorities. Nor was he anxious to be seen as a great "benefactor," the man who distributes alms, mouths pieties, and becomes increasingly smug. He was, finally, what some of his enemies called him, a tough fighter who knew quite well the strength of his adversaries — in this case all sorts of "principalities and powers" that bear down upon children as much as their parents do. With no faith that I could do a thousandth of what he could do, I told Robert Kennedy that I would extend my work to the children he had mentioned, try hard to comprehend the nature of their lives, and evoke for others what I had witnessed and felt to be important.

A promise easier to make than to fulfill, as one learns rather quickly out in that "field" anthropologists and other social scientists refer to. And a promise once almost put aside. In the spring of 1968, as I wrote Volumes II and III, I was convinced that I had done all I could do, so far as "fieldwork" goes — and to no effect at all, if the futures of the children I was writing about were to be the measure of success. I will not deny that things do indeed happen between an "observer" and those who get called the "observed." Learning goes back and forth: the observer's ignorance, arrogance, condescension, and self-regard have to contend with the minds and hearts of those who may be vulnerable, but who can have at the same time a keen eye for the banalities and worse that "more important" people keep uttering. There are, of course, other sides to the "relationship" — good exchanges, reasonably honest times, warm and affectionate moments that light the darkness and at least point in a direction. But for millions of blacks or Appalachian whites, in rural areas or in our ghettos, Volumes II and III of *Children of Crisis* meant nothing, utterly nothing; and I knew that would be the case as I wrote them.

One hopes; one hopes against hope that somehow it will make a little difference; only a little, but still some, if people mostly unknown to almost all of us get better known to more of us. Nevertheless, in 1968 I was doubtful — and I still am. Then came June 1968, the assassinations of Martin Luther King, Jr., and Robert Kennedy, followed by the election of Richard M. Nixon to the presidency. What is the point of studying and writing books about the ordinary struggles of poor and working-class people when the country's leadership is, at the very minimum, uninterested in the fate of such people? Many of the students I knew in the civil-rights struggle of the 1960s asked that question of themselves as they returned to academic life in 1968 — and yet they knew, even as they voiced their bewilderment, that one has to persist, keep loyal to the ideals and purposes one has tried to set clear for oneself. I have no illusions that anything I write will make life easier or better for the Chicano, Indian, or Eskimo children I have come to know these past years. I do hope, though, that it may eventually be of use to let others (relatively privileged, far removed, but interested enough to wade their way through these rather numerous pages) get some sense of how a number of Eskimo, Chicano, and Indian children feel and think.

I am interested in illuminating, as best I can, various psychological, anthropological, or sociological abstractions that have been fixed upon Eskimos, Chicanos, Indians. I have been working with the active assistance of a number of children, who have been patient teachers; they have given me generously of themselves, offered me innumerable interior details, so to speak. Those details, those personal statements, those moments of self-scrutiny, pursued by boys and girls I have spent much time with over the years, may possibly give a certain individuality and dignity to their lives. Or so one hopes. It was after Robert Kennedy's death, in a long conversation with Chicano union organizers in the Rio Grande Valley, that I promised to continue doing the work that ultimately formed the basis of this book. Those men and women, tough and shrewd and fiercely determined, laughed at *me* contemptuously when I told them that I didn't see the point of continuing the likes of my work. Better that I join their picket lines, or stop kidding myself and join the psychiatric staff of a hospital, someplace, anyplace. But they would have no part of my coy demurrers. They insisted that they themselves, as Chicano organizers, often weren't able to understand how many of their own people come to think and feel as they do. (I would later on hear similar observations, almost confessions, at times, from Indian activists in New Mexico and Arizona, or up in

Alaska, from those Eskimos who are trying to alert their own people.) Those anxious to make changes — through protest, through laws — on behalf of others need to know more about their respective peoples.

So much for an explanation of how a "study" that I believed to be finished in 1968 would end up lasting another decade. I had told Robert Kennedy that I'd "go out West"; I told the Chicano labor organizers that I'd stay in Texas and later go west to New Mexico and California. And then there was my family — my wife and our children, who would not have it any other way! As the reader will see at the end, in the bibliographical essay, there is no shortage of books "about" Eskimos, Chicanos, Indians: so much written, so little done! Yet, I did hear from writers and scholars who live in the West and have tried to keep up with the so-called literature that not much has been set down about the way Eskimo, Chicano, and Indian children view themselves, the world around them, and others in it, meaning the omnipresent "white man" or "Anglo." Such a study might be useful to those — even on the "white" or "Anglo" side — trying to change the "condition" of three badly exploited people.

I have tried hard to indicate how the children I have met come to regard not only themselves, their parents or relatives or neighbors, their immediate circumstances, but their *lives* — the future ahead. Once again I call upon children's drawings as a way for younger children (from four or five to eleven or twelve) to "speak." Once again I call upon the children's words too. Once again I try to "place" the reader, give him or her a sense of where the children live, what the land is like, what the "givens" are — the social and political and economic facts of life.

Yet there is, I think, a distinct change of emphasis and tone in this book — as compared to its three predecessors. Since so much has been written about the history of the Indian, or the "culture" of the Eskimos, or the economic struggle of Cesar Chavez on behalf of Chicano fieldhands, I have tried to stay strictly within my own bounds as a clinician — one who has worked with certain children pediatrically (a number of them have been ill and needed medical help) and as a child psychiatrist.

The reader will observe that I have tried to construct a narrative that excludes myself as much as possible, and brings him or her directly to the children — *their* ideas, thoughts, hopes, fears, worries, expectations. I may well have made a mistake, given the limitations of words, not to mention my own shortcomings. But I must confess that it has been a relief, getting rid of myself during most of this book. The book is, of course, a mixture of the direct remarks of children and my attempt to select and choose from years of my own observations. As for the drawings, their significance may be explained either by the children themselves or interpreted by me. Finally, in a separate chapter at the end of each of the three major sections, more or less theoretical generalizations are to be found.

Enough of explanation and self-justification; I hope this volume works a little — helps some children teach the reader a few things and maybe alert his or her conscience to the compelling and necessary tasks ahead of us in this country. I conclude with some acknowledgments of continuing and enabling help: the Harvard University Health Services, where I have had a base, and the Ford Foundation, which has allowed me to wander about, do so in my own erratic way, and not fill out forms or come up with "research designs" or the other endless, sad, exhausting, intimidating baggage of social science "methodology." In that foundation I specifically want to mention and thank warmly Nancy Dennis, Edward Meade, Harold

Howe, McGeorge Bundy. In Alaska, I am grateful to Len Kammerling for his help in the first stages of my work there; in New Mexico, David Grant, for similar help at the beginning; in Texas, Joe Bernal and Albert Pena. As all of those people know, it didn't take long for me to "get lost" — disappear, it seemed, into particular homes. I only hope that the time spent in getting me "going" does not now seem completely wasted. I also wish to mention the friendship of Alex Harris, a fine young photographer who has worked with me in New Mexico and Alaska and taught me a lot about how to look, see, and keep my mouth shut. Many of the people I have worked with are not especially interested in talking — and their silences can frustrate one who is doubly dependent on words, as a psychiatrist and a writer. Alex reminded me often, without putting things in words, that one can be told something inadvertently, by signal, or tacitly, with a gesture, a look — and only much later hear words of confirmation. A photographer's wisdom.

In Cambridge there has been, all along, the attentive, circumspect, affectionate help of Kirk Felsman, of Bonnie Harris. Not for the first or last time, I refer to their utterly essential advice and support. The same holds for Peter Davison, editor and friend from the very start of this effort. His critical intelligence and breadth of sensibility have been a constant, invaluable source of encouragement. In Albuquerque and in the Rio Grande Valley and Kotzebue or Noorvik, Alaska, and in many other towns of the Southwest or Alaska, there has also been, all along, a wife's thoughtfulness and wisdom, her patience and determination — her insistence, really, that we (our entire family) go from place to place and do *our* work. One final matter: I have dedicated each of the volumes in this series to the children I have met in the course of doing the work and to others like them all over the country. I don't think any of them will mind if, in this one instance, I link Robert F. Kennedy's name to theirs. As one goes into many of their homes, and still sees his picture on the wall, and hears comment after comment, it becomes apparent how much he has meant and still means to them. As the boys and girls and their mothers and fathers so often say: God bless him.

CONTENTS

PART FOUR: CHICANO CHILDREN

PART FIVE: INDIAN CHILDREN

PART SIX: REFERENCES

PART ONE

THE SETTING

I

ONCE AND STILL THE FRONTIER

THE AMERICAN WEST still seems endless, untouched, even unknown. The West's land is not the land of the South; it is not a clearly defined mixture of plantations, farms, and copper-red earth covered, mostly, by piney woods. The West's land is not the land of the Appalachian highlands; it is not hollows, for the most part easily walked in a few hours, or valleys that are all too narrowly crowded by hills that may be tough and austere, but are rarely uninviting or unyielding. The West's land is certainly not the open land left in the East, conservation land, small national parks or so-called rural land — meaning, rather commonly, the space between cities that planners expect, eventually, to become more and more settled, to become, successively, "countryside," "developed land," then part of a town, a suburb, even a city. The West's land is not even the land of much of the Midwest: large, formidable cities like Chicago, St. Louis, or Omaha, hardly distinguishable from those in the East; highly developed agriculture — one farm after another, a productive network of family farms, or, in recent years, enormous agribusinesses whose wheat, corn, and cattle spread predictably over the vast flatlands, interrupted by rail lines, rivers, strategically placed towns.

Not that the West doesn't possess with its enormousness, its diversity of weather, land, and people, elements that dominate or characterize other regions of the United States. In the Southwest one can find cotton growing, if not antebellum homes; coal being mined, if not a "hollow-culture" that goes back a century or two; and cities like Los Angeles, San Francisco, Albuquerque, or Denver, which manage to offer and suffer from all that other cities elsewhere in the nation boast and complain of. To be more specific, the West, like the South, is migrant workers, living a life of virtual peonage, if not slavery. The West is widespread, racially connected poverty. The West is, like Appalachia, coal companies and utility companies, intent on taking what is there, no matter the devastation visited on the land, not to mention on the lives of many thousands of people. The West, like the Northeast, is cities with smog, the bewilderment of families newly arrived from farms, the guarded sovereignty of suburbs, each nervously looking at others nearby, and all in mortal fear of something called, these days, "the inner city."

But the West is also itself, much more than the sum of resemblances to other regions. To a degree every region is, among other things, a state of mind. Self-conscious plantation owners of Mississippi's delta or Boston brahmins are not the only Americans who proudly identify themselves by region. Even migrant farm workers, as rootless a people as one can find in the United States (except, perhaps, for some corporation executives) find it important to place themselves, locate themselves not only geographically but by race, religion, occupation, or, in the case of Chicanos, national ancestry. In Florida, among Spanish-speaking migrants, one hears talk of "Mexican-Americans from Texas," talk of how "different" they are — from those who once were themselves Mexican-Americans. Now they have become, at the very least, residents of Florida, if not Southerners. One Florida migrant with such a history makes plain what he has gone through and why he makes a distinction between his past and present situation: "Here it's no Valley; there's no Mexico across the river. When I was in Texas I could always cross over the border and become a Mexican, even if it was for a few hours. We worked for the Anglos, but they were only a few, and they would respect one of us, if he became a businessman and made money. Here we're like the colored; we have to watch our step. Here it's the South. I keep telling my children to be careful — there's no place to go, except to jail. They tried to send us to jail in Texas too; but we could usually slip away before they came. There's a lot more room in Texas than around here."

He goes on to spell out the particular social, economic, and racial problems he has encountered in the ten years he has spent as part of the so-called eastern migrant stream — one of thousands from Texas who have made Florida their base (November through May) if not their home. But as he does so he talks about space, room, a boundary, a river, a nation (Mexico) beyond; that is, he talks very much like those who once employed him, ordered him around, threatened him with the very expulsion from America he both wanted and dreaded. Eventually he expelled himself — from Texas but not America. He heard that he could make more money in Florida. He went east rather than south, where his heart would have taken him, or west, where others like him, not to mention many millions of Anglos (as he calls them), have sought a better life. And, at times, when he is not utterly exhausted or preoccupied with harvesting crops or moving himself and his family to them, he even has what might be called nostalgic reveries in which the Rio Grande Valley figures prominently, for all the economic exploitation and political repression that he experienced there. The memories have to do with people, past events, or experiences; but there is, as the social scientists put it, a context that is broader — as far-reaching, spacious, and immense, maybe, as the Texas land he crossed so many times in his young life: "I'll be working my way up from Florida, through Georgia and South Carolina and North Carolina, and I'll look around, and I'll say to my wife that we're not in the Valley, or anywhere else in Texas. The other day I thought of Amarillo; I don't know why. We'd go through there every year, on our way to Colorado, for the beets."

He stops, changes the subject. He has no interest in imagining Texas, with its dry and lonely panhandle, to be the New Jerusalem. He knows why he left the Valley, why he never sees Amarillo anymore, why he is quite willing to go in and out of Carolina towns without too much annoyance. But he does feel the relative congestion of the East and his own situation as an outsider. The black man is, after all, a Southerner, a natural part of a region's human landscape; hurt and betrayed and badly put upon still, but always there — thoroughly integrated, it can be said, into a once-segregated society. The Chicano receives looks or glances, hears remarks that expose the feeling of white and black alike: that man, his family, his people — they belong elsewhere. And he can only agree: "If I ever got some money saved, I'd leave. I'd go back to Texas. I wish one of my boys could get a job in the Valley and stay there — a job in a grocery store. I have a cousin who runs one, but he can't hire everyone who is related to him. He'd be even poorer than he is. He'd be broke. The market is a small one. Even our Chicano people now go to supermarkets. When I was a boy the Anglos didn't even want us to buy in their stores. All that has changed. The Anglos here aren't the same as the Anglos in Texas. I used to hate the Anglos in Texas, but here they're worse. One foreman told us that his boss doesn't like 'the Spaniards' picking his crops! But he has no choice. The foreman said he hoped I didn't mind being called a Spaniard. I said no; I said I loved being called a Spaniard. I'm a Spaniard from Texas!"

For him and for hundreds of thousands of his people, both in the state and separated from it, Texas is a rather special expanse of land: the rich, dark alluvial soil of the Rio Grande Valley, the hill country to the north of San Antonio, and, not least, the great high plains, known as the Staked Plains or, in Spanish, *Llano Estocado,* of which the panhandle and the west Texas area that abuts New Mexico are a part. The Valley is, of course, for many Chicanos "home," a row of counties that stand like dominoes against the long, winding, somewhat depleted Rio Grande as it works its way toward the Gulf of Mexico. San Benito, Texas, is where the Florida migrant already quoted originally came from — at least so far as the American part of his heritage is concerned. It is a town near the gulf and near the river, a town surrounded by large farms, on which all sorts of fruits and vegetables grow. The climate is semitropical — warm and humid almost all year around. Not only crops flourish; in winter large numbers of ducks, geese, and a variety of birds come and stay until spring: egrets, cranes, spoonbills, herons, and ibises. Not too far inland are doves, quail, pigeons, and the wondrous mockingbird, the officially adopted state bird of Texas. The gulf is, of course, full of shrimp, red snapper, flounder, and mackerel. Chicanos go to San Antonio to visit relatives and friends in the city; they also, like the Anglos, go to the gulf to fish, though they do not have much equipment or boats.

Working westward up the Rio Grande, the communities yield to one another, and within them the towns — a strange assortment of Anglo and Spanish names: Cameron County, with towns like Rio Hondo and Harlingen, as well as San

Benito, and to the south, Brownsville; Hidalgo County, where much of the interviewing for this book was done, with towns like Edinburg, Pharr, and McAllen — balanced by La Joya, San Juan, and Donna; and on up to Starr County, Zapata, Webb, Maverick, Val Verde, Terrell, Brewster, Presidio, and Jeff Davis (a wedge of it barely touching the river), and finally, Culberson (another wedge directed toward the Rio Grande), Hudspeth, El Paso. The point is that these are evidences of cultural intimacy, for all the tensions between those who speak Spanish and those who speak the Texan kind of English. The Chicanos who live in, say, Hidalgo County know people in the other counties along the river, and they know what is going on where: a good Anglo sheriff in one place, a bad one elsewhere; a relatively decent grower or foreman, as opposed to a mean and spiteful one.

The land in Hidalgo County and other counties up and down the river is unrelievedly flat — so flat that one looks with gratitude to palm trees and some tall, pliant pines. Tropical flowers are everywhere — wild sometimes, along the roads, or in carefully tended abundance in the gardens one sees in both Anglo and Chicano sections of the villages and towns. There is oil in the northern parts of some of the Rio Grande Valley's counties, but the nearer one comes to the river itself, the more lush and developed is the agricultural land. Cattle and sheep graze casually, but there is nothing easygoing about the planting, tending, and harvesting of crops — which are especially abundant in the warm winter, when the nation to the north is seized by cold and snow. Apparently endless fields of cotton, corn, tomatoes, cucumbers, lettuce, and beets can be found on the same farm, often subdivided by individual crop into separate worlds, each with its own foreman and "trained" crew of harvesters.

A particular Chicano family may, for example, specialize in

cutting lettuce or celery, as opposed to picking tomatoes or cucumbers. There are machines, astonishing in their size and complexity — the dinosaurs of agribusiness. But human labor is still needed — cheap, more precise, more "reliable," one hears: no sudden breakdown of a piece of equipment that may cost tens of thousands of dollars to repair. Cantaloupe and watermelon also abound, and citrus fruits — enormous orchards devoted to oranges, grapefruit, tangerines. If one favors the slightly exotic, by ordinary American standards, there are papaya and banana trees. And there are flower farms — as well as acreage given over to peppers or black-eyed peas. In the words of one grower: "We are rich here with a good climate — warm, sunny, and plenty of rain. And we have all of Mexico nearby to help us; the Mexicans need the work, and they do a good job. Of course, there are exceptions. But to me the reason we have such good crops is that we have the right people to work here as well as the right kind of weather."

He merges the two, fieldhands and climate, for his reasons; Chicanos do so too — a response to the kind of lives they live. The strong, rarely absent sun, "Mexico's sun" one hears it called sometimes, starts the day for thousands of Chicanos, many of whom have never heard an alarm clock go off. Once awake, the first question has to do with the weather: is it clear, cloudy, rainy, or (in winter) has a freeze, uncommon but deadly dangerous, settled upon the citrus? Soon enough the men and women (and very often, the children) are on their way to the land — *their* land once upon a time, as they often remind one another. The Rio Grande Valley was, in fact, first settled by Europeans in the middle of the eighteenth century at the initiative of the Spanish government of Mexico. Indians had been probing Spanish territory, and the French, who controlled what is now Louisiana, had expansionist designs. To protect its claims, Spain sent its Conquistadores up to and across the Rio Grande, with instructions to clear the land and begin settlements. The province of Nuevo Sontoneer was established, headed initially by Count José de Escondón. Large grants of land were given to certain families, the descendants of whom still live in the various counties of the Valley. These families began to work the land; they brought with them Indians, introduced cattle, sheep, goats, and, not least, agriculture. Corn, beans, and squash were the first crops.

When Mexico broke away from Spain the Valley became part of the Mexican province of Tamaulipas. In 1836, when Texas broke free of Mexico, the Valley was declared part of Texas — by the Anglos, who did not, however, make any immediate effort to move south. Until 1849, when United States troops moved to enforce their claim to all land north of the Rio Grande, there were virtually no Anglos in the Valley. American children, Anglo or Chicano, are usually told what happened in 1847: Mexico was decisively beaten after President Polk instructed General Winfield Scott to take the war into the heart of "enemy country." After Veracruz and Mexico City itself were occupied, the government of Mexico was willing to cede all territory north of the Rio Grande to the United States — the treaty of Guadalupe Hidalgo. Mexican citizens were permitted to choose between remaining where they were and becoming Americans or moving south and starting a new life. Most stayed.

In the latter part of the nineteenth century, as middle-class (professional men, storekeepers, landowners) Spanish-speaking people in the Valley will tell an outsider, a trek of Anglos began, bent on farming, mostly. Land was cheap and plentiful. Often the Anglos were single men, and they often married Spanish-speaking women. The crops were bountiful, and there was a minimum of friction between the Anglos and the old Spanish families. Significantly, the Spanish-speaking people were then proud of their heritage and quite able to absorb Anglos socially and culturally. The daughters of the old Spanish families who married Anglos did so across the border, on Mexican soil and under the sanction of the Catholic Church. Many Texans, accordingly, had Mexican marriage certificates and, even more confusing, their children had Mexican birth certificates because the Spanish families sought out the superior medical care then available in the towns south of the Rio Grande.

In the last three decades of the nineteenth century the number of Anglos markedly increased, and the social and cultural equilibrium of the Valley was upset. Crude and greedy land speculators arrived, buying cheap, selling dear. There were always takers — men who wanted to dig in, try to make a living out of the obviously fertile land. Yet no one was going to get all that rich in the Valley, however good its soil and weather, unless transportation north to the rest of the country improved. Throughout the nineteenth century the Valley was approached by steamboat up the Rio Grande or on horse (stagecoach) through the various cattle trails that had been forged. In the first decade of the twentieth century a railroad connection was at last established, and with it, the possibility of enormously profitable agricultural production. Land speculation increased; a fever of buying and selling swept the Valley. Soon thousands of Mexicans were being brought in by Anglo landowners to clear the land, irrigate it, plant and tend and harvest its crops. A once-picturesque region, inhabited by old, aristocratic Spanish-speaking gentry and poorer Mexican laborers of mostly Indian ancestry, gave way to a bustling, Anglo-run, highly developed agricultural economy. And the Spanish cultural domination ended; the Valley became — socially as well as economically and politically — very much part of Texas and the rest of the United States.

Cheap, compliant labor turned into an obsession with newly rich Anglo growers. Mexico had for a long time been poor; in the first decades of the twentieth century, it was also plagued by a series of revolutions, with their attendant disorganizing influence on the people, thousands of whom crossed the Rio Grande. Better, they thought, the arrogant, demanding Anglos, who at least paid *something*, however little, than the chaos and near starvation that went with constant civil strife in Mexico. And the Anglos were not full of apprehension or self-recrimination, never mind the guilt a bad conscience can generate. They were eager to keep wages low. They had come to a sleepy, relaxed, casual valley, owned largely by a few wealthy Spanish-speaking families and populated by a larger (but overall, not very large) number of other Spanish-speaking people. In a few decades they had turned the place around, making of its land a rich breadbasket — one of the most valuable in the nation. Now the cactus and mesquite were virtually gone. Now the quaint burros and smiling, hesitant people had lost control to strong, assertive, active, and industrious landowners, anxious to make the most of a region beginning to be known (in the 1920s and 1930s) as the Magic Valley.

With the crops came other initiatives: canneries, cotton gins, packing plants, transportation centers, stores that sold machinery, fertilizers, farm equipment of all kinds. At times one can look around Texas and feel oneself to be in Mississippi's delta or in south Georgia or central Alabama: cotton or vegetables as far as one can see, interrupted only by irrigation ditches and, occasionally, a tree-lined road or some railroad tracks; or maybe the squat, flimsily constructed but constantly busy packing plant — a wooden or tin shell to protect dozens and dozens of workers from the sun, as they sort out fruit and vegetables all day long, and sometimes by night too. They pack up boxes or crates full of produce, which are loaded and dispatched by truck or train to the rest of us, who have learned to expect fresh or frozen fruit and vegetables all year.

The "magic" of the Valley is, of course, a wondrous combination of ample sun and water that makes already good land produce so abundantly. The contrast with much of New Mexico's land is rather apparent to Chicano migrants who have had yearly occasion to move from the Valley north and west in search of work. There is not all that much rain in the Valley; the river itself supplies the water, except during the wet season, midwinter, when more than enough falls and gets soaked in. But during the spring and summer it can be dry, almost semiarid, for weeks on end. When Chicano fieldhands first came across the border in large numbers a few decades ago, they camped out. There were, at best, old shacks to house them; they crammed into small rooms, empty save for a mattress or two, maybe an old, rickety chair — as if the buildings too were going to be packed, sealed, and sent off somewhere. "Wetbacks" the people were called, Mexicans illegally in this country: *mojados*. Soon enough they found *el patrón*, and from then on his needs became their obligation — work in the fields from sunup to sundown.

In the summer, though, when the sun is too hot and the Valley's land rests for a few months, the Chicanos move hundreds, thousands of miles north in search of work. They cross Texas, moving steadily uphill with their old cars, and eventually (those headed for the West Coast) reach New Mexico. In west Texas and in eastern New Mexico (referred to as Little Texas) they cross space that is limitless and uninhabited, striking in its rugged, unpredictable appearance. They wonder, on their return to the Valley in the autumn, whether they could ever find a halfway useful or comfortable place for themselves, as Indians have, as other Spanish-speaking people have, in the area near Albuquerque. In a curious way the new interstate highway system has given them a sense of security and confidence; they remember with mixed awe and apprehension the old, narrower roads that brought the traveler closer to the plains, the desert, the mountains, the buttes and mesas and canyons, the highlands and scrubby pine and cactus lowlands that make up the state that has their ancestral home as part of its name. Best to keep moving; in Colorado, or farther north and west, in Oregon and Washington, there is work. New Mexico, as one migrant keeps saying, is "a place you see in dreams; it's strange — like the Indians."

The western sky: immense, boundless, infinite, it seems, while under it. And if one is leaving Texas, moving higher, steadily higher, closer all the time to that sky, the ascent does indeed become unnerving, mystifying. Ahead are grasslands that end in a strange rise of the land — a high table, as it were, awaiting visitors. "God must be there," Chicano children have said with mixed curiosity, surprise, and apprehension. Suddenly tumbleweed comes rushing toward the road, dry and withered almost, yet at the same time round and bouncy and endlessly responsive to the wind. "A skeleton of a plant," a young Chicano child comments; he enjoys his observation, but his mother tells him not to speak like that: "You mention a skeleton and you flirt with Death."

Death is indeed very much present: land that has long since given up hope for moisture; or mountains once boiling with volcanic gases and liquids but now extinct; or arroyos, gulleys, ditches that even desert lizards seem to have shunned. Suddenly, though, deeper into New Mexico, there is a strange shift; the land seems kinder, softer. A few aspens assert themselves — thin, tentative, huddled together against the still, dry, bleak, windswept landscape. How have they managed to grow, to stay alive, to remain standing? A young child, for the first time (at five) conscious (to a degree) of the natural world

outside of his immediate environment — that of a car, a family
on the move — lifts his finger and points and counts: five of
those aspen trees, so fragile and isolated to anyone who comes
from a woody region, but here a surprise, if not a miracle. The
questions begin: how come their presence, and how come no
more? His mother shrugs but has an answer: there will be
more ahead. They have been a sign, those trees, one of many
signs the traveler comes to anticipate in New Mexico. The
state offers an extraordinarily mysterious journey that begs
and defies comprehension.

No one really knows when the Pueblo Indians of New Mexico first made their journey across New Mexico's high plateaus,
cut by deep canyons or interrupted by various ranges of mountains. The Spanish came about 1540, and there is no doubt that
Pueblo settlements like Cochiti, north of Albuquerque and
south of Santa Fe, had then been in existence at least several
centuries. Archeological studies, incomplete but continuing,
date some Pueblo pottery as far back as 1050, and perhaps
before that. Coronado's expedition wandered widely across
central and northern New Mexico, as well as Arizona, and to
the east to Texas and Oklahoma. The Pueblos were approached, surveyed, conquered — without any real opposi-
tion. The Pueblos showed a willingness to make token gestures
toward a Christian God so long as they were allowed to have
simultaneous concourse with the various spirits of their own
faith.

For a while the Spaniards were too busy hunting for gold,
following the course of rivers, and in general sizing up a beautiful, dramatic, inviting landscape to come down hard upon
the Indians. But in time the demand was made: go along
religiously as well as economically and politically. By 1582 the
Pueblos of the Rio Grande Valley were part of an amorphous
expanse of land called New Mexico. Before then the term

Nueva Andalucía had been used. From 1597 onward the territory that included the Rio Grande pueblos was colonized in earnest. Spanish settlers, as opposed to roving bands of explorers or soldiers, arrived; soon churches were built, Santa Fe was founded (1610), and Indians were being converted rather zealously. (By 1624 there were 34,000 Christian Indians.) In 1680 the Pueblos revolted, fought hard and successfully against the Spanish, compelled them to retreat south. But by 1696 the conquerors returned, this time in even larger numbers. They had never completely gone away, of course. They raided pueblos from time to time, burning property and killing people, or taking them away as slaves. Eventually superior force won its victory, and the Pueblos were, in turn, required to help subdue other Indian tribes, the Navahos and the Apaches.

The Hopis, however, were never really reconquered by the Spanish, who had initially stormed the Hopi villages, located in territory that is now northern Arizona, during the early period of exploration (1540). The Hopis had made an effort to defend themselves the first time around, but when overwhelmed, became friendly and generous. The Spanish did not quite know what to make of a people who presented gifts to those storming a village with guns. When the Spanish came back to the Rio Grande pueblos, they continued to engage with, plot against, and try to overcome the wandering Navahos and Apaches, but they kept their distance from the Hopis. It had been the Hopis who had first shown the Spanish explorers the apparently limitless Grand Canyon, which failed to assuage their disappointment at not finding gold and silver but had struck them with awe for a few moments, at least. It was to be the Anglos of the United States, in the nineteenth century, who would gain decisive political control of the Hopis and all other Indian tribes.

The area of land called New Mexico, including present-day

Arizona, was for a few decades part of the Mexican republic, which had been granted independence from Spain in 1821. The Spanish rulers had not wanted some 20,000 of their own people and the 10,000 Indians under their control to have any dealings with the Anglos, who were constantly probing the Southwest. But under Mexican rule trade began to flourish. Santa Fe became the terminus for goods brought by the Anglos — and sold profitably indeed. Other Anglos, from Texas, regarded such successful economic activity as an invitation for conquest. In 1841, and again in 1843, Texans tried to take over New Mexico, but failed. Soon thereafter Texas joined the United States, and an American army, under the command of Colonel Stephen Kearny, took over New Mexico. In 1850 Congress formally set up the territory of New Mexico, and by 1863 had given that territory the size of the present state by splitting off the western half as Arizona, the northern half as Colorado.

During the second half of the nineteenth century, railroads entered the Southwest; with them came an increasing trek of white men from the Midwest and the East. The Indians were gradually "quieted," as it was put then — and not sent to the best land by any means. Texans crossed into New Mexico with their herds of cattle. Mining and agriculture (enabled by irrigation) began to be developed. By 1880 the Atchison, Topeka and Santa Fe Railway had reached Albuquerque, which had been founded in 1706, but grew rapidly only in the latter decades of the nineteenth century. In 1912 New Mexico was admitted to the union, followed (in the same year) by Arizona. The rest is contemporary history — motels, interstate highways, air force bases, nuclear testing stations, atomic research laboratories, and, not far away, Indians on reservations and Spanish-speaking people near villages or on farms or within the barrios of Albuquerque.

For those people New Mexico is something else, not measurable by economists, physicists, or engineers. For an Indian child or a Spanish-speaking child, New Mexico is aspens turning yellow in the early autumn — a gradually unfolding blanket that covers the Sangre de Cristo mountains. New Mexico is sandstone formations in all their strange, eroded, suggestive diversity. New Mexico is a sea of gypsum, of white sand that seems infinite and utterly lifeless. New Mexico is also for such children a field of primroses, a mesa followed by another, a quick storm subsiding and so allowing everything to be lit up again: the cottonwoods, the low adobe houses, the coats of the grazing horses. "See the yellow," one hears a child shout as the sun penetrates the clouds, reasserting a rather common hegemony; and the eyes of the six-year-old girl race from place to place: trees aflame, the sky a furnace, cacti suddenly in bloom, and the side of a building a strange, alive mixture of yellow, orange, red, brown, which together, on blinking, become a blazing fire.

The girl asks: "Will the sun burn them up?" She has in mind that adobe house, so solid looking, so comforting to its inhabitants, so much a part of the landscape. She also has in mind her horse, brown with white spots, but of a different color at certain moments of the late afternoon, after a rainstorm, and under a weakening, reflective sun: chestnut brown, an outsider might say, thinking of a yellow-red hue of low brilliance, but to the girl's eye something else. She can't quite find words for what she is thinking, or so she says. But in fact she can get across exactly what she believes to be the case: "The horse has been under the sun all day. She stands there dozing. I worry that she is hot, that she will get sick. But no, she doesn't want the help of the shed. The flies are in the shed. The sun drives the flies away. The horse is happy. The horse likes the air; the horse's feet like the ground; the horse's coat is full of the day's sun."

Her father, an Indian who moves back and forth, back and forth, from an Albuquerque office building, which he helps keep clean, to a Pueblo reservation north of the city, where he lives, has spoken many times of the sun's "spirit" and the earth's "spirit." The child sees one of those spirits in her horse's coat, as it appears on a particular afternoon, and takes note in her own way of the influence exerted by a particular region's weather and terrain on the everyday life of a people. In the girl's words: "The horse may get tired in the middle of the day; the sun is too hot for her. But she waits, and soon the air is cooler, and she is ready to gallop for miles. That's how we feel, too. I wait for the end of the afternoon; then I know I'll feel better. My mother always tells us to come inside and rest in the first part of the afternoon, and go outside later. She will thank the sun for warming us and later she will tell us that the air is cool and the ground is cooling off, and we can go play. We pick up rocks and throw them into the shade. They feel better after they have landed. They are glad to have the cool air on them."

The air — warm or cool; for her it is something more than a condition of weather. There is a glow to the air, a promise. She is comforted by it, even as outsiders, unlike her in dozens of ways, find themselves immediately struck by something intangible yet recognizable — the extraordinary visual character of the air: thin, dry, clear. In our eastern cities, in California, or in the Midwest, even on a sunny, cloudless day, the air is not what it is in New Mexico. A layer of low-altitude air that is relatively heavy with humidity hangs over most of us; we have learned to live with a certain haze in the air, not to mention the additional and more blatant murkiness that environmental pollution prompts in the atmosphere. But in New Mexico one has moved high up; one is among mountains or on an elevated plateau. And one has come upon increasing dryness, too, apart from the altitude. The result is a crispness of vision, even on hot days, and even after a rainfall. The hazy, somewhat softened, even blurred vision of the coastal plains or the prairie gives way to a clear, bright, almost harsh, sometimes blinding field of view. Air that an outsider has come to regard as transparent suddenly becomes translucent — so sharp, so clean, so light that one feels in a new world or possessed of new eyes.

Scientists know why; the air has lost one-fourth of its weight, as compared, say, to the coastal flatlands of adjoining Texas. The air, too, is low in oxygen, in carbon dioxide, but higher in hydrogen. It is an air that has, to a degree, lost its capacity to refract or diffuse the light. It is an air that seems to bring objects almost too close; they assert themselves strongly, even harshly. But when one is on a hill and looking at the countryside many miles away, it is an air that lends itself to mystery, especially in the evening, when the stars and any speck of man-made light fairly glow before the observer, as if, against all laws of nature, hundreds, thousands, even millions, of miles have been deprived of their meaning, and one need only reach out and touch something in the sky, or nearer at hand, a town's, a house's, a car's lights. Those lights are sharp, pointed, immediate, forceful; there is none of the soft glow one is grateful for when up a mountain or a tall building in other parts of the country. The "big sky" of New Mexico or Arizona is not only a matter of view; it is a striking freshness and immediacy of vision that seem almost God-given — the result, at the very least, of a complicated series of natural coincidences.

Nor is it only the eyes that have to accommodate themselves to a new physical, if not psychological and spiritual, reality. In the late afternoon the sun suddenly vanishes. Warm updrafts leave the earth, go higher and higher, produce clouds as if the sky were ground upon which a whole city was to be built. The result: thunderheads that dispatch bolts of lightning in all directions, followed by a rumble of noise and those brief, scattered, soft showers that settle dust, surprise and awake cactus plants, delight people who regard a full-fledged rain as an unusual event indeed. Indians laugh at the short-lived, noisy outbursts, call them "male rains" — full of pomp and circumstance but little substance. They rejoice at great length when they are visited by the longer, quieter, wonderfully sustained and soaking "female rains." Then it is that a mother tells her child: "The sky spirits want us to have water; they want to feed us. They are mother-spirits. Usually it is men-spirits, quarreling or telling each other off." So much, at least at this point, for the relationship between culture and sexual imagery, not to mention between a region and the psychological development of those who live in it — that is, have to make sense of its weather, its terrain, its physical and biological conditions.

It is an almost timeless environment — endless sky, strangely empty land, and everywhere volcanic spires, reminders of agitation and energy long since spent. It is a gentle, almost unnervingly arresting environment — views that bring life to contemporary clichés: vista, panorama. It is also a harsh, mean, forbidding, ungenerous environment — a violent one too: a summer's flash flood tears through the land, sweeps across arroyos, spills itself wastefully, only to be hungrily absorbed by the land, evaporated by the sun's beating warmth. A child can point to a moment's mud and silt and say: "In just a second there will be dust, and the same old cracks on the soil." It is as if life's rhythms are brutally condensed — ashes to ashes before the comprehending eyes of a boy or a girl. Those children are sometimes casual with a physical world that may excite, surprise, delight a visitor; at other times they can turn quite serious, become preoccupied with the strange mixture of action and stillness they see and feel around them.

The great silence, the solemn loneliness, the provocative suggestion of a surreal and ghostlike world, are balanced by warm, lively winds, by the continuing side-by-side presence of the two oldest cultures in this nation, and by the earthy concreteness of adobe houses, which have themselves become (as they were meant to) part of the natural landscape rather than buildings thrust upon it. No wonder some Indian children talk about home and mean by it a field of cactus, or a tree on a particular hill, or an expanse of semiarid grassland, as much as a building or a street with a group of buildings on it. No wonder some Chicano migrants can pass through New Mexico, on their way from the Rio Grande Valley of Texas to the crops that need harvesting in the mountain states or those of the Pacific Northwest, and tell their children that not only Indians are nearby, but the Lord Himself — and the Devil. The Chicanos may sometimes mean, with respect to the latter, a state highway patrolman; but they also have in mind a God-given terrain — of a kind that strikes them as *too much:* ordinary proportion and symmetry have given way to a supernatural intervention. "It is just too much," a mother dutifully says each year as she looks at the land north of Santa Fe. Her child remembers the description, oft-repeated, from last year's trek and observes: "Sometimes I think my mother thinks everything is 'too much'; she cries a lot. But she is right about this place. I asked the priest if there is some place where Jesus Christ comes and visits the earth every once in a while. The priest said that may happen; maybe He comes to the valley, in Texas. But I don't think so. Why would He want to come there? Here, yes; I can understand why God would want to visit New Mexico."

Up in Alaska there are Eskimo children of his age, eleven, who regard the world similarly. They have been converted to

Christianity, and they believe all too strongly and concretely in an immanent God. He is the God of ice and snow, of a whiteness that is unrelenting, all-encompassing, transcendent. When told by teachers or ministers that some children on this planet never have seen ice or snow, an Eskimo child smiles in disbelief. When asked whether he might want to live elsewhere, in a warm or tropical climate, the same child again smiles: "There is no such place." Like everyone else, he has some utterly rock-bottom assumptions. One of them is that the earth is always covered by some snow, some ice; even in the summer the sun can achieve only a partial victory. And as if to point out that he has the evidence nearby, if not directly in hand, the boy points silently at a distant mountain, one of dozens that stand far away — a perpetual horizon of nameless, snow-covered peaks.

The boy's ancestors came to Alaska, saw its land and presumably mountains, hundreds, maybe thousands, of years ago. Eskimos are light yellowish-brown in color. Their faces are broad, their cheekbones high, their eyes black, their noses flat. They resemble in physical appearance the people of northern Asia: China, Mongolia, Siberia. Archeological and ethnological research connects Eskimos to the Lake Baikal culture of Siberia. Radiocarbon dating indicates that several hundred years before Christ walked the earth, perhaps as much as a thousand years before His birth, Asian families arrived on Alaska's shores and built settlements there. They were a stolid, enduring, patient, lively people. In the face of severe, limiting, sometimes crushing weather they somehow managed to persist. They built crude sod houses out of a frame of driftwood timber and for walls used packed ice: the igloo, now extinct, replaced by today's small frame houses. In the summer they once constructed the tupek out of animal skins; now they use canvas tents manufactured in distant factories. They fished and hunted: the seal, the walrus, the sea lion, the whale. Those who ventured inland, following the course of rivers, encountered the caribou, an additional source of food. And there were berries and roots, in apparently endless proliferation during the short-lived but exuberant summers.

For transportation the men and women relied upon dogs, the legendary huskies who may well have come to North America with the first Eskimos. Sleds were fashioned. Kayaks were built, extraordinarily light and serviceable — an extension, in a way, of those who used them, who were (and are) a people of quick reflexes, sharp vision, and obvious manual dexterity. Decades ago they fashioned the umiak — an elaborately constructed large open boat made of skins and used for hunting and transport. The motorboat has replaced the umiak, but old Eskimos still remember it, not only with nostalgia but pride: a distinct engineering and aesthetic achievement. Ivory carving is another justly famous accomplishment — and, alas, mostly a source of nostalgia rather than everyday self-respect. Some Eskimos, as well as Aleuts and Indians, have also in the past done first-rate basketry. In this century, increasingly, commercial fisheries have commanded the time and dedication of Eskimo men and women and, not rarely, older children. Oil prospecting, and more recently, the building of the controversial trans-Alaska pipeline, as well as (during the 1940s and 1950s) military construction and maintenance, have also been a source of Eskimo employment.

Alaska's modern, recorded history, and with it, a chronology of Eskimo life, goes back to the early eighteenth century. Russian explorers, traders, colonial expansionists had been pushing steadily eastward; eventually the rivers and valleys of Siberia ended: the Pacific. Peter the Great asked Vitus Jonassen Bering (after whom the Bering Sea is named) to find out if Siberia was linked to the continent of North America.

Bering, Danish-born, a man of vision and enterprise, made two voyages; on the second one he explored Alaska's southern coast extensively, not to mention a number of islands, including the one now called Bering Island, on which he died of hunger and scurvy in 1741. But some whom he commanded survived and brought back to Russia the pelts of the sea otter. The result: a new demand for fur, a new surge of exploration, hunting, trapping in Alaska.

Eskimo and Aleut settlers grew to fear the Russian trappers and traders, the first in a succession of outsiders who would arrive with all sorts of demands: food, shelter, goods and services, and, not least, the favors of all available women. In essence, the "natives" were exploited, killed outright, or enslaved. The Russians were followed by the Spanish, the English, the French, and finally, in 1788, the Americans — on the ship *Columbia*, under Captain Robert Gray, a citizen of the newly formed United States, and on another ship, the *Lady Washington*, under Captain John Kendrick. But Russia ruled Alaska in the eighteenth and the first half of the nineteenth century — Russian America, it was called. A number of Russian governors encouraged an active shipbuilding industry, as well as various smaller industries and foundries, sawmills, machine shops. Church bells, for instance, were made in Alaska and sent south to the Spanish missions in California. Agriculture was attempted, but unsuccessfully; the growing season was too short in the southern part of Alaska and obviously nonexistent in the far north.

For a time the Russians contented themselves with intensive explorations of Alaskan territory, but in the early years of the nineteenth century they penetrated as far south as present-day San Francisco and even to the Hawaiian Islands. Yet Russia was only peripherally interested in its North American territory. Its czars and, through them, various governors did indeed issue various ukases, forbidding to other nations "the pursuit of commerce, whaling and fishery, and all other industry, within an area extending from Bering Strait south to 51° of north latitude on the American coast" (1821). Even so, American and British ships were everywhere, it seemed; and they would not be deterred by the wishes of the St. Petersburg court. With the outbreak of the Crimean War in 1854, Russia was even less able to enforce its will in North America. Soon the imperial government was entertaining thoughts of disposal; and in 1857 the Russian ambassador to the United States suggested as much to this country's officials. The Civil War interrupted negotiations, which were begun in 1859. In 1867, however, William H. Seward, our secretary of state, put his signature to a bill of sale — his well known "Folly": Alaska for the sum of $7,200,000.

The Russians left, American troops entered. Until 1877 the War Department ran the territory of Alaska. When Indian uprisings in the West became serious, prompting a need for all available troops, the soldiers left Alaska, and the Treasury Department, with its revenue collectors (whose boats were the precursors of the coast guard), maintained law and order. In 1880 gold was discovered in Juneau. From then on the Eskimos and all other "natives" became relentlessly, hopelessly entangled with one wave after another of settlers or mere visitors from the United States: gold prospectors and, later, miners come to work at the large copper deposits uncovered from 1898 onward; missionaries, who to this day try to convert heathens, educate children, provide medical services, and, sometimes, argue strongly on behalf of the rights of the economically poor and socially vulnerable; federal officials of one kind or another, including, of course, those from the Bureau of Indian Affairs, charged with providing for the "health, education and welfare" of "native" people; and a motley assortment of others — homesteaders, the owners of fishing boats, engineers and surveyors, bush pilots, dreamers in self-imposed exile from the ways (and pressures) of contemporary urban, industrial life, naturalists, and tourists. Many of those people have stayed, become Alaskans; indeed, Eskimos and their distant kin, the Aleuts and the Athapaskan Indians, are now decisively outnumbered by the rising tide of newcomers from "the lower forty-eight," as the rest of the United States, apart from Hawaii, is often called by Alaskans, among them Eskimo children.

The word *Alaska* is derived from the Eskimo *Alakshak,* which refers to *the mainland.* Eskimo children, even those who live far up a river, hence a long journey inland by snowmobile or motorboat, are ever conscious of the ocean. Often they regard the ice and snow around them as, ultimately, the ocean's property, spread over the land by a prodigal (and fierce) nature. The "mainland" for them is the earth immediately under them; the ocean is everything else — as far-reaching and infinite, they believe, as the sky. For Eskimo children who live, say, on the Aleutian Islands, land seems an especially fragile and, for many months, a nonexistent element. Feet walk on ice or snow. Rain pours or snow falls all the time, it seems — over 250 days of the year, on average. Fog is an almost constant companion. The water is insistent, noisy, sometimes threatening and savage. Children wonder whether the sea will claim the islands — even the mainland. And children who live in the coastal settlements watch the ice floes move closer in the short-lived interval between summer and full-fledged winter, see the snow accumulate higher and higher around the houses, occasionally wonder whether the "mainland" won't itself become absorbed into a giant ice floe and get carried deep into the Arctic Ocean.

The children actually know better; they are taught in school

how enormous Alaska is — one-fifth the size of the entire
United States of America: 986,400 square miles, or almost four
hundred million acres, stretching over fifty-eight degrees of
longitude and no fewer than four time zones. The children are
also taught that there is a lifetime of exploration waiting for
any of them who wants to stay in this largest of American
states, a nation within (or more exactly, outside of) a nation. It
is still a quiet, sparsely settled land — about three hundred
thousand people, or only .51 person per square mile. In summer, when outsiders naturally find it easiest to visit, much of
the state seems deceptively warm, approachable, hospitable.
The surface of the permafrost begins to melt, though below
the surface, silt and sand and gravel and rock remain as hard,
as cold as ever. The tundra — a seemingly endless plain, bereft
of large trees — suddenly is no longer brown and dead-look-
ing. Flowers appear, the purple mountain saxifrage or the
array of white flowers: *Dryas integrifolia* — or to Eskimo children, "summer snow flowers"; also the bright yellow glacier
avens — "the little sun" to some Eskimo children — and the
wind flowers *(Anemone parviflora)* with their touch of blue
under the white petals. Grass is everywhere, and shrubs. A
carpet of mosses and lichens covers land that just a week
earlier seemed hopelessly inert.

The tundra gives way to the sea, which is also stirring
— cracks in the ice, currents and eddies that are encouraging
to those who want to see the ocean set free again, but dangerous to navigate. The icebergs melt gradually — mountains to
hills to mounds to an underwater existence; some icebergs, of
course, never yield to any sun, as if the Arctic Ocean will only
go so far in acknowledging summer. The tundra also gives way
to higher country, and to forests: hemlock, spruce, cedar,
mixed occasionally with birch and even balsam poplar. There
are, too, stretches of less imposing willows, and even they fall

off, at points, to shrubs. Berries of various kinds are available, and the grass can be lush, rank, deep green, and triumphant. The combination of heavy rains and long-lived sun, the arrival of swarms of mosquitoes and flies, the constant sound of birds, whistling, crying, croaking, chirping — it all goes to suggest a miraculous, definitive transformation: from a freezing, white death to a tropical jungle's brimming exotic life.

And the animal life confirms the impression. While the steady passage of geese, ducks, and shore birds masks the suddenly open sky, bear, moose, and elk stir, run, seek yet another summer's assertive activity. Great herds of caribou range the Arctic slope, go south, penetrate the woods. And less obvious and awesome, the smaller ones go about their business: fox, sable, ermine, wolverine, mink, land otter, beaver, muskrat — animals whose names evoke visions of fur coats in millions of city people thousands of miles away, people for whom Alaska is also a suggestive name — of igloos that don't exist anymore, of Eskimos who fight long and not always successful battles with giant polar bears or whales. There are polar bears, of course, though it is more often the white man from far away who wants to hunt them and has to be carefully kept in bounds. There are also whales, and they are indeed caught, if less commonly than salmon and halibut.

Mostly, these days, there are village stores with frozen foods, no less, as well as candy galore, soft drinks, and canned goods. And snowmobiles and motorboats; their noise competes with the gentler call of the geese to one another, as flocks of them work their way in stately regiment across the sky. Not that birds don't, under some circumstances, make their own urgent, shrill, even frantic sounds. Near open water, near hundreds of Alaska's ponds, inlets, lakes, male and female phalaropes, for instance, skirt, plunge, jump, flutter, and all the while create a frenzy of sound and motion as they seek one another out, make their claims, adjustments, rebuffs, assaults — the prelude to a new generation. "Do airplanes have babies?" an Eskimo child of four once asked — so accustomed was she to the shrill but important noise of other flying objects, nature's, and to her mother's explanations: mating, then offspring. Why not those planes, too — those larger, even noisier, birds? And even more precisely: why not a link of propeller to propeller — and later, the emergence of a smaller plane out of the belly of one of the planes, whence at other times come mail, packages, and those who carry them?

Soon enough the endless days give way to the dominant and then utterly victorious night. The sky is no longer light blue, has turned black-blue. The stars offer all the hope there is. The birds scurry away, or leave well in advance, an orderly, proud, at times mocking retreat: let man stay where he is; we will have no part of these long, grim, devastating winters. Sometimes the dancing, sparkling, streaming lights of aurora borealis, the northern lights, appear — wild and strange electricity showing a huddled, snowbound people that all is not lost, that there is action, movement, dazzle even, at the least promising and most fearful time of the year. And the silence, the firm, solemn, eerie silence; young Eskimo children pay homage to it, ask their parents, with a touch of desperation to their curiosity, why the snow is so noiseless as it falls. The parents have no explanation, only the reassurance that below and above the ground there is indeed life; and if one is careful to listen, some sounds as proof.

The fox is as agile and evasive as ever through the winter. The snowy owl watches, glides or swoops magnificently, finds its rodents. And fish do not flee heavy snows, thick ice, treacherous glacial movements of a sea, a slope, a whole world of frozen restlessness. Nor, it has to be added, do the Eskimos, who for generations have gone down to the ocean, to the rivers and streams, the wide expanse of a delta, or the marshes and swamps, all so tightly covered by winter, to match wits with the Arctic, with "life," with the fish running underneath and, not least, with themselves, because when the temperature is some fifty degrees below zero, and the winds cut across the tundra, and the snow seems to have become not part of a fall, but an expression of a permanent condition, then even Eskimos, with all the strength of a heritage, can experience a moment of doubt, of apprehension.

It is, as Eskimo children are often taught in school, the frontier that they are part of, and must in various ways learn to live with and, to a degree, master. Even with airplanes and snowmobiles and motorboats, there are days on end of danger, uncertainty, isolation. In New Mexico, too, or in the Rio Grande Valley of Texas, where the weather is so different, the frontier is still either right there or not so far off: the edge of things; the spaces that seem to know no limit; the aloneness that is not the result of self-judgment or worse, self-punishment, but nature's quite natural resistance to any creature's easy domination. Miles of the Rio Grande's loam separate people and towns; miles of New Mexico's hill country keep one Pueblo reservation from another; miles of the tundra, and storm upon storm, make one Eskimo settlement utterly removed from others, even in this age of planes and wireless. "Once it was the frontier here," an Indian child in northern New Mexico says; then he adds, sure of himself in spite of contemporary technology, "it is still the frontier."

So it still is — where he lives, where Eskimo children live, where Chicano children live in various parts of the Southwest; not the old frontier, not the frontier of savage battles, new railroad tracks, smoke-producing trains, daily shoot-outs, anarchic gold prospecting — and anarchic drinking, fighting, stealing; not the frontier of frequent homestead rushes, though in

Alaska they do occur occasionally; and not the frontier of boastful ignorance or dark, even murderous escape from God knows what, God knows where; but as the child says, still a frontier where it once was one — comparatively and substantively. The land has yet to be fully conquered or fully settled. The immense sky is still available, not blocked or shut off by man's various constructions. The woods or rivers or desert or mountains are often untamed, or if brought under control, under surveillance, only somewhat frequented. There are fewer people than are to be found in the settled regions of America; and among those men and women who do live "out there," closer to the earth, farther than all others from our cities and suburbs, there is a responsiveness to that fact, that state of affairs, that state of being, that mixture of physical fact, social circumstance, tradition, memory, and mood: the badlands (once); the hinterlands; the Far Northwest, Southwest, or West still the frontier — and homeland for hundreds of thousands of Eskimo, Indian, Chicano children.

PART TWO

THE METHOD

THE WORK that preceded this book has required from me and my family a substantial amount of travel. At one point we moved to Albuquerque, New Mexico, where I got to know a number of Spanish-speaking and Indian children. My own children did too — at school and in the course of various visits they made with me. At another point we moved to Alaska, and there my oldest son was especially helpful in several villages; he became a fast friend of an old Eskimo man, who undertook to teach both of us a great deal. At still another point we all went to the Rio Grande Valley of Texas, where my wife and sons noticed rather a lot that had escaped me. As I mentioned in the Foreword, I began to work with Spanish-speaking families long ago — in 1963, actually, when I first met and got to know two migrant farmers, a husband and wife, who had come to Belle Glade, Florida, from San Benito, Texas. They and their children moved up and down the eastern seaboard, harvesting various crops, living under the most unfavorable, humiliating circumstances. I have, in *Migrants, Sharecroppers, Mountaineers,* tried to indicate how such people try to manage.

In 1964, after I had known several Spanish-speaking families for a year, the mother in one of them suggested that I go visit relatives and friends of hers in Texas, where she was born, and in Mexico, where her mother and father were born. At the time I had to say no, I could not; I was already overwhelmed, trying to learn how a region's sharecroppers, tenant farmers, and migrants were attempting to live their lives and, especially, bring up their children, against high odds indeed. The mother persisted though — not insistently, but with a kind of shy, tactful patience that I began to realize was itself worthy of some of the "analysis" I was then putting my mind to. Not that other migrants, black or white, hadn't made suggestions to me; I had by then learned at least enough to ask for their advice and assistance: where to go, how to introduce myself, what to say or do. But I wasn't always able (or wise enough) to heed the recommendations I'd been given; and sometimes, they were forgotten by me, as were, occasionally, the men, women, children who made them.

The mother who suggested I go to the Rio Grande Valley and points south was not one to forget what she considered important — or let me forget either. Time after time, as I talked with her ten-year-old son and her seven-year-old daughter, she reminded me that even though they were poor people and utterly without resources, someday, *someday,* there would be a return — away from Florida and from the states to the north, and back to the Rio Grande Valley, where in several counties the population is 80 to 90 percent Spanish-speaking. There were other dreams too — maybe "unrealistic," but nonetheless persistent and, to a degree, sustaining: the ultimate return, in triumph, to a small Mexican village, whence the migrant family had originally come.

In recent years more and more Spanish-speaking families have moved from Texas to Florida and joined the migrant work force; now they make up about a third of it. The dreams of escape, if not victory or triumph, have largely gone away.

It is impossible for even the most hopeful to ignore the presence of hundreds, thousands, of "others," who never themselves get out of the cycle of back-breaking labor for the most meager of wages, constant uprootedness, and a mixture of social ostracism and economic indenture that is unique in the United States of America. In *Uprooted Children* and in *Migrants, Sharecroppers, Mountaineers,* I tried to document the psychological costs of migrant children growing up under such a severe and unjust burden. Among the migrants I had worked with, the Spanish-speaking ones felt strongly that they were "different" — not better or worse but members of a "people," they kept telling me: *la gente.*

In 1968 I made my first trip to the Rio Grande Valley, so that I could begin to get some idea whether the memories I had heard articulated were in any significant way connected to the observable reality of cities like McAllen, Texas, or the towns and surrounding countryside of Hidalgo, Cameron, and Willacy counties. I soon realized that migrancy as a life does indeed make inroads on everyone's state of mind, black or white, English-speaking or Spanish-speaking, those American-born or those here from Mexico or the Caribbean. (Large numbers of blacks are brought over from the Bahamas and other islands to harvest Florida's sugar crop, and some go north to oblige growers who grow a wide range of fruits and vegetables.) But I also began to understand that the mothers and fathers in Florida who had urged me to visit Texas had been right and had actually been telling me something else — about themselves.

One or two of them, more politically conscious than the rest, insisted on calling themselves "Chicanos" and stressed the pride they felt about their background. They would, later on, be active in the still dangerous and by no means completely successful effort to unionize their fellow migrants. I know first-hand the obstacles they faced and continue to struggle against; and I know also how much it means to such men and women that they be addressed as *Chicanos* — not Mexican-Americans or Spanish-speaking people or (an expression one often hears in New Mexico) Hispano-Americans.

As I mentioned in a previous book, *The Old Ones of New Mexico,* no one word or hyphenated set of words will please the millions of Spanish-speaking people of Mexican (and to a varying degree of mixed Spanish and Indian) ancestry who now live in this country. Many of the children I have spent time with are the boys and girls of avowed, proud Chicanos; at this writing I have known them for a decade, and I am inclined to let their particular self-description, learned from their parents, be the one I use most often: in the title, as mentioned before, for obvious convenience, and in the more theoretical sections of the book out of a certain psychological logic — the increased sense of social, political, and cultural awareness that such parents strive for and encourage in their children. It is that awareness, in all its variety and complexity of expression, that I have contrasted with the thoughts and feelings about themselves and their future that Indian and Eskimo children have.

I have to acknowledge again, in this chapter, my admiration for the efforts being made by Cesar Chavez in California; for the efforts, too, other union organizers have made in Texas and Florida. I am no neutral observer when it comes to the terrible social and economic predicament of migrant farm workers, Chicano or black or white. In the case of Chicano migrants, I have testified repeatedly before congressional committees, or those set up by various state legislatures, about the awful conditions I have seen in Florida, Texas, California, and elsewhere. If at times the children I try to bring closer to the reader seem interesting, thoughtful, appealing, I hope he or she will remember that those children are survivors; they have battled every day wretched conditions that have caused many others to die prematurely, unnecessarily, and, often enough, quickly: great pain, high fevers, severe cramps, headaches, vomiting — the sequelae (as doctors put it) of untreated infections that suddenly overwhelm bodies already weakened by malnutrition and constant exposure to faulty sanitation.

I have tried hard to get to know a broad range of so-called Chicano or Mexican-American or Hispano-American children. In 1970 I started working in the Rio Grande Valley. Though I was continuing a previous involvement with migrant farm families, I was also extending my interest and concern to include not only the effect of poverty, uprootedness, social marginality, and economic vulnerability on children, but the significance of what might be called a particular background — a catchall word that, in this case, has to do with class and sometimes caste, with religious, cultural, linguistic, national, and ethnic influences on a child. To be born a Chicano or a Mexican-American means that a particular child has a way of thinking about the world, a way of seeing his or her future, a way of talking, a way of being treated at home and in school, and of treating (regarding, feeling about) himself or herself.

As I kept returning to Texas cities and towns like Crystal City or Edinburg, McAllen or San Antonio, I visited people in their homes, was a guest of theirs. For the children, I brought along toys, games, and always paper, pencils, crayons, paints. We talked, we played, we walked. I was shown around, introduced to friends, was asked more questions, generally, than I asked. I was introduced to new families in the Rio Grande Valley because relatives of theirs had gone to Florida as migrants. Other sources of help were two priests I'd been told to look up in San Antonio, a doctor in McAllen, Texas, and a community organizer in Crystal City. (I am now on the board of a Crystal City clinic set up for poor Chicano families.)

In 1972 I decided to extend my work among Chicanos; I knew that it was unfair to ignore other Spanish-speaking people of the Southwest, and especially the thousands who live in New Mexico, which may adjoin Texas but offers for many of the families I came to know quite a different world. My own family moved to Albuquerque that year, and I began talking with Chicano children in the city, and very important, with Hispano-American children, as their parents insisted they be called, in the rural part of the state — up New Mexico's high country, well above Santa Fe: Truchas and Madrid, for instance. In this region I met people who live more settled lives; they may be relatively poor, but their ancestors have, by and large, lived in New Mexico for many generations and, in some instances, claim descent from the early Spanish Conquistadores who explored the deserts, forests, hills, and mountains of the Southwest before the Pilgrims and Puritans arrived in Massachusetts. In *The Old Ones of New Mexico* I tried to convey some sense of the traditions that help shape the lives of these solid, hardworking, somewhat wry yet vibrant people. In this book I have tried to work into the section on Chicano children the special hopes and fears, the ambitions and assumptions of the boys and girls I was privileged to know for two years in New Mexico.

As in the South and Appalachia, I wandered far and wide on briefer visits — to the barrios of Los Angeles, to Denver, to Tucson, Arizona, to California's Imperial Valley. With the help of community organizers, nurses, doctors, public health officials, activist lawyers, teachers — that network of middle-class men and women that is found among the poor in every section of the country — I was able to meet children I would not get to know well but could speak with, observe at play or in school, and hear about from parents, teachers, neighbors. But the heart of the work with Chicano children took place in a relatively few homes. In Florida I worked for three years with seven Chicano children, four girls and three boys, each from a different family and all under thirteen. I would visit them two, sometimes three, times a week and stay for a half an hour or three hours, depending on how things went. I would tell the children that I wasn't interested in finding out anything in particular, merely knowing, to a degree, how they lived and what they thought about — insofar as it was their inclination to tell me.

I have been asked over the years how I manage to hear children talk so much about themselves, about the life they are living or see ahead for themselves, and what I do with what I hear — that is, how hundreds of hours of conversations get turned into the various sections of this book. As I have indicated in a number of "methodological" discussions, I do not use questionnaires, do not have a fixed agenda of "subjects" that I endeavor to have discussed in the homes I visit. I am not doing "survey" research. I am not even trying to find "representative" families — if there is such a thing. Chicano children have a cultural heritage, a language, a religious faith in common — not to mention the poverty so many of them have to face in the present and, all too likely, in the future as well. Within the constraints of class and culture, occupational and regional influence, men and women still vary as individuals — and thereby frustrate the theoretical ambitiousness of those who want to make social-scientific generalizations.

I struggle to hear accurately what takes place in the particular minds of certain boys and girls, then to indicate how those young people compare with others of the same generation. The comparisons are rendered both implicitly and explicitly — in the course of the narrative and in the more insistently didactic concluding pages of each section. The entire series provides a context for each volume as a whole and for the different parts of each volume, certainly including this chapter. I am hoping, all along, to make clear what characterizes a Chicano childhood, in contrast, say, to an Indian one, or an Eskimo one, or a white, middle-class, New England Protestant one — or the childhood, say, of a black girl who lives in the Mississippi delta, or an Appalachian boy from West Virginia or eastern Kentucky.

I was born to white, middle-class parents, New Englanders, and I am from a profession not always willing to recognize its own biases — and their sources: sociological, economic, ideological. When I say that I have been systematically educated by the various children I have spent time with these past two decades, the fact is that almost every day I have walked away from one or another child better aware of how it goes for him or her and, maybe, for many others — and also reminded of how important it is for child psychiatrists to widen the circle of our human involvements, not only for us to be of service to those who are poor and in various ways removed from us, but for them to help us professionally as we try to sort out the reasons children behave as they do.

I have called upon my "training" in child psychiatry more than ever in recent years, and especially in the course of the work I did in Texas, New Mexico, Alaska. In the South and in Appalachia, in the ghettos of our northern cities, my studies were often connected intimately to ongoing social and political struggles: the effort to achieve school desegregation in the Deep South; the broader civil-rights struggle, in which I took part for several years; the so-called war on poverty, a failure in many respects, but not without a moment or two of significant success — the so-called campaign against hunger, one "battle" of which I had occasion to witness; the continuing struggle to achieve for migrants the same social, political, and economic rights other workers possess. I am not saying I now have no interest in taking a stand, alongside others, on behalf of those Chicanos, Indians, Eskimos who are trying to advance the cause of their people. Even the most committed of activists who are white have found that Chicano organizers or Indian protesters have been wary indeed about any outsider, however earnest and modest his or her intentions.

The entire United States, moreover, has slipped gradually (since 1973) into a recession. The Chicano poor in the Southwest have more company among Anglos than has been the case in many years. The recession waxes and wanes; but even with improvement, it has been hard indeed for Chicano leaders to wage a successful fight for even a little improvement in the conditions of life of their people. And so with Indians; and so with Eskimos.

I was repeatedly told in the late 1960s and early 1970s, as I contemplated various trips and shifts of residence, that there was some reason to study the psychological qualities that distinguish Chicano, Indian, or Eskimo children from one another. Any number of programs aimed at Chicano, Indian, or Eskimo children — educational programs, medical, nutritional, or plain "welfare" — end up limited or useless. The experiences of childhood become for those interested in social or political change quite vexing realities, as opposed to matters of abstract, academic interest. It was especially among the Pueblo and Hopi Indians that this last issue came up. One does not have to be a white intruder to encounter among apparently cordial families a distinct unwillingness to shake one's fist at the world, rise up, and change the social order. It is, perhaps, a reluctance that has to do with a way the young are taught to see things.

The Indians of New Mexico have had considerable experience with anthropologists. They often smile when the word comes up, as do their children. (I know of no other American children who so readily know what anthropologists are likely to be interested in finding out.) When I was well into work in New Mexico with six Spanish-speaking families, I decided to extend my work to several other Spanish-speaking families, related by marriage to the ones I was visiting. In two instances the new families were partially Pueblo, and it was in this way that I was able to reach Indian families. I am a doctor, was quite willing to be of help with medical problems, and wanted to talk with children but *not* observe religious rites or ask questions about this or that "practice," "belief system," and so on. Not that my motives went unquestioned; I was repeatedly called an anthropologist. Thank God for my long interest and training in pediatrics; I was able repeatedly to offer concrete medical help to some of the Pueblo and, later, Hopi children I came to know, and thereby earned at least a measure of acceptance, if not a moment or two of trust.

I must say that the Pueblo and Hopi children I worked with most closely were an enormous challenge to me. As a child psychiatrist I have long since learned to expect weeks, months even, of silence, suspiciousness; then the feigned indifference that masks growing curiosity, and even an interest of sorts — all accompanied by little conversation indeed. Eventually, in many instances (by no means all, though), fear and reserve give way to increasing expressiveness, often through drawings first, but resulting in gradually lengthening conversations. Indian children are, however, in my experience, less talkative than, say, black rural children, Appalachian children, Chicano or Eskimo children. I wish that a writer could convey the long stretches of stillness that take place — when an Indian child not only sees fit to say nothing, but seems strangely, wondrously, unnervingly disinclined to speak. Is he or she "hostile," I have been trained to ask myself — or "troubled," perhaps "sick"? Or is it that some children are brought up to be quiet most of the time, not out of fear or because of various inhibitions and anxieties, but as a quite natural and even active way of responding to the world?

Until I began spending time with Indian children, I had never really had to examine my dependency on words. I had been trained to appreciate the reluctance or inability of younger children to talk with a strange doctor, but I had also learned how to wait for those words — in the meantime to suggest games that might be played, encourage drawing and painting. The children I had long ago treated in the Children's Hospital of Boston had never been all that quiet, even the boys and girls of four or five, who hadn't been to school much and were still struggling for control over spoken English. My clinical experience had taught me that children who come to the clinic *because* they are considered (at home, at school, in the neighborhood) sullen, moodily reticent, disturbingly "uncommunicative," were likely to begin talking rather fluently, sometimes with a push of speech, once the initial impasse was over. The same held for the children I had met in the South and Appalachia. There were indeed barriers, substantial ones, between them and me. But despite shyness, apprehension, an understandable confusion as to my motives and purposes, and despite all the "cross-cultural" difficulties that social scientists, including myself, have written and written about, conversations have not been all that impossible to sustain — as any number of civil-rights activists discovered when they stayed with rural black people in Mississippi or Alabama or Georgia in the early 1960s.

In contrast, I found myself for months wondering what I might do to persuade Pueblo or Hopi boys and girls that I was no enemy, idle busybody, or exceedingly strange and suspect white man — when they were in fact being (so I finally learned from them, as well as their parents and teachers) rather cordial and candid with me. Quite simply, they didn't have all that much to say. They spoke tersely, figuratively. They pointed, smiled, nodded, shook their heads, and willingly drew pictures. But they did not on their own do much extended talking. Had I not, by accident almost and in desperation, begun to have some success in asking the children to tell about what they had drawn, I might have decided that I had best stop trying to have any talks at all in the New Mexican pueblos or the villages of the Arizona Hopi. It turned out that the Indian children were quite willing to use their imaginations, let their pictures prompt a quick story, a short anecdote, a brief observation about the world. It was almost as if the picture, the representation put down on paper, possessed its own authority, energy, and requirements.

For two years I visited seven Pueblo children three times a week; three of the children belonged to a pueblo slightly north of Albuquerque, four to a pueblo well above Santa Fe. I interrupted those visits monthly to go to northern Arizona, where I visited Hopi children daily during the course of a week; and I spent two summers with those children. As with Chicano children, I visited repeatedly a number of other homes — located in each of New Mexico's pueblos, several of Arizona's Hopi villages, and a number of Navaho settlements. I spent many hours, too, in the schools attended by Indian children and in the hospitals to which they are brought when ill. I did the best I could to offer much needed pediatric care to a significant number of young Indian people, about twenty-five in all. I was thereby able to render some assistance, but I was also able to learn rather a lot from the children I was treating. I might add here that the silence, the almost uncanny stillness of the children, was not ordinarily overcome by injuries or pain. I have heard Pueblo or Hopi children cry, but quietly and unostentatiously. Often they did not cry when I quite expected them to scream, shout, indeed vilify me for what I was doing to them. Instead they smiled or stared off — usually toward the sky, if there was a window nearby. And invariably they thanked me kindly for what I had done — by no means a response a pediatrician can take for granted even when working with the best-brought-up children.

While visiting one of the Bureau of Indian Affairs schools, I met an Eskimo youth — sent all the way to our Southwest from Alaska to obtain a high school education. I had been making brief trips to Oklahoma and the Dakotas to get some sense of how the Plains Indians, as they are called, live and bring up their children. I had not imagined myself going to Alaska, however — at least not until I finished talking with the young Eskimo. With no prompting from me, he made many comparisons between his own people and the Indians he was getting to know; and at the time I was contending with a number of frustrations in the course of my work. I was seized with an idea: why not visit his family and others like it and take note of how Eskimo children look at the world? And no doubt about it, at a critical moment in my work out West, it was enormously helpful for me, personally, to leave the Pueblo communities I was virtually living in and travel north, far north, to Fairbanks, thence to Kotzebue, and thence (by a one-engine plane owned by a bush pilot) to Noorvik, on the Kobuk River.

On my first trip I went with my son Bob; he was, at the time (1972), eight, but a rather experienced traveler, at least within the United States, and certainly no stranger to children who looked different, spoke differently, had names unlike those he knew best. It turned out that his presence was invaluable. We went to see the parents and grandparents of the Eskimo I had met in "the lower forty-eight"; through them we were introduced to many other Eskimos in the village — and given the names of others, in other villages. As we were watching some Eskimos dry salmon and prepare themselves for the coming winter (it was September), an especially old Eskimo man came up to us and began talking. He was much more interested in getting to know my son than me, and soon the two of them were good friends. He explained to the boy how the village worked — who did what, when, and under which circumstances. He had had a grandson who would have been my son's age but had died at the age of seven of poorly treated pneumonia. My son's interest in boats, in fishing, in the mysteries of the tundra, had excited the old man — and caused him to believe that, perhaps, his own grandson was paying him a sudden, unexpected visit: the spirit of one child was immanent, the Eskimo believed, in another child.

Eskimos are quite warm, friendly, and hospitable. The Eskimo youth I met in the Bureau of Indian Affairs school had said so — perhaps, at the time, recognizing in me a certain grim determination mingled with a touch of desperation: I will, by God I will, find a way around the inscrutability of my Indian hosts. I *had* by then found such a way, so far as the particular families I was visiting were concerned. That is, I had learned to throw aside words like "inscrutability," "impassive," "mute," and instead sit quietly myself, drawing or sucking on a Life Saver (how the children loved them!) or simply looking across the land to a mesa, up toward the sky, over to a grove of trees. And when a child would tug my arm and point to a cloud but say nothing, I knew that he or she was, in fact, saying a lot — and teaching me a lot about myself, never mind him or her. On a brief visit to an Oklahoma school, however, my perception of a brooding silence in the various boys and girls had returned. The Eskimo youth had watched me making conversation, working harder and harder to do so. He told me later, after a long talk, that he had found it hard to get to know various Indian youths — for a while, that is, until he had stopped trying so hard and simply let *be* the reserve he felt in others, as opposed to taking it personally.

He assured me that if I were to go to his village, to other villages in Alaska, the problem would be quite different: how to deal with the generosity, hospitality, and volubility of my hosts. He didn't use such words; he told me that his people were quite "happy to meet people," quite "friendly." Having only slowly learned to live quietly with the quietness of others, I was all too quick to regard suspiciously the amiable, obliging, accommodating attitude of the Eskimos my son and I met. And when I came back to Alaska and was treated like a long-lost relative who had finally returned, I was full of unspoken hesitations and doubts: *too much,* all this graciousness.

That Eskimo way of getting along, like the relative silence of the Indians, would not go away on further acquaintance — for the obvious reason that both are shared or communal traits, each very much part of a particular people's response to the surrounding world, including one another. I have heard Eskimos talk to fish, and to geese, and to distant caribou, in a manner not unlike that displayed to a white stranger from distant states. As I kept coming back to Noorvik and to towns farther up the Kobuk River, or northward along the Arctic coast, I found myself in a situation quite unlike any I'd ever before had to face: the natural kindness and hospitality of people as a virtual obstacle to my work! I had to learn how to say no: I cannot have supper again and again; I can only see a quite limited number of children; there are just so many hunting or fishing expeditions (or rides on a snowmobile) that I can allow myself, and feel that I am doing what I came a long distance to do — sit and talk with and play with and draw or paint with a necessarily small number of children.

But once I had spelled all that out, I was safe. In fact, I was protected, watched over, virtually guarded — now and then even reminded of my own words, when I found some event or new person more than a match for my obligations, stated previously to the Eskimos I knew. They warned me with a delightful mixture of gravity and amusement: back to work, and never mind (for instance) the division of the whale now proceeding along the shore; or never mind the snowmobile race outside the villages; or the chance to talk with people while they wait for the mail plane to land this afternoon. If I felt torn, annoyed by my own demanding, sometimes overbearing and exhausting conscience, with its firm notions of what must be done, the Eskimo children I was seeing were extraordinarily helpful. Gradually, day after day, they helped me to relax and enjoy our conversations — because, I began to see, they had none of the mixed feelings I had. They were delighted to sit with me and draw, or walk with me and talk, or sit by the stove and answer whatever questions came into my mind — often, as a matter of fact, put there by the child I was with.

The Eskimo children were mostly rather talkative and expressive, quick to take notice of any visitor's habits, worries, intentions — and his shyness. Many Eskimo children made a point, at the beginning, of letting me know that they were quite willing to bring up various concerns of theirs that I may have felt I needed more time before pursuing. I was in Alaska at first for only two weeks at a stretch and worried about hurrying things along to suit the convenience of my schedule. But if we did a lot of talking in relatively brief periods of time, we made a good deal more progress, I believe, during the long summer days, when I could be there all season, for three months. Then the children were out of school, full of life, involved with all sorts of pleasurable, time-consuming activities. And then the children were also inclined to be more reflective — less anxious to keep the words flowing back and forth, less anxious to please their guest or anticipate his interests.

I will never be able to know whether the particularly relaxed, thoughtful, gentle, indeed solicitous, attitude of the children during the summer months was the result of our increasing knowledge of each other, or had a great deal to do with the season itself, its undeniably strong influence on everyone in those Eskimo villages. I tried to find out, I suppose; being an incurable product of Western empiricism, I made it my business during the three summers I was in Alaska to seek out a few children I had only briefly talked with before.

Those "new" children were, to begin with, very much like others whose homes I'd visited — outgoing, talkative, a little too obliging. But rather quickly (was I more easygoing, now that I was up there for the season, and a long one at that, given the daylight we had virtually all the time?) the boy or girl I was getting to know began to slow down a bit, so to speak: less interest in keeping our immediate flow of words going and more desire to show me something that, likely as not, required few words — how to carve, or how to fish, or how to find eggs out there in the vast tundra. Even when I felt that I had to acknowledge that I had already seen a particular feat accomplished, the child would tactfully and respectfully suggest that I go again, go see again, go take part again, go learn again, really — about (I now realize) what I was there to see and hear and understand: the importance to Eskimo children, among others, of a sense of mastery.

In all, I worked closely with eight Eskimo children, four girls and four boys. Six of them came from villages along the Kobuk, two from a coastal village. As with the Chicano and Indian children, I met other Eskimo children in various parts of Alaska, including Fairbanks and Anchorage. I also talked with a number of teachers, as well as, of course, the parents of the children I knew best, and the parents of other children too. I visited Eskimo settlements thousands of miles apart; some were located on small islands nearer the Soviet Union than the United States, and some were way inland and impossible to reach but for those small airplanes that so many people (*white* people) in Alaska possess. One perhaps has to be in an Eskimo village when a winter storm strikes to understand the relationship between "fieldwork," Alaska's size, and Arctic weather. On some occasions I found my original intention — to spend a few days talking with a few children — converted by a blizzard into a rather intense and sustained experience, wherein "observation" became quite something else: days of good and close friendship, along with the shared responsibility of work.

There was snow to shovel; there was water to be obtained; there were dogs to be fed; there were sick people to be attended to. In joining up, so to speak (I was always asked, quite politely, whether I wanted to "watch" a particular activity or "join up"), I came to know the children who were my working companions (or themselves "observers" of a kind — of me!) in a rather special and, I believe, instructive way. For me the work I did in Alaska was challenging, stirring, and sometimes quite dramatic. The sheer logistics of the "research," the weather in all its striking variety, the experience of being transported again and again by bush pilots (themselves — their lives, their personal stories — worth a book or two of sympathetic and grateful narration), and not least, the insistence of the various Eskimo children I met that I be educated about their world, made the experience of working in Alaska and with Eskimos quite unlike anything else I have done in the course of my studies in the United States.

The children in this volume of *Children of Crisis* are indeed children; that is, they are by and large unaccompanied in the text by words from their parents, grandparents, teachers, or even older brothers and sisters, so-called adolescents. In all I worked closely with a few more than thirty children (Chicano, Indian, and Eskimo) and saw another fifty boys and girls at least ten times — for my kind of work, alas, a mere beginning, but still an opportunity to see, hear, and be taught. None of these children was over thirteen. I arbitrarily, and for a number of reasons, set that age as an upper limit.

What middle-class white people regard as "adolescence," yet another stage in the long (and seemingly, lengthening) period of "childhood," many Indians or Chicanos or Eskimos regard as the beginning of a person's adulthood. Few of the families I met had ever sent a "child" to high school; and if one had gone off, the parents and the youth regarded the experience as very much an *occupational* opportunity, not unlike the way older people do in the suburbs when they undertake a period of "vocational education" to qualify for a new job. There were other reasons that prompted me to spend even more time than usual with younger children — and less time with adults: the particular circumstances under which I worked, the time, the historical moment.

Although I more or less stumbled into the first Chicano families I met, when I decided to work in Texas and later in New Mexico with Spanish-speaking people, and got to know their children not as "migrant" children but as children whose parents were offering them a particular world-view that had to do with a culture and its values, I wondered for a while whether there was any point at all for me to do the kind of study I was trained and had learned by experience to do in the South and Appalachia, as part of a protest movement — the civil-rights struggle or the war on poverty. Now there was no single dramatic political or social issue, such as school desegregation, for me to observe, with the knowledge that I might be of some practical help to the harassed participants. The so-called hunger issue, while always alive with the children who speak in this book, is no longer part of a strenuously fought political struggle, as was the case back in 1967. In the late 1960s and in the early 1970s, people who call themselves Chicanos and Eskimos were mostly poor men, women, and children, trying their hardest to make do, sometimes succeeding barely, sometimes failing sadly, but engaged in no social and political assault on the status quo comparable to that of the late 1950s and early 1960s.

It is true that a number of Indian tribes have had a series of confrontations with white power, though the Pueblos and Hopis mostly have not been among those protesting, demonstrating, or taking part in "occupations" or boycotts. And, as the Indian activists know quite well, it has not been possible as yet to generate the kind of momentum among Indian youths or older people that southern blacks and their white sympathizers got going over a decade ago; nor have the millions of white people who make up the majority of the population been alerted and become well-wishers if not out-and-out allies, as was the case during the 1960s for a few luminous moments like the march on Washington, or the Selma bridge, or the Mississippi summer project of 1964. Finally, those Indians, Chicanos, or Eskimos who are now struggling politically — or in the courts, or economically, or for the cultural and social assertion of their people — are not anxious for a lot of white outsiders to march with them, speak up for them, fight alongside them. Quite the contrary; the general trend is for those taking a stand against the existing laws and economic and social practices to do so rather insistently on their own: no white middle-class college students wanted, however earnest and well-meaning; no white ministers, professors, or even doctors wanted either.

At one point, before beginning to work in Texas, I spent two days talking with a group of Chicano political activists, and a week later, another two days with their Indian equivalents. I also went to talk with a number of sociologists, economists, anthropologists who had been much involved with studies of Indians, Chicanos, or Eskimos. A year later, in Alaska, I had a candid, to say the least, meeting with a group of Eskimo political activists. In all three instances I was told, right off, that the time has long since passed for white social scientists and writers to come poking and prying around, asking questions, and accumulating data and more data, in the barrios of San Antonio, or out among the Chicano agricultural workers of the Southwest, or on Indian reservations, or up among Alaska's Eskimo settlements.

The books, the astonishing number of books that have been written over the decades! One Indian leader thrust several lists of them in front of me — hundreds of titles! All I could do was say that I did not intend to do a traditional study but rather had come to certain families as a physician, a trained pediatrician, anxious to be of *service* to those families and as many others as I could also assist, but also anxious to obtain some idea of how the children regarded the world around them — and not, it was to be hoped, to fit whatever was seen and heard into one of those theories or "perspectives" that somehow turn the people being described into caricatures of themselves.

I was eventually told to go ahead, but to do justice to the children I was meeting — that is, try to be a mediator of sorts rather than someone intent on fitting them into the requirements of my own various formulations. Then at the least I would cause no harm, and I might possibly be of help to those doctors, nurses, teachers (mostly white, but increasingly in the future Chicano, Indian, or Eskimo) whose job it is to work with children. One Indian activist, for a time a graduate student in anthropology and sociology, reminded his friends and me that there wasn't, for all the research done with Indians, any study of the kind I hoped to do as a child psychiatrist.

I have shown no great interest in stressing singlemindedly the psychopathological side of the lives I have encountered. It is true, I was trained in hospitals and clinics, where there is every reason to look at the psychological troubles, often crippling, that even young children can develop for one reason or another. Yet psychiatric work with children, however disturbed and incapacitated they are, often fails unless the doctor and the patient together find a way to build on the strengths and achievements, no matter how fragile, that children almost invariably have managed to demonstrate. In fact, as Anna Freud has pointed out repeatedly, children especially require from their psychiatrists extreme caution when it comes to authoritative diagnostic and prognostic statements. The most ominous "pathology" can quickly recede, and the most "normal" child can suddenly become a serious worry to his family, and maybe to a doctor called in as a "consultant."

If such "fluidity," not to mention ambiguity, characterizes the emotional life of children whose parents are reasonably well-to-do, well educated, and not especially tormented (by inner problems) or harassed (by the outer world), then children born to a life of hardship, malnutrition, ostracism, or worse deserve even more cautious appraisal from those of us whose lives are so different. (Since there are only a few hundred child psychiatrists in the United States, I doubt very much that there are now *any* Indian or Eskimo child psychiatrists, and at the most there may be one or two who are Chicanos.) And even the most suspicious activists among the three groups identified to me the "problems" they have seen among their own people — a high rate of alcoholism, suicide, depression — and expressed their interest in any connections I could

discover between the thinking of children and the later behavior of adults.

Needless to say, it is precisely that kind of generalization
(however appealing and, at first glance, seemingly of "practical use" to activists) one like me ought to try hard and long to
avoid making. I do offer some comparative remarks that move
beyond the individual children I know; but I am, or at least I
have wanted to be, exceedingly wary about categorical, over-
inclusive descriptions and, certainly, causative links: *this* (in
the home, the culture, the larger society) leads to *that* in
Chicano (Indian, Eskimo) children or adults. What I can offer
is my "direct observations," to use Anna Freud's much favored
words, and following them, for each group of children, some
comparative ("cross-cultural," as it is put) analytic comments.
But if those more abstract remarks are the essence of what the
reader ends up taking away from this book, then I will have,
by my lights, failed miserably. The whole point of this work
has been to put myself (body, mind, and, I pray but cannot at
all be sure, heart and soul) in a position, with respect to a
number of children, that offers them a chance to indicate a
certain amount about themselves to me, and through me, to
others. But each life, as we ought know, has its own history, its
own authority, dignity, fragility, rock-bottom strength.

On the other hand, I have also recognized, as I have gone
from home to home, and then from group of people to group
of people, certain qualities of feeling, certain states of mind,
certain assumptions (maybe the best words to use are *ways of
seeing*) that seem shared.

In each of the three main sections of this book, I have tried
to make some general remarks — at the end, after the reader
has met and become somewhat familiar with a number of
particular children. Sometimes I compare the given children
(Chicano, Eskimo, Indian) to other children who live nearby,

or even within the same family (other Chicano, Eskimo, Indian children); sometimes I try to indicate differences between, say, Indian children and Chicano and/or Eskimo children; sometimes, additionally, I make contrasts between the children of this book and those I have worked with in the past.

There has been, no doubt, a certain tension in my mind as I have done the work that has ended up as this book. On the one hand, I have tried to be, within my limits as a person, no more or less than a quiet and interested observer. On the other hand, I am a doctor, a child psychiatrist. I have wanted to know how a number of children think, feel; what they very much hope for, fear exceedingly. I have had medical and psychological interests to pursue. Students in various universities where I've lectured repeatedly ask me *what* my work is: please give it a name, or a series of names, so that it can be put in a category, defined. Have I been doing social science research, fieldwork? Have I been a participant-observer? Do I write nonfiction novels? Am I practicing oral history? And so on.

All this talk about "method" is rather ironic coming from someone who has no great interest in the subject. I am an observer who has chosen to spend time with children in a certain setting — as they live their lives in the midst of everyday circumstances. The children know me as a doctor who practices pediatric medicine, as a doctor interested in the way the mind works, and, not least, as a man who talks with them, plays games with them, draws with them (they and I *both* draw pictures in the course of our acquaintance), and, finally, moves from writing them postcards, when away, to showing them and their parents what I have been writing in the course of return visits to their homes and other homes near or far away.

As for the mechanics of my work, I do *not* go lugging around tape recorders as I get to know children. For months I simply sit with them, walk with them, play sports with them, ask them to draw, or draw for them. When I leave a particular house I write down what I have seen and heard. When I know a child rather well, and his or her family also rather well, I may ask to leave a tape recorder around — the kind that runs for a long time and requires no relatively frequent changes of cassettes. When I do decide to use the tape recorder, it is mostly to have with me later when I try to convey the "rhythm" or "tone" of a child's speech as much as the content.

I would be the last to deny (or want to deny) the subjective element in this work. I have no statistics to offer, don't know what a computer is, and am short on sweeping generalizations. I have been making, if one wants an expression for it, a child psychiatrist's and pediatrician's naturalistic observations. Nor would I deny a so-called humanistic, even literary side to the work. I have, so far as the "method" of writing goes, tried to embrace, within my limits, the tradition of the social essay.

Years ago I spent a lot of time reading and learning to appreciate Matthew Arnold — what he wanted from his fellow poets by way of social and political responsiveness. He hoped that those in what we now call the humanities would move a bit closer to the day-in, day-out realities of the marketplace, the factory, the rows of tenement houses. Today he might, alas, look askance at the work of those of us who have done so and are called "social scientists." We have a lot to learn, those of us who do "research," from novelists and poets — their capacity to see, evoke, and, indeed without apology, celebrate the ambiguities, ironies, inconsistencies, and contradictions in people.

I suppose this book is a mixture, then: clinical observation, narrative description, oral history, psychological analysis, social comment. Insofar as I draw upon widely different experiences with a number of children, insofar as I condense the remarks of children, arrange and rearrange what I have heard, let one child be representative of others, pick and choose my way through the human scene I have been so lucky to witness, then I cannot deny the novelistic side to the work. One has to *present* — a word I used to hear in medical school when we were asked to tell about a particular person's medical "complaints," but also her or his personal life — the *story* of someone's life, as it has been told to the doctor, and as he has chosen to put in words what was spoken.

Do the children one meets in the Rio Grande Valley, or in New Mexico, or in Alaska, "usually" speak as they do in a book like this? I have heard questions like that for years; and the answer, of course, is yes and no. If a stranger comes to those children, he or she hears, most likely, nothing at all. But in time shyness, reserve, suspicion, annoyance give way to a certain curiosity, a certain willingness to try the person out, and exchange words, thoughts, feelings with this "outsider." Later, there may develop a real bond — and more words, more thoughts and feelings. Or little may develop; only longer and longer silences or idle, polite talk. Needless to say, I don't learn much (does anyone ever?) from the children I don't get to be rather friendly with, for one reason or another. Oh, I suppose I do learn — learn why it is that with some children I don't get along: a series of negatives about myself and them. But the children whose voices have become part of my thinking and later were very much "with me" as I wrote this book are those whom I kept coming to see, because our involvement (once more, through games and crayons and paints as much as words) seemed to keep going along well.

One last comment. Apart from those first few pages and these here that make up this chapter, this book is quite free, I believe and hope, of the vertical pronoun. More than that,

I think there is a certain tone in this book (if I may become my own critic) that distinguishes it from its predecessors. It is a tone that first appeared, not accidently, in *The Old Ones of New Mexico*; it is a tone I learned from the Indian, Chicano, and Eskimo children themselves, as well as from their parents and grandparents: a certain detachment toward the world and themselves, a tendency toward ironic self-effacement, not unrelated to a keen and ever-present realization that the land is vast, the mountains numerous and high indeed, the sky enormous, the ice permanent, the sun powerful, and man (as one Indian child kept telling me) "a real small part of everything."

The reader may detect a resemblance in the "world-view" of these children to that presented to viewers by Chinese and Japanese painters of long ago: man portrayed as overshadowed, if not on the verge of or in danger of being overwhelmed. I have tried to stay out of the narrative presentation of these children; tried to let them move toward the reader on their own. If overly "objective" and statistical, "research" can risk becoming arrogant, dry, and cold, the kind of work people like me do can risk becoming effusive and sentimental. Years ago, when asking William Carlos Williams about his short stories (so many of them based upon and devoted to the lives of the poor he treated in New Jersey), I heard him say: "The stories develop their own energy; they take over — leaving me behind. I read them, afterwards, and hope I will forget that it was me, me, me — me going to visit patients, me glad when I could be of help to them, and me driven to write about them and proud that I could. If I've managed to get rid of myself as an annoyance to the reader, but still give the best of myself and what I've experienced to that reader — then the effort has been worth it, and is a success."

One can only agree, and try to follow in that tradition. Perhaps the last thing needed by the children whose lives this book aims somewhat to illuminate is for them to become foils in the hands of yet another self-enhancing, constantly intruding observer-writer. I hope that my work, as well as my words, will prove worthy of a certain old Pueblo Indian woman's approval. A grandmother of eleven boys and girls, she gave me this advice as I began to talk with boys and girls she knew: "When you go to our children, try to become a friendly tree that they will want to sit near. Enjoy them. Forget yourself. If we all could only forget ourselves a bit more — then our children would feel free to be a bit more themselves. Sometimes we get too close to our children; we scare them with — with *ourselves*. They can't become themselves. It is *them* we should try to know."

PART THREE

ESKIMO CHILDREN

I

CUSTODIAN OF A SPIRIT

WIND, strong and uninterrupted, hits the old man, pushes the girl of five backward. She holds her grandfather's hand tighter. He wants to reassure her; he points to the river, as if to say: it is only a matter of yards, so let us keep going. They reach their destination in a few moments, stand silently at the water's edge. They seem oblivious to the mud that moves quickly to cover their boots. The wind, which had fought them so hard, now seems to let up a little. As the old man has told his granddaughter several times, they have reached one of the sources of wind, the river. The girl looks closely at the ice. She points with her right hand, smiles, says quietly: "Many cracks." The old man smiles back and nods his head. The girl does not say a word more, nor does the man move, for about ten minutes. Then he squeezes the child's hand, pulls his feet out of the mud, turns around. She follows suit, and soon they are on their way back, hurried along just a bit by the wind that now is a friend.

They continue their silence. The man looks straight ahead. The girl tends to look downward, except when she suddenly lifts her head all the way up — to catch a glimpse of her grandfather's face. He quickly responds each time she does so — he seems to sense her glance toward him rather than see it;

he smiles at her, lifts his chin noticeably, using it to point ahead: we will soon be under cover. When they have reached the top of a gentle incline, they both turn around and look again at the river; it is April, the ice is beginning to break, they are excited and pleased to have taken this particular walk. The old man at last begins to talk with the child; he tells her that the wind is coming in from the ocean, sweeps up the river, leaves it for the banks on either side, takes a lurch upward to get on top of the slope, even as they have done so, rushes through the village and out across the tundra. The wind is not an enemy, though; the wind is part of life, he tells the girl, who is listening carefully to his every word. She moves her head emphatically up and down as he talks, not necessarily following a particular thought but indicating a sort of general acceptance of his authority and good judgment. When he has finished his mixture of description and explanation, she stops indicating her assent and says one word: "Home?"

Soon they are there, slowly unburdening themselves of their coats, hats, gloves, boots. The man watches the child as he takes his outdoor clothes off but makes no move to help her. She is agile, fast; she is done before he is. He is quite pleased, pats her back, smiles, goes back to his boots, which he makes no effort to clean, simply pulls off — a bit of a struggle — and puts them down beside the door on an old, torn brown bag. The two of them are cold, but they make no effort to warm themselves near the stove. They sit down on chairs that face one another and for the first time since they prepared to leave the house about an hour earlier, look at each other intently and with a certain persistence: a full minute. The silence is broken by the grandfather; he tells the girl that she is a good companion, a sturdy walker, and that she has taken her grandmother's place in a ritual he has performed for years and years, since he was a young boy himself, having learned to do so by walking with his grandfather: the walk to the river to catch a glimpse of the ice beginning to break.

The girl had, of course, walked to the river many times that winter; she had gone with her father, with her older brothers, with her grandfather — to fish, to watch the snowmobiles move on the ice, or simply to meet other children and play. But this was a special walk, and she had been honored to be asked. Her grandmother had died the year the girl was born. At the age of five she knew a lot about her family; most especially she knew that her grandparents had been quite close and that her birth, coming as it did three months after her grandmother died, had meant a lot to her grandfather. In fact, he once told her — she was maybe three or three and a half — that her grandmother's spirit may well have moved into her. He had no proof; he simply had a feeling, and he wanted the little girl to know. Not that he made too much of such a conviction; he avoided seeming portentous when he made his announcement (the girl's mother tells me), and he has since then avoided going out of his way to mention it. Still, upon occasion he has reminded his granddaughter that she resembles her mother's mother and that when one of them left, the other arrived. And so doing, he has given the child a special sense of herself. She watches him more carefully, with more regard, than his other grandchildren do. She asks her mother about *her* mother more often than her brothers and her older sister do. She asks, too, about "the time before" — her way of referring to her grandmother's span of life. She knows that when her grandmother was five or six, snowmobiles were not in existence, nor were airplanes commonplace in Alaska. Now they cross the sky every few days and land weekly on the ground near her village. She knows there was no electricity a few decades ago. She also remembers that her mother and her grandfather both have remarked that her grandmother died glad she had lived when she had and had not been born much later — in the girl's words, "these days."

The girl is glad to be alive now. Her name is Betty, but she has decided she likes Betsy better. She has been called that by a schoolteacher, a white man who lives in the village and has come to know her rather well, even though she is not yet six, hence not old enough for school. The teacher has told Betsy's parents that they have a smart and likable daughter — all very pleasant to hear. The parents say thank you over and over again, sometimes reminding the teacher of his observation with respect to their daughter so that they can, once more, express their appreciation. The parents also remind Betsy of the judgment that has been made about her, and she delights in hearing the outsider's prophecy. She connects his analysis with her grandfather's attitude toward her: if she is indeed a continuation, so to speak, of her grandmother, then she naturally would possess some of the old woman's intelligence, wit, and common sense, all of which she was reputed to have in abundance. She has heard about the old lady: "She was tired a long time before she went away from us. My mother said one day she woke up, and her mother was calling her. My mother went to her, and her mother told her that before the sun set, she would be gone from us. My mother believed her mother; and she did go away just as she said she would. It was early spring, so the sun set a few hours later. Everyone said that our village would be in trouble, because no one was smarter than my grandmother, and no one knew how to fix things and settle arguments better than she did. But my grandfather disagreed with people; he said that he knew that his wife would stay with us and people would remember her; and then he decided that she passed me as she was going away: I was coming here, and she smiled at me — that's what he says he's sure happened."

There is just a touch of uncertainty, maybe confusion, in

Betsy's voice as she makes that assertion. She has tried to learn exactly what her grandfather believes happened when his wife died and his granddaughter was born. But the man waves off her questions, not brusquely or angrily, but with a gentle vagueness she finds it impossible to get beyond. If not he, then his daughter, the girl's mother: what does she know, and, just as important, what does she believe? But the mother is even less helpful; she tells Betsy that she knows nothing — that it is the grandfather who must be asked. If he has no more to tell, then that is that. But the girl has herself to turn to; she has a lively, imaginative, speculative mind, and she calls upon it to answer questions others shirk altogether or respond to, it seems, unsatisfactorily: "I think I know how I got to meet my grandmother. She was being carried away by the wind, and suddenly the wind stopped. Everything was still. Then I was born, and she had a chance to breathe her breath into me, and then the wind came up again, and she was gone. I saw my uncle lean over his son, and he kept breathing into him, but my cousin died anyway. My father said that sometimes it helps, when you see someone who isn't breathing, to breathe for him. A teacher at the school, who used to be a nurse, taught us all to do that kind of breathing."

Someday, Betsy thinks, she might become a teacher. She looks forward to school; she will join her older sisters and brother. They are not all that enthusiastic about the time they put in as pupils, but that is a mistake on their part, she knows. Her grandmother had told her mother to encourage all her children to go to school. The Americans from "the states" would be coming in increasing numbers to Alaska during the next few years, and the Eskimos had best be ready for the influx. The mother repeats to all the children what she was told, but Betsy listens most attentively. Her older sister, aged nine, reprimands her, tells her that she needn't be a slave to their dead grandmother's every word. Betsy denies being a slave to anyone or anything. Besides, who or what is a slave? The older girl talks about black people and their fate as Americans in the eighteenth and nineteenth centuries. Betsy is neither interested nor impressed: "I'm not a slave. I don't want to go to school because my grandmother wanted me to go. I want to go because *I* want to go. I'm only a slave to myself! Don't tell me any more about slaves."

She turns away abruptly. She goes to the window; how are the dogs? She looks at them, decides out loud that they don't need food at that moment, but keeps looking at them. Meanwhile, the sound of a snowmobile can be heard, and she listens carefully. Betsy turns to her mother, who is frying cut-up potatoes, with Spam to follow, and asks whether (and if so, when) they will get one of those snowmobiles. The mother says no. She says they are expensive, and only the rich people in the village can afford them. But there are a lot of rich people, the child retorts, with a mixture of annoyance, envy, and incredulity. Not so, the mother insists. Anyway, the machines make so much noise that a handful of them dominates everyone's hearing and, maybe, thinking. They are an exaggerated presence. The girl is not persuaded. She mentions four children she knows whose parents own snowmobiles. The mother casually mentions ten or twelve whose parents don't and then, both teasing the child and making a sensible, generous suggestion, tells her to go ask her various friends for a ride; surely their parents will oblige. Betsy is both grateful and quite stubbornly aware of her mother's ironic, if not sardonic, proposal. She does not underestimate the hospitality of others, but she wants something for herself. She conveys her feelings by apparently changing the subject, by asking a question rather than making any further comment, and by shifting the discussion to a different level of abstraction, arguably a more pointed one: "How do you get rich in the village?" She seems ready to wait patiently for hours after that request for information, but when her mother does not immediately respond, and indeed appears lost in thought — will the potatoes burn, or will she ever be able to tell the child how a few prosper while others are lucky to get through the winter alive? — another effort, this one more personally directed, is made: "Will we ever be rich?"

That is enough for the mother. She hits the stove with her spatula and tells the girl to go clean up. The girl does not often hear such a demand, and she knows to obey quickly. The mother is smiling at her, but the eyes above the smile are hard and glaring, and Betsy does not speak another word or prompt any further injunction. She moves directly toward her bed, an old iron military cot, and with her hand brushes crumbs from the sheetless mattress, arranges the blanket neatly, dusts off the small pillow, and then with her cupped palms gathers what has fallen on the floor and carries it to a basket near the stove. As the old crumbs, a couple of lollipop sticks, and an empty orange soda-pop bottle get thrown in, the mother remarks, in a soft voice, that the rich have learned to take good care of themselves, to be tidy and prompt. The girl now does a philosophical about-face; she says she hopes her parents never become rich and that she would give away her money if she had a lot. Then she has a second thought: "I'd buy everyone in the village a snowmobile, even the smallest baby. Then no one would have one while other people didn't. It's not bad to have a lot of money; but it's bad to have it while other people don't have it."

Betsy has heard that point of view expressed many times by her grandfather, and by her mother and father, too. When the mother hears her daughter speak so, it is as if a threatening war had been replaced by a pact of friendship and mutual support. The child finishes her chores; the mother moves close to her, helps her straighten out the particular corner of the room that she has responsibility for, pats her lightly and with obvious tenderness on the back. Betsy had thought of going outside before, but now, acknowledging her own shift of mood, announces that she will stay in and try being of help, if she can, to her mother. As the girl helps cut up some fish, which will be fried in deep fat, the mother responds to questions about the history of the Eskimo people. Betsy wants to know how long they have been in the village, and how long they have had snowmobiles in the village, and how long they have been visited by airplanes once a week. The questions continue, are answered briefly, factually. They are both general and specific, have to do with matters of faith and conviction or with technology, both primitive and highly developed. Motorboats interest the girl, but so do rowboats and kayaks.

Eventually there is silence. Betsy decides to draw a landscape. (Figure 1.) She makes no effort to look outside and remind herself what there is to see, nor does she close her eyes first — a gesture some children make, as if to summon up for themselves what they want to represent. She simply sets to work, quickly and forthrightly. She makes the sky first, a light blue, lighter than the sky other American children make. She omits the sun altogether. She works on a river, setting it off with the thinnest of black lines. The ice is breaking, she observes. Consequently, blue water interrupts the snow. The white crayon is used most, and she worries that it fails to evoke the visual reality around her. So she abandons the picture when it is done for another attempt. She decides to let the white paper *be* her accomplished landscape, except for a few interventions with blue for the sake of the sky. That does not work either; she decides to abandon hope of picturing the tundra and nearby river. Instead Betsy turns her attention to a nearby hill, whose pine trees offer a limited relief from the endless white, flat land she had been trying to evoke. She is ever so delicate with the trees; they are each fragile, yet obviously strong and flexible: they survive the winter, as she remarks when she is done. (Figure 2.) She is told that she can use black paper, cover it with white — a visitor's suggestion, a "technique" explained. She shakes her head. She will have no part of that idea.

Betsy's mother smiles, admits she will never be an art connoisseur, but is appreciative of her child's ability. The girl asks the mother if she has ever drawn a picture. No, she hasn't. Has her grandfather? The mother says she is always reluctant to answer for him, but she is sure he hasn't. The girl decides to try her hand at a snowmobile. She has just heard the noise of one, and she is sure it is going down toward the river. As she works, using a black crayon for the machine, her mother looks outside: some birds, no doubt just returned from their winter stay to the south. Betsy does not get up to catch a glimpse, but she does turn her attention away from the machine to the portrayal of a sky. Soon it is filled with birds, each one small but in their sum a virtual blanket. The snowmobile is eventually completed; it was going to be small, anyway, but now, in comparison to the birds, it seems quite insignificant. (Figure 3.) As a matter of fact, the mother remarks that the machine looks like a fallen bird. Yes, that is not such a bad idea, Betsy muses: "The snowmobile is like a bird that wants to fly, but can't, so all it can do is make a lot of noise and try to go faster, faster, but it never takes off. Why don't the white men who make planes give wings to their snowmobiles?" She pauses only briefly before she comes up with a reply to her own question: "A snowmobile isn't a plane; they're different." As she looks at her picture, she decides to pursue, almost as in a reverie, the subject of differences. "An Eskimo is not a white man. The teacher told my brother that we're all like animals; we were once animals. But then we became people. My grandfather said the white man comes from one place, and we come from another, even if now Alaska has a lot of white people. When my grandfather was a boy, he said he didn't see too many white people; and *his* grandfather had told him there were no white people around most of his life — only at the end. The teacher told my brother that today girls are the same as boys. My father laughed, and my grandfather did. But my mother said she knew what the teacher was saying!"

Her mother at first says nothing in response; she is putting on her outdoor clothes to go get some more fish, kept frozen in a small cabin removed from the main house. As she leaves she tells her daughter that Eskimos have seen their whole world change in recent years, and there is, no doubt, more to come — more people, more machines, more alterations in customs, habits, beliefs. The birds somehow survive, despite the continuing turmoil beneath them; and the fish still are to be found, for all the motorboats that have made the river far from the quiet place it used to be in the summer; so, Eskimos will also manage to survive. The girl is unhappy with a certain fatalism she detects in her mother. She has heard the same attitude expressed by her grandfather: stand firm, and somehow we will stay around, and the generations will follow one another. Betsy has other ideas; she is convinced that the snowmobile and the motorboats, if given even further reign — if owned by more people — would make Eskimo life better, easier, more pleasant. The mother will hold her ears when one of the snowmobiles goes by; Betsy listens to the noise quite eagerly.

Not that she is infatuated with the machines or allows their presence to change her overall sense of perspective. While she draws, she thinks: the machine is no match for the natural world in all its threatening, awesome, and occasionally quite beckoning presence. The machine is a help, even as the dogs are. The dogs, those Arctic huskies that are almost taken for granted by her and the other children of the village, are still (as her grandfather has often reminded her) the mainstays of village life. For a machine even to be compared with the dog is, in itself, noteworthy. But the child knows enough not to get hypnotized and fooled by Western industrialism. More planes might mean faster mail, a more varied and plentiful diet — assuming the continued willingness of the state and federal government to provide a subsistence economy with welfare checks, food stamps, surplus commodities. More planes might mean a greater intimacy with the outside world, something intangible, yet quite real to an Eskimo child: "We would see a lot of white people; there'd be more movies brought in, and we'd hear more news." But there is no likelihood, Betsy knows, that machines will overcome the long Arctic winter. She has seen dogs penetrate the coldest weather. She has seen machines rendered useless by weather she herself considers, at the very least, unsurprising. The dogs are utterly essential; without them life seems unimaginable. The motor-driven boats, the snowmobiles, and the airplanes belong to another world — one that has steadily encroached upon her existence but not one she wants to see replace the essence of Eskimo life.

Is there still such an "essence" that a child like her can confidently and persistently know — even put into words? In her own way she both asks and answers that question: "I think I will paint a picture. It is better to use paint than crayons; I've decided that if you want to show how we look, especially in winter, then it's best to use the paint set." She ambitiously undertakes a study of the village in midwinter, well before the weather begins to moderate. She ignores the sky, even the snow and ice, at first; she uses black and a touch of green to indicate the houses of the village, some nearby trees, a store, and a school. Then she surrounds all she has done with white — flat stretches of it, hills of it, flakes of it. There is no sky. There is no sun or, for that matter, moon. (Figure 4.) When she is finished she recalls what her father once told his family: "He has a cousin who went to live in the city, a long way from here. Then he left Alaska; he went to the lower forty-eight. He was in the army, I think. They sent him to a school down there. When he came back he said he knew how other people live: they look at the sun, but we look at the ice and the clouds. My father wasn't too happy with his cousin. He said we look for the sun, too. Now that the weather is getting warmer, we will see more and more of the sun. My father says that the Eskimos are like our dog: we know how to live here. The white man, he comes here and then he leaves."

But Betsy knows that white men, too, have remained in various parts of Alaska. They may not, by and large, live in small villages, under the circumstances she takes for granted. They may come, dig in, dig the earth out (for gold, for other minerals, for oil), and then leave. They may retreat to southern cities as often as possible — to hotels and motels, to buildings that are large and made of brick or concrete. But for limited periods of time even some of those people have endured the Arctic at its most oppressive; and there are some white people, she knows, who have done so for years at a time. Her grandfather and her father have told her about one such family. She speaks of them as if she knows them, though she has never met them: "They came to our village. They asked our people if they could join us. We said yes. They get their mail here. They buy at our store. They come to our meetings. When the ice melts, we always look for their boat. My grandfather asked them once if they would like to live closer to the village, instead of upstream and away. No, they wouldn't, they told him. He said he is sure that they have the spirit of our people living in them. He said maybe they are Eskimos who look white, just like there are some of our people who look like Eskimos, but they have the white man's spirit in them."

Betsy is halted by her own, vivid remark. She considers, silently, what she has said, resumes in a minute or so: "One of those Eskimos with a white man's spirit came from our village. He was married to my grandfather's sister. He took her, and they went to the big city: Fairbanks. He works for the government; he has something to do with the planes that bring us mail and food. He came back here two years ago; I don't remember him, but my mother says he was not very nice. He kept on telling all of us how dirty we are, and how clean we should try to be. He didn't even like our new school. He said we are not good at school; and it didn't look neat, the way it should — and he told people he'd talk to the important people he knows in the city. My father told my grandfather not to be so unhappy with his sister and her husband. Finally, my grandfather could smile; he told my father that he woke up in the night, and he realized what was wrong: his sister had married a white man; she'd married a man who thought he was an Eskimo when he was a boy, but pretty soon, when he was older, he turned out to be white. Or maybe he'd been taken over by some white spirit."

II

ARCTIC WANDERLUST

THE GIRL'S older sister, Ann, aged ten, is skeptical of talk of "spirits." She has asked her teacher, a white man, about them, and has been told it's all nonsense. Ann describes the sequence: "I went to him, and told him that I'd heard that there are spirits, and they take over a person; you can be an Eskimo, and a spirit comes, and you're white, even if you still look the same. He laughed and said no, no. I started telling him more, and he still said no, so I decided to stop." Ann is very fond of the teacher. She wants to be a teacher herself. She wants to stay in school until she is eligible to help educate her own people. To do so, she knows, will mean leaving home, going to a boarding school hundreds of miles away, run by the federal government for those Eskimo children who want a high school education — in her village a very small number. Meanwhile, she contents herself with another kind of departure from the village; she reads books about distant places, including the rest of the United States of America, and she looks at maps and learns how to spell the names of cities, rivers, mountain ranges, state and national capitals. Her teacher has called her a bright, eager, responsive student, and she has found in his approval a sense of hope: the future will be different for her than it promises to be for many of her friends.

Ann is not a strange or eccentric girl. She does not want to leave her village in order to turn her back on her own people. She has a critical eye, though; she reads a lot, has listened closely to her teachers, remembers what they have had to say about the Eskimos and Alaska. They, in turn, have tried to be critical without being condescending or arrogant; or so Ann insists — aware, no doubt, how proud and sensitive her people are. She often prefaces her remarks with a defense of the school she attends: "It is a good place. The teachers there have come here to this village to try to help us. They don't want to interfere. My uncle told my cousin to tell the teachers that they should go away, because they make *us* want to go away, but my cousin didn't say anything to the teachers. My uncle told him he was glad; he said it is wrong to be unfriendly to outsiders, even when they make mistakes. But it is my uncle who doesn't understand; the teachers are trying to help us, and that's not being bad. My cousin said his father shouts at the teachers, but not when he's near the school, and he could be heard! My uncle thinks the white people have brought nothing but trouble to us. But my father doesn't agree with him, and my grandfather remembers all the troubles our people had, before there were white teachers here in the village, before any white people had come here, even for a visit."

Ann is tempted to go on, but she decides that it is hopeless: some people feel one way, some another — and she is not old enough to be heard with great respect. Her girl friends warn her that if she doesn't learn to keep her opinions to herself, she will get into trouble later. A girl is not one to speak about the issues she keeps mentioning. And a woman ought be grateful for each day's reasonably bearable news — rather than constantly be coming up with criticisms, complaints, invidious comparisons that make Eskimos seem, at the very least, an ill-fated people. Ann's friends have a way of teasing her gently into silence; she admires them for their tact. But she knows what they think, what they have been taught to think: "My mother is like the other mothers in the village, so I have a good idea of what my friends hear. They are told that the school may help us, but it is a dangerous place, too, because we end up thinking that the only people who know anything are the white schoolteachers. My mother sees the teachers, and smiles at them, and she would serve them the best supper she could make, and would give them her own winter jacket, if they needed one and couldn't find one. But she would be unhappy with them after they left. She would call us to her, and she would warn us that we will get into a lot of trouble if we don't keep our eyes half-closed while they teach us at school. She once asked a teacher if he would like to go fishing with us and then dry the fish; he said he would, but he doesn't like the taste of fish, and he buys his food at the store, and he has some sent in by the airplane every week — mailed from Fairbanks, or maybe Chicago, where his family lives. My mother wouldn't let us forget; she kept on reminding us that the white teacher tells us about everything, because he knows so much, but he wouldn't be alive a week here if it wasn't for the airplane and what it brings.

"I told her I didn't agree. If the white people wanted to live here, a lot of them, they would build their own village, and they'd stay alive, they'd get their food somehow. They'd learn to like fish, if they had to! But she was unhappy with me; she told me I must not argue with her. Later she called me to her and said she knew I didn't agree with her sometimes, but a mother has to have quiet in the house — no arguments — or the younger children will be upset. I told her I *did* agree with her about that! She smiled. She asked me to help her with the cooking, and I did. While I was cutting the fish, she said she wanted me to know something. She said that when she was my age, she used to see the boats come up the river, bringing

supplies and mail during the summer. She'd wonder where
the boats came from. She'd wish she could go on a trip and see
the big cities she'd hear about from the men who worked
on the boats. She and her friends would ask to go aboard the
boats, and they'd look around, and they'd ask what it was like
to live in a city, and then they'd go home and tell their mothers
and fathers. My mother once admitted to her mother that she
wished she wouldn't live the rest of her life here, in this village. Her mother said she knew my mother would change her
mind, and she did. My mother said she's sure I'll change my
mind, but she wants me to know that if I don't, she won't be
unhappy, because she remembers how she used to feel when
she was young, and she knows that it's different today —
the airplanes, and the big icebreakers, and the snowmobiles.
And we have our school here, and the planes can get through
more and more, except in the worst weather. And the radios
are so strong, you seem to be able to hear people from everywhere. My mother said she heard the shortwave radio in the
store, and she kept on thinking about it later, when she came
home, and she told my father that if we had a set here, she
wouldn't be able to do anything, because she'd be listening all
day long. But my father said no, that wouldn't happen —
except for one day, maybe."

Ann decides, one afternoon, to draw a picture of a city
— Fairbanks, perhaps, or Anchorage. She remembers photographs of Alaska's cities, and she has heard her teachers talk
about them; and besides, she has her own ideas about what
urban living is like, based on various books she has read or has
heard read in school. If she could do a good job, her mother
would be pleased, and even (the girl hopes, a bit desperately,
perhaps) won over to another view of the future — the artist's.
But Ann has trouble figuring out how to do the drawing or
painting. She starts with crayons, abandons them. She uses the

paint set, abandons it. She decides to do her own village first — using paints, and, yes, even trying black paper for the first time. She will get herself warmed up that way. She works efficiently, knowingly, sensitively; she paints, does a careful job of suggesting the outline of the village, but does not distinguish any particular building. The sky and the land become a stretch of white. Trees are put to one side of the village, which is rendered fragile, small, vulnerable: strands of brown in a corner of the enormous white expanse. (Figure 5.) When the time comes to turn to the picture of a city, she hesitates, decides that she is thirsty, sips a Coke, begins — only to stop quickly: she cannot do it. All the more reason, she muses, to go on a trip, to see for herself; then she will be able to draw, and draw well.

Ann decides to do something else, though; she returns to the white paper and sketches with a black crayon the plane that connects the village to the outside world. She has trouble doing so; she makes the plane too small and fails to remember the details of its appearance: how many windows, how many wheels. She is rather upset with herself. She has seen that plane so many times, yet she cannot draw it to her satisfaction. She decides that the next time the plane comes, she will take the crayons and paper with her, go sit near the plane, and draw it. But her mother is not at all happy with that idea. She stops sewing, begins to give her daughter a lecture: why does she want to draw a plane in the first place? Why does she want to draw a picture of some distant city? Outside spring is struggling hard to establish itself. Outside a few hardy birds, pioneers and scouts, have returned north and soon will be followed by others. Is it not enough to look at them? Why bother drawing or painting them? And the sun, the growing, lengthening sun, how can anyone do justice to it with a crayon and a piece of paper? The sun is warmth on one's face. Let someone try to show that with a few crayon marks!

Ann hears her mother, throws up her arms, surrenders. She puts aside her project, asks her mother if she can be of any help. The mother is pleased but worried; she did not mean to hurt or humiliate her daughter. A person is entitled to have pride, to feel that no one will go too far when it comes to personal remarks. So, after a few minutes, the mother brings up the subject of drawing and painting again. Why doesn't the girl try to draw a picture, after all — before it is time to help prepare supper? The girl smiles, begins a drawing, works hard at it, tells her mother not to look. It turns out to be a sketch of the river, with some fish swimming in it. The summer has arrived, the snow and ice are gone. The sky is clear blue, has a sun. The tundra is brown-green, flat, inviting, with its frequent nests of eggs. The mother is gratified. Now that the river is beginning to stir, now that the ice is yielding to the gradually increasing length of the days, the diminishing cold, summer is indeed foreseeable. The mother expresses her enjoyment by staring a full minute or two at the picture and by saying "soon." The girl repeats her mother's word.

They talk about the seasons. Ann tells her mother what she has learned: about the four seasons; about the sun's varying distance from the earth; about the tides and their influence on the coast; about the origin and destiny of rivers. The mother nods, says yes, smiles, occasionally shakes her head — to emphasize a point her daughter has made rather than indicate disapproval. After about fifteen minutes neither of them has any more to say. They work well together, cutting up fish, boiling water, frying potatoes. The mother at one point makes a point of acknowledging to her daughter that the white man has influenced Eskimo life in many ways — that it is, after all, foolish to direct accusations at a school and its teachers, when there they are, the two of them, frying potatoes, and all the while sipping Coca-Cola. Ann thanks her mother for saying what she did. The avid student and would-be world traveler is impressed: her mother's reference to Coca-Cola was right on mark. And her mother had stopped frowning at an institution many children don't regard as restrictive, boring, or demanding.

Not that the school is all that special. It is a rather conventional place, and only one or two of the teachers even claim to be especially interested in capturing and fueling the imagination of the children. Yet that is what happens; boys and girls become excited almost in spite of the teachers. Ann explains why candidly: "When we're in school, we hear about places far away. I'd like to go on the plane one day; I'd like to see where it stops after it leaves here. The teacher says it stops at a village like ours, but that when it's emptied all the mail and packages, it turns around and goes to Fairbanks, and that's a big city. And she says planes come to Fairbanks from far away; she showed us on the map. I stretched my hand, and the planes came from places even farther than I could reach — two hands, maybe, or more. We have books; the pictures in them show places where the sun is hot, and they never have snow. They have the American flag, too. My friends and I are taking care of the teacher's plants, and we have some turtles — flown in. The teacher says she wants us to learn about the whole world. We have tropical fish in the room, too. The teacher shows us what children in other places read about us; it sounds funny, hearing about yourself, your own people. The teacher asked each of us to choose a place, any place in the world, we'd like to go visit. I didn't know where to go, but then I saw Chicago on the map and I chose it. There's a pilot, he flies in here a lot, and he's from Chicago. He told me that he doesn't care if he ever gets back there, but when I told him I'd like to see some city, he said Chicago was very big and had tall buildings, and he remembers where they are, so one day I can just get in the plane, and we'll head for Chicago! I guess he was joking!"

Rather obviously he was; but he knew that he was touching a responsive chord in her, because Ann had several times asked him where he'd flown, where he'd like to fly — and how many passengers he could carry. She loves to go to the landing strip near the village to watch his plane suddenly appear, out of the clouds, slowly circle, then approach and land. She says there is no greater pleasure than observing the pilot get out of his plane and the crew begin to unload. If she could fly a plane, she would never want to stop for very long; she would go from village to village, from nation to nation. Once her mother asked Ann what she would do after she had visited every landing strip in the world. The girl had no difficulty answering: she would start all over again seeing various places a second time around. The mother was surprised, saddened, but eventually able to laugh — and to begin teasing her daughter: we will miss you, but we will be getting picture postcards day after day, and when you come back, you will be an experienced pilot, and we will wait near the landing strip and expect to be taken for a ride, high above our village.

Ann does not enjoy such comments all that much. She senses a streak of anger and disapproval in her mother's humor; she also begins to realize, as she hears her daydreams being caricatured, how unreal they are. Once she was drawing a picture of the sky. She had decided to portray a snowy, cloudy sky, and she had finished doing so. At the last minute, she added an airplane, a two-engine mail plane. Ann talked out loud as she tried to decide whether to make the plane a mere dot in the sky or whether to have the plane ready to land, hence low and large: "I like to see the plane when it is high up, and it could be a bird. I like to see it when it first comes out of the clouds. But it's fun to see it get nearer, and then it is larger and larger, and you see the wheels coming down, and then you try to see the wheels touching the ground. My brother used to like planes, but now he doesn't care about them at all. He goes hunting with my father; he goes fishing with him. He has told me that I'll forget there are planes in this world when I am as old as he is. But he is only two years older than I am, and I think that I'll never forget about planes. If we all forgot about planes, we'd forget about our mail, and our food, and supplies for keeping the house warm, and furniture. Everything is flown in to the village. Maybe if I went up in the airplane once I'd never want to try it again. There are times when I agree with my mother: the airplane is noisy, and it is dangerous.

"One plane crashed near our village, and it burned, and nests were destroyed, and fish died, and the river became dirty for a few days from the oil that was brought to it. They sent another plane here, to see what happened. They said it wasn't the pilot's fault. He died. My father keeps reminding me that Eskimos have been here for hundreds of years, long before there were any airplanes. Even the teachers in school tell us that they are worried, that the white people are going to destroy the state of Alaska; they'll dig for oil, and then send it over our land, and a pipe will break and the oil will spill, and birds will die in their nests, and fish will die in the water, and animals will die, and it will be harder for us than ever before. We all walked to see what the plane that crashed had done — everyone in the village. My father felt sorry for the pilot; it was a plane with only one engine. My mother asked me if I wanted to go nearer; they didn't want to get too close. I said no. I said I'd probably never fly in an airplane. Maybe some day I'll get to climb a mountain. I could see far away, and then I could go down."

A year ago Ann took a long sled ride with her mother, father, and older brother. Her grandfather stayed with the

younger children. She recalls seeing the foothills of a mountain range. She recalls telling her father, then, that planes have
trouble going over very high mountains. Her father had
laughed and said he was glad that planes can't go anywhere
they please. Later a plane had passed over them — and
headed for the mountains. But the girl had felt no triumph; she
had felt sorry for the people in the plane. They were missing
the fun she was having: the joy of being pulled by huskies
across the land; the joy of helping her father dig a hole in the
ice, then catch fish, one after the other; the joy of watching the
wind sweep snow down a hill and out toward the tundra
— the swirling clouds of white that move relentlessly toward
everywhere and nowhere.

She has asked her father if he thinks she will one day go to
a boarding school; then she would have to fly to her destination. He said no, she will not — unless she very much wants to
do so. Some of her teachers encourage the children to pursue
a high school education, but most of them don't: what for? She
wondered at one point whether someday she might become
a teacher. Her mother and father had not encouraged the
idea. They had no notion, anyway, of how one goes about
becoming accredited to work in the village school. After the
girl was discouraged from teaching, she began to wonder
about pilots: are any of them women? Her acquaintance, the
man who flies in weekly with mail and food, said yes, or maybe;
he knew none, but he was sure that somewhere in the world
women could and did fly planes.

One day as Ann stood beside her father, waiting for the fish
to bite, she repeated the queries: might she leave, get an
education, return to teach, or might she learn to fly? The
father said he would never stand in the way of his children.
The winds come, carry off what they can, stop. Children come,
stay, leave, remain away, usually return — even as the winds

also come back. Had not her aunt gone away, lived in another village — but appeared late in life, to die where she was born? The girl insists that it is not simply a matter of wanderlust. She wants to roam the world, see places she has read about, learn how to teach so that she can tell others about persons, places, and things unfamiliar. She has heard her own people, girls older than she, talk about how dull life is, how bored they are. When she tells her parents what she has overheard, they nod, smile at her, tell her to continue to dream, to study, to try to find a different life. But they also shrug their shoulders, begin to huddle together, as the wind bears down on them. Cold, hungry, worried about the possibility of a new blizzard beginning, they turn apprehensive, guarded, gloomy in their talk. Ann feels far less hopeful than she did only a few minutes earlier.

One evening Ann reminisces, tries to sort out what she has heard and thought: "I know about the couple from our village who went to the city. They went to two cities, to Nome, then to Fairbanks. They were just married, and they decided to leave. The man had gone to a boarding school, and graduated. His wife was glad to leave here. My mother says I remind her of the wife. She came back to us with her husband; they did not like living in the city. The man had a job in a city school; he swept and cleaned. If he'd been a teacher — if he'd learned to be one — maybe they would have stayed. But the wife said they would have come back anyway. She is friendly with our teachers at the school. She goes there with her baby, and she has coffee with them. They talk about cities, I think. Sometimes, in the winter especially, the teachers want to leave; they speak of other parts of the globe — and in class they tell us what it's like to live in a place where it's mostly warm. Or they tell us about New York City; one of the teachers lived there. They show us movies — about New York City or other cities. I'd like to go to New York, but I'd prefer Chicago. The pilot says in Chicago the people are friendlier. My mother is afraid I won't forget about those cities and that I'll leave. She reminds me that the man and his wife from our village left — but not for long. I don't think I'll leave. If I could just go once on the plane, I'd be happy."

Ann is rather pleased with herself; she has struck a compromise. She reminds herself of all the kind and approving words about Arctic life she has heard from teachers, from the pilot, from government officials — the white visitors she has met over the years. They have come to Alaska, have stayed there, because they find its weather, its people, its hurdles and challenges and opportunities, preferable to life elsewhere — life in the lower forty-eight. The more she thinks and talks about it, she realizes that she does not have to travel all over the world. But she continues to be taken with the idea of a city: many people; moviehouses and places where one may go out to eat; tall buildings; automobiles going up and down paved streets; several or more airplanes coming each day. And she continues to say, openly, that she would like to leave once, however briefly.

Ann decides to draw a city, calling upon what she has heard, read, been told. She reaches for the white crayon but puts it back with an ironic smile: force of habit! She seems at a loss to know which crayon to use. Finally she takes the brown one and begins to construct a building with it. She compares the building to a mountain, and she makes the building look like a hill — wide at the base, gradually narrower toward the top. She puts in several windows — arranged as if part of a house — and one door. After a long pause, she decides to provide an airport, which turns out to consist of a single runway, no terminal, but with two airplanes standing by. She looks at what she has done for a minute or so, then puts the drawing aside:

finished. (Figure 6.) She knows, however, that there ought to be more. She considers doing another one, but no, she will not — cannot: "I don't know how to draw a city, because I've never seen one. The teacher says we should make it up in our minds — something to draw or paint — and then go ahead and put down on the paper what we've thought up. We try. I close my eyes, like she says, and I try to think of a city. I see a building, and it's tall. I try to draw it, but I don't do a good job. Then the teacher shows us a picture of New York City, with the tallest building in the world, and it looks like a tree, only no branches. So, I'll draw that — a trunk of a tree."

She does another version, quickly and confidently; she takes a black crayon, works on what indeed seems to be a trunk of a tree, tapers things off at the top, and calls it quits. Then she remembers her teacher's admonition, draws another skyscraper, and another one: *there,* that is New York City, where more people live than in the whole of Alaska, as well as many foreign nations. But she never seems able to talk about New York without mentioning Chicago. The pilot came from there, she reminds herself yet again, and she would prefer the nation's second to its first city, were she given the choice of a visit to either. As for what she would do in Chicago, she knows quite well, having had talks on the subject with the pilot: "It is next to a lake. We could go fishing. We could go to a place where they have fish in a building, and see them swimming — like the tropical fish the teachers brought up here to show us. We could even see pictures of Eskimo people in another building. I asked the teacher if she thought we should have pictures of people from Chicago or New York here in the school, and she said no. We have pictures of children from Brazil on the wall now; they live near the world's longest river, the Amazon."

Ann's mind now moves toward the ocean. She has heard the

pilot talk with awe of the ocean — how much he loves flying over it. She has heard her teachers give names to different oceans, and she has had to memorize those names. She recites them: Arctic, Pacific, Atlantic, in that order — she cannot recall the others. She has also heard the oldest woman in the village, a great-aunt of hers, talk about the ocean. And she has compared what the old, weak, tired woman says with what the young, energetic, well-informed women who teach school have to say: "She is my mother's aunt. She was the oldest, but she outlived everyone, four brothers and four sisters. She says she is ashamed of herself, but she will not take her own life. She tells my mother that in the old days she would have killed herself, or been left to die, because there would not have been enough food, and the young people have to live their lives. But now she can stay with us until her brothers and sisters call her. She says she must have been very selfish, or they would have called her a long time ago. She says they are somewhere in the ocean. I asked her which ocean, and she laughed: there is only one ocean. I said no, that's not right; there are four or five oceans. She said I was being silly, I was talking as if I was half my age. I told her what our teachers say. She said she never went to school, and she is sure she should have gone; then she'd know a lot more than she does. But she laughed at the teachers and the names they have for the oceans. She is sure that there is only one ocean and that all the water in the world is connected, because the creeks and ponds lead to the rivers, and the rivers go to the ocean, and if there is another ocean, it is part of the one our river goes to.

"When she was a girl, her grandmother and grandfather took her by sled to the ocean, and told her that just like the fish, we have come up from the ocean, and live near the river, and we will go back to the ocean. She can remember her grandmother pointing beyond the ice, to the water; she was sitting on her grandfather's shoulders. They bowed their heads toward the water, and they asked her to do the same, and she did. Every year, just before the ice begins to break, my mother and father take her to the ocean. She looks at it and bows her head. Then she asks to go home. On the way, she says that she'll probably live until the next time we take her. She says that all animals were once part of the ocean. I asked her if she meant that once people were like the fish; she said she didn't know, but she believes what she was told by her grandparents, that once there was just the water, and then some land came. I told the teachers what I'd heard from the old woman, and they said there's no way to be sure. They said there were times when there was more land than water, and times when there has been more water than land. They said they don't believe that when you die, you go to the ocean to live. They said my father's aunt probably doesn't really believe that, either.

"I was going to ask her whether she did, but then I decided that I'd better not. She would be upset. She would tell my mother and father to take me away from the school. She's told them that a few times. She heard me talking about the airplane pilot, and she said I was going to leave the village and end up miles and miles away — inland, further and further from the ocean. Then I wouldn't be the same person. I'd be a white man, like the Americans from far away. They used to come and talk with her, she remembers. A minister came, and told her about the Bible. They built a church in our village, and they wanted her to come to it. She wouldn't go. Finally, they started bringing food to her, and she gave it to her children, and to her sisters and brothers, and she decided she would go to church because the minister was nice. He told her she should believe anything she likes, but she should agree that Jesus Christ was a good person, and He was God. My father and mother say they don't know if Jesus Christ is God; they say they don't think there is a God, but there may be one. The old lady says she has never worried about God: either the Christian God is above us, or He's in the ocean someplace; and if He's no place, then it's too bad, because the minister believes in Him and says He's the one who decides if we're good or bad. The teachers say they don't know, either; they say maybe there is no God."

She is rather confused; since no one seems to know for sure about the Christian God — does He or does He not exist? — it is hard for her to make a definite commitment to Him. Mostly, she thinks about the earth, rather than Heaven or Hell. But she does go to the church with her parents, who find the minister there now as generous as his predecessor: food baskets, friendly advice and support in connection with any encounter with the white world that may be necessary. The village needed a more secure and ample source of electricity; the minister, who moves from village to village, was quite helpful. He is also anxious to teach children, show them all sorts of Kodachromes. A number of active, self-reliant children, ordinarily not likely candidates for a church school, eagerly have joined up, look at the pictures, listen to stories, say yes, they are good, true stories.

III

YOUNG LEADER

ONE of those children is a twelve-year-old boy who also likes to talk to the pilot who comes to the village. John is a boy whom others of his age, even those a year or two older, regard as a leader. He talks to the minister like an equal. He challenges him on matters political, theological, philosophical. He asks him if God favors white people over Eskimos. He asks him if God likes the Bureau of Indian Affairs and the schools it sponsors. He asks him if God is on the side of the storekeeper, who makes the most money in the village, or on the side of the elderly people who have nothing to their name. The minister rallies to the defense of the poor, the weak, the vulnerable. But the boy is not easily persuaded to let up his scrutiny. What is the church like in the lower forty-eight? He wonders that aloud at one meeting, after a series of Kodachromes show the Eskimo children some stunning pictures of the California seacoast, as well as interesting, attractive San Francisco. The minister acknowledges openly that the Christian Church, in its various expressions, forms, structures, has betrayed Christ over the centuries. He tries hard to explain himself and his own purpose — to serve a number of villages in a particular section of Alaska.

Later, in his own home, John both defends the minister and

continues his critical appraisal: "He's a good person. We all
like him. He wants the Eskimos to live better. He argues with
our schoolteachers. I've heard them; it is fun to listen while
white people argue! The teachers didn't realize for a long time
that my friend and I were listening; when they did, they
stopped. I don't blame them. When my mother gets angry at
my father, she says nothing until they can be alone. She
doesn't want everyone to know how much pepper she can
have on her tongue. Later I told the minister that I'd heard all
he'd said, and I was on his side. He was glad I was. But I told
him that he should go talk to other ministers, not to the schoolteachers in our village. He should tell the rich, white people
that it's wrong, the way the Eskimos are pushed around. We
don't have much to say about how we're going to live —
even the teachers admitted to him that he was right when he
said that."

John goes on; he repeats much of what he had heard the
minister himself say. But the boy and the boy's father and
grandfather have said the same things many times. The minister is, however, a white man — and to hear such self-criticism
from white people is not an everyday experience for Eskimos,
the boy knows. He says *that*, too — indirectly but with unmis-
takable emphasis. For the boy, white people are powerful,
hard to speak to, a source of confusion. They introduced, on
the one hand, snowmobiles, airplanes, frozen foods, electricity, welfare checks; on the other hand, alcohol, drugs, jails,
schools where children learn to look down on themselves,
other schools located hundreds, even thousands, of miles
away, to which children are arbitrarily sent. The particular
village this boy belongs to has banned alcohol, but there is
another, larger, village nearer the ocean where alcohol is plentiful — along with work during the summer season at a commercial fishery, where the river's salmon are cleaned, cut,

salted and packed — to be sent "down there," as the boy refers to the lower forty-eight.

The boy has heard his grandfather complain endlessly about white people and what their presence means; the boy both agrees with and takes issue with his grandfather: "The white people are everywhere, so I guess we can't expect them to stay away from here. The minister showed us a map; all the places where America has air force bases were marked; they're all over the world. Air force planes land down the river; they never come to our landing strip, though, because it's too small. The big pipeline, carrying the oil, won't come near us; but I have a cousin who lives near where it will run, and he's waiting to watch the machines come in to dig. They've come to his village and talked to the people. I'm in favor of the pipeline, I think; the Eskimo people will get some money. My grandfather says that money is like liquor — you end up waiting for the checks, just like you end up drinking every day. My father doesn't drink anymore. But he used to, and my grandfather doesn't forget. He told my father that if he didn't stop drinking, then he'd have a funeral to go to — his father's! My grandfather was going to kill himself! That stopped my father, and then he went around the village, asking people to join him in getting rid of liquor. We had a vote; the people from the state government came — and we won: no liquor is sold here. Men go and buy it in other villages; they bring it home and we can hear them getting drunk. But at least you can't just walk to the store and spend your money there on whiskey, instead of food. The store owner wanted to pay each person who voted five dollars so that they would say yes, we should have the whiskey here. And he is an Eskimo! I keep reminding my grandfather of that, and he turns away. My father said to stop reminding the old man. My mother said not to stop, because if I remind someone else I remind myself! A lot of Eskimos drink when they get to be fifteen or so, and there's nothing to do."

John stops talking. He looks at an empty whiskey bottle his father insists upon keeping on a table near his bed — a reminder to him of the bad times he used to have. His wife has repeatedly objected. She would have thrown the bottle out a long time ago. But the man has his reasons, and his son has heard them being turned into the basis of an argument: "My father took me once with him; we were going to catch salmon, then get them ready for drying. We started setting up the racks, then we got our nets ready. Before we went out on the boat, Father told me how glad he is to get up in the morning and be without a sore head and a sore stomach. He told me how he used to feel when he'd been drinking; he felt terrible. But he couldn't stop. He'd try; each morning he'd try. But each morning he'd end up taking one drink, then another. He'd hold the bottle to his lips. He never used a glass. When my mother offered him a glass, he broke it. He said that if he could wait long enough to find a glass and pour the whiskey into it, he could keep himself from taking the whiskey. He either grabbed the bottle and drank from it, or he kept away from the bottle. But he stopped my mother from throwing the bottle out. When she did, he shouted and threw the dishes and pots around, and we were scared.

"My mother would tell us, in front of him, to leave the whiskey alone. My grandfather said that my father had fallen under the power of the white people, and that one day he would 'break out and be free.' My father smiled when my mother told us that. My father was drunk, but he said she was right! When he did break out, he said he was sure that he'd never have another drink. My mother wasn't so sure, but my grandfather told her not to worry. He had gone with my father to get firewood, and my father told him that he would *never* drink again. My father hadn't said that before; he refused to promise because he didn't want to break his promise. He's never made a promise that he couldn't keep. Now he talks to men who still drink; they smuggle in bottles, and you can walk by their houses in the summertime, and you can hear by the way they're talking that they're drinking a lot. My father tells me to go home, and he walks right into the house of a man who is drinking and he starts talking about how sick he used to be, and how sick he gets now, just thinking of the past. Then he'll tell the man *not* to stop until he is really ready to stop.

"The man's wife will get very upset; one wife told my mother that my father must be getting five dollars from the owners of the store where the men get their whiskey. My mother was very upset, but the woman was only teasing her. The wives wish my father would be a better preacher. I asked the minister why he doesn't help my father become a better preacher! The minister said that preachers don't stop people from drinking. I told my mother what he'd said, and she shook her head and said that you can't let a man drink and drink. But I think she knows now that the minister is right. She tells the wives of men drinking that you should try to stop a man from drinking, but if he won't stop, no matter what you say or try to do, then you should sit down and even lift the bottle for him, if his hands and arms are shaky. Then pray the day will come that he learns to say no. If you get him to promise every day to stop and he doesn't, then he'll be a man who can't keep his promise, and he'll drink because he'll want to forget that he made promises and couldn't live up to them.

"When my father and I went to catch salmon, and he talked with me about the drinking he used to do, he told me that when he was very sick, and when he thought he wouldn't live very long, he promised himself that he wouldn't say he'd stop until he was ready to stop. He told me that when you promise someone you'll do something — yourself or another person — then you are saying the most important two words in the world: I will. He said never begin with those two words unless you know you'll be able to do what you say. When he decided to promise my grandfather and my mother and all of us that he'd stop drinking, he took the bottle off the floor — it was half-full — and put it on the table and said he'd never again take a drink. And he hasn't. Then my mother picked up the bottle, and she was going to empty it and throw it away, but he said no, she must never touch the bottle. He wanted it to stay near him! A few days later, he emptied the bottle, but he's never going to throw it out. He says it reminds him of the promise he made. My mother doesn't understand why he needs to be reminded, but she never argues with him. I think I understand. He told me; he said that the bottle on the table is the bottle he beat. He said he fought with the whiskey in the bottle, and he won over it. He said it's like going out with a gun, and there are a hundred white men, and they have their guns, and they have their fast planes, but he is the only Eskimo, and he just tells them that they can kill him, but they can't take him a prisoner and put him in their jails, so he'll just stand there, and let them go ahead and do what they want, but if they try to touch him, he'll shoot himself. They don't know what to do. They just stand still. The white men only know how to fight, not how to stay away from fights."

John isn't so certain, it turns out, that he would want to be faced with the challenge his father described. He is a tough, combative boy — or so his teachers describe him. They consider him unusually assertive, as Eskimo children go. As teachers, of course, they welcome such a trend; they have come to the village — whites from the lower forty-eight — to be themselves an "outside influence," to bring change. The boy agrees with them; he refers to them as "white people" and is sure that they will one day leave — having taught Eskimo children a lot about places they have never heard of and will never see. He disputes the emphasis they place on themselves, the high re-

gard they have for their "influence." He considers his forceful-
ness to be a quite traditional trait, acquired from his grandfather, who is one of the most respected men in the village and,
for that matter, other villages.

The grandfather is well known to many Eskimos, as the boy
makes clear — and not only to boast about a man he is proud
of: "The teachers ask me why everyone looks up to my grandfather. I tell them I don't know. My grandfather said I give the
right answer! One teacher said he had an explanation. He is
an Indian, and he wants to stay here for a long time. He told
the other teachers that my grandfather is a leader and that's
why everyone pays attention to him. The teachers asked why
my grandfather is a leader; the Indian answered: why is anyone a leader? I told my grandfather and he laughed. He said
he'd be glad to talk with the Indian teacher I like, but they
haven't talked much. They say hello when they meet, but my
grandfather has not been feeling too good, and he does not
want to talk with strangers. He believes that he's alive for a
reason; each day he tries to do what he believes he's here to
do. He says he'll die when there's no longer any reason for him
to be here. He helps my father get wood. He helps my mother
with the fish; she says he's better at cooking than she ever was.
He takes me out for a walk and teaches me how to find wild
birds' eggs and how to collect moss. He knows how to keep
warm, and he tells me and my sister and my brother how to
keep warm. He makes sure I know how to put the moss in my
boots when it is very cold. He told me that he hopes he stays
alive until he has taught my youngest brother how to take care
of himself. Then my grandfather will leave us.

"My mother says he almost died a few years ago — and
many times he's been sick, and people have given up, and told
themselves that he's soon not going to be here. But he stays
with us, and it's because he wants to make sure we hear every

story he knows! Everyone believes that he knows more about the village than anyone else. Even faraway people will say that if you want to know anything about our village, go ask my grandfather. He will sit down and explain how the village was built, and why his grandparents built our house here, and not further up the river. He should have been a teacher — that's what my favorite teacher, the Indian, said. My father said: your grandfather *is* a teacher. But when I told my grandfather what the teacher said, he didn't get annoyed. He said he can remember when the government built the school, and when they brought in the first teachers from outside, and how hard it was to persuade the people to send their children there every day."

The boy admires the old man's pride, his tact, his unwillingness to take any statement or controversy personally. He remembers once when younger going for a walk with his grandfather, hearing him talk about the snow, the ice, the long sunless winters. The boy wanted to know why — why are other parts of the world warmer, easier to live in? The old man had no answer for a long time; he told the boy he would like to think about the question. Finally he told the boy that there was no point asking whys, only a need to get through that day, then the next, and all those that follow, until the end comes. The boy was not at all satisfied; he wanted to know whether his grandfather had ever thought of trying to live elsewhere. The grandfather said no. The boy asked *another* why — why not? The grandfather suddenly turned the tables on his grandson: why was he asking all those whys? The boy didn't know how to answer. He said he didn't know; he was, quite simply, curious. The grandfather replied that he didn't know, either, why he couldn't come up with satisfactory explanations; perhaps it was because, quite simply, he *wasn't* curious. But the boy knew how eager his grandfather was to search out eggs, find geese, hunt seals, go fishing, scan the skies, spot the first crack in the ice, watch the sun rise or set, discover some good thick moss that he could cut, dry, and use to pad shoes, and thereby keep his grandchildren warm. Why did such a vigorous, independent, thoughtful man refuse to allow himself the ruminative, speculative moments the boy felt prone to?

The old man never would answer such a question, but John had his own way of finding out what he wanted to know: "I asked my mother and she said I was being foolish, because when you are born in a place, you have to live there, and no one knows why one place is different from another, so I'd better stop wasting my time asking. My father said he'd wondered, too; but he said he was told by his mother that it was once hot here all winter, then it got cold, and one day it might get hot again. My grandmother told my father that there was a big fight long ago between a white bear and a brown bear, and the white bear won, and that was when the snow came to our land. She heard stories like that when she was a girl, but she didn't really believe them, and she was happy to see that my father didn't either. She told him that the winds bring bad weather, but they can change and bring good weather. I asked my grandfather if he'd let me tell him what I believed; and he said yes, he'd much rather listen to me than talk. So, I told him about the winds — that I'd heard they cause the snow and ice, and if they changed, there would be different weather here. And he said I was right, and that was the secret he hadn't told me — about the winds."

Not that the grandfather went any further. John remembers asking about the winds: where do they come from, and why are they so harsh, and when will they let up, go elsewhere, try hurling their force on other regions of the earth? Whereupon the old man told the boy something he has never forgotten: "He told me that I had better stop asking him questions like that, because no one knows the answers to them — even the white man, and he thinks he knows the answer to every question." The boy has heard words to that effect over and over again; he has, upon occasion, repeated them to the one teacher (the Indian) he trusts. The teacher listens respectfully but disagrees; he tells the boy that there are causes, effects, reasons, explanations. The boy smiles, nods his head, says nothing. As he compares in his mind his grandfather's way of regarding the world and his teacher's, he decides to make a drawing. A blast of wind has reminded him of what he has heard at home about Arctic weather; he decides to show the tundra under siege — a fierce, snow-bearing wind sweeping across the land. He announces that the first snow is the one that he finds most exciting, so he will attempt to show how it appears to him, as he thinks about the early autumn months when suddenly, overnight it seems, summer turns into winter.

He draws the tundra with great care and obvious affection. He works hard on the grass. With a mischievous look, he sketches a nest, full of eggs. He tells his mother that he has drawn some eggs, and they are not far from the village. She laughs. It is an old source of tension as well as humor between them. The boy is supposed to keep an eye out for eggs, and sometimes he comes home, after an extensive search, claiming that none are to be found. His mother then goes out and, invariably, stumbles upon a nest of eggs even before undertaking the pursuit formally. As the boy tells of his mother's sharp vision, her successes, in contrast to his failures, he decides to put aside the larger drawing and do another one: more eggs. He makes them big, spotted; he puts them in a bed of grass, then works at the tundra — flat and without trees or shrubs. He loves to go find eggs, loves to bring them home, loves to eat them. He has learned at school that children elsewhere merely have to open a door to find a dozen or so eggs before them. But he has also been told that they are chickens' eggs — and far less attractive to look at, and of a different taste.

John would not like that kind of life, he says firmly, as he puts his drawing aside — unfinished. He also seems uninterested in working on the previous, more ambitious, one. The soft, easy life of other Americans interests him; he has heard it remarked upon, criticized by his father and mother, his elderly grandfather: "They have told me that we will no longer be Eskimos if we have all our food here at home, and have forgotten how to go out and find food for ourselves. That is how the white people live, and that is how some of our own people have begun living — in the cities of Alaska. My friend's uncle lives in Nome. He went to visit his uncle and his aunt and his cousins. He said that they have a television set, a refrigerator, a snowmobile, a motorcycle. They have a stove that is electric. They have a motorboat. They are talking of moving to Fairbanks because they'd like to own a car, and they say in Nome you can't go too far with a car. My uncle was in the air force, and now he works for the government. He may get a job from an oil company. Then he'd go north by himself and send all the money home. My father says that his brother is ruined. He keeps telling my father to come visit him. He lives in Nome too. He sends us letters. He says it's too bad we don't have telephones in our village. My father says that when we have telephones and television, it will be time for us to leave. He won't go see his brother anymore. And his brother won't come see us. But they write to each other. My grandfather says that when he dies, the two brothers will stop being brothers. My brothers and I will never let that happen to us."

John has immediate second thoughts: maybe, one day, he will travel, and will like a certain country, and will want to stay there, and so will lose contact with his family. He would never want to live elsewhere in *Alaska*, but the teachers have showed him and his classmates pictures taken from the *National Geographic,* and he has to admit that some of them have whetted his appetite. He especially responds to the tropics, to stories about and pictures of the Amazon, the African jungle, the Pacific islands. What is it like to live under a hot sun, to be able to dress so lightly, to fight sweat and mosquitoes rather than chills and frostbite? He has a slight idea; summer comes to the Arctic too — however briefly. It is never an unbearable summer — to outsiders, like pilots, teachers, government officials, the white people who visit villages like his. But for him warm weather can be strange, unsettling, even unnerving, and he knows quite clearly some of the reasons why: "The sun never leaves us, and we keep telling ourselves that we should enjoy it while it's with us, but after a while we get so tired. We are tired because we can't sleep too well when it's light all the time, and we are tired because we have been doing too many things and forgetting to go to sleep."

He muses out loud about the tropics; he wonders whether he would be especially vulnerable, were he to go there on a visit. He has seen white people come to Alaska and become sick, weary, constantly fearful: can anyone possibly survive a particular storm, never mind an entire season of winter — a half-year of temperatures at or well below zero, and of heavy snows, relentless winds? Just after he observes that he would probably learn how to live with one hundred degrees, day in and day out, he reminds himself that he ought to finish his abandoned, large drawing of a windy, winter storm. White people have learned to survive Alaska's winters, he comments as he picks up his drawing again. He contemplates it, seems ready to work at it, then puts it firmly aside. He will start all over again, and this time he will finish what he starts. He reaches for the largest piece of paper available, reaches for paints instead of crayons, and works long, hard, silently. The result is an astonishing painting — really something in the abstract expressionist vein: thick white upon thin white, streaks of black, lines of white and black, and nothing else. (Figure 7.)

John is apologetic, yet determined as he tries to indicate what he hoped to accomplish: "The wind comes from the mountains or from the sea; we get winds from both directions. We sit here and my grandfather laughs when we ask what it is like outside and go look through the window. He says that we'll never see anything standing in the house and looking; the only way is to go outside and look — or else close our eyes and stop talking and listen and picture the snow up in the air, speeding across our village like airplanes, millions of them, only even faster than they go. I remember closing my eyes, and besides the wind, that shouts at us, and never loses its voice, I could feel the snow touching my face, and I tried counting the flakes, but I gave up: too many. Once I asked my grandfather what would happen if all the flakes came together, because there were so many of them. He said it is a mystery — how the air can hold so many flakes; but perhaps that is what the wind is for: to keep the flakes away from each other until they fall on the ground. Sometimes when I see a heavy snowstorm coming, I joke; I tell my grandfather that the snowflakes are coming *together,* and it's *all white* out there, it's falling big *pieces* of snow. He smiles and says he hopes so! I think he'll like this picture, even if we haven't had *that* much snow. I guess I could have done better, but the picture shows what the wind would do if it was so strong it made snow come down in big lumps."

Snow and the wind that carries it are apparently taken for granted by him but are really a continuing source of wonder and awe. John has been taken down the river to the sea over and over again, yet the sight of giant icebergs still captivates him. He would like to go exploring on them. He would like to watch them break up, yield slowly to the spring. But they never yield completely, as he keeps reminding himself, almost with pride: "The teachers tell us that in a lot of places the snow doesn't last too long. When I was younger, I used to tell my mother, when we came back from a trip to the ocean, that I was worried that the icebergs might melt during the summer, and there would be only the water to see. My mother would laugh and repeat my words: *only* the water! She loves to walk to the edge of the river. She loves to walk on the shore, near the ocean. She collects stones or shells, and brings them home and keeps them in a box. She says she doesn't care about the ice; she is glad, I think, when it leaves the harbor and goes further and further back. But I like the ice, and when it is far away, I tell my father that I hope to come back later, when I can see no water, only the ice and snow."

He has heard from his grandfather stories of his ancestors, who used to live by the ocean and only recently (the generation of his grandfather's father) moved inland. He has been told of expeditions through dangerous waters, of ice floes that shift, appear suddenly, disappear strangely, only to return so that lives are threatened or lost. He makes no pretense of concealing the excitement he feels when such accounts or stories are told: "My grandfather remembers being in his father's boat; they were coming in after fishing, when suddenly the wind came upon them, and it brought the ice from different directions, and they were cut off, so they couldn't land. They stopped rowing. They thought they'd be crushed to death, but there was a narrow channel still open, and my grandfather can remember his father saying that they should keep moving, and follow the channel. They could have been crushed to death at any moment. But they didn't become scared; they used their arms and they talked to the ice, and the ice never cut them off all the way, so they got to shore. I don't believe that the ice heard anything they said, but if they didn't keep moving, they could have been killed."

John is excited as well as impressed; they were skilled, able people, his ancestors, and they faced natural elements more strenuously than he will probably ever have to. He and his friends have heard the stories, though, and have attempted in play to recreate the moments. They build walls of snow, the bigger the better, and imagine themselves navigators, with their lives at stake against the whims and excesses of ice floes. When their parents or grandparents have a moment, the children ask for new stories, or the repetition of familiar stories: struggles against the elements, including floating ice. And sometimes a picture makes a statement about the sea, about those floes, about Arctic life in all its savage or fragile beauty. The boy particularly treasures one painting he did at school. (Figure 8.) His teachers questioned him closely when he submitted it to them: had he seen ice floes that enormous, or was he making something up on the basis of hearsay? No, he was making up nothing; he had gone to a village near the sea, stayed with an old great-aunt, his grandfather's sister, seen exactly what he had tried to represent. One teacher had told him that he made the ice floes seem like skyscrapers in a city like New York. He had looked at pictures of American cities, heard about the tall buildings in them, but he had never realized that they were *really* tall. He had estimated them to be, maybe, as tall as a water tower he'd seen in one seacoast town, or the tower on top of a small airline terminal building he'd seen at the edge of that town, but he had never thought any building could rise to the height reached by massive floes.

He paraphrases his grandfather's memories as he looks at the painting he did for his teachers, took home and showed to his parents, and then put aside, against the advice of his teachers, who wanted him to hang up the picture at home —

after he had refused to let them do so at school: "My grandfather remembers when he saw a picture in a church school of the ice in the harbor of the village where his father and his grandfather had been born. It was a photograph, I think. He went home and told his parents; they did not want to go and see the picture. They told him that as long as they had eyes, they would go look at the harbor. The white people would rather look at a picture than anything else. They go to movies, and they have television, and they have cameras. All the white people we see have cameras; and in school the teachers tell us about movies and television, and they get movies and programs flown in here to show us. My grandfather tells me to sit down and close my eyes, while he closes his. He sees the ice in the harbor, and he tells me what is happening — the wind is beginning to move the ice, and everyone is trying to take his boat back to the shore as fast as possible. I tell him what I see — the ice is moving in, but there is no one fishing and no boats are out, and he and I are standing and watching the ice. The sun makes some of the ice so bright I can't look too long. So, I open my eyes — and I'm back in our house again!"

When John says that, he stops talking. He looks outside. He lifts his eyes upward, scans the sky: the poor, weak, short-lived sun. The boy has imagined himself to be an ice floe, the wind, the river, a salmon running it, but never the sun. He pities the sun, even the summer sun, that brings the tundra to life so poignantly: "The sun must get cold. The teacher told us that the sun is so hot it would melt anything, but it doesn't look very hot. My mother used to tell us that she can feel the sun shivering, and the moon, too. The sun goes south, just like the birds. My sister sees the birds going, and she calls to them, and tells them not to forget the sun. When my friends and I told the teacher what we thought about the sun, she was very upset. She told us that we had to learn the truth, that the earth goes around the sun, and it doesn't run away, and it's always very hot, even when it doesn't melt our snow and ice. They must be right. They told my older sister that *we* make up stories, but *they* tell the truth! I'd like to go see other places, where the sun is hot; then I'd know they're right. In the summer it gets warm here, and it's hard to believe that the winter will ever come back. But before long the birds are flying away; they know. I wish the teachers would invite our parents and grandparents to school, and explain to them what they know. My father says the teachers are right, but they wouldn't be much help if they had to leave school and work with us. They would walk on top of a lot of eggs; they would plant flowers in the summer and hope to see them bloom in the winter."

Such sarcasm, such episodes of bitterness and scorn, are relatively infrequent and, it seems, self-limiting. The boy likes to go to the village store sometimes; there to sit and say nothing at all, only watch intently and listen, as the teachers, among others, gather close to a wood-burning stove and talk, eat, drink, even doze in public. A father or grandfather offers stories about the past, information about the tundra, the nearby river, or the ocean, at once dangerous and inviting. The schoolteachers, or the visiting pilot and a passenger or two, offer stories about the outside world, the lower forty-eight. The white people are more relaxed in the store. The winters bring everyone in the village together. The teachers sing, drink, avoid self-important pronouncements. The children are endlessly fascinated by the difference — by what they hear in the store as opposed to what they hear in school.

IV

YOUNG OBSERVER

O FTEN it is Miriam, at thirteen slightly older than the
younger children (under ten) but not regarded as a full-
grown woman (of fourteen or fifteen), who dares talk to teachers or various white visitors right to their faces; she points out
contradictions or inconsistencies. She is a shrewd, observant
listener. She talks with both animation and precision. Her
father knows of her outspoken friendliness with the store
owner and teachers; to them he jokingly refers to himself as
"Miriam's father." The mother will call herself "Miriam's
mother," but is not at all happy doing so. When her husband
introduces her as Miriam's mother, she goes through the motion of taking a bow — as if to mock the idea that anyone in
the village needs to be introduced to anybody else, including
weekly visitors, like the pilot. A moment later she frowns,
turns her head away. As Miriam, customarily, dominates the
scene, the mother finds a diversion: canned goods to inspect,
a baby to restrain or scold, a woman to begin talking with.
Occasionally she makes reference to her daughter's virtues; it
is done with a mixture of pride and annoyance that defies
analysis. Neither emotion predominates.

The fact is that Miriam both pleases and angers her parents;
sometimes she even frightens them. The girl knows why: "I

should keep quiet; my mother always told me that. She says I was born a noisy child! She says I was born staring at people! She says that her sister took me into the world, and I cried right away, with no slap, and I kept looking around and crying — until my father said I must be very sick, and I would die soon. But my mother knew better. She said that I was very strong. I've seen two brothers be born, and they died soon afterwards; my mother would ask me to go touch them, and breathe over their face, then maybe they'd shout like I did. But nothing happened. Soon they weren't breathing at all. My mother was very glad to have them taken away. She said some children have never wanted to live up here, and they leave as soon as they can; but some children love our people and our village, and they will stay, and they will never want to leave, even when they are very old. My grandmother said she wanted to stay here until she was too sick or too old. She said I will feel the same way when I grow up, because I'm like her. She says she knew I'd be like her the moment I was born; so she told my mother to call me Miriam, the name she got when she was baptized. The minister gave her that name because he liked her; it was his wife's name. They called my grandmother their first daughter, and she still goes to church, and the new minister likes her, too. The old minister said she is like a minister; she makes you believe her when she talks. She says I'm like her — I give sermons, too!

"My mother and father don't like her to give sermons, and they don't like her saying I'm like her, and they don't like my sermons! My father says I'll get into trouble; I might even get arrested. He showed me the jail in the town, the last time we went there. Later he told me they'll come and take someone away, who steals from the school or the store, or who talks too much. They'll take the person on a snowmobile or a canoe down the river to the town. They'll lock you up: nothing to eat, just water to drink, and a piece of bread, maybe. I said it was wrong to lock someone up. It's wrong to make you hungry. My father said I shouldn't talk like that; it's not up to me to say something bad about the jail. I told him I'd go ask the new minister. My father said he'd lock me up in the house, and the house would be a jail for me, if I said anything to the minister. My father told my mother that my grandmother has spent so much time with the minister and his wife, she's become a white woman. And my father thinks my grandmother won't leave here; when she dies, she'll come and live in me!"

Miriam knows that her grandmother will indeed soon die. The girl also knows that her mother and father admire the old lady, though they find her confusing. She seems more in touch with white people, for all her age, than are they, or even many Eskimo youths, who love the sight of snowmobiles and airplanes, but feel quite shy in the presence of a white person. Miriam has learned from her grandmother to enjoy white people — eye them carefully, by no means take them for granted, but take risks with them: initiate conversations, exchange jokes, take the calculated risks of teasing, being critical, even playing practical jokes. She knows that her parents find her a bit odd, but she has the sanction of her grandmother's life — lived so intimately with whites, yet not at all deprived thereby of its own character, not to mention integrity. When her father threatens her with jail, she knows that he is telling her to be careful, but also expressing his sense of her uniqueness: a child who is very much his daughter, but who carries on at the store and in the school as if she came from Fairbanks, maybe even Seattle.

Miriam wants to go to Seattle one day. She has heard about the city from the man who runs the fishery; he is an Eskimo who, like her grandmother and her, has become rather friendly with white people. The fish brought to, worked on, and packed at the fishery are shipped to Seattle, and once in his life the Eskimo man was flown there. He has never forgotten or stopped talking about the experience, which lasted four days. And his most avid listener in recent years has been Miriam. If only she too could go there! It is an exclamation she utters silently as well as in the company of the manager. Occasionally she has told her parents of her desire, but they are not sympathetic, only puzzled. Even the young men of the village, who dream of flying and speeding on a motorcycle, don't imagine themselves leaving Alaska. But Miriam would like to go up an elevator; she would like to see a large church; she would like to go into a department store — and stay in a hotel. She would like to walk down streets, look in shops, eat in a restaurant. She knows about all those manifestations of urban living, knows about them not in the rote, abstract way that a student does (in cities there are stores, theaters, skyscrapers, and so on) but in response to her wondering mind's eager interest and her wandering heart's strong inclination. The latter does not escape her parents' notice, and they become frightened (what will *happen* to her?) and troubled (what have we done to let this come to pass?). After all, even the girl's grandmother has had no interest in travel.

Not that Miriam is regarded as a potential traitor, someone intent on abandoning her own people for the sake of others. She is a dutiful and affectionate child, whose wanderlust is regarded, more or less, the way educated white people in, say, Seattle, might think of a genetic anomaly: why this strain of aberrancy? And the girl is, at times, quite willing to view herself as somewhat possessed — driven by forces she only vaguely understands. On the other hand, she can erupt with impatience, insist upon her right to be considered no one and nothing else but herself: "I am not my grandmother, and I am not the favorite of the teachers. Just because I want to travel, some people say I am turning away from my own people, and I will be punished, or I *am* being punished, because anyone who wants to leave Alaska is being punished by having that hope! That's what my aunt told me, and she told me she felt sorry for me, because she's heard bad stories about Eskimo people who have gone away, and then come back very sick — or maybe never come back, just died far away. I want to live right here, most of the time. If I had a lot of money, I could take an airplane trip once a year. I could see the world, and tell people here what I've seen. My teacher says that her mother and father used to do that; every winter they flew from Indianapolis, Indiana, to Florida, or to Mississippi, then they came home with stories. She showed us on the map where they went — the Gulf of Mexico. It's cold and there's a lot of snow in Indiana during the winter, so her parents left for a vacation. I told my mother, and she told my father, and he said that there is no such thing as a vacation here; he said that even when he feels very bad and he can hardly get up, he does. They brought a doctor to the school last year, and anyone could go see him, and my father did. The doctor told him that he needed medicine, and maybe he should be put in the airplane and go to a hospital. He would be in a city then, for a long time, the doctor thought. My father said he wouldn't go. He told us he didn't mind taking medicine from the white people, but he couldn't sit in a bed all day and all night without wanting to go out and shoot himself."

Mention of a gun prompts silence and reflection. Then memories of walks with her grandmother come to the fore and, with them, the words the old lady would use when she talked about guns. She detests them; regrets their all but universal presence among Eskimos, old and young; blames white people for the fact that such has happened; and wonders out loud whether someday (God willing) guns might go, never to

return. The girl has disagreed. There have been arguments.
The grandmother has shouted that one can like white people
without approving of their every whim and fancy, not to mention a serious evil they have inflicted on the world. It is wrong
to use a gun, the grandmother believes — cruel, harmful,
noisy, frightening, dangerous. Even the ministers, old and
young, have disagreed with her: a gun helps an Eskimo kill a
seal, a polar bear — or, inland, a deer. Why the disapproval,
the horror?

She has argued with them, quoted Christ to them, told them
they had the Devil in them when they justified the unjustifia-
ble. A net is not a gun; a spear is not either. A gun is "unfair"
— it lifts the struggle of man for food from a matter of survival
to one of cold, impersonal, wanton murder. The ministers
have shaken their heads: what is there to say, when an old,
proud, stubborn woman gets an *idea* in her head? The granddaughter also has given up in confusion — but tried hard to
understand what might be going on in the lady's mind: "She
worries that it's not *fair;* that's what she says most of the time.
I see how she can think that. Before the gun came, our people
made nets and knives and harpoons right here in the village.
My father says he was taught by his father how to sharpen
rocks, but he has forgotten now. I think my grandmother
wants to see the animals or fish have a chance of escaping. She
watches when they put out the nets in the river, and she says
she claps her hands for the salmon that escape. But she doesn't
want to go without food! She admits that when my mother gets
upset with her! She doesn't like to see the geese rounded up
either. She leaves when the men do that. Then she eats the
geese when my mother cooks them!"

It is difficult for the grandmother or Miriam to reconcile
their strong interest in the white man's world with their real
pride in their own, Eskimo people. But they can find some-

thing to do that does not compel them to feel confronted by a choice of one or the other set of values or assumptions. The grandmother for years worked happily in the fishery; there she could be an Eskimo woman, exerting herself knowingly in a rather traditional if commercialized way, but also someone who was much admired by white visitors, who were, of course, the owners of the fishery. For young Miriam the school serves both to affirm her as an Eskimo girl and connect her to the whites who have come to teach. She carries messages from parents to teachers, from teachers to parents; she tells the teachers what she has heard, what they would do well to think about; she receives their admiration, while at the same time she is known by the people of the village as someone who commands the attention of outsiders, no matter her age. She has been told to go to a boarding school when she gets older, become a teacher herself, maybe stay in the lower forty-eight, there to serve as an adviser and educator to those whites who will, increasingly, be going to Alaska — geologists, engineers, physicists, as well as teachers and federal officials. But she wants to leave her village on her own terms, and not before she is quite ready. She loves her family, her village, her people, even as she admires and is endlessly curious about white people. Her dreams take this form: "I woke up and I said to myself: you had a long airplane ride, and you landed in Washington, D.C. — right near the Lincoln Memorial. Then, I remembered that our teacher showed a picture of it to us, and said it was the nicest building in the city, she thinks. When she is in Washington, she goes there and stops and prays. The minister says she is right. I thought I'd tell both of them what I dreamed. They both said I couldn't have had a better dream."

Miriam decides to draw the Lincoln Memorial. She wonders aloud whether she ought go to her teacher, ask for a look at the picture, then come back and begin. But no, she can remember enough to start on her own, and she does. She chooses the paints, virtually circles the paper with the brush, as if uncertain where to land — and finally the plunge: a line of white, which she describes as the "bottom" of the monument. Slowly she works at building it until at last she is satisfied that she is done. (Figure 9.) She has used only white, has felt no need to place the monument on the ground or under a sky. She looks at it for a few seconds, then becomes her own stern critic: "It's not very good. I wish I could draw the way the teachers do; I've tried, but I can't. They say I could if I had some lessons, but they're not art teachers and they don't know how to teach us art. So, they show us pictures, and they tell us to look, and to like what we've been shown."

The painting is put aside. It will be discarded, she declares, unless anyone wants it. Some paintings and drawings have been exhibited at school, but the teachers have a way of discouraging the children, and the children, in turn, have a way of dragging their feet during the "art period." Miriam was told a year or so ago that even *she* draws like an Eskimo: everything looks like a mountain of snow. She resents that observation bitterly. There are times when all white people seem to her just what some of her friends say they are: full of themselves and, really, quite ignorant. She has in mind the drawings she has made of salmon. Nothing about them reminds her of a mountain of snow. She knows what salmon look like, and her drawings remind her of — salmon. Why don't the teachers try their hand at drawing salmon? For that matter, why don't they try their hand at drawing *something, anything?* They are so willing to find fault, so anxious to correct others. All they do is tell the children that they are slow with numbers, or they don't read as well as they ought. And the children don't even get discouraged. They shrug their shoulders, smile. For their seeming indifference, she has a certain annoyance, if not outright contempt. Moreover, she gets tired of being singled out as good, as better than her classmates, as the best there is in the school. She wonders how she would do if there were white children in the school with her. She wonders what the teachers say about her in the privacy of their room, the so-called teacher's rest room, to which she has been invited only once. Is she, in their estimate, really the best — the best of an exceedingly bad lot?

Miriam has second thoughts; she recalls the many times she has heard those same teachers speak with sympathy and understanding of the educational problems facing her and her classmates. They are hardworking, well-meaning teachers, she knows; and not one of them need stay in the isolated, impoverished village she and several hundred other Eskimos call home. She has earned the confidence and respect of those teachers, and they have shared with her, openly and often, their doubts and misgivings. Ought they be there teaching at all? Ought she and others like her even bother to go to school? Would it not be wise for all white people to stay away from certain parts of Alaska, thereby leaving the Eskimos to themselves? Miriam has mostly argued with them; and they have come to admire her even more, because they know quite well how hard it is for Eskimo people to take issue directly and vocally with outsiders.

Miriam knows that characteristic of her people, knows that she has come to be somewhat different: "My mother heard me talking to the teacher in the store — I was telling the teacher I thought she was doing a good job, and she was telling me that she wasn't, and she would probably leave at the end of the school year. My mother didn't like to hear me say anything 'against' the teacher. I told my mother that I wasn't 'against' the teacher; I just didn't want her to think she was bad, when she's a good teacher. My mother still was upset; she said that if the teacher wanted to feel that she'd been a bad teacher, then that was up to her, and I should keep quiet, or nod my head and let her know that I'm glad to agree with her. That's what my mother and father do; when they meet the pilot or a teacher, they listen to what they say, and then they say yes, yes, and they keep on moving their heads up and down. Later, when we are alone together in the house, my father will laugh to himself, or my mother will shake her head back and forth, instead of up and down.

"My grandmother used to tell me that I should try to be like my parents. She would put her hand on my mouth when I told her I didn't like one of the teachers at school. Then she changed her mind; one day she said she could see that I was never going to change, and that I'd always be like her. She admitted to me that she had once told a white man who came here, a friend of the pilot's, that he was not very nice, and he should leave. The pilot was very upset when he heard what my grandmother had said. My grandmother told the pilot that his friend had said some bad words about our village; he'd called it a swamp, and he'd said it was dirty, and he'd said he would rather be in jail than live here. My grandmother didn't say anything until she saw two Eskimo women, friends of hers, smile at the man after he said that — as if they wanted him to know that he was one hundred percent right. Then she went up to the man and told him that we had no jail in our village, but if he stayed here any more than one day, she would begin building one with her own hands, and she wouldn't stop to eat or drink or sleep until the building was done, and then he could stay in it forever, or until he died, and so he would have his wish! The man left a little later, and everyone in the village kept talking about my grandmother and what she said to him. Her sister was alive then; she was very angry. She said the man should have turned his back on my grandmother. He didn't. He laughed, and said he was sorry about what he said. My grandmother asked me what I would have done, and I said I hope I will speak like her if there ever is another time when an outsider comes in and talks like that man did. She said every village needs at least one person who barks like a hungry dog. I guess I'll be the one when she leaves us. Until then, we have two in our village. And we have a jail now."

But Miriam cannot let the matter drop there. Her parents can't either. Her mother has told her many times that silence is eminently preferable to sharp words. Why not walk away, saying nothing? At least then one is not being rude, insolent, inhospitable, *outspoken.* But Miriam is not by nature inclined to be reticent. She has tried though; she has listened in respectful silence to her mother's insistent argument that respectful silence is the only permissible response. Even unfriendly thoughts, not expressed to a stranger, but shared with the family, are frowned upon. Miriam hears her younger sisters and brother being instructed, at times warned, by their parents, and she notices that what is said to them is meant for her: "My sister just started school, and she comes home and tells my mother about the teacher. My mother tells her that she must smile when the teacher looks at her, and do what the teacher says. My sister said a few days ago that she doesn't always like the teacher. My mother explained to my sister that it is bad to think like that. Now my sister even smiles at home when she talks about school. I'm the only bad one in the house! My friends at school tell me they like watching my face, because sometimes I look as if there's a polar bear ready to attack, and I'm going to shoot first! I tell them that *they* look as if someone has a gun pointing at them, and is telling them that if they don't smile, they'll die. But they laugh and tell me that everyone knows I'm only pretending to look unhappy, and that I like the teachers more than anyone else in the school does.

"It's true; I'm friendlier with them. But I can't be nice to them when I don't want to be; and my sisters never let the teachers know the truth. My nine-year-old sister and I are always talking about the boys we like and the boys we don't like. We went to the store, and her teacher was there, and so was a white man, who was counting all the people in the village. He was working for the government. He had a notebook, and he was asking the store owner questions. My sister put the empty bottles on the counter and waited for the money. She wanted to pay for some food too. My mother needed the food right away, but my sister wasn't going to say a word. I didn't like that; I spoke up. The store owner didn't like hearing me; he paid no attention to us. My sister smiled and waited. I wanted to leave. She wouldn't go. She was upset with me, not the store owner. I could see: he wasn't going to help us until that white man had left. But she didn't care. She didn't want to hear me in her ear; I was telling her I was leaving right away. I did leave, but she wouldn't follow me. When she came home she told our mother that I had caused trouble at the store. My mother didn't even ask what trouble. She knows; it's the only trouble I ever cause! By now everyone in the village laughs when they hear that I spoke back to someone or walked out of the store again. But if I had been there alone, the store owner wouldn't have been able to ignore me. I would have kept telling him that I needed the food, and I would have asked the white man to wait, so that the owner could take my money and give me the food and the matches and the cooking oil."

Miriam is both outraged and amused. She doesn't expect her friends to follow suit, to go along with a form of behavior everyone else dislikes. She realizes that her people have a right to their own habits and values. Her grandmother actually has warned her not to become provocative or teasing — not to make an issue out of her insistence that she be heard

and noticed when she is unhappy with someone or about
something. But she notices how white people behave toward
her own people, and so far, at least, she fails to find within
herself her grandmother's calm acceptance of the difference.
She has talked to her grandmother about their respective attitudes. The old lady says it is a matter of time: the girl will grow
up, will become more circumspect, even as the grandmother
will never feel genuinely inclined to welcome strangers, however arrogant, and smile at them, no matter what they say or
do. But the girl thinks Eskimos are changing, that she is merely
a few years ahead of others. And she has not failed to discover
some evidence for her position.

Miriam has heard white people talk about urban Eskimos,
who live in Fairbanks, Anchorage, Juneau, Nome. She has
heard those Eskimos described as bold, forceful, grim, insolent, uncooperative, sassy — not at all like the "good" Eskimos
of the seacoast or inland villages. She has pretended self-
absorption, or a consuming interest in a certain task, obligation, game. But she has listened hard and gone later to her
grandmother's for another of their private, emotional, and
somewhat extraordinary conversations. The old lady has occasionally given in, acknowledged that a rebuff deserves a rebuff,
that inconsiderate people do not deserve unlimited hospitality. But what is the alternative? The old lady can think of none;
and she is not satisfied with her grandchild's conviction that
the demonstration of the cold shoulder, or more assertively, of
retaliatory impatience or irritation will have any effect.

Yet Miriam has listened; the old woman's fatalistic psychological accommodation to the social, political, and economic
status quo has prompted in the child a certain guarded resignation of her own: "I can't make my grandmother agree with
me, and sometimes I don't even believe what I tell her myself!
One of the air force planes will fly over us. It goes very fast;

and it makes so much noise that even with my hands over my ears I can hear it. They showed us pictures of the war, and the planes, and the bombs they dropped, and while I was watching I thought to myself: what would happen if they decided to send all their planes up here, and drop their bombs on us? I never told my grandmother about the movie. I knew she'd become very unhappy. She would probably cry. She likes some white people, but she knows a lot of them can be very bad, and very dangerous. She's the only one in the village — except me — who won't smile at white people all the time, no matter what they say.

"The teachers tell us how dangerous it is to live up here, because the weather is cold, and the wind gets so bad in the winter, and people can die, because there's not enough to eat, and they can't fly food in, and you can freeze to death. But the white people have brought us more trouble than the winters. One teacher admitted to us: more Eskimos die because of the liquor they sell in the stores than because of the weather. And we don't make our own liquor; it's all brought up here — from Seattle! I wish I could visit the places where they make liquor and ship it to us. I wish I could tell the people that they should stop, and if they won't believe me, I'll ask them please to come up and see some of the villages. Even in our village some of the men get liquor. We voted not to have any in the store, but the men wait until the weather is better, then they go get some of those bottles for themselves. My grandmother said it's our fault; and she's right — but we didn't invent liquor, and we don't make it up here. My uncle drank himself to death. There are some days when I wish no white people *ever* came here."

She knows what a "nice" white person would say in reply; she has heard her teachers deplore the use of alcohol by Eskimos, even as her father has wondered what in his brother, in other men of various Alaskan villages, prompts such an unrelenting need for alcohol. And why do Eskimos keep drinking whiskey when they see what it does to themselves and others? There is no answer to that question — at least none that makes the pain, humiliation, and sorrow any less. The girl knows that, knows when she blames the white man that the repeated acts of will, the *choices* are made and made by Eskimo men (and increasingly, women) who, after all, are not compelled by anyone's law to drink. If, on the other hand, she feels inclined to blame her own people, she cannot stop reminding herself of the historical account her grandmother has passed on: the trappers, hunters, gold seekers, and all they brought north, including cheap liquor, which they virtually gave away to Eskimos, in return for labor, information, shelter.

When all is said and done Miriam doubts that the future will be very different. When she is old, she predicts, the village will be very much the same — a few more gadgets, machines, buildings, maybe, but no transformation in the essential situation facing the Eskimos, which she has described to her grandmother: "I have told her that our people will not move to a big city; they will stay here and hope to get by the winter, and then the spring, and then the summer, and then it is winter again. My father says that the next season is as far ahead as he can look; he doesn't even like to think *that* much into the future. He is glad at the end of the day to see us eating supper and to know that there is food for breakfast — and that he has dried and put away plenty of salmon for the days to come. The minister tells us to think of many years ahead — to think of our lives after we die; and the teachers tell us to plan; and the government sends people to do tests on the ground, and to tell us the same thing — plan. But my father comes home and says he has been thinking and planning all day: will we all have a good supper? And he has known the answer: we will. That is good enough for him.

"My little brother is just like my father; he is small, but goes everywhere with him and copies him. I guess I copied my grandmother when I was small. I don't remember, but I must have. In a few years I'll agree with her on everything; then I'll be nicer to white people! But I'll always look them right in the eyes — like she does. And I'll say *something*. My teacher says she's glad that I speak up; but she *is* surprised when I do. I just raise my hand and talk. She told me after school that she's surprised because I'm the only one who ever does 'talk back.' She says she would like the others to speak up. 'Speak up,' she'll say, sometimes, and we all smile and say nothing — even I do, mostly. I wish my cousin at least would *look* up; he won't, though."

V

YOUNG HUNTER,
YOUNG FISHERMAN

HER COUSIN Joe is a month younger than Miriam but taller and obviously stronger. She cannot understand why it is that he avoids white people so much, but tells her she is brave for not doing so. The teachers may consider him just another, shy, Eskimo child; he knows better, and says so: he is afraid. He doesn't know why; and he has no interest in finding out why. His mind turns to other matters: seal hunting, the nets that catch salmon, and polar bears. He has never seen a polar bear, but knows that he well might, when he gets older and able to wander far from the village, toward the ocean. He would like to be a hunter, be a successful fisherman — someone who brought fish, perhaps, to the fishery, but never had to work there. He would also like to build himself a swift kayak, travel far up the river, so far that he would be away from the influence of schoolteachers and airplane pilots and salesmen who come to sell supplies to a store owner or a school principal. He has heard from his father, from others, that some Eskimo villages are remote enough to be spared white people. Let his cousin feel sorry for such places: no schools, no churches, no mail delivery, no access to an emergency airplane, with a nurse or even (sometimes) a doctor on board. He has other ideas of what it means to be out of touch, out of reach, really: "My father doesn't want a snowmobile, and I don't, either. We don't buy nets in the store; we make them. My father owns a gun, two guns; he says he is glad the white people brought us rifles. Once I saw the pilot pass a bottle of whiskey to someone in our village, even though we have voted to keep whiskey out of the village. I thought: what if my father's rifle just showed up here and began shooting at the pilot, and no one could stop it until the bullets were all gone!"

The thought of a rifle doing that, a mere moment of fantasy, prompts an apology and silence. Joe is sure, of course, that no rifle would behave in such a manner. White people are coming up with a lot of gadgets, capable of doing a lot of strange things (he has learned in school from his teacher); but a rifle that had prejudices and acted on them of its own accord would be something terrible to contemplate! As if to emphasize a pastoral alternative to the nightmare he has heard himself forecast, the boy scans the tundra, remarks upon its rich, green color, soon to give way to the brief yellow and brown of the autumn, followed by the white and more white of the winter's snow. He is a boy, he remarks — intent on stating the obvious for a reason he then reveals: "I like to go find berries and bring them home. Some boys won't go; they say it is a girl's job. They would rather make noise with the snowmobile. They dream of owning a motorcycle. They say they will try to go into the army; and the reason they will do that is to save money so they can come back to our village with a motorcycle or with a snowmobile. Then they will need the gas to run their motorcycle or snowmobile, and gas costs a lot of money, and there are very few people here who can spend money on gas, because only the store owner and the postmaster make a lot of money, and the people who work in the fishery. My father and I walked far away yesterday; at last we couldn't hear any noise from the motorcycles. We listened to the birds and ducks leaving us to go south. A mother and father bird were calling together their children, telling them to hurry up and keep up and stop being so slow! That's the kind of noise my father and I like to hear! We waved to them, and my father said good-bye, and we both told them we hoped they have a good winter somewhere (in Texas, the teacher says). I'm glad we don't go to Texas!"

Joe has no interest in going anywhere — except, maybe, to the Aleutian Islands. He would like to be a thoroughgoing fisherman. He would like to know how to shoot seals and whales, catch all sorts of fish, and, very important, know how to navigate a kayak through stormy waters, around dangerous ice floes. He knows that he would be lucky to have a motorboat; there is a limit to the aversion he can feel toward the white man's technology. He has even, it turns out, admired fast motorboats — but only under certain circumstances: "I like to watch them when they're far away, and I can see them moving fast, but not hear the noise. I went with my father last week down the river to the ocean. We stood and watched three motorboats; they were far off, but we could see them, and they must have been racing each other. I asked my father if he'd ever buy one; he said yes, when we can get the money together. It's not easy to do; we've been saving for a long time. But my mother and my father don't spend every day feeling sorry for themselves. My mother doesn't want a new stove. She doesn't like the white man's 'machines,' she calls them. She tells my father that a motorboat would bring us trouble as well as luck. What if the motor broke down? Who would fix it? The white man can trick you many ways; it's not just with whiskey that you get caught by him! Once you have his 'machines,' you have to call him in to fix them. The snowmobiles break down. The electric generator they have at the school breaks down. They have a lot of trouble fixing it. They curse it and wish we were back in the old time. But when it's working again they say they're glad it's not the old time. I don't want to live in the old time; I just like going with my father hunting and fishing."

The old time — Joe refers to the past with those words often. He is young, not given to nostalgia; rather, he simply likes the world that stretches beyond the village — a world that requires competencies old Eskimos remember, young Eskimos (brought up with "machines" everywhere) often fail to acquire. His father now and then talks about the old time — a period in Eskimo history when each man stood virtually alone against the elements, though confident that relatives, neighbors, fellow human beings, would be willing to offer whatever help was available. The boy stresses the reason for his apparent refusal to go along with others of his generation in the village: "I'm not against the white people. I like the pilot better than some of our own people. The worst person in this village is the man who owns the store. He is the richest person in the village; all he wants is money. He spends his money on motors and on furniture. He has furniture flown in here, and he fills up each room of his house with tables and lamps and chairs. My father went there, and he came back and told us that he had to think of something very sad, or else he would have started laughing, and never been able to stop.

"The store owner pays us to bring in grass, or weeds; then he sells them. My father hates to offer him anything we've picked; but we need the money. My father said that if he had one wish it would be that we had a world without money. Then we would all try to take care of ourselves, and no one would sit back and collect money, and not do anything else. The store owner was given money by a white man, and that's how the store got going. Then the white man got his money back, and now the store owner sits on his chair and the people come in and buy, and they leave after paying him, and each year he gets richer. He doesn't do anything but look at pictures of furniture in catalogues. He is always buying gifts for his wife and his children — and himself. His brother works for him; he's the one who orders the food and makes sure he has enough of everything. He only gets a salary, though; he complains that the store owner is stingy. To be stingy is to be a white man, my father says. Most Eskimos don't like to watch others go hungry, while they sit on a hundred cans of spaghetti and a hundred bottles of Coca-Cola, and a hundred bars of candy, and a hundred bags of potato chips and a hundred boxes of frozen french fries. The store owner only *looks* Eskimo! I'd rather eat the berries we pick than any of the food you can buy in that store. I'd rather eat the salmon we catch. I'd rather go hungry than go to that store all the time."

There are compromises to be made, Joe knows. The store is part of everyone's life, his family's included. The store has food when families begin to run out of fish that has been dried, roots or berries that have been put away. And the store offers candy, which for many of the children is not unlike (as an object of passion) the whiskey craved by certain Eskimo men and women. This boy detests candy — so much so that he is the talk of the school. His teachers at first applauded the good judgment he demonstrated. His teeth would last longer, they pointed out, and his diet would be better balanced. But after a while they began to sense in his preference (or rather, his outspoken, almost militant lack of preference) another kind of judgment: candy as a symbol of the white world's values and habits. Consequently the schoolchildren of the village, or at least some of them, heard a new, more qualified message from their teachers: a little candy isn't so bad; the point is not to eat "too many sweets."

Joe remembers a particular teacher's repeated use of those three words; he is scornful of the teacher but also amused: "She and her husband came here and told us they were on our side. They said they may be white people, but they want to help the Eskimo people — us. I told my father, and he said I should pretend to believe them, even if I don't. My mother told me to avoid talking with them if I could; but try to be friendly. I have; I don't want them to think I don't like them. They're good people; they're better than the pilot and his friends, or the people who come here and inspect our school and tell us we should clean up the village. But sometimes they can be just like the pilot and his friends and the government people; then I have to remind myself of what my father says, and my mother. One teacher asked me why I was 'against candy.' I said I wasn't *against* it; I just don't care to buy it and eat it. I wanted to say that I could remember what they told us last year — how candy is not good for us to eat. They heard me saying the same thing, and they changed their advice; they started saying that I was making a mountain out of an anthill. I wasn't. I was telling my friends that candy is as bad as whiskey, and our people didn't know anything about candy or whiskey until the white people came here. The white teachers didn't like it. I guess I should stop talking, and smile more. One of the teachers asked me why I don't smile as much as everyone else." Joe smiles as he talks about his own smile, or the absence of it. He comments on the teachers' situation: outsiders who want very much to be considered insiders; but also outsiders who have a definite moral bias, which they want to persuade young people like himself to adopt.

He treasures most those moments when he is away from school, away from that part of the village where the church is, the store, the landing strip, and near the river, the open tundra. He has proposed to his father that a few families go off, try to start another village — one that would proudly uphold the old Eskimo traditions. But the father both educates and disappoints his son by pointing out to him the virtual impossibility of a return to the old ways, or at least all of them. Even if the store owner is no friend of the father's, it is helpful to know that in the event of an emergency, food and some medical supplies are available, with a shortwave radio set to call for more. Nor is electricity, for all its uncertainty during the winter months, something to be dismissed, as even the boy, less interested in compromises than his father, is willing to admit: "We miss the electric lights when they go off. We have no school in the winter a lot of times because the electricity stops working. Then I miss being with my friends. They joke with me when we go back to school; they ask me what I'd do if I lived up the river, in the middle of the woods, and there was a storm, and it kept up, and I ran out of everything: food, and oil for the lamps, and bullets. I tell them we'd sit in our house, and we *wouldn't* run out of food, because we'd know enough to put away a lot of salmon before the winter started. But they say we could make a mistake, and then we'd starve."

Joe is not convinced, but he gets the message. He pulls back from his radical critique of village life into a more balanced, cautious position: self-reliance, to the extent possible. Who wants to risk death, when it is possible, relatively speaking, to avoid doing so?

Joe has learned to ask himself that question; has not learned to come up with a satisfactory answer. He finds himself buffeted by contrasting moods, interests, inclinations. One day he goes with a friend to watch the village's generator being fixed. It is about fifty below zero outside. The boy is intrigued by the competence the repairmen show, even if they don't get immediate results. The next day the boy goes to the river with a simple line and the patience, the determination needed to cut through ice, endure cruel winds, catch a few fish. Later he talks about the fish as if their problems are not unlike his own. He has just finished drawing a picture of the tundra, the river that works its way through the land to the sea, when he thinks of a network of nearby small ponds and of the estuaries that mark the juncture of the ocean's tide and the river's current. He has not the ability, he declares, to do justice to the way water spreads itself over land. But if he were a fish he would make certain decisions. He would stay in the ocean; or he would stay in obscure inlets or ponds; or he would go right by the various villages, try his hardest to escape capture; or if getting old, he would prepare to get caught, even invite his own death, on the theory that if he did, others would be spared.

His mother long ago had explained to Joe that some fish, some animals, are more elusive than others — even as some people appear to be tougher, more persistent, stronger than others. The boy had wondered why Eskimos don't run Alaska — or why they haven't moved south, tried to take over villages in states like Washington, Oregon, California. His mother knew why: Eskimos are different from white people, even as some fish (instinctively, it seems) know to stay clear of dangling bait. The boy perceived the thrust of the comparison and did not like what he heard. "I wouldn't want to go live with white people, but some of them want to come and live with us. Our people don't say no. We are like the fish who never say no; they see people standing with nets, and they come to them, or they see a piece of food and they try to eat it. Even if their mouths get hooked, but they break away, they still come back and get hooked again, and this time they are caught. They seem to know they are going to get caught. They must know. The priest who comes here told my mother that fish don't know anything, only people do. But that's wrong;

he's wrong. Some rabbits will run away and stay away; some will come right back, even though they've seen you, because they're curious, or they're friendly, or they don't realize that you hope to catch them, kill them, eat them. They're not dumb rabbits; and the fish that get caught aren't dumb. They're probably the nicest fish, the nicest rabbits. It's too bad!"

Silence, and a frown on Joe's face; he lowers his head too. His mother addresses a question to him (has he fed the dogs?) and he answers reluctantly, tersely: yes. She moves away, quite ready to grant him his mood without recrimination. In time he has recovered enough to offer help: might he go get some firewood? There is always a need for it, and his mother is delighted. So are the dogs, when they are let loose, harnessed, sent off, the sled and the boy behind them. When he returns, with a neatly arranged pile of scrubwood, he is full of good humor and a willing talker. He speaks of the low bushes and trees beyond the village; it is a miracle that year after year there is enough firewood. One has to go a distance to get near the wood; from the village one sees nothing but snow and more snow. The boy reminisces — goes back to last spring when he went whaling. He wonders aloud how long to the coming spring. He answers his own question: "Not too long, because the sun has returned and is staying with us long enough for the teachers to keep the lights out in school part of the time. It is not as cold as it was a couple of weeks ago, when we had a storm that didn't want to leave us, and so much snow that we thought we'd never again see the sky. The teacher said it had gone down to seventy below, or lower, but my father said not to listen to all that talk of numbers. It's foolish to describe our weather with the thermometer they have in the school! My father says that if the teachers woke up, and the sun was out, and there was no wind, and the birds were overhead, returning to us for the summer, but the thermometer at the school had gone way down, then the teachers would never go outside, and they would write their letters, lots of them, telling their friends in the lower forty-eight how much below zero the column had dropped, and how *cold* it is outside!"

Joe is worried that he may have gone too far. He hadn't intended to be so sharp or critical; certainly he is not by inclination sarcastic. His father, who often reminds his children to be polite to the rudest of outsiders, had made an observation, and the boy had simply heard it, declared his agreement. But he senses in himself something else, a long-standing resentment, suddenly kindled. He gives expression to his own feelings by defending his father against an anonymous critic, whom he eventually identifies as a teacher. "One teacher told us that the Eskimos have been teaching her as much as she's been teaching us. I liked what she said. But then they'll tell us in school that we are behind other people in the United States, and we should learn more, so we'll be better off. I don't like to hear our teachers talk like that. I'm sure that if you don't have a thermometer, you don't know how cold it is — not *exactly* how cold, anyway. But my father knows; he knows how his face feels, and how his chest feels when he breathes, and he can tell the temperature by how the snow feels when he walks, and he can tell by the dogs. The dogs keep moving when it's cold, but when it gets warmer, they enjoy the sun and get lazy! I know one of my teachers wouldn't like to hear what I just said. She would say that I'm not being a good scientist. You need to be exact if you're a scientist. You need a thermometer. My father forgets that the white man needs thermometers, even if we don't. I know sometimes we are wrong, and the white man is right.

"I don't want to stay in school — I only go because my father says I should go, until I'm a little older. I would like to learn to shoot the way he does, and cut up a seal the way he does. He is teaching me, but I'm not as fast as I should be. Maybe the teachers wouldn't mind if my father came to see them and told them to live here without their thermometers! They all bring them up here, and my father laughs when he hears them talking in the store: they have a number for every day. They'll say yesterday it was forty-five below zero, but today it's only twenty-five below. My father laughs at them, and I guess they laugh at us. I told one teacher that there are times when I'm not just speaking for myself, but for my oldest brother; he died, and when I was born I was given his name, Joe, and my mother says she knows he is inside of me. He loved to go with my father to the ocean; he loved to watch the seals being caught. That is why *I* love to go with my father and watch the seals being caught.

"My father is good with the harpoon; he'd rather use it than shoot a gun. The teachers have told him a gun is better: you can get the seal when he is far away, if you know how to aim. He argued with one teacher in the store; he told the teacher that he liked using the harpoon, and he didn't like using the rifle, though he does sometimes. I would like to be able to throw the way he does; but I'd like to be able to shoot the way my uncle does. My uncle could shoot down a star if he wanted to! I've seen him look at the sky, pick out a star, raise his gun and tell me he's going to knock the star out of place — and then laugh and shoot at the target he's built. He doesn't need daylight to hit the mark! My uncle, with his gun, is the equal of any white man. My uncle has a thermometer in the house. He says he'll try anything the white man tries.

"I told my mother that maybe *we* should get a thermome-ter. Then, every day we'd be able to know what degree it is below zero, or above, and I could go to school and tell everyone, and they'd think I'm one of the better students. Maybe they'd think I was being 'fresh,' though. They say my 'attitude' isn't too good. I saw the words they wrote about me. I looked when there was no one in the room but me and my friend. His name is Joe too. My brother Joe would be getting ready to go whaling now if he was alive. He *is* getting ready to go whaling — because I am, and when I do something, he does; I can feel him telling me he's glad I'm doing what I'm doing. I tried to tell the teacher what we do, my brother and I, when we wait for the seals, but the teacher thought I was talking about my *friend.* The teacher is like the minister and the priest who come here every week; they think their God is the only one who can talk with someone who has died."

That is that; Joe has, perhaps, ventured a little further into the realm of social criticism and theological analysis than he had intended. He decides to draw a winter landscape, then changes his mind. He will sketch a whaling scene — a view of an event he took part in a year ago. He begins with the snow: white paint and more of it — so much of it that one wonders why he even bothered. Might he not just as well have left well enough alone — the entire piece of paper, so white to begin with? But he has a complex vision in mind, and a story to go along with it. As he begins to use blue paint, thereby cutting up the ice and snow, he allows his mind to wander back over the months: "My father can tell *here* what is going on way over *there.* He steps outside and comes back in and says we must wait. I watch him, and before he comes in I can tell by his face what he will say. He asked me yesterday what I thought. I told him what I thought: not now, but soon. He said yes. You can tell by the weather. I've been trying to practice standing still; I spent most of the day being still after we got out of school. If you move when the seals are coming near, they see you, and you come home with nothing. The whales are hard to catch;

they are fast, and my father warns me that I must say *nothing* when a whale is spotted. Sometimes people get excited and make noise, and move — they forget themselves — and the whale gets away. I would like to shoot a whale first; then it would be mine. It would be my brother's, too. He is waiting for me, for us, to kill a whale, and bring it home; then the pieces of food would go to everyone, and my father would say: in the name of Joe and Joe. I will write that down on the paper: *'in the name of Joe and Joe.'* "

He had stressed the words as he spoke them; he underlines them after he has written them. He puts aside the picture — unfinished. How to draw whales, a man or boy hunting them? He is no artist! He has learned to write though. For all his apparent lack of interest in the education he is receiving, he pays careful, if rather wary, attention in class. He volunteers nothing. He speaks tersely, with no great emotional expression to his voice. And he is unlike many of his friends, who smile when the teachers address them. As a result he is known to those teachers as "the grumpy one," though they haven't told him directly what they call him. But he has heard; the store owner, for instance, has a glib, gossipy tongue — and in winter, especially, gossip is one of the store's chief commodities. But the boy doesn't mind being considered grumpy; he enjoys the critical description. Haven't some teachers complained to the store owner, the visiting minister, and others that Eskimos are *too* friendly? And haven't those teachers wondered out loud what Eskimos *really* think or feel?

He has heard the teachers doing so, as he explains in connection with, of all things, his aborted drawing of a whaling expedition: "When you go whaling, you have to become part of the ice; my father kneels and he says to himself that he will not move, even if the pain makes him feel like crying. He tells me not to cough and not to sneeze. We are as quiet as we can be.

Once there were sea gulls, and they landed, and they moved closer and closer, and they must have decided that we weren't people, because they came so close, we almost could touch them. Then a seal came toward us, but my father didn't want a seal; he wanted a whale. So did I. For a second I was going to say something, but I saw on his face that we shouldn't even move our eyes, if we could help it, so I stared at the seal, but I didn't say a word, and I didn't smile. I was going to; I like seals. I like to hear them talk. Later the whale appeared, and suddenly my father was awake and throwing his harpoon. I was so used to being still that I didn't know what to do — stand up, run, lie down, stay as I was.

"In school I once sat at my desk. Everyone else except my friend Joe and I had gone outside. The teacher thought we'd *all* gone out. She was standing in the hall; I could see her back. She was talking to another teacher. I was ready to stand up and make some noise, but I decided to sit still and say nothing. Joe and I agreed to do that — by the look we gave each other. He looked at a book; I looked at a map of Alaska on my desk. That's when I heard the teacher say I was 'grumpy,' but she *liked* me for being grumpy! My friend was going to get up and laugh, I could tell; and so was I! But we didn't. I remembered what my father always says: keep quiet at the right moment, and you can have a long laugh afterwards, and you can run and talk and shout. So I sat there and thought to myself: wait until I come home and tell my father what I heard the teacher say about me!"

Joe says things about himself; he can be rather gloomy as he looks ahead and thinks about his life. He watches men sit idle through the day, talking about the past — when Eskimos had to keep on the move all the time to survive. Now some of those men move only to the store, sit by the stove, and talk, pull cords, see lights go on, hand over food stamps, receive canned goods, hear what their children covet: a motorcycle, a snow-mobile, a motorboat, a series of lessons that will result in a pilot's license, a stint of military service. Is someone who at ten or twelve or fourteen turns his back on such hopes peculiar, maybe even disturbed? In his own way the boy answers that question: "We do a lot of fighting; we wrestle and box because the teachers say we should get exercise in the winter. I tell my friends that no one needed exercise a long time ago up here; there was a lot to do in the winter. One of my friends says he wants to leave the village, because he can't sit here all winter inside his house and inside school. His father should make him go fishing, or go collect wood. But his father works for the state of Alaska; he tries to keep the airstrip clear, and he helps out at the school. So he gets good money, and his kids are soft. They sit around in the summertime, too. They're fat, and they're lazy. I wish the whole family would move to the city. They belong in Kotzebue, or Fairbanks!

"My friends say they'd like to go hunting. They wish they knew how to live the way our ancestors did. But they don't. My mother is right: a lot of our ancestors died before they were as old as I am. But the ones who lived knew how to take care of themselves! My father says that when I'm his age, we'll all be sitting here in the village, eating frozen fish we've got from the store in the summer — through food stamps — and playing checkers during the winter and complaining that it's too hot in our houses. I woke up the other morning and it *was* too hot. My older brother Joe must have been smiling, and my grandfather, because they both had my name before me. My older brother used to tell my father that he wanted us to be able to get through a winter without buying food at the store, and without buying oil or kerosene either. My father would tell him that it's too late for us to live like that; we're different people than our ancestors were. But my brother said we could be the kind of people we want to be. He died before he could prove his point.

"I think he had his eye on a girl from another village. She came to visit her cousin in our village, and my brother met her and he liked her. My mother says he came home, and told her he wanted to marry the girl, because she told him she hated every Eskimo village she'd seen, and she wanted to live alone in the woods, or near the ocean. I think my brother was my age then; a year later he died, and then I was born three months afterwards. I haven't met a girl like that, but if I did I would come home and tell my mother the same thing. I hope I wouldn't get sick, though, like my brother did. The nurse who came here said she thought he had blood poisoning; she wasn't sure. Then we had bad weather, and no one could fly in. My brother woke up one morning and he felt very sick. He threw up the bread my mother gave him, and the coffee. He told her he was sure he was going to die. He wasn't unhappy, though. He asked if she would name the baby she had inside her after him, if it turned out to be a boy, and she said yes, she would. Then she went out to the store, to see if they could reach Kotzebue by radio, and maybe get a doctor here. When she came back my brother was dead.

"My father had come back with some fish, and he was hoping to cook some for my brother. He found him on the floor, and he wasn't breathing the way you should, and suddenly he stopped completely. When my mother came in she knew my brother had died. My father had picked him up and moved him to the back of the house, because he thought he'd tell my mother first, before she saw his face. She said that she'd come running home, because while she was in the store she'd had some pains in her stomach, and she was sure that my brother had suddenly become even sicker, and so she was hoping to be with him before he died, but he left before she could get to him, and she's told me a lot of times that the pain in her stomach was me: I must have known that my brother was dying, and I must have tried to tell my mother by kicking her. I hope I can meet a girl like the one he met, and she and I can build a house near the ocean, and we can learn to go whaling together, and catch seals and fish, and we can build our own sled, and have a large team of dogs. And we won't *buy* sleds for the children. We'll *build* sleds for them. My friends agree with me; they say they'd like to be Eskimos first, and not white people who look like Eskimos! But they say it's too easy to let the white people come and show us how to live like they do!"

Nevertheless, Joe's friends are not lazy, or lacking in enthusiasm for the traditional tasks of their people. They have all gone whaling, and they all would love to keep on experiencing the challenges and satisfactions of negotiating the ice pack, finding the edge of the floe, spotting and killing and taking in and, not least, cutting up the whale. They remember especially the feel of the whale, so smooth and cool; the sight of the whale, so clean and shining white. The more they recall whaling, hunting, fishing, the more they assert their loyalty to old-fashioned village life. But the more they hear the roar of a snowmobile, or a plane landing, the more they turn enthusiastically to America's twentieth-century technological culture. If one boy says no, they must not turn with their hearts in that direction; dozens of other voices say yes, why not! Most persuasive, in this regard, are the slightly older boys — youths of, say, fourteen or sixteen, who are, by and large, without jobs, but driven by many hopes and fears of a kind their parents don't quite understand. The younger boys watch the older ones, listen to them, learn to follow their example: cut wood not to make something, but simply to chip away, chip away; ride a snowmobile, anyone's that can be begged, borrowed, or, for a few hours, stolen; listen to records all day long — and in the summer, all night long as well. There are also flights of fancy that become very much shared by a number of youths and, in imitation of them, by younger boys: the dream of a trip to a city, where one can buy records and more records; the dream of a trip to a larger village, where it is said that there is a television set, and where more movies are brought in than is the case in one's own village; the dream of a trip on an airplane to — anyplace outside of Alaska, but the larger the city the better.

VI

A MODERN GIRL

ESKIMO GIRLS are not without their own moments of boredom, irritability, dissatisfaction with themselves and their life. One girl in a small Arctic village has just turned thirteen; Mary sympathizes with those who yearn for the old days and ways, but she is not about to turn her back on today's "progress." She is an expert on rock music, has a stereo set, wonders when she will get to a city, dance in a dance hall. She has finished school, does little to keep herself busy, resents the fact that her father is, by Eskimo standards, rather well-to-do — but can offer her only a limited version of the future she would like for herself. If some of the village's more proper, conventional people find her self-centered, even insolent, she has some thoughts about them, among others: "My father worked with the white people; he helped them build the airstrip, and he was the one who showed them where to build the school. He can fix the generator, if anyone can. Other people are jealous of him; and they turn on my mother and me, just because we like to wear clothes that aren't like their clothes. There are some old women in this village who are very mean. They spend all their time exchanging gossip; and when there isn't any to tell, they make some up.

"On our radio I heard that in places like California, women

are living different; they aren't bowing before men, and taking orders all day from them. I'd like to go to California. Or maybe the gossiping women of this village, all of them, should go there! My father heard that my mother and I are 'friends' of the pilot — that he comes here on an extra trip every week, just to 'visit' us! Of course, everyone can see and hear that plane landing — so if he came in secret he'd have to be quite a pilot; he'd have to be like Superman in the comic books! When he *does* come he is greeted by the whole village, and he's never out of everyone's sight. But the women sit and sew and say that he's my mother's 'special friend,' and that when he gets tired of her, he turns to me! That shows what is going on here in this village: nothing! I wish the pilot would go 'visit' those old ladies and do something for them! They are worse than the minister and the priest put together! They are always calling me a 'modern girl' — and then they sneer!"

Mary cannot bear hypocrisy, and she is convinced that next to some of the gossipy village women, the most two-faced people in all of Alaska, maybe the entire world, are the pair of ministers who come to her village on weekly visits and who have long been objects of her derision. Often she wonders why in the world those men even want to visit the village. But she has figured out the reason and is most adamant when she comes forth with it: "They don't like their own people, so they leave them and come up here to be with us. I heard one of the ministers say that white people are 'plundering' Alaska; but he's up here, talking us into believing that he knows what's best to believe in. And he'll call you a bad person, and tell you about Hell. How does he know there's such a place? My mother says he's never been there, and no one has who's alive, so it's all up in his head, that there's Hell and Heaven. The ministers both expect to be in Heaven one of these days; I'll be glad to be in the other place, if that's how God will divide people up.

"I don't want to hear one sermon after another forever. Anyway, I'll bet they did something wrong, before they ever decided to come up here. They keep talking about the Eskimos they haven't converted, and how they want to convert them; but I think they ought to go back to the cities they come from and stay there, and stop telling us that it's wrong to drink and wrong to swear and wrong to do anything, except go and pray in their churches. The older minister asked me last summer where I got the dress I was wearing. I told him I ordered it in the Sears catalogue; but he looked very unhappy with me, and I was almost in a fight with him. But I was younger then; I was a little scared. If he dared say something like that to me again, I might pick up a rifle and aim it at him and tell him to go radio Kotzebue for that pilot who flies him in here!"

Mary doesn't really ever intend to talk like that to the minister or to any other grown-up; at least she can't imagine herself doing so. She recognizes the difference, even in someone as relatively outspoken as herself, between a thought and the actuality of words uttered — meant to be heard, taken quite seriously. But she is not really joking, either; nor is she being fresh and sassy — without taking the risks of putting herself on the line, so to speak. She has dared tell her teachers what she thinks, knowing full well that she has accepted their invitation to say candidly what is on her mind, but at the same time risked offending them. They have wondered aloud why she is so adamantly interested in urban life, why she seems so anxious to join what one teacher quite explicitly called "the rock culture."

She immediately challenged the teacher to describe that "culture," and the description given prompted a rather strong response: "I told her she was not right about me. I decided to say what I was thinking. Most of the time I don't. *All* the time the others in class don't! I know I'm sounding conceited; that's what my best friend said to me. She said I think so much of myself that I make the teachers feel uncomfortable — and her, too. We had a fight. I tried to explain to her why I say what I say. But she was too upset to listen; she said I shouldn't talk to people like I do — especially to white visitors who come here to teach us. But that's what I told the teachers; I said it's not right for people like them to come here to this village and talk to us the way they do. They think they're acting like Eskimos; they think they're saying what our parents say, and what we'll say to our children when we're parents. But they're wrong. Is it wrong for me to tell a teacher she's wrong — or he's wrong? My friend says yes; she says that you should stay quiet and smile and try to agree with what you've heard. I say that it's wrong to pretend to agree when you don't. But maybe my friend *does* agree! She says she agrees with the teacher when the teacher talks, and when I talk, she begins to agree with me! My friend says *I* should be a teacher!

"All I said was that I thought the teacher was trying to sound like an Eskimo; I mean she was talking like she *thought* an Eskimo talks, or like she thought we all *should* talk. Even my grandfather doesn't talk like that. He likes the electricity the white people brought to our village; and he likes to listen to my stereo; and he likes to go on a ride in a snowmobile. He says that if he was only younger he'd learn how to ride a motorcycle himself! He wasn't kidding me, either! The teachers are white and they come here from Chicago (one of them does) and New York (another one), and last year we had a teacher here from Portland, Oregon. They all say the same things to us; they tell us that we're good, but the white people are ruining us, because they're bringing in movies and radios and motorcycles and snowmobiles and potato chips and bubble gum, and we're getting lazy, and we no longer have our own 'culture.'

"Don't ask me what that word means: *culture*. I asked the

teacher, and she explained, and I still couldn't figure out what she was telling us. So I asked again. That was my first mistake. My friend says I was being mean by asking, but I swear I didn't understand the explanation. I asked my friend what *she* thought 'culture' means, and she said she wasn't the teacher, and she couldn't talk like the teacher! Oh, did I laugh at that answer! Then I told her *she* was conceited because she was so proud of what she'd said! All I'd wanted, anyway, was an explanation from the teacher that all of us in her room could understand, and take home to our parents and give to them. What's so great about living in an igloo, and not having a store where you can get food in the middle of the winter, when it's fifty below and the wind is getting ready to carry the whole village into the ocean? What's so great about living here, when there's no doctor or nurse who can be flown in, with the medicine they bring?

"My younger brother would have died if they hadn't brought in a nurse, and she gave him penicillin, and he lived. I agree with the teachers about some things. The ministers don't belong here, and they don't really respect us. They ought to close down the church here and leave us alone. We don't need their sermons. But my grandfather disagrees; he says there was a lot of fighting, a lot of bad trouble here in the village *before* the white man came, and it was the church people who tried to make us get along better here, and he thinks they succeeded. He remembers that the old minister, who lived here for a long time, would go and talk with one family, and then with another, and he'd turn enemies into friends! He was a kind man, my grandfather says, and he brought food to people all the time, even people who never wanted to listen to his sermons, or go near his little church."

Mary is taken aback by her own capacity to emphasize ironies and inconsistencies. She laughs at herself, declares herself to be a touch mad. Her friend, in fact, has warned her that she will become the village eccentric if she doesn't watch out. She wonders out loud why she doesn't just go along, yield to her teachers, to the many neighbors and their children who retreat in embarrassment and dismay from her unashamed militancy, her willingness to speak out, on issues and dilemmas others are content to ignore or tolerate. She holds on tenaciously to a lively interest in the outside world, is determined to visit places most of her friends or classmates have no interest in seeing, can be self-deprecating as well as sardonic: "I heard one teacher call another one a busybody. I'm a busybody. I'm always watching what's going on; if I lived in a city, I'd have to stop because there are so many people. But here I can keep my eye on everyone! There's not much else to do here! A lot of my friends agree with me; they'd like to go live in the city for a while. They wish they had as many records as I do; they bring theirs over, and we play them and play them, until my mother says she can't let us go on, because she feels like walking away from the house and never coming back.

"That's what her uncle did; I guess he was her great-uncle. He was old, and he was sick. One day he got up and he was in pain. My mother tried to help him. She made him tea, and she gave him some bread and jam. He turned away from her food. He said he wanted to go out; he was sure that the cold air would make him feel better. He got dressed and went out. He never came back. Later that day we all went looking for him, and we found him up the river. He'd found a small tree, and he'd sat down under it and died. When we brought him back everyone was sad because he had always been a good person. One of the teachers said we should have told her, so she could get a doctor here. But the old man would never have let a doctor look at him. He told my mother that the day would come when he'd go out and lie down and die, and he did. My

mother told the teacher what her uncle had said and done; the
teacher thought it was 'beautiful.' My mother admitted to me
later that she felt like laughing at the teacher but didn't. I
would have laughed. It's stupid to say our uncle did something
'beautiful.' He wasn't painting a picture. He was dying, and he
knew it. But maybe the teacher didn't mean bad. I guess she
likes Eskimos."

The person she feels closest to is not her best friend, or
either of her parents, but a younger brother, aged nine, who
has severe nearsightedness, complicated by astigmatism, and
who has relied upon her heavily in the past for vision —
literal and figurative. The boy had no glasses for a long time.
His parents accepted his near-blindness as something fated.
His sister urged her parents repeatedly to go talk with the
state officials when they came by, as they do often enough for
one administrative reason or another. Finally she took the boy
herself, telling their parents that they were simply going out
to play. She stood with him at the airstrip, waited for the plane
to appear and land, and went right up to the pilot, who stood
watching and smoking while the mail and various supplies
were being unloaded. Did he know when someone from Fairbanks, someone who could help her brother, would be flying
in next? What was the boy's problem? His eyes — he can't see
well. When he is five or six, the teachers will pick up the
trouble and get it corrected, won't they? But that is in the
future, and there is so much the boy can't do right now! Oh,
all right! He told her to be standing exactly where she was,
with her brother beside her, one week to the day, the hour.

They obliged. With the pilot this time came a doctor, who
had agreed to change his schedule of visits to the various
Eskimo villages. He did not only come for the boy, but the boy
was seen first, at the school, where his vision could be tested.
The child was measured for glasses; he has worn them, mostly,

ever since. On very cold days, however, or wet days, or snowy days, they become a hindrance; they fog up in response to changes in temperature, become themselves wet and snow-covered, hence a barrier rather than an aid. And the boy has not always been able to get his glasses fixed; they become loose, bent, eventually useless. Mary describes what happens in the winter, when the planes throughout Alaska have a hard time responding to the most routine and urgent of village requirements: "My brother says to me that he likes my eyes better than the glasses. He says he is glad it's winter, and he'll be on his own — or sticking close to me and my eyes! I take him with me when I go to the store, and I read the labels on the cans and packages I buy there, and I tell him what I can see in the sky — a lot of stars or only clouds. And we play a game we call *Wish*. In the game he makes me guess what he's wishing — that he could be someplace, or that he could have something. If I guess right, it's my turn; if I'm wrong, he tells me. He's easy to play with; he always has the same wishes — that he could see better, or go out and catch a seal or a whale. He's afraid that because of his eyes, he may not be able to do a lot of hunting or fishing.

"A lot of people here need glasses, but they don't want to get them. A friend of my mother's asked me if everyone in the city wore glasses, and I said I didn't think so. I don't like questions like that; they are stupid. I keep telling my brother that the day will come when we'll fly out of here, and it won't be to Kotzebue, except to change planes. We'll go in a jet, and we'll visit a city in Washington, or Oregon, or California — those are the three states that face the Pacific Ocean, like Alaska does. When we're down in the lower forty-eight they'll fix my brother's eyes so he won't even have to wear glasses. A teacher told me they can put something in his eyes, a very small piece of glass, and he'll be able to see the way other people do. Then we could go look around; and we could buy some records. We'd have some money we saved up. You can only order certain records in the catalogue.

"My mother says she's worried that all I'll ever do is listen to my records, but I tell her I'd like to get a job in some city, maybe working in a store where they sell records! The pilot told me I could get the records cheaper that way. And I could get myself a new stereo. It would cost a lot, but if you choose a set that isn't too expensive, and you get it even cheaper, because you work at the store, then you've done pretty good. If I brought the set back here — had it sent back on the plane — I'd have a lot of visitors. Even kids who think I'm strange because I want to leave here tell me they'd like to have more records and a big stereo. They'd all come over here, and they'd not only listen; they'd want to know what my brother and I saw down there in the lower forty-eight. We'd tell them. I'd let my brother do most of the talking because he'd be real excited, telling the kids what *he* saw."

She smiles at herself — a little critically, a little indulgently. She suspects it would be hard, after all, for her to keep quiet for long, even though her brother would have so much to tell. When she was much younger, maybe four or five, her grandfather told her that she talked too much; he was sure, accordingly, she would be a great favorite with the white schoolteachers when she started the first grade. But he had not realized how much the particular teachers in that village school admire what they keep calling "traditional Eskimo culture." A child who likes to talk a lot, and who, even at five or six, was intrigued with the shortwave radio because it made available "dance music" and news of other villages, distant cities, and countries would hardly be the traditional Eskimo child.

Mary rather soon discovered that her interests were not

those of her first-grade teacher. When the teacher tried to point out how strong and proud the Eskimo people are, this one pupil of hers observed that children who lived in other parts of America were lucky. The teacher asked why. The child remembers well her answer — and the consequences: "I spoke quite loud, and she was surprised. I told her that I wouldn't mind living near a city in the United States of America where there was a Sears Roebuck store. She asked me why, and I told her why. I told her my mother sits with us and lets us look through the catalogue; and we point at the pictures we like, and she tells us how much money we'd need, and then we keep looking. The teacher said there was so much around us up here that we could look at, and we don't have to pay any money, just go and look — so why think the pictures in the Sears catalogue are so good? I didn't answer her back, not then; I was too young to know what to say. I did tell my mother what had happened between the teacher and me, and my mother told me not to tell the teacher what *I* think but to find out what *she* thinks.

"That is what my parents and my grandfather and my aunts and uncles have kept telling me, all the time: that I shouldn't speak my mind to the white people; instead, I should ask them what they believe and what they want, and be friendly with them. But it's hard for me to pretend I like a person if I don't really like her! Anyway, the white people who come up here aren't the only white people in the world, and if the pilot is right, the white people we see are different from the white people in the lower forty-eight. Once the teachers decided to come and talk with my mother and father; they decided that I was different from everyone else! They asked my mother if she was happy with the school — was I learning a lot? She said yes, she was happy and I was. She said she was glad all of her children were learning to read and write, and she hoped we went as far as possible in school. The teacher thanked her, and I remember my mother offering her tea; we had teabags. The teacher said we certainly had everything! My mother didn't know what she meant at first. She looked to my father. I think he knew, but he only smiled and asked the teacher if she wanted some sugar in the tea. The teacher said no. We gave her cookies, too; but she didn't want any.

"Later, when I was older, I could figure out what had happened. The teacher didn't expect us to serve tea and cookies; I guess she'd only recently come up here to Alaska, and she thought we had completely different food than the kind white people eat. In the past we lived on what we could catch in the water, or find on the land. But it's different now. She had seen the store, I guess, but hadn't gone visiting us yet. It's strange: some of the teachers don't really want us to live the way we do. They want us to be even poorer than we are! My grandfather says a lot of white people who come here would like to see us living in igloos. He jokes; he says he's going to build an igloo, and go live in it, and then he'll be the teachers' hero. I'm not sure he would know *how* to build one! Maybe he would. My grandfather sometimes says he doesn't know how to do anything, except fish, and dry out the fish, and eat; but other times he tells us long stories about the things he used to do when he was younger. Then I wish the teachers were here to listen. They'd really love him, because of what he says."

VII

CHILD OF THE ARCTIC WILDERNESS

THE TEACHERS would certainly love the people of another village quite a distance away from the one Mary
and her grandfather live in. It is among the less accessible
Eskimo villages and is known to interested outsiders as a place
where Eskimos have become less "corrupted" by Western
cultural inroads. The people don't live any more "primi-
tively," but they have no snowmobiles or motorcycles, tend to
make their clothes rather than buy them, and are less interested in Western packaged food or the arrival of an airplane,
bearing the latest goods from Sears Roebuck & Co. Several
white people have come to the village though — as in the case
of other Alaskan villages — to teach, to help with problems of
sewage or disease, to carry out ecological surveys, and occasionally to go fishing or hunting. Always the Eskimos are
friendly, courteous, full of warmth and kindness. They are
relatively less likely to refuse help or advice than those who
live in many other villages; and their children are less likely
to be cynical, knowing, or obsessively interested in the lower
forty-eight.

A twelve-year-old girl from this village smiles at an account
of another twelve-year-old Eskimo girl's interests and ambitions; finally, she apologizes for seeming to be indifferent or

amused: "I didn't know what to say. I was silent because I was wondering if I'll ever try to leave our village, except to go visit my aunt and uncle. It takes us all day and half the night in the spring to get to their village. We go when the days have become longer, but before the ice melts. The dogs are very fast, and they know by now that my uncle will give them a lot to eat when we get there. They have been good to us, so we are good to them. I wouldn't want to live someplace where I couldn't get on a sled and be pulled by our dogs. My father asked me if I want to fly in a plane one day, and I said no. He doesn't want to go up, either — and there have been several chances. Our town has one man who talks with all the people who come here by plane, and he told my father that a hunter was willing to hire him and my older brother. They could have gone in a plane the man had. My father said he'd like to help the man out. We were getting ready for the winter though; we had to go out by ourselves and do a lot. The man told my father's friend that, even so, he wanted to come with us. But we were going to be building a new rack to hold our fish. We had to cut some bushes up. My father told us when he got home that he didn't think he could do enough for the hunter. He was afraid the man would be very disappointed, and my father didn't want to take the money, either. In our village we don't really use money. We have to spend a day getting to a store in the next village where we can spend money."

Jane is not being facetious or sly when she describes her father's persistent refusal to be of help to an outsider as based on a sense of personal inadequacy — that it was not possible to do justice to the white man's wishes or needs. Her father had shared his apprehensions with his family. He had told his wife and children that he would have liked to go out hunting, or fishing; would have liked helping an earnest, friendly white man shoot and cast to his heart's content. But the Eskimo had visions of failure he could not shake off. He was sure he couldn't live up to the expectations of white people — so best to say no. He was not refusing with a sense of irony, or with sarcastic reservations in mind. He honestly believed that his people are no match in many ways for white people, so it is best to follow their lead, or learn from them, or keep a certain polite but respectful distance from them.

And his children have learned to feel a similar mixture of awe, apprehension, and deference; in Jane's words: "I know that Alaska is part of the United States, and we are second to no nation. We are the strongest. I haven't seen the tanks we have, or the big planes, but I heard about them in school. My grandfather built the largest sled in the village. Each time he puts the harness on the dogs, he jokes with them; he tells them they'll never, never be able to pull the sled he made — and him. He pats his stomach and says it is too much for the dogs! But they don't pay any attention to him. They are only waiting for him to remind them that they will be eating very well when the ride is over: he throws them a little bit of fish. The white man wanted a ride in my grandfather's sled, too. He told his friend that the dogs looked sick. The dogs don't like white people! I think the man just wanted a ride for fun! White people have their own airplanes, and motorboats, and snow-mobiles. But they want a ride on our sleds too. They want everything! There are a lot of rich white people! I don't think there are any rich Eskimos; maybe in the cities. My mother says no; she says that even there our people have to worry about the white man, because he's the one who owns every-thing. But they mostly leave us alone here. We like their visits; when they come they are usually polite, because they want to ask a favor of us. We try to do the best we can. My father says he always offers to show them around, and they come with him. I've seen him walking with them, pointing at our houses, and the road we made between them, and at the ponds we have near us."

At such times Jane's impulse is to keep her distance; she is shy of white people, including even the schoolteachers she has had. She has come to various conclusions about them and, by implication, herself. They walk so fast. They are always going *somewhere.* They meet her and ask her where she is going; she says, invariably, nowhere; then without being asked, they tell her where *they* are going. She has asked her mother, who is soft-spoken, retiring, quite hardworking, why white men and women behave as they do. Her mother has no explanations that banish further inquiry; in fact, is quick to point out that she doesn't know why Eskimos and white people look different, talk differently, walk differently. One evening her mother did go so far as to say that the girl is a "child of the tundra," the white man a "child of big cities."

The girl has heard an itinerant minister talk about God, and His decisions, but she does not regard herself and others as "creatures of God's." Let the minister have himself in mind when he uses the phrase! Nearer the mark was a teacher's description of the girl: "A child of the Arctic wilderness." She liked that. She has been told by elders in the village that there are many spirits to be reckoned with: in the atmosphere; up the top of distant hills; hovering over the vast water. Those spirits are often on the lookout for entry (or really, reentry) into this world — through the medium of childbirth. Some spirits choose Eskimo children being born; some choose whites. It is a matter of luck, chance, fate. Or is it? She remembers her father saying that there are Eskimo spirits and those that belong to the white people — all of which simply moves the mystery of human differences back in time or out into the world of rain, mist, clouds, snow, oceans, and mountains.

Usually Jane keeps busy at home, helping her mother care

for three younger sisters, or at school, doing the assigned work. But she has her reflective moments — the best of them, she believes, with her mother: "My mother wants me to sew with her; she calls me in and tells me to sit down beside her, and help her. She asks my sisters to go to our aunt's house nearby; they are glad to go! She gives them chewing gum. My mother will not let us have chewing gum. She says it's not *bad*, it's just that she would rather have us chew food and swallow it — and she doesn't like to see gum on the floor or outside near the house. The white people come here, and if they're not smoking, they're chewing gum or candy; even their mouths never stay still for very long. In school the teacher sometimes asks: What are you thinking? I say: I don't know. She wants us to be thinking of what we have learned, or what we plan to learn next. My mother says we should try to have something to say, so that when the teacher asks what we're thinking about, we can tell her — we can give her something, and then she'll be happy with us. The teacher *is* happy with us, though. She tells us we are good people. She says she is glad she is here with us. She thinks my father is very good with his knife; he carves wood and the teacher likes to watch him work. She asked him to come to school and show us what he can do with his knife. We all know what he can do!"

Jane does not speak those last words sarcastically; a bit quiz-zically, perhaps. One more indication that at school mysteries continue to abound. She is happiest, she believes, when she is at home, sewing alongside her mother, and not talking much, or thinking much. In spring she can watch icicles melt for a half an hour, an hour, and not think of anything, or feel that she ought be doing something else. Her mother has reminded her that white people like to talk, and like to tell each other what they are doing, and will be doing. It is different with Eskimos; she and her mother go about their business without announcements, admonitions, inquiries, or even at times a single word. At times, when the girl is persuaded to talk, her memories of those shared times with her mother come across as somewhat mystical: "We were sitting at the table. We were making a jacket for my youngest sister. There was no wind. It was very quiet. I felt the house talking to us. Something was happening outside. I looked up, and there it was — a lot of snow. We hadn't noticed. We hadn't even looked out. I think my mother wasn't happy with me for interrupting with the news of the storm. She looked at the snow and said she wasn't surprised. But she remembered that the sun was out only a little while earlier; so she realized we might be getting a very heavy snow — the kind that comes very fast and leaves a lot behind by the time it's ready to go. She admitted to me that she was surprised.

"We were going to wash the floor, but we changed our minds — it would be a waste, because everyone would come home covered with snow, and the floor would soon be wet and dirty. Maybe it snowed because we said a few days earlier: The floor must be washed before the minister comes here again! When he comes, we want the house to be as clean as possible. The teachers don't say anything about our floor, no matter how it looks, but the minister and his friends tell us that the floor is clean — or they look hard when it is dirty. I asked my mother why the minister comes to see us; she said because he wants to be friendly. The snow comes to be friendly, too; my grandmother told us that. The sun leaves us in the winter, but not forever. The snow gets higher and higher, and you begin to think it will never go away. But the sun is strong, and in the middle of the summer you cannot believe there will ever be a winter here. When the flies and mosquitoes come, we wish it was a little colder. When a blizzard hits us, we dream of the summer: my mother says it can be a real pleasure — a mosquito trying to get inside the ear! In the summer she reminds us how nice it is to be covered with clothes, and still feel cold! That is why we have seasons, my grandmother says — to make sure we are never without a good memory, even in the middle of a blizzard, or even when mosquitoes and flies are covering up your arms and face."

Jane especially loves the summer. She remembers hearing a teacher say that Eskimos know how to live under extremes of winter weather that other people would find impossible to survive. She remembers hearing another teacher remark upon the joy she sees on the faces of Eskimo children when the snows come, the estuaries and ponds freeze: sledding, games, sliding. She remembers hearing that teacher praise the winter — a time when the valuable and hard-earned skills of Eskimo people are put to use every day, and help prove a people's competence, dignity, integrity. She is not cynical when she recalls those remarks, and others like them, made by earnest, sensitive, kind whites, intent on helping to affirm in the minds of children like her a sense of personal worth. Still, she has no great love for school. She bears no animus, either — toward teachers, toward white visitors, toward the advancing Alaskan technology, glimmers of which even the people of her village (a relatively remote one) have kept seeing in recent years. Nor is it a matter of a girl quite set in her ways — the ancient and established ways of her village. She does indeed cherish those ways; she sees herself as, eventually, a woman very much like her mother. She is, as she puts it, "just herself." She was not, as she puts it, "born to study or live like a white."

Jane has no great desire to travel, even to larger villages, a few hundred miles away. But she does have her own streak of independence, of assertiveness; in the summer she parts company with her friends and family, certainly with her teachers, when she goes for a walk and allows her mind to wander: "I like to walk far from the house; only in the summer can I do that. I like to swim in the water of a pond; only in the summer can I do that. I like to lie down, and the grass is a bed, and I see how near I can go with my eyes to the sun, before it tells them to stop; only in the summer can I do that. I like to watch the sun when it gets weak, and it almost sets, but doesn't; only in the summer can I do that. Most of all I like to sit down and keep so still that the birds come closer and closer, and the geese come so near I could reach out and catch them, but I don't; only in the summer can I do that. Only in the summer can I go with my sisters on a walk, and we take some fish with us, and we don't come back for a long time, and when we do we are sleepy, even if the sun isn't. We bring flowers home, and we look at them, and say good night to them, and good morning. I wish the summer would never leave us. I wish I was a bird; then I could follow the summer. I wouldn't like being far away from here for too long. If I was a bird, my mother and father would be birds — and I could always come back here, like the birds do, every summer. It would be hard to leave, but the summer is worth a long trip — the only reason I'd ever want to go so far away.

"My sisters and I dream of the summer; that's what we can do — hope, wait. I ask the teacher sometimes to point out on the map where it's summer — it's very cold out when I ask. She smiles, and she tells us how hard it is to get through the summer near the Equator — a lot of diseases, and mosquitoes that carry germs, and the temperature so hot you don't need a stove to cook. I'm ready to leave for the Equator! I wish I could go there, and bring the weather back and keep it here. One teacher had a friend of hers come visit us; he was from Arizona, I believe. He told us that the ice might melt in the North Pole, and we would have warm weather all the time. He said it takes thousands of years, but that because it's cold here now most of the year doesn't mean it will always be cold here. We could lose our winters. Maybe I'd miss them; but I don't think so."

Jane knows that she is a bit different in that regard; many of her friends find the summer enjoyable enough, but confusing: the endless days; the surprising warmth and, with it, the hordes of flies; and worst, at least for many, the stillness and wetness of the air. She likes to feel and see herself sweating, likes it to be quiet outside. But she knows what her mother means, or what some of her friends are getting at, when they claim themselves a bit undone by a calm, muggy day. And she does like the wind, so she has to become somewhat guarded, tentative, as she continues with her comparative remarks: "I wouldn't want to be where there's *no* wind. The wind is the sky talking; sometimes spirits up there try to send us messages. My father says his grandfather would listen to the wind, and he'd come in and tell them what they were doing that was right and what was wrong. I'd like to be able to do that, but my mother says you have to be quite old — that's when our ancestors may start whispering to you, because you're almost ready to go be with them. The best winds are in the summer because you don't have to run away from them. You don't have to turn your back or bend your head. You can stretch yourself and you can feel the wind all over you, and the sweat gets carried away, like snow in winter being swept across the land and piled on the hills.

"I like the hills in the winter. The snow is on them in a big heap, and we dig in, and make a house or a fort. The winds are stronger in the winter, and they're with us every day then. In the summer you can begin to wonder if there will ever be a wind here again. You can begin to wonder if the sun will ever leave us, and if we will ever see snow or ice. My father always reminds us that if we wanted to walk very far, we could get to the ocean, and if we followed the coastline up north, we'd see ice and snow on the ocean, even in the middle of the summer. The men who fly planes can look at the icebergs, and look at the sun shining on us — and see the winter and the summer at the same time. So can some of our people who live farther north. But I am glad that we live right here. When we see the winter getting tired, we can talk to the sun, ask it to get stronger and stronger, and we know that it will melt every snowflake and all the ice. The birds know the summer is near, too. They stop here and don't go farther north. The birds love the water; not only the ponds, but the melted snow, the muddy water all around us. The village is wet in the spring; my mother wonders why fish don't begin to swim past our door. It would be easy, then, to catch our supper! But I'd still want to go near the pond, and be so far away from the village that I don't have to keep quiet if I don't want to; I can make all the noise I want, and try to make the birds think that I'm a bird myself, a strange bird that's much bigger than they are and, like some geese, can't fly, only make a lot of strange-sounding noises."

Jane is amused at the prospect of being mistaken for a bird by other birds — or by some person (a stranger, a white person) who might come within hearing distance. If she has any complaints about life in the village and its surrounding land, they would be directed at the anonymous outsiders who aren't especially interested in the village and its inhabitants, but who are to be encountered with increasing frequency well beyond the homes and other buildings. The girl knows who the men are, what they want: geologists, biologists, ornithologists, ecology-minded investigators, engineers, and, not rarely, determined vacationers, anxious to get away from the many parts of Alaska (even) that are now well traveled. She has several times asked her parents when (not whether) they and

others in the village will begin a trek north, south, east, or
west: someplace, anyplace private. It is possible, of course, to
move in any direction, though a hundred miles west would
bring the ocean, and she has heard a lot about life there: "If
we went to the ocean, we'd have more people than ever near
us. The white people have ships and airplanes in the towns
there. The air force planes we see land on a field near the
ocean. My father says the towns there are like the big cities we
have — Fairbanks and Anchorage: a lot of our people, a lot of
white people, a lot of drinking."

The very mention of the word causes her to feel troubled,
sad, perplexed. She has never seen alcohol, but she has heard
about it. The elders of her village will not permit alcohol to be
sold; nor is there any demand for it, only a great deal of fear
that somehow, someday, this village will go the way of others,
be infiltrated, undermined, destroyed by the presence of bottles and more bottles. If so, one of the proudest, most intact,
least "Western" of the Eskimo villages in Alaska will have
yielded to "progress," all of which the girl knows quite well:
"My aunt comes from far away; my uncle met her because her
sister married one of our people and came to live with us. (The
man was in the army, I believe, during one of the wars America has fought.) It is that aunt who always warns us about
liquor. She is not the only one who knows about liquor, but she
saw what happened to her people — her father, and her
brothers, and even her mother, she says. We are lucky, she
tells us; but my father doesn't like to hear her say that. He says
we have worked hard to keep our village to ourselves. White
people come everywhere; they have come here, and they
have made different offers to us. They have stopped for a
while, my father says, because we have become known to
them as people who are happy with our life, and don't want
to build a longer airstrip, and open up a liquor store, and allow
a fishery to be built near our town.

"Some white people who have come here tell us we should be glad that we aren't like other Eskimos. The teachers tell us that. A man who works for the state of Alaska came here, and he told us so, too. He said we're lucky we're not near the pipeline they're building, and we're not where the air force or the navy want to build a base, and we don't have any gold here, and there's more fish to be caught in other places than near our village. My father kept saying yes, when the man spoke. The man would ask my father if he was right, and my father would say yes, he was right. When we got home my father told my mother that the man didn't give us any credit for being able to say no to the white man. But then my father admitted that it's best to say yes, if someone wants you to say yes. In our village the birds and the fish, even the bears, don't care whether you agree with them or not! And if an Eskimo from another village comes, he doesn't care. But if it is a white person, and he's from the city, and he's with the government, he'll expect you to agree with him.

"If it's a white man who wants to hunt or to look around and take pictures and go fishing, then he'll probably not be any trouble. He'll ask your help, and you'll give it to him. We like to have people come here, if they want to look at our village and go visit the birds nearby, in the summer. The teacher says we have millions of birds here then, and some men have come from a university, and they have big spyglasses, and they know a lot about birds. I took two of them to a place I know; the teacher told them *I* know a lot about birds, too! They said I must have spent a lot of time watching birds, to know how to go near them without scaring them. I told them I didn't want to scare them, and I try not to, but you can't get too close, or you will be seen moving, and off they go. The men asked me if my father or my grandfather shoots birds; I said no. They asked me if my father or grandfather taught me how to creep up on birds, to *steal* up on them, they said; I said no. I just started listening to the birds one day, and I didn't want to stop them from talking, by making them go away, so I stood still, or if I came nearer, I went step by step, with a rest in between each step. That's how I learned."

One of the men wanted to take a picture of Jane near the birds, but no, she wasn't interested. He jokingly offered to fly her to Fairbanks, where she could tell some interested university students how she observes "Nature," but no, she wasn't interested. When he told her that he didn't actually mean to be taken seriously, she became confused and, it can be argued, angry — though she becomes increasingly apologetic and self-critical as she allows her resentment to be expressed: "I thanked him for telling me he would like me to be a teacher in Fairbanks for a day, and when I did he smiled, and told me I wasn't getting his joke. I didn't think he was so funny! I thought he was trying to tell me that I know a lot about birds. The teacher explained that he was trying to be friendly. I guess I wasn't too friendly! I should have smiled. I forgot to. I was sorry later. I told my mother. She said I should remember the next time to be nice to the visitors. I will try. But when the visitors are gone, I always want to leave our village and go visit the birds. I am like them; they don't like people coming around. They fly away."

She is quite ready, if only it were possible, to fly away herself — not simply to the nearby tundra but (in her mind) much farther north, where (she has heard it told) some birds like to go during the summer months. Her village is a relatively isolated one, but no village in Alaska is now as isolated as she and some other Eskimo children she knows would like to be the case. And when she is told by her parents or at school that she had best resign herself to the pressure of more outsiders, more government officials, more scientists, pilots, teachers, or hunters, she smiles (as she has been told to do) but also turns her eyes skyward.

One of many drawings Jane has made of birds shows how she regards them and their fate. (Figure 10.) The bird soars, is high up on the paper; below stretches the sky. She sees no reason to furnish her drawing with clouds, never mind land. She decides to indicate the nighttime: a half-moon instead of the sun, and some stars. She loves the evening sky, loves those birds who don't rest at night, loves the village in the spring and the fall, when the evenings have their own authority, have not become the endless extensions of the day or its total replacement. In April or September she will walk outside after supper, look up at the moon, wonder about the stars — and think of her own life as well as the lives of birds: "I used to ask my mother why the birds don't try to fly to the moon and stay there. She said she was sure the birds can't get there. I asked my father why. He said *because*. That means not to ask him again! My grandfather said he agreed with me: it's too bad the birds can't fly higher, and go to the moon and the stars; then the sky would really be theirs. As it is, they live in the sky, but they have to watch out for airplanes, and they can't go anywhere they want. It's the same with us; we aren't free the way we once were, my grandfather says. He was told when he was a boy that he could go all over, and no one would stop him.

"Now the state of Alaska has signs on land not far away from us: don't enter. And there will be a big pipe coming down — not right here, but not far away, a day's ride, maybe, on our sled. We won't be going near the pipe. Some boys I know want to go see the pipe when it's built, but I don't. I'll bet the birds will fly right over the pipe and not pay any attention to it. If they decide to land, though, and they see the pipe, they'll change their minds and go right back up. When the teacher told us that American men had gone to the moon and they had a bike or a car with them, and they looked around, I was glad that no birds live up there. It would be a bad thing for the birds if they were up there, and all of a sudden they saw a machine coming, and it made the noise of an airplane, and it landed, and then the men came out, and they started spying, and they had their flag, the American flag. The birds wouldn't know what to do: to fly away, and try to reach a star; or fly back to the earth; or stay where they are, and hope the men will go away before long."

VIII

CHILDREN OF AN ARCTIC CITY

HER SKEPTICISM toward the white man's world of increasingly powerful technology, her preference for, her virtual requirement of, a large measure of privacy, her interest in and response to birds, the sky, and the least frequented stretches of the tundra, are by no means the psychological inclinations of another Eskimo girl, a few months younger, who lives in a coastal city — no match for Anchorage, but by Alaskan standards a rather heavily populated place. Her father works for the coast guard, and her mother occasionally works in a restaurant-bar as a dishwasher and cook. Jean goes to school, plays with her friends afterward, upon occasion accompanies her mother to work and helps her in the restaurant's kitchen. She also helps her grandmother take care of a younger brother and sister. She has lost two sisters from pneumonia. A brother died of a mysterious disease that puzzled a military doctor; he eventually told the parents, just before the seven-year-old boy's death, that he was probably suffering from a form of leukemia — "bad blood," the parents to this day call it, and the twelve-year-old girl does too. She had hoped that her brother would be sent to Fairbanks or Anchorage, even to Seattle, as the doctor was planning to do just before the boy suddenly hemorrhaged massively and died.

She would have stayed close to her brother, would have comforted him, reassured him in the face of danger and a sudden
shift of environment. But she would also have seen an even
larger city, and she will not deny that such a visit was attractive to her — to the point that when the doctor thought, for
a while, that her brother was getting better and would need
no further treatment, never mind diagnostic evaluation, she
was quite disappointed.

Jean does not, however, want to leave her hometown per-
manently. She is quite satisfied with her life there. She has a
specific career in mind and has been so consistently interested
in that career (for two years) that her mother is convinced she
will achieve her wish. She would like to be a waitress. She
would like to be one at the "best place" in the town —
a place where only white women serve drinks and food to
white men (mostly), but also some white women and children.
She is sure she would be especially helpful to the white children, because she has done some babysitting for white families
with children younger than she and has been complimented
highly: a capable and competent young lady. She has come
home less inclined to praise the children she has watched; they
have impressed her as unlike her own sisters and brother, or
her cousins, neighbors, friends. She has trouble putting her
opinion into words that amount to an explicit, concise declaration. She hints, probes with a question or two, withdraws,
abandons her effort, only to resume again: "It's not the same,
being with white kids. I thought it would be, but I was wrong.
They know how to ask for something! They'll want a 'snack'
before they go to bed, and I learned not to get in their way.
They have so many toys, I can't figure out what they do all day,
except try to keep busy playing with the dolls, and with the
trains and the blocks. They all have Lego; they bring it up from
the lower forty-eight. They want to make towers — taller and

taller. They ask me what they've built, and I say a tree, and they laugh: no, a skyscraper. I've asked them which toys they like best. They change their minds; one day it's this, the next day it's that. They tell me about the toy stores they've been to. It's their father's money they spend! I've asked if they'd let me have some of their toys when they get tired of them. They say *no*. I'm only kidding, but they don't get the joke!"

She abruptly turns to her father's work: does he have a good time, she wonders, helping keep a small lighthouse and a radio dispatch room in a presentable state? Does he like being with the uniformed men, who seem to her, at times, rather austere? She doesn't know. She has asked herself those questions repeatedly — and asked them of him. But her father is a silent person, and so is she, often enough. She has only learned in the past year or so to have a reasonably sustained conversation with another person: "I've spent evenings with the white children, and they want you to talk. My mother says I am different when I come home from an evening of babysitting. She says I keep opening and closing my mouth, and words come out as if there's a river of them inside me, and it's spring, and the river is in a hurry to get to the sea. So I stop; I tell myself not to say one more word! Then my mother says I'm back to being myself! Then I start talking again; I'll remember something I heard at the house I was minding, and I tell my mother — what the kids said, usually — and she smiles. She likes to hear my stories, and I like telling them. But my throat begins to hurt, and my mouth gets dry, and I'm tired. I'm not used to talking so much. White kids talk and talk! They're always telling me something, or asking me something. I can't keep up with them.

"In one home the father has a clock that has a radio, and you can go to bed, and the music keeps coming, and then it stops. You have to know which buttons to press, or else the music won't stop, and you'll wake up in the middle of the night and there's still music playing. I told the kids we don't have a radio. My mother likes living in the city, here, and so does my father; but they don't like radios. They don't mind my hi-fi; it's theirs, too. They listen to the records. But with the radio you have to listen to a lot of talk, and they say only people should talk in a home! When I was younger, and I'd have a pain in my stomach or I'd get a sore throat, I'd go to my mother and I'd try to tell her what was wrong. She'd know right away. She'd say I could just point, and she'd know. She'd say that the more I talked the less she knew! I think I confused her. That's what she told me later, when I was in school and learning new words; she said that it's good to learn the words, but if you use them too much, you mix people up!

"In the restaurant my mother hears the white people talking all the time: first it will be a joke, then someone says one word, or another word, and the next thing, there's a bad fight, and they're shouting and they're going to kill each other, you'd think. When my mother and father don't agree, one of them goes outside, and after they're away from each other for a while, they come back together, and it's all right. The best thing to do when there's an argument is to stop talking. I try to tell the kids that when I babysit. I tell them that the more they say to each other, the worse it'll get. Once you've said something, it's no longer yours; the words belong to everyone who heard them. And you can't get them back, even if you ask the people to forget what they've heard. People don't forget words. I try to; I mean, I come home, and I've been listening to the kids I stay with, and I say to myself: start in all over again — as if it's the morning, and you've just got up and there isn't anything on your mind. But I can't. I'm still thinking of Lego, and of what one kid said to me, and another kid. I have to go to sleep; then I forget everything."

Not quite; she has vivid dreams, which she remembers, and by day she is a bit of a dreamer. Despite a family prejudice, often stated, against long-winded statements, she easily obtains her parents' interest in her mind's various reveries. Her mother's grandmother had been a village seer of sorts; she made forecasts about the weather, the migration of caribou, the onset of the first thaw, the arrival of birds from the south. She would have a dream, tell it to her husband; he would then tell their neighbors, and they would come to see the woman who had the dream to hear her interpretation. Each one in the village asked the same question, the great-granddaughter has been told: "What shall we think of your dream?" The old one would say what she thought, and others would feel in the presence of wisdom.

Many years later a descendant of hers has a much more limited audience, both in numbers and degree of credulity, and she knows why: "My mother says that today, if her grandmother was alive, she wouldn't be dreaming at all because she'd be so unhappy. She loved the village where my mother and father were born, and she never left it, and none of her children did. When my mother and father decided to leave, they waited until my grandmother died. She wouldn't have come here. I had a dream about my grandmother the other night. She was right here with us, and she said she'd stay, and she was glad that we had an extra bed for her. When I woke up I was scared that she was there, on the couch. I got up to look; but she was gone. She came to visit us, I guess — to see how we're doing. She said hello to me — that's when I had the dream about her — and then she left. When I told my mother of my dream, she said she has had the same kind of dream. My mother is sure that her mother's spirit visits us in our dreams. A week ago I had a bad dream, and I wasn't going to tell the dream to anyone, not even my mother, but she said I looked as if I was worried, and I knew I was, and she asked why, so I told her.

"In the dream I'd gone to school, and was just getting out; it was in the winter, because it was dark. I started walking home, when suddenly I heard a lot of noise, but I couldn't figure out what was causing it. I decided to go home as fast as possible. I began to run. But the noise got louder and louder, and before long I could see what was going on: a herd of caribou had come right into the town and was running through to the other side of town. Someone shot at them, I guess, and instead of running away even faster, they stopped and turned toward the person with the gun and ran toward him. He emptied his gun; a few caribou fell to the ground. But there were hundreds of them, and they kept coming at him, and soon he was on the ground too. I thought they'd turn around and come after me, but they didn't. Instead, they headed out toward the ocean! They must have been in a lot of trouble. Something was wrong with them, I know. I tried to shout at them: no, turn around, go inland! But they wouldn't listen. They went into the water, and they didn't stop until — well, I guess they drowned. My mother heard me calling to them: Stop, stop, stop, I was shouting. She woke me up. She asked me what I was dreaming. I told her, and my father. They didn't like the dream! My father asked me why I would want to have such a dream! I told him I didn't know.

"Sometimes I wish I could stop dreaming! I've had good dreams though. I keep having one: I'm with my parents, and we're eating a large supper at the restaurant where my mother works. In that dream we're the only Eskimo people there; all the other people are white. But they like us, and don't mind us being there. I think one of them wanted to know why we didn't eat at home, but my father asked her to leave us alone, please, and she did! When I told my mother and father that dream, they smiled. My father said we should go right away to the restaurant and order supper! My mother said they'd be glad to have us there, but the only problem is money: the prices are very high, and only white people who are air force or army or navy officers, or who come here to visit and look around, can afford to pay so much money for food. And it is meat they eat. I can't eat meat; I don't like it."

She has no memory of eating meat. Her mother remembers when the girl was smaller — say, about four or five, though time has made everyone uncertain of the exact age — suddenly, one late winter day, she refused to eat caribou meat, any meat. The girl has no such memory, only recollections of constant teasing from her parents. They reminded her that if they were all living at another time and in another place, she could not afford the luxury of an intense dislike for meat. She is, in fact, the first person in their family and, indeed, of their acquaintance, who has a dislike of *any* food. And so they are puzzled, even apprehensive. So is their child: "I don't *want* to stay away from meat; I wish I *did* like it. My stomach turns when I see others eat meat. My mother says that I'll never be able to be a waitress, if I can't serve white people steak; that is their favorite food. I hope I can learn to smile and serve steaks one day! I asked my father once if he thought I should eat meat, even though I don't like it. He said no. He said that as long as we lived here, it made no difference. He has a good job. He is told by the white men at the base that he's 'a lucky Eskimo.' They say he's 'the luckiest.' We go to the store for our food, and he doesn't even fish much — just in the summer, when he feels like it.

"He comes back and he tells us that he's done some thinking: he's become a white man, because he fishes for the fun of it! But I think it does bother him, and my mother, too, that I don't even like the fish he catches! I'd rather eat the frozen fish; it's sent up here. My mother gets angry, and then I eat what she serves. She buys a lot of potato chips for me, and with them I can eat anything, except for meat. I like apples and oranges. I like candy. I like ice cream. I like, best of all, french fries. I like a Coke or orange soda or Seven-Up. I like coffee and tea. I like scrambled eggs. I could eat scrambled eggs all the time, and nothing else, except potatoes. And catsup; I love catsup. I understand the white people put it on their steaks. My father thinks that if I tried some meat with catsup, I'd be a different person, because I'd like meat again. But I haven't followed his advice yet! I know I should. I hope I do someday."

She hopes, someday, to go on a brief trip to Hawaii. When she was six years old she heard her father and a naval officer talking about the cold Alaska winters. The officer reminisced out loud: he had spent the best years of his naval career in Honolulu; he has tried to get back there once a year — and he hopes to retire there. The girl could not forget the man's strongly felt descriptions; nor could she forget the postcard he sent to her a week later with an inscription: "I hope you will get to see this beach one day." That stretch of sand, surf, and sun has been for years a closely guarded possession of hers. She keeps the picture of it on a table, where her clothes are to be found. She and her mother often look at the card wistfully, and with some incredulity: can there be such a place, so pleasant all year around? At school the girl has done her best to obtain the facts needed to discredit a romanticized version of Hawaii. She learned from a teacher that Hawaii can also be crowded, *too* hot, muggy, a haven for greedy, noisy tourists; and that there is some tension on those islands between people of various backgrounds. She told her parents what she had heard. Her father was saddened: a child had lost an illusion. There is plenty of time for that to take place — the later, the better.

Her mother was amused, was moved to express a few thoughts, which the girl has never forgotten: "My mother said I shouldn't be disappointed. She said there's probably some girl like me in Hawaii who has a picture of Alaska: snow and ice and maybe a whale being caught. The tourists come here from all over, too — maybe not as many as to Hawaii, but enough of them to fill up our town's hotel every day during the summer. All the visitors want to see us capture a whale! Some of them want to see igloos! They are disappointed. My mother said that people always like to dream of a place where everything is good and nothing is bad. If it's cold here, they dream of Hawaii. If it's hot there, they dream of Alaska. If it's crowded in California, they dream of coming here, and they think they'll be happy here — until they land, and they look around and they decide that they'd like to leave as soon as possible and go home! She hears them talking in the restaurant: I can't wait to go home, they say! But even so, they keep saying they want to tell their friends what they saw here, and they're glad they came. I guess I'd want to come right back to this town if I ever got to Hawaii. But I'd be glad I got there."

She likes to watch television — in Alaska mostly old movies and serials, long since shown in the lower forty-eight. Her parents bought a set when she was eleven; she has had over a year of exposure. In the beginning the whole family watched at every available moment, and then some. The parents and children would arrive at work or school late, much to their own surprise. Finally the set was declared a tempting menace — something to be watched only with care: no more sitting on straight-back kitchen chairs, seeing one "I Love Lucy" program after another. Who is this Lucy? Jean wondered. Who are all these people who appear and talk? Which state do they live in? Is this their *lives* we the viewers are witnessing, or are the teachers to be believed — that people are paid large amounts of money to *pretend?* She wonders about such matters, wonders what it would be like to live in the homes she sees on the screen, wonders how it came about that her people, her town, came to be part of the same country those television actors and actresses call their own.

Jean knows the *facts*, knows what teachers have said — about Seward's Folly, and all that followed. But she wonders how Alaska's various visitors have regarded the land, the people. What have they felt over the decades — the assortment of missionaries, gold-hungry explorers, sportsmen, tourists, scientific investigators of one kind or another, and yes, idealistic schoolteachers or social and political activists? What would she feel like if she came to live in suburban Los Angeles or Chicago or Atlanta or Philadelphia — wherever those situation comedies on television are meant to take place "in real life"? She has heard that expression used by teachers: television as against (or as a supposed mirror of) "real life." She wonders whether her life is a "real" one, whether any program will ever try to convey how it goes for her and her family and their neighbors. Certainly the television cameras are not likely to penetrate the small, isolated villages up or down the coast or inland; she knows that. But there might be a chance they will one day arrive on Wien Consolidated, the Alaskan airline whose planes land several times a week just outside her town — and begin their work. If so, she has some suggestions to make: "Why don't they build new buildings, and we all could move into them? Then there wouldn't be the bad houses. They told us oil would be coming here, that there'd be ships coming, too, and they'd take the oil away, and the oil company would build a new town, and my father might get a job working for the company. Then they could show us on television, with our new houses, and my father would show me where they'll put the oil. My father thinks it will go into large barrels. Maybe he would get me a ride on an oil tanker."

She changes her mind immediately. She doesn't want to go on such a boat, should it appear in the harbor; and she has no interest in appearing on television. She wishes, every once in a while, that her parents would one day become tired of the city, despite its advantages, and decide to return to the life of her ancestors. Other Eskimos, she knows, live such a life, more or less. They have a relatively clear-cut idea of what the future holds for them. In contrast, she is torn by various ideals or wishes, to the point that she finds it hard to say anything very important without soon thereafter contradicting herself or undercutting the thrust of what she has said. She gives voice to the contradictions she feels within herself — and all around her too: "I was told by one teacher last year that after a while there won't be any Eskimos left in Alaska. I mean, we'll still be here, but we'll be like all the other people in America. I said I didn't think so, because some of our people live far from the city, and they won't want to live the way we do here. But the teacher said that they won't stay in the villages too much longer; and besides, even now the people there don't live the way they used to live, and if they didn't get money from the state of Alaska, and the planes didn't come with food, they'd be in trouble, and they'd all move here. My father says she is right. He says a lot of Eskimos are having trouble; they don't know how to live the way our grandparents did, but they don't know how to live like the white people do.

"I think my mother and father live the same way white people do. My father says he'd like a better job at the base, but they don't have any. My mother says she heard that when the pipeline is built, there will be more jobs for our people — because there will be offices and a refinery, maybe, and big places to store the oil. And the company wants to be friends with our people. Sometimes I hope the company will come here tomorrow, and take over the whole city. Then they'll make us equal with the white people, and they'll have jobs for everyone, and we'll be like the people on the television programs. They might even have a television program made right here in this city! But the next day I'll be talking with my friends, and we decide that we want to go out way beyond the city, and find someplace where we could stay and be away from people here — except our mothers and fathers. All the older boys want is to ride motorcycles. All the older girls want is to fix their nails with polish, and get their hair set, so that they have curls for a day or two. In a year or two, that's what we'll be like, too, unless we get out of here! My mother says that when she goes to bed, she worries all the time about us. She's afraid that we'll end up in trouble. She's afraid we won't be Eskimos, and we won't be white people, and we'll always be taking orders from the navy people, or the people who come here from Fairbanks or Anchorage. I told her not to worry: we can escape; we can go to Hawaii! She doesn't like my jokes. I don't know what else to say.

"I wish there was a place where we were left to ourselves, the Eskimo people — but where we lived in good houses the way white people do. It's no good to be poor! I agree with the teachers when they say that. It's no good to be sick all the time, either. I got sick last winter, and they took me to the navy base, and I got a needle, and soon I was all better. I might have died, if it wasn't for the doctor and his medicine. The same with my aunt; she was *very* sick, and they had to take her to Fairbanks, and she had an operation. Now she is better. She says that she owes her life to the white people. My grandmother says the worst thing about the white people is that they make you think the way they do, and you get greedy for every minute of life, and you forget your ancestors: you won't let anyone else's spirit come into the world, because you're here, and you won't leave, and no one can take your place until you do! They told us in school that my grandmother is wrong in the way she thinks. You should try to live as long as possible — and there aren't spirits waiting to take your place. I don't know who is right. I don't even want to tell the teachers what I hear at home anymore. If you do, you get a lecture, and when you go home and tell your parents what the teacher says, they don't say anything back; they only nod or shake their heads. My father will only say: In school they know one thing, and outside of school we know another thing. But he tells us later to go by what the teachers say because we're living here in the city, and we have to get our education, and if the teacher isn't on your side, then you can get into trouble. Maybe if I was a boy it would be easier when I grow up!"

Jean is convinced that if she were a boy she would be trying hard, later on, to get a good job on the base where her father works, and that as a result she wouldn't be vexed by some of the considerations that now seem to confront her from time to time. But she knows better, actually; she knows that a cousin of hers, a year older, thirteen, has the same worries she has. Jean has heard his dreams of a future success become qualified by expressions of apprehension: will he ever get any kind of job, and how will he live — as an Eskimo, an Alaskan member of an urban community? Right now, he seems all taken up with motorcycles and snowmobiles. But he does have other preoccupations. Several times, right in her presence, he has challenged her to change some of her notions about what the future holds. Relatively tall for an Eskimo, quite thin, he is no slouch as a speaker. He starts in, fires his words off, stops only when he is through. "Don't you see," he often prefaces his remarks with: "Don't you see that it doesn't make any difference whether you are a boy or a girl here? I don't even think it will make any difference that we are Eskimos, not in a few years. They tell us that once the pipeline is running, only a few people will be needed to make sure the oil is coming and that there's no leak. A lot of people are coming up here now, but they'll leave, later on. My father says we were here for a long time before anyone else came here, and we'll be here a long time. When all the whites have gone, we'll still be around.

"I'd like to leave and go to Anchorage; a lot of people live there, and you can sign up there, and go into the air force. The teacher doesn't know whether there are any air force pilots who come from Alaska. All the pilots who fly up here come from California and Illinois and places like that. A lot of white people are moving up here. There are some white kids at school whose parents have been here a long time. My father went back to the village where he was born, and nearby a white family was living, and they were almost a part of the village. They went to meetings there with our people, and to church. Here, we go to church with white people. The minister is one of our Eskimo people; he went to California and studied there. It used to be that the church sent up somebody, a white man, and he stayed here a few seasons, and then went back, and another person came up. If someone is sick, our minister knows how to get a doctor. He knows the people at the base; they will do him a favor. He has written letters to our governor and our senators, and they try to help. They always come here when they are running for office, and he takes them to us and introduces them. He tells us the best one to vote for! My father asked him if he was going to run for office himself. He said no. Then my father told me that I should run for office when I get older! I'd have a good job, if I got elected."

Meanwhile the boy sets his sights much lower. He hopes his father will be able to help him get a job at the base or at a nearby fish-packing company. He will leave school in a matter of months, has no interest in a high school education. He has held part-time jobs — loading and unloading, sweeping floors, all at the airport — and wouldn't mind turning those jobs into full-time jobs. He has become friendly with a mechanic and watched him for hours work on airplane motors. But the boy has no great confidence in his own ability to follow suit. When the mechanic suggested a high school education, with an emphasis on practical courses so that the boy could learn a craft, the answer was no. When the mechanic asked why, the boy said he didn't know, but the answer was still no. The boy explained why: "I don't think I could ever learn to work on the engines the way the mechanics do at the navy base or the airfield. My mother agrees; she says we have different blood! The teacher says if we all stayed in school, we could learn anything that white people have learned. Maybe; I don't know. But I don't like going to school, and I won't stay in school for years and years more. I may hitch a ride to Anchorage, and see what luck I'll have there. The pilots say they can always take me for nothing. One pilot said I could go to a store in Anchorage, and ask for work. I could pack and unpack. I could help ship things from Anchorage to here! I could write messages on the boxes, and my friends would be here, unpacking the boxes, and they'd see my writing.

"The mayor of our city is married to a cousin of my mother's, and he says he's sure I can get a job in Anchorage. I could go out to sea on a fishing boat; there are jobs like that, if you want them. But if I had my choice, I would work in a big store. I could sell hi-fi sets and records. I could sell refrigerators, television sets, electric toasters, and lamps. Maybe I could get the things I'd sell for nothing — if I worked hard enough and sold a lot. But the mayor said no: you don't get anything for nothing in Anchorage! The small villages are the only places in Alaska where the people will give even a stranger food and a place to sleep. The trouble with our people, according to the mayor, is that we will let outsiders have all they want, but we never ask for anything. But that isn't so, not here, and not in Anchorage. The Eskimos in the city have become like white people. My mother says she's forgotten what she used to be like. She tells us that when she was a little girl, she'd see new faces coming toward her, and she'd smile. If they came nearer, my mother would ask them if they wanted to see her parents, and point to the house. Now, she tells us that we should always tell a stranger to go see the mayor or the people at the base. In Anchorage, the teacher told us, you see our people lying on the ground, and they are bleeding, and they have thrown up their food, and people are stepping over them and kicking them out of the way. Our town is not yet like Anchorage."

He has no great confidence that the time is far off; soon enough, he believes, most of Alaska will resemble Anchorage — or perhaps the fierce winter will stage a last-ditch struggle with the white man's technology and win, in which event Anchorage will be abandoned, and all Alaska will be left to a handful of persevering small-village Eskimos, who will have remembered the ways of their ancestors, and so be in a position to survive. A teacher's effort to let children know something about their past and their possible future (the "ice age" that was and might well come again) becomes for the children something else: a means of social and economic analysis.

The boy has good reason, he is convinced, to fear Anchorage. He might well become someone lying inertly on a sidewalk, dazed, and out of touch with everyone, including himself. Even in his town bars have opened, catering to residents and visitors, Eskimos and whites, the engineers or geologists, and the recent arrivals from Eskimo villages who have spent little or no time in a classroom. He has heard his parents remark on the difference between drinking in a bar and drinking at home. True, the result is the same — drunkenness; but it is one thing to collapse on one's bed and be cared for by one's family, and quite another to be thrown out of a bar (after having spent all of one's money, of course) and to end up on a sidewalk, in a ditch, or in a jail. He hopes never to be a customer, standing with a drink inside a bar — but he is also quite anxious to go in one, see what the place is like. If he were in Anchorage or Fairbanks there would be dozens of bars to visit, he has heard. He wonders how men and women make a choice — of a bar, not to mention the place where they live, the work they do, the way they live. His father has told him often to wait and see, to have patience and be trustful, because life has, mostly, improved for Eskimos in recent years. The boy is glad to hear such advice, and remembers it — along with the stories he hears from his father and others about bars, derelict men and women, confused youths, crowded jails.

IX

GROWING UP ESKIMO

N O ESKIMO CHILD, however isolated his or her village, is immune to the tension generated by Alaska's fast-changing social and economic climate, not to mention the Arctic climate, which so far has not changed at all. A snowmobile can give a child the sense that distance means little, that one is not really subject to Nature's power. A snowmobile can also present itself to a child as a pathetic giant, full of noise, bluster, and capability one minute, but strangely immobilized the next — when a midwinter cold spell (with, say, temperatures of fifty or more below zero) renders oil and gasoline useless. But not the sleds and not the huskies; they are ever present, reminders in even the more "developed" villages or towns, possessed of a bar or two, a restaurant, an airport (as against a landing strip) and some television sets, that Alaska is not just another of America's states.

Eskimo children are generally interested in the lower forty-eight. Even Hawaii, which seems sadly excluded by the term, comes in for some attention: another exile of sorts, far away from the mainland; an opposite to Alaska so far as weather goes, and therefore a place that serves the dreams of children who want to leave home for one reason or another. Eskimo children are quick to wonder about other kinds of weather:

what is it like, and what difference does it make in the lives of the people?

When compared with Chicano children of the Southeast and the Southwest, or Indian children of New Mexico and Arizona, Eskimo children emerge as the most persistently curious with respect to the white man and his ways. On the other hand, these same children exhibit strong nostalgia when, for a moment or longer, they tell what they have heard about igloos and caribou hunts and lonely vigils over ice holes in hopes of a fish. The weather persists — a link of sorts between the old habits and the ways of today. Life in an Arctic village can still be fragile, hard-pressed, isolated.

When anyone arrives from outside, friend or enemy, familiar or a stranger, a he or a she, the Eskimo's impulse is to go look and wonder *why*. It is one thing to be born in a village above the Arctic Circle; another to seek out that same village (especially in the long winter). Moreover, for all the exploitation inflicted upon various Eskimo villages by those hungry for gold (or oil), by those intent on preaching the Christian gospel, or hunting or fishing, or taking a long and esoteric vacation, Alaskan "natives" (as they are often called by the state's white people) have not been systematically, massively assaulted, then subjugated both militarily and politically, as was the fate of all Indian tribes. Nor have Eskimos been adrift on the land, and treated as aliens in the way Chicanos have known. Treated as "ignorant," yes, or as worthy of being lied to, cheated from; but often out of necessity acknowledged as people who have their own authority, competence, and skills, the last helpful indeed for many whites who have ventured north and found themselves in jeopardy.

Eskimos are different in the way their parents, by and large, tend to bring up their children, and consequently, the way those children tend to regard both themselves and others, whether friends, neighbors, relatives, or thoroughly strange and different-looking visitors. Those children are taught to be fearful — but not of other human beings so much as the possibilities nature presents. Even the most disturbed, anxious, and guarded of people have their moments of relaxed self-confidence, their favored friends who are regarded without much suspicion. When subzero temperatures, ice floes, driving snow, and a barren tundra are the enemies, and when there are for company only a handful of human beings, of whatever "color" or background, and they, too, must face the common enemy, Arctic weather, there is less likelihood that individual men and women, and through them, children, will take on "others" as enemies. Moreover, the Eskimos have for generations been a kind and thoughtful people, quick to respond warmly, generously to outsiders who arrive for whatever purpose. The Eskimos have also developed for themselves a resigned acceptance of life, an acquiescence in the face of a relentlessly impersonal, grim environment — so that any stranger's evil words or deeds seem like a mere annoyance when compared with the life-and-death struggle that is daily life, week after week.

Eskimo children are masters of the faint smile, the slight grimace that never goes any further. They are usually quiet children, more controlled than Indian or Chicano children. Often in an Arctic village a small child is discouraged from talking too much — by parents who may strike a visitor as taciturn, even forbidding or surly, but who have their own reasons to distrust words and more words, or "emotional" people. In the clutch, when the weather is worst and the danger of starvation, illness, death the greatest, the person who is moved to talk a lot, move around a lot, become demonstrative and excited, may well be the person who misses whatever chance there is for survival. One must learn to be careful, controlled — able to husband emotional as well as physical energy, able to sit and wait, or move at all costs. A fierce outer world is resisted successfully only by a finely regulated inner world, wherein words and the emotions that generate them are watched as closely as the next blizzard, days or weeks long, that may at any moment make comment, conversation, expressions of "feeling" a dangerous indulgence at best.

The mind has its own life, however. Spells of wary silence do not undercut the work of eyes and ears, do not thwart the capacity children have to make sense of the world and try to affirm in action (even if indirectly, quietly, unostentatiously) what that sense has turned out to be. One word can take the place of dozens of sentences. A look, a gesture can be an eloquent response, on a child's part, to life's demands or opportunities. In many Eskimo villages, especially those still more or less removed from the full thrust of the white man's influence, each day has to it a regularity and predictability that seem to give the child little room for independent activity. In the Arctic those who would survive must learn to work together and, quite literally, huddle together. There are, really, no Eskimo loners, only some who are a bit more introspective than others. Loners are white men, hunters or fishers, bush pilots or missionaries — whose solitariness often confuses or mystifies rather than repels Eskimos. How does this or that white person live like that — and why?

There is not much time for questions, however. One must attend to living, including the instruction of the young. Boys are taught how to fish — not only the mechanics of the effort, but the patience required and, again, the silence one must learn to feel comfortable with. A talkative fisherman is apt to become inattentive, and soon enough will needlessly move about, alerting the fish below. Four- or five-year-old Eskimo boys, counterparts in age to the noisy, active children of the

American white middle-class world, can be seen standing still and quiet near an ice hole in coldest winter for fifteen minutes, half an hour, an hour — unnerving almost, unbelievable, just about, to a white outsider, especially one who has his own ever so agile and talkative sons. Hunting, too, requires disciplined wariness — and a capacity to keep one's muscles and mouth under firm control.

When Eskimo children learn how to walk, they are encouraged to walk immediately behind their parents — in file, so to speak. They are also encouraged to learn how to stop quickly, stand still for increasing lengths of time. And they are encouraged to look around themselves as they walk — rather than simply enjoy the discovery of movement. As a matter of fact, the children are not hurried into the "toddler period" of childhood; a crawling child is very much appreciated and enjoyed for what he or she is — someone who can be taught to crawl and *stop*, crawl and *look*, crawl and *listen*, rather than crawl as a prelude to walking (and the sooner the better). Crawling children are told that animals crawl, and do rather well for themselves under the circumstances! Crawling children are sometimes told not to be in any hurry to stand, never mind walk. Often the child is somewhat discouraged, for a while, at least, from standing and walking. The idea is to let children learn thoroughly what they already know — and must know — rather than encourage them to move on.

As infants, Eskimos are breast-fed to their hearts' (and stomachs') content. They are also kept especially close to their mothers — carried on the back or held tightly with one arm while another does a particular task. When the children get fidgety, they are put down, allowed to crawl, but given firm limits: here but not there; for this length of time, but no longer. The point is not to curb the children or make them obsessively time-bound or self-consciously hesitant, but rather to show them from the start that "outside," a word often used in Eskimo homes, there is a demanding and difficult word that sets its own limits. There are habits, controls, sets of restraints that simply must be learned. Crawling children learn to do so in a straight line, do so quietly, do so and then stop, await further instructions. Newly walking children learn to move only so far, then halt, peer in every direction, say not a word, heed whatever command is issued.

Not that Eskimo children aren't talkers; they learn their words — their English words, these days. But words, too, can be taken a step at a time. Young boys and girls often avoid sentences, because their parents are quite content to use a word or two, rather than make a statement or ask a question or give a command. The tone of voice can, of course, be important, decisive. The child gets up, hears the word *river* used, knows full well that soon there will be a virtually silent trip, followed by fishing, again without much talk, and a return home. Or a child can wake up and hear the word *wind* used by a parent in such a way as to indicate a matter of grave interest: is the wind favorable or unfavorable, strong or weak, apparently a brief one or likely a continuing one? And the particular words that a child first learns to use easily and familiarly are, naturally, those that have to do with the activities of the household — *river, fish, whale, wind, snow, ice, caribou.* Those words are used somewhat solemnly; one doesn't just laugh and savor the use of a word. One learns to say a word, mean it.

If a child wants to be very much a playful, carefree boy or girl, it is not through sounds, language, or even large-scale physical activity that his or her inclination will be expressed. A carved piece of wood will serve well; the child knows it, fondles it, puts it aside, rediscovers it, makes of it, in sum, the kind of toy the white man's child possesses, not rarely by the bushel. An Eskimo child usually plays more sedately, more circumspectly, than not only white children, but Chicano or Indian children. And the same child is a more careful eater — fewer "messes," less noise at the table, less impatience or restlessness. The whole world, needless to say, bears down on Eskimo homes, on entire Eskimo villages, for long months of the year; that being the case, one has no leeway — streets or backyards, the desert or the fields in which other children can be let out, allowed to work off their apparently endless reservoir of "surplus energy." Eskimo children are not much berated, are not browbeaten or punished with physical force. They are often stared down, told in a word or two what to do, or not do, and looked at intently (to an outsider, sometimes, it seems *fiercely*) until a parent's wish becomes a child's command.

For instance, a child is prompted to pay attention to the wind by a mother who points outside, herself listens obviously, carefully — ear cocked, eyes open and knowing, and mouth firmly closed. Why talk? Why compete with the wind for a young one's attention? Should not both parties stand in simple, silent awe of one of nature's elements? Later, yes; later children hear parents, or more often, grandparents, talk a lot about the wind, the river, the tundra. The river is the source of life itself; the river is a link with other villages, with the sea, with everyone and everything. Without the river, one imagines, there would be no Eskimos, at least in this or that part of Alaska. As for the wind, children soon learn not to underestimate its power of significance. The wind brings movements of the "spirits" of people, voices from the grave and vice versa, messages from the living to the dead. An Eskimo mother may often talk briefly, intermittently but evocatively, to the wind, and make sure a nearby child understands what is happening: a dead ancestor, maybe, is speaking and being spoken to.

Often when a grandparent dies, the grandchildren are told that his or her "spirit" was borne away — by the wind. Where to? No place and every place — or, more precisely, up and over the tundra, toward the sea.

There is no Heaven, no Hell — at least not of the Eskimo's making. There is only the vast, apparently limitless space that is land, that is water, that is, most of the year, snow and ice. As for Christianity, it is both everywhere, and upon occasion, nowhere. Eskimos are perfectly capable of taking their children to an Episcopal or Quaker or Catholic service, then coming home and telling them about the "spirit" of a nearby river, a spirit that just then seems importunate indeed: the wind coming headlong off the water, screeching and whining and threatening everything in its path to be sure of notice. No wonder, sometimes, in school Eskimo children seem "lost," seem uninterested in what is being told them, seem in a world of their own. In fact they are paying the closest heed to a wind their teachers have long since managed to ignore.

When home, the children are anxious to compare notes with their parents, and thereby learn to have a common view of things. The intense wind, with its urgent or dire warnings, must be quickly appraised — compared with the gentle, reassuring winds, harbingers of spring. But not only weather is thereby comprehended; a household's particular crises, psychological struggles may be connected to natural phenomena, and merely worked on. An uncle lies ill, for example. His niece is in school, being taught the American Civil War: who fought whom over a century ago and why, or over what? Suddenly the girl turns her eyes toward the window, then back to the desk in front of her, then down toward the floor. She mutters a word or two, inaudible to her classmates, and certainly her teacher. Then she stands up, quickly sits down, raises her hand, tells the teacher that she is "sick," and had better go home. The teacher has a moment of doubt or concern, maybe both, but has learned not to try to fathom the child's "mind" — or her bodily symptoms, either. The child wants to go home, and the child had best be sent home. On the way home the child stops every once in a while, as if taking the measure of the weather, or the immediate environment around her; or so a white outsider would imagine — unless, that is, something more grim, even sinister, came to mind: a *very* disturbed child! Soon the girl is home, and more than likely, her uncle has just died, or will shortly do so. The girl, in a matter-of-fact manner, tells her mother that she "heard" her uncle dying: a wind brought her the message, and another wind seemed on its way to carry off the uncle's spirit. The mother nods; she too had noticed one, then another, gust of wind and had the same thoughts. And the uncle himself had wondered aloud, before dying, when he would be "taken" — not by God, but by the wind. All very confusing or "superstitious" or mystical to a white teacher or bush pilot or doctor. Not at all incompatible with attendance at a Christian missionary church and with an appeal for modern medical advice and treatment.

By the same token, a river may be negotiated in a motor-boat, challenged for its fish or nearby game by every mechanical device known, in the way of rods or guns, landed upon by an amphibious plane, studied or brought under a certain control by engineers or biologists who come from far away, but at certain moments be seen by Eskimo parents and children alike as a great "friend" who has a "voice," who resists the winter as well as surrenders to it, who "knows things" that mere mortals don't, and reveals things those same mortals would do well to remember as important, even life saving. What do the Eskimos "really" believe in connection with the river? What do they attribute (psychologically, religiously, philosophically) to the river, and for which reasons? No Eskimo is ever going to find words for those questions, even if some visitor has the nerve or subtlety to phrase them in such a way that they appear inoffensive, uncritical.

Eskimos teach their children and have themselves been taught not to make a lot of inquiries, not to ask one why or what or how after another, but to immerse doubts, worries, questions into activities that have obvious, practical value and, as well, a symbolic function. Walking to the river or the ocean for a child becomes a ritual, an act of dedication, even though the child seems merely on the way to go fishing. The parents have stressed repeatedly the importance of the water — and the importance of recognizing that importance. The child has been told not to challenge the judgment of his parents, and so most Eskimo children don't have to be reminded again and again what their parents have said. The risks and dangers of ordinary living are apparent, even to young children. There is little time for discussion, and usually there are no alternatives, only one possible plan of action — or else quick disaster. Moreover, parents are constantly with their children, and so have the leverage of affectionate companions who don't have to spend minutes, if not hours, trying to prove their credentials, elicit respect or affection, and so on. The child has learned to trust his or her parents; learned that in moments of danger, when hunger and severe cold threaten, there are ideas forthcoming, plans of action — followed by at least some relief.

When Eskimo children walk toward a river and, even at four or five, say nothing and stare ahead with solemn attention, they are taking part in an almost religious procession, surely one in which the energies of young and old are about to be consecrated to nothing less than survival itself. One need not get fancifully existential at this point and recite an observation of Heidegger's ("Being close to death can teach man how to live in a strangely peaceful way"); one need only see the quiet seriousness of vigorously alert and sometimes energetically active children as they do more, really, than march seaward or down the banks of a river. They march toward life itself.

Eskimo children are quick to look at the sky, examine it, as a doctor does a patient: what is going on up there, and what might soon go on — within minutes, actually? At seven or eight, children have learned to scan the horizon, comment upon the shapes and sizes of clouds, and what they portend, so far as weather goes. Often a child may say, quite openly, that bad weather is ahead, and so he or she must be ready to work hard, help out, and be in a good mood. Eskimo parents sometimes remark upon how low or sad they get in the summer — but not in the middle of the winter, when sheer survival demands every ounce of psychological energy available.

Boys and girls have acquired a similar inclination. They gird themselves constantly in January, say: errands; trips with a father, uncle, grandparent; the journey to school — all undertaken against the odds of heavy snow, or extreme cold, or a brooding, fierce wind that strikes suddenly, devastatingly. But in June or July time lags, bears down like an oppressive burden — how best to carry it? The child may even complain to a parent — too much light, too little that is obligatory. And the parents don't know how to prescribe mere busywork, something to distract the child, keep up a rhythm of responsible activity. In summer the children are not only sometimes "let down" by the sudden leisure they, along with everyone else, face; there is a certain apprehensive incredulity that many Eskimos, young or even old, find in themselves. A fear, for instance, that an especially warm and pleasing summer will give way to a severe winter. A worry that there won't be another winter, so warm and triumphant seems the sun — and, as a result, a whole way of life will have to be forsaken, or turned upside down, or modified beyond recognition, and maybe, beyond the psychological capacities of those involved.

It is strange, the lethargy and even dour edginess young Eskimos can demonstrate when the world appears so delightfully beckoning. Nor is it long-restrained "depression" finally surfacing, after the fact, so to speak — the long winter's trial. During the winter the children have not at all, by and large, been "depressed." They have been hard at work or, if very young, they have been observers of those hard at work. When summer comes there is, initially, much excitement: warmth, lengthening days, an outburst of natural beauty. Nothing is scarce any more; everything is in profusion — except the challenge of an immediate and compelling task. Boredom strikes, a north wind of a kind. Children have to remind themselves how to play easily, how to lounge about, frolic at night even, when the lingering day prevents sleep.

And the reduced amount of sleep exerts its toll. People go to bed for brief periods, doze in fits and starts rather than for long, uninterrupted hours. The result is a cumulative weariness of both a physiological and psychological nature. Will the warm weather take away, drain, or sap, in some manner undo, the resilience, drive, and ingenuity that are inevitably associated with severely cold weather? No wonder Eskimo children are a bit wary of the short-lived Arctic springs, which create difficulties and, often enough, outright chaos: almost impenetrable mud; treacherous conditions on rivers or the sea because of melting snow; temporary flooding; and so on. Winter becomes an object of nostalgic reflection: the short days, in which a lot has to get done; the long nights that bring complete rest; the delightfully close quarters of family living.

Then there are the summer mosquitoes and flies. They come with a vengeance and in hordes; make winter seem like a distant oasis, long since left and, one hopes, soon to be seen again. Children in the lower forty-eight often escape the psychological wear and tear of those flies and mosquitoes. Up in Alaska children also try to be forbearing, uncomplaining, indifferent — willing to scratch themselves but shrug their shoulders; so it goes for a few weeks. But commonly the air is so filled with noisy, potentially hurtful flying objects that boys and girls, especially small ones, whose memory goes back weeks or months rather than years, do become quite frightened. All over, Eskimo boys and girls pray for the magic of the wind to assert itself. When that happens, there are suddenly no bugs for a while; a gust has risen from the water and carried them off or brushed them aside. Badly bitten children know to say thank you; they have been taught by parents never to take any of Nature's kindnesses for granted. But the wind eventually exhausts itself, and soon the mosquitoes are droning again, diving for blood, even clouding the air, so many are they. The children have listened to the mixed reaction of their parents: sadness that life is harder up in the Arctic, even in the summer; a certain pride, though, that nothing, in any season, has yet managed to drive the Eskimo people away from their village home.

Children brought up by such parents have a strong attachment to the land in and near their village, and are quick to identify outsiders by reference to that land — people who were born elsewhere and have lived elsewhere. Such people are "different" — do not, that is, know how to thank the wind, or smile gratefully at the river; do not know, too, how to think a season ahead. When summer comes, winter is already on the minds of many Eskimo children; the fish they help dry are for future use. Even an ordinary, full meal in August can be an occasion for anticipation; a January supper will be leaner, so best store up now. Most young people are not usually inclined to think of the future. In this regard Eskimo children, even at four or five, are remarkably different: never altogether willing to live from moment to moment, or even day to day; inclined, rather, to remind themselves of what might be, could be, will be — but not with foreboding so much as a candid recognition of life's realities.

As a matter of fact, those realities make for introspective, contemplative children. When starvation is not very far off and when parents openly discuss such a possibility, children are apt to have a lot of questions on their minds. At four or five Eskimo boys and girls wonder why it is not possible to leave, go elsewhere. At seven or eight they consider a departure unlikely, but talk at length about death — and the chance that one might be born again, appear on this earth as a "spirit" that will, in time, become part of another person.

To be an Eskimo, those children have often been told, is to brave the Arctic winters in a particular village, and each spring to come out alive — maybe alive by the skin of their teeth, but alive. To live in a city is to live so differently that one begins to wonder who one is, what one ought be called, and yes, why one has been willing to make the shift. Children use their imaginations, try to provide answers to various life-and-death questions. One child can be heard telling another that the sun is losing its battle with the ice, the snow, the freezing blasts of wind, and so soon all Eskimos will have to leave for a warmer climate. Or there are stories with a glimmer of fact joined to fancy: outsiders arrive with orders that the village be evacuated because a giant tidal wave threatens; an earthquake threatens; a government-sponsored project may come; an oil company will buy out the entire area. Some children become more mystically apocalyptic, speak of a "bad wind" that will one day lift the entire village away, drop it on the outskirts of Anchorage.

Not that those children have any doubt in their minds that

if there were the will, the determination, they would be able to stand fast, endure. There are days, however, when the will seems lacking — in parents and, soon enough, in children. Usually those days are not ones of explicit crisis, but rather occur in the midst of a quiet spell when food is relatively plentiful or, at a minimum, assured for a matter of days. Then it is that a grandfather begins to wonder out loud, in the company of his grandchildren, about the point of it all — struggles and more struggles, with no victories, only respites. The children listen and ask little; the old man seems engrossed in himself, recites stories of hardship and suffering almost as if everyone and no one is there listening. But he casts a glance occasionally toward the grandchildren, and if one of them seems on the verge of falling asleep or paying no attention, the old man raises his voice, adds a touch of emotional intensity to the narrative: someone got killed in the fierce struggle with a whale just mentioned.

He asks the boys and girls what they would have done. They would, of course, have done nothing different. He is wise, they know. Anyone who has lived as he has had to live, year after year, and is still alive, still there, in the village, with white hair and a wrinkled face, has to be wise — and tough, and shrewd, and resilient and ready for just about anything. Yet the man is saying that even when younger he had moments of hesitation — when all the effort seemed to avail very little, if anything. The children say no, he is too strong, even now, for such moments. But he wants them to realize something — in fact, that a man like him must once in a while talk aloud as he has, question everything, life itself. The children are not exactly sure what he means; he is not exactly sure himself. But the point must be made: when things are going reasonably well, one ought be allowed the privilege of letting one's hair down, giving expression to the whys that an exceedingly hard life is bound to generate in those who live it.

No wonder some white schoolteachers in Eskimo villages comment on an almost uncanny kind of self-scrutiny certain schoolchildren demonstrate — usually with one another in the schoolyard rather than in the classroom. The mystery of human existence itself gets discussed, candidly and for five or ten minutes at a stretch, a long time for a child. With death and extinction either imminent or around some corner, boys and girls are both anxious and inquisitive. Is there some reason, for instance, that they as Eskimos have been "put" where they are, asked to endure the challenges of the Arctic? And what about the Eskimos who die young, or who get sick and never quite recover — linger on several years in pain and sorrow: what kind of justice is there in that? There must be a larger "spirit," many boys and girls conclude — a God who decides that some people will live comfortable lives, and some people will die early in life or be tested day after day, year in year out.

Many young Eskimos have heard their parents' version of Rilke's assertion: "Survival is all." Elderly relatives insist that there is only the triumph of endurance — the proof each Eskimo thereby offers that he or she has lived up to the demands of the "spirit" within himself or herself. And that "spirit" is held to be a restless, forceful, demanding one — hence, its presence in the Arctic. Other "spirits" go elsewhere — seek out warm, oceanside resorts, or mild spots in the lower forty-eight. Other "spirits" are quieter, weaker, more pampered, less hardy. It is as if Eskimo parents have decided that Charles Darwin was right: the fittest do indeed survive Alaska's long winters.

Even the airplane, that most enormous of all mechanical presences that have come to Eskimo villages, must be endorsed with a certain controlling "spirit," and not only by children. An Eskimo grandfather tells his granddaughter that when the plane arrives once a week with mail and provisions, he is sure that "spirits all over" pay attention. And why not? Life is maintained by that plane's work; and kin kept in touch with each other. The roar of the plane, its descent and ascent, are striking, vivid, summoning events — proof, surely, of a scheme of things that defies explanations (of the rational kind that teachers offer in classrooms) and has to do with what the existentialist philosopher Martin Heidegger called "the mind's lust for the dramatic evocation of Being." At times Heidegger pleaded with himself and others like him — educated Western people of the twentieth century: if only it were possible to leave behind one's wordy, fact-minded side, "return to Being," as he put it — meaning "the questions Being asks of us" and also "the images of Being." It is the latter, perhaps, that Eskimo children try to construct, even as their parents have tried to do so — the airplane as a testimony of sorts: man against nature, but also man as part of nature; man as the one who soars, even as the ocean does, who glides like the clouds, and lasts, like both.

Some Eskimo children make a point of saying that when a plane leaves the clouds for the land, it must say good-bye to those clouds, promise to return soon. As for seaplanes, they are the most wondrous of all the things man has wrought because they place him (literally) in intimate touch with the clouds and the ocean or the rivers; he thereby strides the universe. And so, when an Eskimo child is told by a missionary minister or priest about Christ walking the waters, it is not incredulity and not blasphemy and not sarcastic unfriendliness that prompt the simile: "like a seaplane." The mind struggles for "synthesis," those who live far from the Arctic tell themselves; and Eskimo children can only agree, as they draw upon Nature's whims, Christ's life, Western technology, and their own "everydayness" in a continuing effort to make sense of life and, maybe more ambitiously, find order in the confusions of the universe.

At times those same children ridicule themselves and their rather grand meditations. While they play and talk, boys and girls tell each other, in sum, that there are no spirits, only gullible people who believe in magical notions that "everyone" knows to be fatuous. And sometimes the child who is most imaginative, articulate, and taken with the mysteries (and paradoxes) of life is likely to be the most criticized or, rather, teased. Teasing is, actually, a psychological specialty, one might say, of many Eskimo people. Since parents rarely shout at their children or scold them openly, tempers must be kept on a rather short leash. Outsiders find themselves stared at when they raise their voices, scream, shout. A tantrum at the landing strip on the part of someone in a plane's crew can be a subject of discussion among Eskimos for days. And children who have witnessed the tantrum will refer back to it weeks later — as a terrible "storm," as a wild assault by a "bad, bad spirit" that took over the person, maybe as a portent: ugly weather ahead.

When Eskimos drink a lot, they don't usually let loose, show a truculent, nasty, mean side. They seem as quiet and considerate as ever; still courtly, a touch diffident, a touch amused at the world's ups and downs, but not about to shake their fists and hurl invective or spleen at anyone. On the other hand, alcohol does increase the amount of teasing one sees or, actually, hears among Eskimos. Children who want to indicate that their fathers or mothers, or both, have been drinking may well do so tactfully by making reference to the significant increase in the family "jokes" being perpetrated.

They are not really "jokes"; they are exaggerations or distortions of reality, presented to the child in a slightly mocking way — as if to say: the world is crazier than you think, and it is best that you begin to realize that, and the sooner the better. Often the "joke" comes in response to something the child has said, asked, done. And often the parent has in mind making a point, teaching the child, letting him or her know that a grown-up has experienced enough impatience to speak out. For instance, on a bitterly cold day, after a heavy snowfall, a child returns with his father and seems disappointed because they have caught "only" one fish. The mother sets to cutting and cooking the fish, and all the while smiles at the child, who has supplied a running account of what transpired before luck arrived with a tug of the fishing line. Suddenly the mother looks at the child and says that she is delighted with the fish, but knows that tomorrow will indeed be better, because then the child will go out alone and come home with a hundred fish, maybe a thousand, and even though that number, too, will be unimpressive, so far as the child goes, everyone else will be rather grateful. The child smiles, gets the point. The mother says no more — for a half-hour or so. But she is not finished. As she gets ready to serve supper, she again makes the point: tomorrow will bring abundance beyond one's dreams.

Teasing can be gentle or quite relentlessly tough. Fathers tend to challenge their sons by suggesting to them a particular project that is obviously beyond their competence, in the hope that the boys will catch the implied lesson: try to do the best you can, but don't bother or criticize those who can do what you can't. Sometimes the son is almost ready to do what his father teasingly recommends, indeed, the boy nervously tries to oblige: I will try to do it with all my might. If he succeeds, he has earned the right to tease his father back — by suggesting that the older person himself do something outlandish. It is a way of saying that the challenge has been met, thereby earning the younger person a prerogative of his elders. He too can express his annoyance or resentment, his self-confidence or pride, through the medium of a joke. He, too, can tease.

Fathers are less inclined to tease their daughters. A man may tell his wife that a particular daughter has not been respectful enough. Soon enough the mother has thought up a way of getting the point across for the child: suggest that the girl has too many responsibilities, has been working too hard and conscientiously at them, is in need of some assistance — which ought to arrive soon. Before the girl can ask about the nature of the assistance, she is told: twenty white women from Seattle, friends of the schoolteacher who hails from there and has been at the village school for a year. The girl gets the message, smiles, shows new energy and commitment as she does her chores. She thanks her mother — may even do that by coming up with a clever tease of her own, a continuation of the joke: how wonderful it will be then, having so many white people around to keep the house clean — but how burdensome it will be, too, because it can be a heavy labor, directing others, coordinating their work, and dealing with them as human beings. The mother loves the rejoinder, feels complimented that her daughter has not only listened carefully, understood what was intended, but found the mode of conversation and discussion congenial. A child who can pick up like that on a tease is a child too intelligent and honorable to slip back into laziness or indifference, the original difficulties in the first place.

Mothers can tease their sons rather hard, too. A boy who is beginning to throw his weight around with his younger sisters or brothers — at age ten or eleven, maybe — will more likely be teased by his mother than his father. When the boy comes to the table, for example, he finds before him an enormous meal — more meat or fish, by far, than anyone else in the family is getting, including his parents or grandparents. The boy may have had a similar experience before, so he knows what his mother has been thinking and has wanted to tell him. Or this may be the first time, so he makes note of his serving, innocently enough, and gets an immediate comment in reply from his mother — to the effect that a person who talks so big, behaves like a bossy one, if not a tyrant, must need a lot of food indeed. A sheepish grin on the boy's face records his acknowledgment of the criticism. He glances toward those who have been pushed around, smiles knowingly, apologetically at them. The subject is quickly changed — lest the boy be humiliated. Eskimo parents generally want to avoid doing that, rubbing things in so that their children feel attacked directly and to the bone.

Eskimo parents constantly encourage their children to be curious, while at the same time the point is made that Nature is inscrutable, impassive, unpredictable, and, of course, potentially life-threatening. Similarly, children are encouraged to be cordial with strangers but are also told to observe them warily because they have their own reasons for coming so far north. No question, the more isolated the Eskimo village, the more "innocent" the people — the friendlier to outsiders and, consequently, the more vulnerable to exploitation or manipulation. But even in the larger and more established Eskimo towns (as opposed to villages) Eskimo children have a hard time being cold and detached for long.

In contrast, Indian children of the Southwest have no trouble being aloof from and suspicious of the various white outsiders who come along. Why the difference? For one thing, each Eskimo village has had its own experience; and visiting whites have not always been mean or cruel. Unlike Eskimos, Indians have a continuing sense of their history, the details of which are handed down to children as a principal part of their psychological and cultural inheritance. Eskimos, though not completely ahistorical, are far more concerned with the present — with the day-to-day maintenance of life itself. Recent or past social and economic injuries inflicted by Alaska's white people are not forgotten; but in the face of constant adversity, there is no inclination to sit and remember the affronts, insults, and worse of an earlier time.

The Eskimos never as a people fought the white man; indeed, it can be said that the Eskimos have never really fought anyone. They don't really fight among themselves — not in the sharp, explicit way many whites do, or Indians and Chicanos do. Even within the family there are few arguments or confrontations. Disagreements tend to be rare. Teasing is one way for individuals to give vent to their antagonisms. Another mode of expression is moodiness; even small children know to say that a particular parent has "gone away" for a while — a departure that is not physical but psychological. No effort is made to placate or appease such a person, or try to draw out him or her. The withdrawal is respected, even considered a gift. And understandably; a person who feels bitter or angry, for one reason or another, has decided to spare others evidence of those emotions and move away, mentally at least, for a matter of hours — rarely days. There is no room, no time, for extended gloom or despair. The realities of Eskimo life demand a certain rhythm of activity — a ritual of obligations each person learns when young and never outgrows.

Do some Eskimos get so grim and melancholy that they forsake involvement in that kind of life? Yes, especially those who have become heavy drinkers or alcoholics. Or, sometimes, those who are quite old and have recently lost a husband or wife. Children are told about X or Y, who "went away" and never came back — stopped eating, exposed himself or herself carelessly to the elements, died rather quickly. But their numbers are few; in fact, the stories told children about them, in many villages, have an apocryphal quality to them — as if the teller isn't really convinced that a particular person actually lived (and died) in such a way but feels that, validity notwithstanding, there is a purpose to letting children hear about a mind gone amok. And an understandable analogy, too, with what happens to animals sometimes: a frenzied bear off by itself; a caribou lost and forlorn and ready, apparently, to lie down and die; a bird or a duck that is ailing physically and decides to leave its flock. For Eskimos, the flock, so to speak, has everything to do with one's life; privacy as white middle-class people know it is virtually nonexistent, undreamed of. It is a measure of "normal" Eskimo life that its most abnormal expression has to do with the assertion of privacy — a person's decision, for one reason or another, to break radically the bonds of family, kin, community.

It is no surprise that Eskimo children rarely play alone, and Eskimo youths are not the solitary, brooding adolescents that many American upper-middle-class parents have learned to take for granted as "normal." When an Eskimo child plays, there are other children around to play with; a child is seen alone only when on a specific errand; and even then, one hears the boy or girl ask for a companion, or sees one found rather quickly. Cousins are an especially important part of family life; they provide company to the first and second children, whom parents recognize as "alone," or, to the Eskimo's way of thinking, in jeopardy. A people's experience with the world around it becomes distilled into a psychological and philosophical approach to child rearing.

An Eskimo child is not someone who needs to be given a sense of himself or herself, who needs to be shown special attention, given particular strength, protected now and then from the vicissitudes of "sibling rivalry," granted sanctuary from the competing demands of other children. An Eskimo child belongs to certain parents, certain grandparents; and, too, is connected (so some believe) to certain "spirits." And the individual Eskimo families are not themselves set off, each distinct from the others. It is not only a question of kinship, of

the relatedness in a relatively small village, where marriages
have over the years connected everyone. A village is itself a
family, and the children in it learn to regard other children as
not merely familiar, as occasional playmates or as schoolmates,
but as village brothers and sisters.

A whale caught is divided among a whole community of
people. The same with caribou and, to the extent possible, fish.
Children are encouraged at an early age to feel warmly toward all other children, not only the members of the household. A baby just born is put among its cousins, close or distant
by blood, as well as children of its "own" family. And mothers
ask many different people to help care for their infants. If a
boy in a village has proven himself an agile hunter or fisherman, he is likely to be called over by neighbors when a baby
boy is born and asked to "keep an eye" on him — all very
informal and not to be confused with a religious practice or a
ritual, but a very significant moment in the life of a family. The
hope is that a certain competence will mysteriously communicate itself to the baby. And when visitors come from other
villages, as friends or as relatives, they don't ordinarily visit
one family; they are met by many people, hosted by many, and
bidden farewell, often, by a majority of the village, commonly
assembled in a circle or a semicircle. Nor do the people
quickly leave when the visitors begin to move away. A child
of four or five must stand, smile, wave for many minutes
— as long as the departing people are within sight, and so able
to gain strength from a lasting farewell. If Eskimo villages are
isolated from the outside world, they are in many respects one
intimate family coming to terms daily and in various ways with
the surrounding land and water.

There are tensions in such a life, psychological ones as well
as those obviously related to physical survival. It is all too easy
for a white outsider to emphasize the strong sense of "commu-

nity," to look almost with awe upon the bonds children forge with one another, in defiance of the strict and sharp familial lines that set so many middle-class boys and girls apart in the lower forty-eight. Unquestionably Eskimo children are far less combative or scrappy with each other; are not so envious of one another as middle-class white children, or Indian and Chicano children in Texas and the Southwest. But some Eskimo children are indeed more forceful, winning, clever, than others, and tensions result between them: rivalry or envy or resentment. Though those people are in certain respects quite lovable, peaceful, courteous, and psychologically disciplined, they have not by any means discovered a New Jerusalem, a heaven on earth.

The ways those tensions are handled by the children, however, are characteristically Eskimo: silence; an effort to change not the subject but the particular activity going on; a valiant try at praise, in which the person who generates rivalry or inferiority or envy gets lavishly acknowledged as not only the best person (in a certain respect) within the village, but all over Alaska. Misery thereby obtains a good deal of company; and the one who excels is obviously acknowledged as virtually godlike, hence no real judge of a particular (worried, saddened) child's own worth. It can be uncanny, listening to a sudden silence — the prevalent response of children to the tensions that arise as they play or help their parents do various daily chores. One child will go "dumb," as parents sometimes put it, and accordingly set off a chain of dumbness — until, saving grace, someone laughs. That is the end of that; the laugh is a statement of sorts: let's forget it and get back to getting on. And a silence lasts — in the sense that for an hour or two any subsequent difficulties between the children don't have the disabling effect they might have; the air has been cleared and is not ready to be regarded (emotionally) as once again tense.

And then there are the birds, those summer visitors whom Eskimo children remember well in wintertime. A child who feels tense may stare at the sky in hopes of spotting a bird. If it is summer, the child may focus on a single bird and follow it. If it is winter and there are no birds, the child may imagine one. Parents often tell their children that a bird is lucky, can at will take off, can remove itself from danger, from a problem, at least temporarily. And those parents go further, make a connection for the young, suggest that they "be" a bird for a moment or two, under certain circumstances. Also recommended at such tense times are fast-swimming fish; they can help a young person "leave" for a while. A boy or girl who has not quite measured up to the demands of a certain occasion may be seen gazing downward, peering intently at the ice and snow that cover a river. The birds and fish are of great help. But the child knows that a return is necessary; birds come back, fish do too.

Psychiatrists talk about "ego-boundaries," which stretch and constrict but which no one has ever seen. They talk of "identifications," "projections," "introjections," or "reality-testing," also imaginative constructions of sorts: metapsychology, so called. Eskimo parents and children have their own ways of coming to terms with the mind's activities, including a child's unhappiness or wrongdoing. If there has been a difficult experience with others, there are birds and fish for solace, or watching, interested, protective "spirits." If there has been an error committed, a failure of will or persistence, an abdication of responsibility, the child is told so bluntly. But grudges are virtually unknown. Grudges require precious time, demand a view of "life" that is relaxed enough and casual enough about the possibility, indeed the actuality, of a "future" to enable one person to ostracize another psychologically. Eskimos cannot live that way: they work hard in the present, hoping that the present will stretch and stretch

— that one day will be followed by another. And they need one another, depend on one another; raise their children to know that, feel that.

Time for Eskimo children is not what it is for middle-class white American children. Even Indian and Chicano children follow, to a degree, the definitions of Anglo schoolteachers: seven years old in the second grade, eight in the third, and so on. And conform, albeit sometimes reluctantly, with the "developmental" chronologies of various child psychologists and child psychiatrists who have definite notions of what should be done by boys and girls. In some Eskimo villages it is frequently otherwise; the white teachers yield to Eskimo parents and children, learn to forget about the number of hours in a school day, the number of school days in a year, and so on.

Eskimo parents often observe that white outsiders expect two things of Eskimo children — that they learn to keep a certain kind of time and that they dwell on themselves in a way that strikes those parents as unseemly. Many Eskimos have come to understand the white person's view of what a person is: someone who begins to learn when young a high order of individuality. To Eskimos white people act like raging introverts, hopelessly caught up with themselves and therefore fatally at the mercy of the natural environment.

For their children the world *is* reality; the mind's life is but one aspect of a complicated environment that, even six- or seven-year-old children know, may well one day be entirely free of human beings. Not so many miles north, after all, year-round human life is impossible. Those who go north may stay for limited intervals but only with help from the outside. When young children know that, they know something about themselves — their relative importance in Nature's scheme of things. Eskimo children are taught *never* to make judgments that ignore others, that are not, really, part of a community's

judgment. The emphasis is on *us*, as opposed to *I*. It is dangerous, they learn, to cultivate oneself; true, one learns to distinguish one's own life from those of others, but with none of the
intense psychological assertiveness, even imperialism, that
some other American children generate.

There are, on the other hand, moments of reverie, of self-
preoccupation, for children and parents alike. Especially in
the summer, the brief period of topsy-turvy abundance: a sun
that never goes away; a strange proliferation of life, both animal and vegetable. No wonder Eskimo parents sometimes
pronounce the summer "dangerous," tell their children not to
be "taken in." When life is so vulnerable, can be wiped out so
quickly, one takes risks, during a summer interlude, to pay
inordinate attention to oneself. In winter, meaning most of the
year, children are taught that the eyes, the ears, the mind all
must be fastened endlessly, relentlessly, utterly on what is
happening, on who is doing what, on tasks and obligations that
are quite literally life saving. And existential necessities have
a way of becoming psychological preferences, philosophical
values. Eskimo parents, generally, don't like what those in
another world call a show-off. A child who begins to be petulant or self-serving is regarded as not in need of close supervi-
sion but threatening — someone who bears a potentially con-
tagious disease.

There is no time in Alaska for histrionics, for the narcissistic
indulgence some other American children seem to assume as
a birthright. No time, no tolerance, no sanction; Eskimos quite
deliberately discourage in young children expressions of personal preference or pique. Toddlers are taught to work alongside their parents and grandparents, brothers, sisters, cousins,
neighbors: pick up wood, help keep the house straight, go seek
eggs in the nests on the tundra beyond the house, or simply
watch others do those tasks. Those children are solemnly

warned, at two, three, or four, of the perils that go with self-assertion and militant independence. A child who wants to lead other children, who beckons them a lot and begins to exert a strong spell over them, is himself or herself put under scrutiny and, maybe, a spell or two — a grandparent's stern desire, expressed in silent meditation and prayer, that a child's mind be rid of a "bad spirit."

The grandparent may take the child for a long walk and tell him or her what is wrong and what must change — or else. The alternative is not the "or else" other children, elsewhere, hear about: the penalties, physical or psychological, of the white middle-class world. The alternative may well be the child's death, the death of others, even an end to the entire village; and the boy or girl is candidly, starkly told so. Elderly Eskimos put much faith in a sustained, serious (if also kindly) stare — managed in such a way that the child is not frightened but rather intrigued. The old one, in essence, goes into an intense, spoken reverie, tells the potentially errant child why a certain community of people, trying against great obstacles to survive, cannot put up with a lot of idiosyncratic expressions and postures. And that encounter is followed by the reality of everyday experience. The child has not been given a rebuke, then sent away; rather has been prepared for participation in a vital task — a trip to the precarious ice, perhaps, where a fishline must be held in mandatory, prolonged silence. It is astonishing how quiet, cooperative, and obliging even two-year-old children can learn to be under such circumstances.

There is obviously an apocalyptic side to Eskimo life, and children are bound to be affected. Perhaps that is why in those small and still quite vulnerable communities boys and girls can speak with astonishing directness and candor of death — their own, never mind an animal's, or an elderly person's. Their remarks are at once evidence of detachment and an earthy, blunt appreciation of what may well be around the next corner. And their drawings and paintings even more tellingly, precisely, unnervingly, indicate an accommodation to a dangerous and risky life. The resemblance, for instance, between the pictures Eskimo children make and those done by our so-called abstract expressionist painters is especially instructive. And so is the willingness of Eskimo children to give titles like "A Storm Nobody Survived," or "The End," or "Lost Moments of Our Village" to their hauntingly un-populated sketches or paintings: black and white mixed wildly or with all too careful control and order; or green and brown hemmed in by encroaching black; or blue fighting its way through white, white everywhere, so much white that one can only encircle it with black, and thereby make a final, brooding statement about at least one portion of Arctic life: the endless fight for the next breath, the next morsel of food, in the face of snow and ice and cold that threaten to turn flesh black and blue, render it yet another inert surface for the white land-scape to seize.

But the child who has had to acknowledge death as an im-mediate and constant companion is also a child who appears to be cheerful, gracious, quite confident about the things of this world. It is a delicate task and an altogether remarkable achievement — to bring up children in such a way that they have a lusty appreciation of and responsiveness to life's pos-sibilities, but at the same time an urgent regard for its severe limits. Even the rather well-known friendliness of Eskimo boys and girls (and their parents) has to be qualified by circum-spection and wariness: the apparently innocuous or gentle outsider, like all else, can turn into a terrible threat. Still, Eskimos have no desire to recoil, become cynical, withdrawn, brusquely indifferent to others. They know that a people ex-posed overwhelmingly to the world cannot risk turning in on themselves; that way is death.

Even in winter, when the temptation to stay inside is strong, whole families venture out every day — for food, for the sake of the dogs, who require food, and to keep up with the job of clearing the snow. Thereby those people keep in touch with others. There is a psychological side to such activity: one must face the Arctic elements at all times rather than give evidence of being on the run. An especially hard-pressed people must take care not to slip into a defeated, passive mentality. So it is that boys and girls laugh at the snow, go out and sing to it, shovel it quite gaily and enthusiastically, speak to it — as though saying over and over again that no kind of weather will overcome their trust in themselves and their ability to emulate others: the old ones who have faced down one Arctic winter after another and not only survived physically but, very important, kept an ability, an eagerness even, to enjoy the challenges of winter.

The sense of humor old Eskimos have, even in the face of the worst, is a crucial element in the character formation of their grandchildren. It is the older Eskimos who often take the children in hand and, day by day, encourage them to feel hopeful about life — to enjoy the severe stress of a winter storm or a long spell of waiting for a fish to bite. The phobias one sees so often among white middle-class children — of school, of the dark, of thunder and lightning — seem strangely absent among these boys and girls who, ironically, live in great jeopardy a large part of the year, and know it. Also virtually absent are the food problems child psychiatrists come upon so commonly in the lower forty-eight — disturbances with respect to choice of what is eaten, or amount, or the necessary conditions for any intake at all. Also absent is clinging, so often part of a young child's phobic life — even though, of course, an Eskimo child is constantly warned by parents to stay close, lest he or she go off alone, in dead winter, and die. More than warned; the child is chided well before any thought has been given to straying. The parent has sensed a wandering eye, a touch of curiosity, an impatience with the slowness of a particular project.

To an important extent, it is the old ones who soften the effects of such experiences — interpret, really, the reasons a mother, father, older brother, or older sister has been sharp, blunt, critical. Often a parent directly turns over a child, reprimanded a moment earlier, to a grandparent — without a word spoken but with a clear message in the eyes: make things clear, justify what I had to do, so that there will be no lingering resentment, sadness, conviction of failure and worthlessness. There is, indeed, no such conviction in most Eskimo children; they seem almost uncannily at ease with themselves. They also seem convinced that they will survive, come what may, or if not, others like them will, so that the Eskimos will be part of the Alaskan seacoast and the interior water network from generation to generation.

Perhaps such an assumption is a mix of braggadocio and self-deception — the illusions of children who have learned rather well how to whistle in the dark. But as the children talk about their kind of life, they do not appear blinded to its realities or unaware of the considerable battles each day presents. Nor are they swept up in a mystical way by a religious faith, a cultural outlook, that together aim to make the best of a bad situation by emphasizing its redeeming virtues. These are children, after all, who are not, most of the time, gazing into space, indulging in dreams of glory and conquest (as many of their age-mates in other parts of America do routinely in their games with toy guns, slings, swords, knives). Nor do these children deny, when asked, the very real struggles of their people; quite the contrary, the children are very much a part of those struggles. It is their grandparents, most of all, who manage to convey to them a certain wry and ironic manner, a sense of proportion about themselves that comes across, quite often, as self-mockery — not ordinarily seen in children of seven and eight, or even ten and twelve. An old man, for instance, walks with his eight-year-old granddaughter and tells her of a confrontation he once had with a whale. The girl is sure the whale was eventually caught, and so she is delighted as she hears more and more about how difficult the effort at capture was. But suddenly she hears otherwise — the whale got away. She looks up at her grandfather, and he is smiling. She is quickly told why: as the whale disappeared, there was a brief moment when it must have known of its victory. The old man remembers that moment well, will never forget it, because the whale's eye, full of triumph, met the eyes of his would-be captors, or so they believed. As the whale disappeared, they all celebrated on its behalf: *good!*

The child is delighted, and her grandfather too. He won't let the matter drop, though. He uses the story as a point of departure, a means of talking with a girl about Eskimo life, its virtues and trials. He tells her that the whale is a neighbor, and not something to be hunted down at will. He tells her that he has always felt pain when catching a whale; the injury to it has been felt by him, too. The answer is not to abstain from fishing and hunting; they have to be done, or there would long ago have been no Eskimos around, including the two of them. On the other hand, it is no occasion for pure joy, to kill a whale or a caribou, to pluck a fish out of the water. Fish, animals, birds, they are all part of Arctic life, and if enough of them can survive, along with the Eskimos, then so much to the good.

The granddaughter will not forget the heart of the message — his smiling face, his kindly regard for all life. Later, on the way home, she sees some salmon on a rack, drying under the warm summer sun. She is sad; she wishes, out loud, they had been able to wink at an Eskimo and escape. The old man sighs, agrees. But he tells her not to be downcast. The salmon can take care of themselves; they are quick, daring, persistent, inventive, and yes, beautiful — as beautiful, he tells the girl, as she is. Some die so that Eskimos will live; but most salmon, the old man insists, live full lives, love the Arctic waters, and don't at all mind the occasional challenge a fisherman makes for them: how to slip by? And when they do slip by, there is plenty of laughter; those Eskimos, so smart and so patient and so agile — once again they have fumbled, have been no match for an adversary. Surely the salmon are delighted as they move along, safely out of range. By the time the old man has carried on so, the girl is smiling. She knows that salmon don't really "think" or "talk" or have emotions like pride; she knows that whales don't smile. She knows that her grandfather has really been trying to tell her about himself and herself rather than about the "reactions" of nonhuman Arctic life — about the requirements of civility, about the need for modesty and humility.

The same old man has often told her, told all his grandchildren, that a brisk, sweeping, impatient wind usually stops all of a sudden because it, too, doesn't want to take everything in its path — but rather is swept along by the mysterious alchemy of Nature, and so to a degree compelled to live out its own destiny, as is the case with a whaling crew or a fisherman standing on the thick ice of the Kobuk River. The children are told, when the wind is blowing hard, to come and listen: a howl softens, becomes a whistle, or a rustle. Why? The trees have spoken up, have told the wind to behave itself — or, alternatively, the wind has, on its own, begun to do a little smiling, begun to realize that noisy power requires restraint. After all, the old man reminds his grandchildren, if the wind "took" everything before it, there would eventually be no one, nothing to stop the wind. Then the wind would lose control of itself, go howling across the earth endlessly. There is, there-fore, a smiling and careful wind as much as a howling one.

All quite vivid and, with Eskimos as with many Indians, anthropomorphic. But not so out of ignorance, gullibility, or superstitiousness; out of guile, yes — the shrewd hope of an elderly gentleman that his descendants will develop some quiet, thoughtful sense of balance about the world around them. But he is willing, at times, to be introspectively voluble rather than imaginatively preoccupied with ascribing human qualities to the natural landscape or the animal environment. He stops telling hopeful, ironic, charming stories and instead talks about the extreme moments he has lived through. He speaks anxiously, pessimistically about the future of his people. It is no one thing; it is everything: the pipeline, the jet planes, the increasingly powerful tractors, the snowmobiles that each year roar more and defy the elements just a little more suc-cessfully, the shortwave radios, the radar screens, the talk of "modifying" the weather, and, too, the talk of new kinds of buildings, new kinds of food (a whole winter's supply in a package or two). And the talk of the cities — jobs there, all-year-round ones, and money, lots of it, and stores in which dozens of things, hundreds of things, *everything*, can be bought. Maybe one day the wind will have less reason to re-strain itself; the salmon will all be caught, by new machines; the whales will disappear from the earth, victims of the white man's technological genius and triumphant greed.

If all that happens, the old man has no hesitation in saying that it will be too bad, but not the end of the world. He is not inclined, at any time, even when most tempted, perhaps, to take himself or his people or their traditions and history and memories and values all that seriously; he is not inclined to stop smiling at himself. He shuns the ideas of a sermon to "the young": don't leave here, don't become like the white man

— because that would be tragic indeed. The thrust of his stories, of his articulated self-scrutiny, works against the notions
of tragedy; there are only tragicomedies, or tragedies with
comic overtones for someone, something — for a person like
him, perhaps, who has the desire to regard the world as he
does. And he can only have such a view because of the quality
of self-regard, which seems astonishingly unthreatened. An
appetite for irony gets directed inward by a mind that all the
time has to keep its wits directed outward. That is why he
punctuates his speculations about what animals, fish, birds, the
wind, or the falling snow "feel," or his own expressions of
opinion, of hope or regret, with casual looks in various directions, with a raised eyebrow, a furrowed forehead, a slight
constriction of his nostrils, a shuffle of his feet: something may
be about to happen and he is not one to talk on, not if some
event will imminently bring danger. Words, ideas, thoughts
— they can easily be put aside, interrupted. No one ought take
himself, no people ought take themselves, all that seriously.

Such self-effacement, not the product, however, of an absence of self-respect, has a decisive bearing on the way Eskimo
children are brought up; when very young as well as (more
obviously) when older — ten or twelve. In fact, it can be argued that an Eskimo parent's sense of himself or herself as
worthwhile (hence the continuing struggle to live) but not as
the very center of the universe is the single most important
psychological influence on his or her children — the influence
that most significantly determines the way those children behave and come to think about themselves. It is not that Eskimos don't recognize in themselves or in their children petti-
ness, truculence, spite, meanness. They have no desire to be
angels — even though to many white outsiders the Eskimo has
become a romanticized reproof to all other human beings.
Eskimos stumble when the white man comes, fall prey to

alcoholism, despair, prostitution, apathy. They turn harshly on themselves rather than on others — thereby demonstrating the special way in which their "innocence" can be corrupted.

When white middle-class American parents tell their children the rights and wrongs of the world, or tell them how to do various tasks, they by and large assume themselves, as grown-ups, to be knowledgeable: mothers and fathers, hence the child's first teachers. When the child has trouble, the parent keeps trying, hopes the lesson will eventually get learned. If not, the boy or girl is judged slow, or declared in need of more time, or not quite "ready," or maybe, in possession of a "problem." Through discipline, through repetition, through persuasion, and by God, if necessary (at least in some homes), through "therapy" of one kind or another, the child will eventually learn. In contrast, Eskimo parents have quite a different manner of approach. They take small children with them, aim to teach them, of course, but put the burden on themselves rather than the children. The point is to *be* with the child, and try to *earn* the child's attention and responsibility. Children are rarely told they have failed and are rarely criticized directly or personally. And are rarely spanked, shouted at, called on the carpet, told to shape up or else. But they are not coddled, either — or endlessly "understood." In fact, very little explicit instruction is given children by their parents nor are there those "discussions" children elsewhere know as a daily, maybe an hourly, experience. Instead, Eskimo boys and girls hear memories, stories, reflections — narrative accounts by older people, in front of younger ones, about what happened and why at certain times and under certain circumstances. And those accounts are usually given as the grown-ups and children work together on a particular task.

If a child does not seem to be listening or minding, one of the grown-ups (a parent, a grandparent, an uncle, a neighbor)

works harder at getting a message across. The voice is raised,
not in censure but to attract the child's ears. And if it is a story
being told, often the case, the teller improvises, becomes a
touch dramatic, sharpens the narration, engages the boy or
girl through questions, through anecdotal humor, through
sheer dogged insistence or clever charm. Often the gist of the
story is self-critical: a person's attempt to master a task, and the
inordinate length of time required. But there is an implied
message of encouragement, all the more persuasive for its
indirection: eventually one learns the knack, and then one is
quite pleased and happy. And there is frequently an interesting boast made in the story: no one, absolutely no one, will
ever be slower, more awkward, more self-defeating than the
narrator once was! The child or the children are virtually
asked to laugh at the one who is talking. Not laugh in a scornful
or nasty way; not even laugh out loud; just laugh to themselves.

If for some reason the lesson doesn't go too well, it is the
adult who develops doubts, begins to wonder what went
wrong, how things might go differently next time. The child
is told that soon it will be different, soon the grown-up will
have learned enough himself or herself for the child to gain
the particular skill in question. Sometimes another child, older
and able to do what the younger child has yet to learn, is
brought into the picture. Eskimos encourage their children to
work together and play together, to teach one another, too.
Upon occasion a parent or grandparent will be quite forthcoming with a boy or girl: we didn't succeed, but you and your
older brother (or sister) will do much better! Perhaps, the
parents acknowledge to the boy or girl, age has made them
forget how to help someone else acquire one or another skill.

On the other hand, Eskimos are not afraid to be quite tough
and stern with their children. It is an interesting and alto-

gether effective combination — a refusal to accuse the child, make the child feel bad or to blame, coupled with a manifest determination that the child learn what has to be learned. When the child is told to keep doing something, or stop doing something else, the older person may acknowledge his or her failures or inadequacies; but in no way does he or she send out a signal that indicates surrender, indifference, guilt, or ambivalence. Life is at stake; death never far away. No one, really, is bad, everyone has had moments of weakness, and one ought to be ready to smile at oneself and others, however grim the occasion — but there are things that must be done, from day to day, and the child had better catch on to that necessity, to life's rhythms and his or her part in them.

If the air gets thick, psychologically, if the child fails to respond, or gets nasty with other children, or tries to implicate them in his or her troubles, then the response is quick and brief: stop it. Eskimos can be astonishingly peremptory with their children, order them to stop being sullen; to start being pleasant and considerate; to refrain from telling tales about others. The children are not appalled by the substantial size of the psychological requests. Instead, they by and large oblige. If they don't, they are told again what is expected of them — and again and again. The parents don't shout, rarely lay a hand on the child, but make it clear, sometimes quite abruptly, that there is no going back on a requirement, that there are obligations and responsibilities that simply have to be learned and met. It is no one's fault, after all, that Arctic life bears down on people as hard as it does, but it is everyone's commitment of time and energy that enables that life to go on.

As for what happens to those Eskimo children who grow up and leave the various Arctic villages for the American urban life one finds in Fairbanks or Anchorage, there is no generalization that quite does justice to their fate as youths, as adults.

Some become, by their own account, very much like the whites who live in those increasingly crowded (and slum-ridden) places: industrial workers; men and women accustomed to the technological pace of urban living, its advantages and its demands. Others falter, grow weak, tired, sick, melancholy, and die spiritually, psychologically, physically — in that order usually. It is often precisely the strong points of Eskimo child-rearing that work against Eskimos who have left the villages for the cities. It is hard enough for any newcomer in any American city to find a job, a friendly neighborhood, a sustaining network of friends or relatives who enable a satisfactory transition from one way of life to another.

But any Eskimo who has learned to be kind, obliging, and self-critical is no great competitive antagonist in the urban life of the industrial United States. A person who smiles philosophically, has misgivings about himself or herself (even as his or her parents and grandparents once admitted they did), is all too vulnerable, is susceptible to the assaults, the accusations, the deadly serious manipulations of others — for whom life is, often enough, a matter of getting what one can, laughing at those who don't rather than at oneself or one's existential situation or predicament, and, in the clutch, throwing blame anywhere and at anyone, except oneself. A person who has learned to burden himself with grace and dignity — and without psychological jeopardy, because others in the village do likewise — is a person who has to take special care when everyone else is on the prowl.

Still, in the villages, at least, things have not come to such a pass. Hints, yes; portents that worry Eskimo parents — until they see their children grow up, and so far, emerge with the same values and ideals. No question, today's Eskimo children in most of the villages feel the tug of the new world; and some wait longingly to leave for it. But in their minds they are, even in the 1970s, and even with the pipeline looming close and large, American children who have been brought up by parents who are strong in their beliefs and never, it seems, wishy-washy in the saying of them, the transmission of them across the generations. It remains to be seen how long and how well a particular way of getting on with children (and in turn, enabling them to get on as members of a family, a community, and not least, as inhabitants of a very special region) will hold its own in the face of changes that are coming, coming, coming to all of Alaska, even its unfrequented, remote, secluded parts.

PART FOUR

CHICANO CHILDREN

I

IN TEXAS: CARMEN

THE HEAD is fixed in position, tilted slightly downward. The feet are slightly apart, and they do not move. The forearms are held tightly behind the back, the hands clasped. The eyes look straight ahead, as if focused on infinity. The only discernible movement in the body is an occasional blink; the force of a shock, it prompts in others a glance, raised eyebrows, a shift of vision. Suddenly the silence is broken: "You may go." No more and no less than those words; again and again, over the days, the weeks and months, the father uses the expression — permission for his sons and his daughters to leave, to resume whatever activity had been interrupted. And always, before the departure, there is a brief acknowledgment of gratitude: "Thank you, Papa" — three words in exchange for three words. With that accomplished, the head becomes unlocked, the eyes move to the door, and, finally, in a burst of movement that defies anatomical specification, the body comes alive, and in seconds has disappeared. Then it is the father's turn; he has been standing still himself, a mirror image, save for his eyes, of the child. As the child leaves, the father's eyes hold fast to the moving body; when it is out of sight, his gaze for the first time searches out the long view that a window offers. "A child who goes without discipline becomes an animal." Then there is a brief pause, followed by an important qualification: "No, I do not let my animals go wild. They must watch themselves too. We all must." He throws a quick glance at the mirror, pulls back, checks the clock unnecessarily ("I don't need to be reminded of the time; I have a machine that keeps good time in my brain"), and is on his way.

As he leaves the house he catches up with the child he has just reprimanded; they exchange greetings as if they had not seen one another for quite some time. The father quickens his step when he sees his nine-year-old son, is at the boy's side in a few seconds, stands there for an additional few seconds with his right hand on the child's left shoulder. The man says nothing. The child says nothing. They simply stare at one another, and a squeeze of the hand is acknowledged by a slight responsive turn of the boy's body — toward his father. They show smiles simultaneously. They break away from each other at the same time — the father in the direction of the street, the son toward the house. When the son is out of sight, the father again permits himself a few words: "He is a good boy. He behaves himself. God smiles on us through a child's eyes."

And the observation leads to a qualifying afterthought: "They are the eyes of a boy; they seem wild with greed sometimes. But that is as it must be. I must help him see what is right and what is wrong. Otherwise he will turn out to be a man blinded by his passions. A father does his best. A father is the law. A mother is love. A father's love is important too, but it cannot be given as fully as a mother's. My own father taught me how to grow up, and now it is my turn to teach my children. When I become too strict, my wife speaks up. She knows how to make her point without stirring anger in me. She begins telling me how much she respected my father, and she reminds me how gentle he could be with her — and with us, his children. She has made her point. I tell myself not to forget her words, and sometimes they will come to me as I am telling one of the boys to behave better."

He claims not to need such reminders when he is disciplining his daughters. They are different, girls; he dares anyone to tell him otherwise. As if someone might be near at hand who would indeed try to make such a case, he launches into a justification of his opinion, summoning in exquisite balance personal experience and a theoretical position he readily admits having been brought up to maintain: "One of my daughters is ten; she was never in much trouble. She is now so grown-up — it is hard to believe that she is but a year older than her brother, or two years younger than her older brother." He stops at that point to reflect and, it turns out, gather some ammunition: "My wife feels that I am partial to the girls. When I ask her if she knows any father who is more just than I am, she is quick to say no, I am a man, and there is no other reason for the way I act. She then tells me that she is quite sure that she favors our sons.

"I think she is wrong. I have a strict code; I was educated by both my mother and father to look upon myself as someone God uses. He uses all of us, I know — why else would He place us here for a few years of His time? I try to keep my eyes open; when I see a child of mine saying something wrong, making a mistake, I speak up. I don't enjoy what I have to do; it is my job as a father to be alert to my children, and I try to do what I am supposed to do as successfully as I can. I will admit that I have some prejudices. Who doesn't? I wanted all boys — and all girls. Does that sound crazy? If so, I know why; I am hopelessly divided in my loyalties. My sons, they are me — I know no other way to say it. My daughters, they are not only mine; they belong to others — to the men they will marry, to the children they will bring into this world, to our people: Mexican-Americans, they call us, the Anglos whose state this Texas is, whose country this United States is."

He stops again; it is as if he has slipped into a slightly awkward grammatical construction to give himself time to think, as well as place his emphasis on a certain political and economic set of circumstances. He does not, however, allow the United States to thwart him, at least on this occasion. Even if he were a citizen of Mexico, of Spain, he is convinced that he would have the same ideas about children and their upbringing. The church transcends all nationalities and races, he reminds himself; and too, there is a certain common sense that is part of one's nature — a biological given, he takes pains to point out: "I am not very good with words, and anyway, I know some things that I can't put into words. I try; my wife and I start talking about our children — and soon, about ourselves when we were children. We try to say what we think, but it is hard. A man is not a woman. A boy is not a girl. A father is not a mother. A child is a boy or a girl. A boy has it in him to stretch his arms, to run when his sister would be content to walk. A girl wants to hold on to her doll. Let the brothers throw away the sticks they have just turned into slingshots — an hour or two of time spent; a girl will keep faith in every single toy she receives — or makes for herself. The boy will marry; he will learn to keep faith too. But his mind will wander, and there is no stopping it. My wife doesn't even admit that I am telling her the truth when I say that *my* mind wanders, not just any man's. It is not within her power of imagination to understand what I am struggling to explain to her. I always end up shrugging my shoulders. There is more to life than she and I can discuss. That is what life ends up being — silences that mean a lot."

One of them, several minutes long; and a body's stillness; then his voice chords again: "I keep saying that I can't find words for my thoughts. That is what happens to me; I'm sorry. The priest has told me that Christ Himself knew when to give up — hold His tongue and pray to our Lord without saying anything. It is very strange: I will talk too much with my daughters and not enough with my sons. I stop myself sometimes, when I am alone, and ask why. I never come up with the answer. Once I turned to my wife: why the difference? I wanted to find out why a man is a different person with his wife, his sons, his daughters. My wife suggested that I go ask our children — take them into my confidence and let them teach me. I did not like her suggestion. To tell the truth, I was angry."

He becomes angry remembering his anger. He flushes. He turns restive. For a man who can be so immobile he suddenly seems to have the jitters. He will never turn his children into "witnesses." Children are not meant to talk about the rights and wrongs of the world; that is for parents to do. Children must learn to behave — must master in their daily activity the kind of moral tact and ethical discrimination he as a Catholic parent strives to convey, day after day: "It would be terrible for a child of mine to be asked what he thinks of his father, what she thinks of her mother. The boys, the girls, mine or anyone else's — they all would wonder what has happened to us, that we have no trust in our own beliefs. A father needs his standards. My wife is not so sure of our standards. Are we perhaps wrong, she wonders? I tell her no, but she keeps on questioning herself and sometimes even me, though I don't want to give the impression that we are unhappy together or that she is rude to me. I have my suspicions that often she has discussions with the children that I do not want to know about or hear. It is best sometimes to ignore what, in any case, one cannot change."

A nod of his head, as if to say he agrees with himself; then a wink of his right eye — and the right forefinger directed toward the outside. There his wife is hanging some clothes. The sun is strong over the Rio Grande Valley of Texas, so it will only be a few hours until the clothes are being removed and taken back inside. They are mostly children's clothes. "And why not?" the mother asks, as she looks at the large number of shirts, pants, dresses, and socks she has put on display, as the wind comes and goes. She knows her brief question has come out of nowhere, has meaning only for her. She explains herself, apologizes: "I sometimes think that I am a slave to washing these clothes. I am always collecting them from the floor and scrubbing them on the board, the same one my mother used. It is a miracle that the board still exists, and that my knuckles have not become jelly or powder. But then I catch myself; I ask myself *why not* — that is what must be done if children are to look halfway clean. We are poor, but we take good care of ourselves — the best we know how and can afford to. I never went to school, but my parents taught me how to live a decent, God-fearing life. Can many of the rich Anglo landowners say as much for themselves?"

She is surprised by what has come out of her mouth. Her husband, she is certain, would not at all like hearing such talk. He has often cautioned her to stay away from political remarks. Who knows what lackeys of which Anglo county official or grower might be near at hand? The priest, too, has advised silence; there is no point, he has preached, trying to fight the guns of the Texas Rangers — and their well-known willingness to use them. Best to obey God's commandments and trust in His will — which, one is told, "will be done," if not now or indeed within the foreseeable future, then when "time" is exposed as a mere construct of mortal man. None of that is too abstract a way of regarding Catholic theology for this mother; she has her own way of indicating the breadth of her vision

— as it fastens upon eternity or the utterly concrete and immediate issue of children and their laundry: "I think of God often; I talk with Him often; He is with me, I believe. But I know that I have no right to expect more of Him than anyone else. We all make our mistakes, and He has to judge us. That will happen in the very distant future, I know. I throw my hands in the air; I give up wondering when that future will come. Not in anyone's lifetime. I am certain that a thousand years from now we will be no closer to that future. I told that to my husband one day, and he laughed: 'You are invading the priest's land,' he said. So I told the priest what I believe, and tell my children — about the time when we all will be saved or damned. He said God alone knows when — it could be tomorrow or thousands and thousands of years from now. I told the priest I was sure it wouldn't be tomorrow, and he looked annoyed with me at first, then he broke out into a laugh. I said that the only thing I was certain tomorrow would bring is washing — more clothes to scrub and soak and put out to dry.

"Once I had a dream; I was dead, and a shadow — instead of myself, here, with this body to house my soul. Suddenly I started to laugh, in the middle of the dream. I realized that I was still alive, only dressed up in bed sheets, like those on the clothesline the wind has just been whipping. I woke up and I was amused with myself; but I was also frightened. I told my husband the dream, and he waved me aside: 'Don't make more trouble for yourself; we already have enough.' I was afraid to confide in the priest. I told my oldest child; she is thirteen, and I can open my heart to her, and she to me. She asked if she was anywhere to be seen in the dream, and I said no, not to my memory. She was disappointed. She said that God was probably whispering to me, when I was asleep; He was telling me that if I did a good job every day, I'd be all right.

I didn't understand what the child was saying — oh, she is no longer a child, I know it. Then my younger daughter, who is only ten, mind you, spoke up: 'I hope the sheet you were wearing was clean — not a single spot on it.' Then I understood myself better; my little girl had revealed my mind to me!"

The girl is not so little, her mother realizes. The girl is watchful, active, helpful, if at times a touch morose. She is given to solitary walks; they worry her parents. Why should someone ten years old want to leave her family and her friends for the sake of paths that lead to the wide, cultivated fields? The mother will not talk with the girl about this habit of hers. Even a child of ten is entitled to her own preferences, her willfulness; even a girl: "My husband worries. Let the girl be like everyone else. She *is*, of course — most of the time. Occasionally she wants to go off, be alone. Is that so bad, such a terrible wish? I envy her the good sense she has. She avoids arguments and fights with the other children that way. To be honest, I think I was the one who taught her, a year ago, to leave a scene of noise and trouble. She listened to me; she took me seriously when I gave her a suggestion. For doing so, her father frowns upon her, and to her face calls her strange. But she will not easily break; no, that child has a mind of her own. At times I think to myself: she has a man's spirit in a girl's body. Maybe she will be unhappy later on. Maybe she will try not to let a man be the boss. But if her husband tells her never to leave on long walks by herself — then there will be a struggle; and I guess she will know to surrender."

She slumps in the chair; mention of surrender, even if the word came from her own lips, has surprised her and weakened her. She admits to periods of sadness: a woman's life is hard. Not that she wants to compete with her husband; his life is hard too. Once he was a fieldhand; now he drives a pickup truck for a grower. Wages are slim. Anglo authority and power are a constant, unforgettable presence. And he is sick, that burly, forceful, hardworking man she married sixteen years ago. He gets severe headaches; often, inexplicably, has fits of hiccups and vomiting and shortness of breath. Neither of them has ever seen a doctor for any complaint. Their children were delivered by a midwife. They pray when they feel ill — and go on as best they can. For the man it is a matter of work that starts at six in the morning and ends around seven at night. For the woman there are children, always requiring her attention.

The woman who has suddenly appeared tired and worn is not one for self-pity — or invidious comparisons. Her troubles are neither heavier nor lighter than her husband's, she is quick to insist; they are different troubles. The ten-year-old daughter is a somewhat special person though; it has been upsetting to contemplate the child's present characteristics or her likely fate in the years to come: "I wonder whether she will be as contented as the rest. She is too smart, I sometimes think. But the teachers don't agree. They have told me, year after year, that she is like all the others in her class, no better and no worse. But how are they to know the truth about the children before them? They have no use for us anyway: Anglo teachers. I return the sentiment. My husband tells me that it is just as well the children meet Anglo teachers in school who are unfriendly; then our sons and daughters will be prepared for the world. I think that is what my ten-year-old girl isn't ready to accept now — the life she will have to face later on.

"My husband wants me to be tougher with the child. I hold my ground though. His word is law; I believe it should be. But a mother has her own way of enforcing the law! I tell him to be patient, and the child will come around; she will get tamed. She is a bit of a wild horse. But even a wild horse needs to learn

to watch her step — or soon someone will tame her. Our children belong to this world; they learn about what it offers them
— each differently. I would not have it any other way. My
husband is less patient. He sees the child standing up for herself, walking off to be alone and collect herself, and he worries
that she will get in trouble — at school now or later on when
she goes shopping in town by herself. Someone will tell her to
step aside; someone will call her a name — one of the Anglos
— and she will glare and speak back, or she will run off. The
police cars, with their lights and sirens, will catch up with her
in no time, of course; her father knows that. Well, so do I
— but I am ready to take a chance: the girl will catch on, as
I did, as her older sister already has, as one must."

She is now feeling stronger; determination lightens the burden of a resignation that never quite leaves her. She wants to
talk about herself; she wants to explain why it is that she is
quite content that all the difficulties she has to count on will
never leave her, at least while she is on this earth. She insists
upon her essential good humor: a willingness to smile when
things are at their worst — a quality she is certain she obtained
from her own mother. But to her own surprise she finds herself
making a more general kind of comment: "Women are not
born to fight the world, as men do. Women are born to suffer.
We must stand back and remind ourselves that there are others, whose daily needs require attention — so there is no time
to become bitter. I think my husband is afraid that if our girl
becomes too much of a fighter, then she will not only get in
trouble herself, but her children will suffer even more than
the children of our people have to suffer, and that will be sad.
I repeat myself: a woman has to suffer. To bear a child, to give
birth to it, to know in one's heart what is ahead for it, to hear
it cry and not have enough food for it, or good clothes, to think
about what it will hear in school — memories of one's own
past: that is to suffer.

"There are times when I wish I was a man. I have a dream: I am my husband, and I find some wild horses and tame them, and I give one to each of the children, even the smallest. And then, miraculously, they can all ride safely, and they do — no saddles, only us and the swift animals. We all ride off — away, away from this terrible Texas and the Anglos; back to Mexico. We find a village, and the horses graze, and we build a house, and we live quietly, and that is the end of the dream. I tell it to my husband each time I wake up and remember what I have been dreaming — always the same. He is annoyed. He thinks I am silly for repeating and repeating myself during the night. But what can I do? I have fallen asleep, and the rest is up to the Holy Ghost. I am quite sure that it is the Holy Ghost that puts things into our minds when we are lying on our beds at night. And there is one thing I don't like to mention to my husband; I did once, and he has never forgotten: in the dream we lose him, the children and I, as we are riding on the horses. He is with us for a while, but all of a sudden I look around, and he is nowhere to be found. My ten-year-old daughter goes looking for him, but no luck. She seems glad, and I ask her why. She says that we can have a good time on our own. Later we can go find her father. He will show up, she is sure. That's the part of the dream it isn't easy for me to think about."

Her ten-year-old daughter has the name Carmen, and loves it. She was told once that she is indeed a Carmen — by an Anglo schoolteacher who wasn't being all that complimentary: "She told me that I was like a woman in an opera, flirting with all the boys. I wasn't doing that; I was just playing with them." She doesn't tell of her disagreement with shame; she was not upset by the teacher's criticism. In fact, she wishes one day to see the opera that bears her name. Meanwhile there is school to finish, and a daily life to live: "I don't like school. The teachers don't like school, either. They look at us in the morning as if it's our fault that they have to show up. But they need the money, like everyone else. I heard one telling another that if she only could find another job, she'd take it, because we're no good, the Mexicans. The principal calls us Mexican-*Americans* in assembly. But he's not very friendly either."

She is a thin, active girl. When she stops speaking she is ready for some other kind of activity. She flexes her thumb, waits a couple of seconds, unbends it. She moves her feet about as she sits. She looks at her dress, examines closely the pattern on it, then stares at the window: what is happening outside? When she is given a wish, any wish she might possibly come up with, there is no period of anguished hesitation: "I'd ask for a horse. I'd have it and ride it. I'd stop school and care for her. It would be a mare, like the one my father used to ride. Now he drives a car." Her father rounds up not cattle but men; he makes sure that Chicano farmhands stay together and work on certain specified stretches of land. He is always afraid of losing his job, and his daughter Carmen knows exactly why: "My Papa is not cruel enough. He does not frighten the men to death. That is the only way to make them obey, but he won't be an Anglo's bad man. So, he's afraid he might be fired."

The girl looks around. Her mother is outside with the chickens, and so not able to help explain what her father does all day. Carmen can't understand how anyone would ever be unhappy with him, even the men he has to keep in line: "My father is a good man. He loses his temper only when it is right that he get mad. I have earned his temper a few times; I have disobeyed him. He has let me know that he won't be fooled. He can tell when we are not doing as we should; he says he can tell by my face whether I have been good or bad. I try to practice in the mirror: how to smile, even when I don't feel very happy. But my mother says that the truth comes out, through our eyes, whether we want it out or not."

Carmen closes her eyes briefly, then opens them wide and stares at a mirror across the room. She acknowledges shyly that if no one were there, she would examine her brown eyes with the greatest of care — an occasional indulgence that affords pleasure. Talking about her appearance has made her self-conscious; she moves her glance from a table to a picture of Jesus, to the mirror again, and finally, to her own legs, her knees: "I fell down a year ago, and split my right knee open. The blood would not stop coming out. I thought I would never walk again. My father got very upset with me when I told him that. He was standing there, shouting at my mother to press harder with the cloth, and I said she was hurting me, and please to stop. He said no, continue; then he shouted that I had better start learning right away about pain. My mother said no, it was the wrong time for me to have a lesson. My father did not like to hear her disagree with him. He picked up my brother's slingshot and threw it at the door. He said my mother and I are alike, and I will be a spoiled wife to some man, if they don't tame me. I thought he was going to hit me; I even thought he was going to hit my mother. But she ignored him; she kept the pressure on my knee, and she told me to help her in putting both my hands on the cloth, and then she put her hands on top of mine: four hands — and they won out over the blood."

With the mention of blood, she touches her knee, pulls the skin over it tight. The scar is still there, a tribute to her body's ability to heal — and without the aid of stitches, which other children, of different background, would unquestionably have received. She begins to talk of the future. Will she again fall down and hurt herself? What would happen if she had broken a bone, as indeed her father had thought was the case? How much blood is there in the body — more than the amount needed to fill a Coke bottle? Two such bottles? She is sure, as a matter of fact, that she lost one bottleful at the time of that accident. As for the subject of fractured bones she recalls an incident: her brother had hurt his arm so badly that he screamed incessantly for a whole day and through the following night. Finally the father took him to the Anglo boss, the foreman, who in turn had driven the child to a hospital ten miles away. The arm was put in a cast, and eventually the boy had to return for the cast to be removed. Carmen had wanted desperately to go with him, to see the inside of a hospital, to watch the cast being put on. On television she has seen nurses taking care of patients, and imagined herself one day as a nurse. Outspoken child that she is, she once asked her teacher if she might study subjects that would help her become a nurse. The teacher was surprised and annoyed: no, not then, and not next year, and actually, never. Nursing requires a high school diploma, and Carmen was told she would soon enough be dropping out of school, just as others of her kind do all the time.

She was not really made angry by that prophecy, even as, upon describing what took place, she does not stop and ask for reassurance by looking hurt, or through a self-pitying remark. She brusquely slaps her knee, as if to show how strong it has become, gets up, and announces that she doesn't like school, may stop going, but would stay and stay — for years, if necessary — were she actually to decide to become a nurse. No Anglo teacher is going to tell *her* about what the future does or does not hold in store. When her father makes his predictions she takes exception, even if, out of fear, she doesn't speak up. She tells her mother later and in confidence what has crossed her mind. The mother advises caution — but, significantly, does not chastise the girl or give her the impression that she has thought something wrong: "My mother says that you have to keep quiet about a lot of things, or else there will be trouble. She says even at home you mustn't say everything that you think of saying. I ask her why, but she shakes her head and says she won't explain anything to me; I'll just find out. I know what she is thinking. She is thinking that if you're not Anglo, you'd better be careful. You can't be too careful, she tells us. But my older sister says you can't just give in, all the time give in; the Anglos take, and we stand by, but if we fought them, *they'd* have to watch their step too. My father heard us talking one day about Anglos, and he didn't say a word; he just stared at us, and we could tell that we had better go out and play. I hope my brothers grow up to fight the Anglos. I'd like to fight them too. I don't think my mother should always put her hand to her mouth and tell us to be seen and not heard."

She has been speaking rather more softly than usual; and now that she has made her strong opinion public, she has some misgivings. Perhaps there are indeed reasons for her and others like her to learn to live with silence. Are not her parents older and wiser? Have they not gone through years of living, and thereby obtained a certain kind of education? Is it not presumptuous of her to challenge them so? Even now, as a grown man and a grown woman, her father and mother defer in dozens of ways to their own parents. And if Carmen's parents are cautious and easily made apprehensive, her grandparents, she knows full well, are thoroughly circumspect, and never in any doubt about their fate, if not destiny: "My grandmother tells us that when she was young, and my mother a little girl, the Anglos wouldn't let us walk on the sidewalk. My grandmother has a lot of bad memories. I tell her that the world is getting better, but she doesn't believe me. I tell her that we should call ourselves Chicanos and stand up to the Anglos. She tells my mother that I have the Devil in me, and there will be a lot of trouble if we don't get rid of the Devil. She wants the priest to stand over me and ask God to help drive the Devil out of me! My sister and I just laugh to ourselves; but we look very serious when our grandmother is nearby. She would be upset if we didn't agree with everything she says."

How about her mother — does she also regard Carmen's rising political consciousness and activism as the work of the Devil? The girl is emphatically sure of the answer: no. There is a difference between the generations, Carmen is quick to point out. The state of Texas is still no great welcoming friend, but its customs and laws have changed over the years. Carmen is, of course, brief in the comparisons she makes, but pointed too. She summons imagery that is connected to her daily experience: "Once we hid behind the trees; now we walk out in the open." She knows that there are many exceptions to the observation she has made. She knows, too, that even in her own family, among her sisters and brothers, there are different hopes, worries, doubts. Her older sister has given up on the United States, would like to return to Mexico and spend her life there — no matter how terrible the poverty. Then there is Carmen's older brother; at twelve he is anxious to leave Texas for a northern city, the larger the better — perhaps Chicago. He is aware of the risks — idleness in a strange, cold environment; but he believes that in far-off cities there is a different America: "He thinks it is better to leave and try to find a place where people are so busy, they don't worry what you look like."

Carmen tells her mother upon occasion that she can't help it, she isn't as proud of her appearance as she'd like to be. She half wonders whether there isn't a way for her to look different. One day she spends more time looking at herself than she feels comfortable acknowledging; the next day she denies herself any self-confrontation through the mirror. She notices the way various Anglo or Chicano women do their hair, dress, walk, talk. She wonders how she will look and act later on, when she is herself a wife and mother. Then she refers to those arbiters of all taste, the Anglos: "If you look like an Anglo, you'll be treated better by the teachers. There's one girl, her father is an Anglo, and her mother one of us; she's light, and in school we keep hearing how smart she is and how she has the best manners of anyone. Then some kids want to beat her up later, after school." She is not one to want to do that; she senses the envy, the rivalry generated in herself and others. She becomes sad rather than angry or resentful. In a picture she made one afternoon, an hour or so after she had come home from school, she draws her school, and beside it, her teacher — whom she dislikes, but also holds in a certain awe. Near her is the half-Anglo classmate, and quite a bit farther away is the artist, Carmen, who isn't hiding behind the trees she has placed in a noticeable clump, stretching to the edge of the paper, but who at least has available the option of that refuge. (Figure 11.)

When Carmen draws pictures of herself away from school (at home, out in a field, near a road) she seems less demure — or apprehensive, depending upon the interpreter's point of view. (She herself insists that she is "just watching" in the school scene.) Gone is her stiffness, shyness, and relative inconsequence. Now she is at the center of the viewer's (and her own) attention. Her eyes are more in proportion to the rest of her face and, similarly, her head is made to fit her torso, not be dominated by it. Moreover she is quite willing to talk about what she has drawn: "It's just me; that's who it is in the picture. I'm going to play, but I've stopped to rest, because I was eating a piece of bread and jelly, and I wanted to get the jelly off my fingers before I met my friends. We might go to the fort we built. It's strong, and we are making it bigger." (Figure 12.)

There is such a fort — a rather sturdy place, made of tree

trunks and branches and other pieces of wood, along with some sun-baked mud. Boys and girls alike use the place, and if some of the girls want to pretend to be good, compliant housewives, Carmen has other notions of what she ought to do: "I like to be like my mother; if I had a lot of dolls, I'd bring them to the fort. But a girl can fight too. I tell the boys, when they choose sides, that they're crazy not to take some of us girls and use us to fight. It's better to win than to have half your people sitting there, praying and sweeping the floor." Does she, in fact, pray or clean house when she is in the fort? Do her girl friends do so, even if she chooses to go with the boys? In "real life," she points out, mothers stay at home and tend to their traditional duties, but at the fort even the least out-spoken or forceful of her friends end up joining the boys in the various contests and struggles that take place — all of which prompts a moment of reflection and analysis: "It's my mother who says that a girl shouldn't get herself into trouble outside the house. It's not our business, she tells us. But even my father will disagree; usually he is the one who laughs when my mother speaks up, but when he's feeling very bad himself he turns to her and tells her that maybe if she and all her friends would stand up and fight, maybe if the *women* spoke up, then the rich Anglos would back down. Isn't that a great idea! But he does not really mean what he says. He reminds us later that he was joking."

She takes him seriously, however. She smiles, claps her hands, pretends to be in possession of a gun: bang, bang, about ten times — and a few dead Anglos. She quickly apologizes: she did that once in front of her parents, and they were quite disapproving — her father, it turned out, more than her mother. He had told her that women don't go shooting guns; and that, actually, if he walked around with a rifle, there would soon enough be trouble to pay. She elaborates on her father's words: "He said that Anglos have guns, and we must never forget that. He said that when our people have tried to fight the Anglos, we have lost. I asked him why, but he said I should stop asking my questions, because they bother him, and if I don't know the answers to them by now, then I'm in big trouble. Later my mother told me that there's no use trying to figure out the world because only God can do that. I asked if Anglos ever wondered how they got to be the bosses over us, and she said no, they have their inheritance, and they're too busy enjoying it to ask questions. Then she asked me if I'd be worried and ask questions if I was on top, and others were below me, and I had the guns and they didn't. I wasn't sure. I said I hoped I would."

A long silence; she looks steadily at a clump of trees, then her eyes shift to her own feet. She notices that her shoes have yet again become untied, and she hastens to do them up. She looks at her knee, feels the scar, then decides that she would once more welcome a chance to draw. But she has a change of heart; it is the paints she desires to use. She chooses the largest kind of paper available and sets to work. She appears to know exactly what she wants to portray. She speaks only briefly and intermittently — for example, to express her annoyance with the relative slowness of painting, as opposed to drawing, when one can use the crayon without the need to keep dipping it in water. When she is finished she is not especially anxious to display her work, a contrast with other times, when she quite eagerly holds up for inspection what she has accomplished. She gives the painting one lingering silence, then announces that she has a chore to do for her mother and will be back in a few minutes.

The paper has been almost completely covered, mostly with a vast blue sky. (Figure 13.) There is no sun, however — unusual for her. Birds are all over, rather broad winged and with prominent beaks. They hover over a stretch of land that lacks houses, trees, flowers; only one person is there — standing, or rather leaning against a pole. She is looking skyward and has her right arm raised. At first one notices how many birds are above; eventually it becomes clear that they are mostly at the edges of the sky rather than right over the lone woman in the picture. When Carmen returns she needs no encouragement for a remark or two about her work: "That is someone who is trying to decide whether she'll stay where she is, or go someplace else. The teacher told us that in Texas, a long time ago, people would come and find some land, and they'd claim it for themselves, and they'd fight, if anyone came and tried to move in. No one has come yet, and she's trying to decide: should she begin to build a house, or should she go get some food, and prepare it over a fire? But there are some vultures, and she has to scare them off first, and she does."

Why are the vultures there? Carmen is not sure; she thinks that vultures are "almost anywhere." But vultures or no vultures, she is convinced that a Chicano who wants to stake out land and build on it is in for a fight of one kind or another. Perhaps those birds aren't even vultures, she adds; perhaps they are hawks. She has heard her father talk about hawks with great admiration; they can manage such a long, smooth glide, and they seem to rule over all the terrain below them. Maybe there are some Anglos nearby; they have not yet appeared, but they will, and the woman in the painting will have to settle with them. How would she do so? Without a moment's hesitation, the answer is forthcoming: "I didn't put the rifle there, but she has one, and she'd have to use it. There's no other way. She'd have to shoot the Anglos or shoot the vultures, if they didn't take a hint. She would do so; she would defend herself if she had to." Is there anyone she might call upon for help? Nobody right there; but Carmen is not willing to leave the woman all alone forever. There is a husband, but he has gone into town to buy some food; and he will no doubt go to the hardware store and purchase a hammer and some nails, so that the two of them would be able to put up a house. Meanwhile he has left his wife to defend their new-found land, and she will do so effectively — let there be no question about that.

Two days later Carmen has come home from school and is full of rage; a teacher asked her when she was going to change her dress, and she had felt embarrassed. She wants to talk about the incident, but she also feels that her pride is at stake — to discuss what she went through, even with her parents, never mind anyone else, would be to emphasize the sense of weakness and humiliation she felt. Her mother had tried to talk with her as soon as she mentioned the encounter with the teacher, but no luck: "Carmen didn't want to say anything — except to let me know what happened. When I tried to make her feel better, she became quite angry — with me! Sometimes it is best to let the dust settle, then come back and try to be of help." But Carmen did not really agree with that line of reasoning. Carmen has all along felt that her mother and her father are inclined to be excessively comforting, let too much dust settle. Three hours after she returned from school and had her brief discussion with her mother, she was no more anxious than ever for reassurance, for affectionate support — but she did quite explicitly and knowingly decide to use crayons as a means of getting something off her chest: "I'd like to draw a picture of that teacher."

She is quick and rigorous as she picks up the various crayons and makes the figure she has in mind. (Figure 14.) She spends a good deal of time with the woman's dress and also with her face. Suddenly she leaves the woman to start another person. For a while it is not clear whether it will be a man or a woman;

it turns out to be a child, a girl. She is holding on to a rake and seems to be doing some gardening. There is grass and even a flower or two at her side. A thin, blue sky looks down upon the two figures, and a modest sun. Just as the picture seems completed, Carmen reminds herself that she has an addition to make. She adds one rather large, black bird. Then she begins putting away the crayons.

A minute or two goes by; she has nothing to say. She seems curiously calm — no movement of her hands and legs or her head. She is staring at the wall — or so it seems. Suddenly she springs to life. She stands up, crosses the room, takes hold of a picture on a table — her father in an army uniform. A few seconds later she releases her grip on the picture, begins to talk: "My father fought in the war; it was in Korea. He was shot. They sent him to Japan. They got him better, and he came back here. My brothers always ask him why he didn't keep his gun. He says because — because it wasn't his, it was the army's. He says he'd get shot again if he tried to escape with army property. My brothers say he should have put the gun under his coat and walked away. I don't agree. They would have caught him. Once my sister and I decided to ask him if we could save up our pennies and try to buy a gun. We said we'd leave school and help him with the crops. We'll soon be doing that anyway. Never, he said, never. He won't have us working in the fields if he can help it, and he won't have us buying a gun. His brother has gone to El Paso, and he works in a factory. Another brother and sister are in San Antonio. Maybe he will also go to a city. I would like that. My brothers say that in a city you can laugh at a teacher if she puts on airs. Here you have to keep your mouth shut.

"The sheriff drives by the school every day on his way to the fields. He makes sure all the Chicanos know he's nearby! My father has to give him a cup of coffee; that is his job. I wish my father could steal the sheriff's gun. I'd like to draw a picture — and show the sheriff and the teachers in jail and my father standing outside, and he'd have the keys on a chain around his neck and two guns, one on each side, and he'd be talking with the sheriff and the teachers, and he'd give them a cup of coffee, but that would be all they'd get for their lunch, and for supper they could have what they give our people in jail — stale bread and dirty water. My cousin is a brave man; he tried to work for the union people, and they arrested him and they beat him up and threw him in a cell and kept him there for a week, and when he came out he was half himself and no more, and my mother said she went to confession and told the priest that she wanted to go kill the sheriff, but the priest said she mustn't have thoughts like that, and besides, she'd never get very far because they'd catch her and throw *her* in jail and never let her out, until they decided to hang her. My cousin left, and he's in Chicago. He doesn't like it there — no work. But he's afraid to come back here. My father says you're a fool to fight people who have all the guns. But there must be a way you can stand up and fight that sheriff and his people. I'd like to learn a way. My mother and father don't want to hear us talk like that; but our cousin told us a lot, before they arrested him, and he said he hoped we never forgot what he was telling us."

There is just so long that she can sustain that kind of grave, reflective, and combative mood. She decides to put on her radio; it is small, not very strong on pickup, inexpensive. She loves to play it when she goes to bed and when she wakes up. She listens to a local, Anglo station — music and more music, mostly rock, interrupted by commercials and brief episodes of news. If she had a better radio, she would be able to pick up Mexican stations, or Spanish-speaking ones located in San Antonio or El Paso. She would like a record player and some Spanish music to play — but that is a dream for the future.

Right now she can live rather comfortably with Anglo music and Anglo voices: "I've wondered if I'll ever get to see a radio station. The people who play the records sound nice; I wish they taught school. Some Anglo people are real friendly. They are the good ones. There are plenty of bad ones; not one of our teachers is any good. My cousin told us he hated Anglo school-teachers, and I agree with him. My father doesn't like us say-ing bad things against schoolteachers. He says that the only way we can get ahead is to stay in school. My sister and I whisper to each other: No! My mother says we must not dare speak back to our father. I wouldn't dare! But even he will shout that many times he is afraid to say what he really be-lieves. Sometimes my friends and I want to go and get some guns and dare the Anglos to try anything, just dare them."

Carmen's attention returns to the Anglo voices on the radio. They are, she is sure, people who themselves don't like much of what their own people do. The same goes for the people she watches on television, the people who take part in serials or read the news or tell about the weather. They come across, to her at least, as reasonably fair-minded, thoughtful men and women. She is certain that they are not the sheriff's kind of person: "I've seen him. I've seen his men. They are very bad. You can look at them and see how mean they are. They snicker, but they don't smile. God must have been asleep when they were born. They must be the Devil our priest always talks about. They must be related to the disciple who betrayed Jesus Christ. I saw one of them, the deputy sheriff, coming out of one of the Anglo churches — our Lord must have seen him too. I asked the priest how such a man could be allowed in a church. He said that the nails on Christ's hands and his feet — they are still there, and they will always be there, until everyone is judged by God."

She has become more philosophical or theological than she

cares to be. She laughs and says that she sounds like the priest himself. She envies him for all the answers he seems to have. There are times, she acknowledges, when she feels quite uncertain, even confused. She wonders why God allows so much injustice in the world — and why those who inflict the injustice manage to show up so confidently, faithfully at church. Her cousin often remarked on that irony, to say the least — that source of scandal, one might say. He would scoff at all churches, his own Catholic Church included. For Carmen, however, as for her mother, it is sad to think of his estrangement from the sacraments. Carmen's mother has often remarked upon the high price of rebellion — not only imprisonment, but bitterness, self-laceration, and a kind of unrelenting despair. The girl has her own way of trying to take account of the turmoil, exploitation, and meanness she is often witness to: "My father says you can't bang your head against a stone wall without causing a lot of blood to flow. My mother says that if you try to climb a mountain, and it's too high, you either give up and come down, or you die from cold — because you get so tired, you are no good anymore, and your head stops working right. I'd like to go up to Chicago, where my cousin is. Maybe I could live there. Maybe I'd find a job there. There's a horse I see a lot; she is brown, and very fast. I've watched her galloping. She belongs to one of the growers, to his girl. I would take her if I was going to leave. I would ride her north! They'd never catch me! I could find a place to keep her in Chicago; someone would have a barn there. Maybe we all could move up there one of these days. I asked my mother once, and she said no. I guess my parents will never leave; they'll stay, and we will. My cousin isn't very happy up there, my aunt says, but he hasn't given up hope."

She is going to add a few more thoughts, but she abruptly stops herself, and also stops the radio, which has been on, at a subdued level, while she has been speaking. It is time for her to help her mother with the supper. She and her older sister like doing that; at times they prepare virtually the entire meal, while their mother sews and watches closely. But upon second thought, there are a few minutes left — time to do a final drawing. It is to be of the sheriff; she knows that, and indeed has been preparing herself for the occasion: "I've wondered what I could do to show him up; he is our enemy, and I would like to make sure he comes out that way when I draw him." She takes the paper and makes a pretense of covering it with black, while in fact leaving it empty. (Figure 15.) Then she settles down: a big face, a circle at first, followed by the details of his features. The eyes, she points out, are very large, because he is always looking, looking — for any trouble he can find. When he finds none, he makes some up. The ears come next, also large. He is a busybody, an attentive troublemaker. Moreover, he knows whom to seek out — and whose orders to follow. Hadn't her cousin pointed out that the sheriff never does anything without first going to the big growers and asking them what they want done? A man who is under someone else's orders has to have good-sized ears and a willingness to use them well.

Finally she offers her subject a nose and a mouth, the latter with large, pumpkin-like teeth. This is a sheriff who is constantly poking around, on the hunt for "trouble" — any sign of unrest among the "Mexican-American fieldhands," as the local Anglo paper refers to various neighbors and relatives of Carmen's. This is also a sheriff who is big, fat, and quite content with himself. The result: a large stomach to go with a large, open, toothy mouth — and for good luck, as well as for the sake of accuracy, a beefy pair of arms and legs. And that is that: no land, grass, sky, trees, flowers — only the big, powerful man. And a few final reflections: "I hope my children are all like my cousin. I probably won't go to Chicago. I'll stay here with my sister, and we'll be as close as my mother and my cousin's mother are. My aunt says that she is proud of her son, even if he can't get a job in Chicago. At least he stood up and looked the Anglos right in the eye. If I had one son, and he did that, I'd feel I had done a good job. If I had five or six children, girls and boys, and they *all* did that, I'd feel as if I was a great success in life."

II

THE BROTHER, DOMINGO

CARMEN'S BROTHER Domingo is two years older and no more sanguine, really, than she. Like her, he has occasional dreams of glory, power, and victory; one day, perhaps, his people will have a much better life in Texas — that is the hope he keeps expressing in words and through the drawings and paintings he makes. But after he has given expression to his wishes, to his moments of speculation and affirmation, he becomes resigned, tries coming to terms with the brute realities around him: "I don't see how the Anglos will be made to become better people. My father gets very upset with me when I tell him we need a Zapata here in the Valley. He laughs and says the United States can win over anyone. Even if my cousin was right when he said that the weak can beat the strong if the weak are right and the strong are wrong, he didn't know what to do when they came to get him, except to surrender. Then, when they let him out of jail, he left here — for good, I think. I don't want to leave; I want to be near my family. I'd be afraid to travel across the country. I just hope my own sons will be able to figure out an answer. My cousin and his friends, they'd come and talk, and say that if you knew what was wrong, you were on the right road, and you'd be a lot better off pretty soon. But that's not what happened. The sheriff just came and told my cousin he had to go to jail. He never even had a trial. They told him they'd already tried him, and he'd been found guilty!"

Domingo slumps in the chair, lowers his head. He moves his hands toward his knees, holds on to them. After a few seconds he releases his grip, stands up. He wants some potato chips, goes looking for them. As he eats he acknowledges the despair he feels: "I don't think my people will get too far in Texas. I don't think we'll get too far anyplace in the country. This is an Anglo country. You have to be an Anglo to be President. The Anglos run everything. My friends say we can fight the Anglos and win. That sounds good, but I don't believe we'll ever really beat them. I'd like to go away from here, but I don't know where to go. I'd miss my family; I know that. My cousin isn't doing so well up in Chicago. I guess I'll end up working for the growers. If I'm lucky, they'll pay me a little more, and they'll have me shouting at my own people; that's what my father says he does. I'd like to do something else. Maybe I'll go into the service. You can see other countries that way. I'd like to see South America. A teacher told us that there are a lot of Americans in Venezuela, I think; they own the oil wells there. They must be Anglos, like the ones who own the wells here in Texas.

"If the Mexican government had the atom bomb, then maybe the Anglos would be more careful about what they say. Our teacher, she told us that we don't learn the way we should. She said we're not 'natural students,' that's what she said. I wanted to raise my hand. I wanted to ask her what she meant. I wanted to tell her something. I was going to get up and walk out. But I'd be in trouble. My father would punish me; my mother would cry. The priest would tell me that you mustn't speak back to grown-ups. That teacher doesn't like us. She likes pushing us around. She likes rubbing our faces in the dirt.

She brings in some dirt every day and rubs our faces in it — by saying something. All she can tell us is that everything was wild and no good here in Texas, and then came the Anglos, and now it's a great country, and if you go up to Houston and to Dallas, they have the best art museums in the world, and *they* built those places. I hope I never get near any one of them. I might want to bring in some of the tomatoes we grow here and throw them at the pictures, and then I'd be in jail like my cousin was."

He is ready to go outside. He looks at his own house as if it too is a jail of sorts. He observes that the weather outside is quite good, sunny and warm — so it is foolish to stay inside. He wouldn't mind making a drawing though. He wouldn't mind taking some paper and crayons and using them on the ground, aided by a clipboard he happens to have. He knows that he is not the likely owner of such a possession, and so he is quick to tell what happened: "The Anglo foreman has me doing errands for him. Sometimes he calls me 'kid'; sometimes he calls me by my name. He will even say 'hey, kid,' and add, 'hey, Domingo.' He once told me that he liked the name 'Domingo,' but he wouldn't want to give one of his sons a name like that because people would get the wrong impression. They'd think his son was a Mexican; that's the word he uses for us. He's always saying that he has a tough job, 'keeping the Mexicans in line.' But he looks at me and tells me I'm different, because I do what he tells me to do right away.

"He gave me the clipboard as a present. I was looking at it one morning, and opening and closing the clip, and he came in and he asked me what I was doing, and I told him nothing, and I was sorry. But he just laughed and said I could have the thing, and it's called a clipboard, and he has an extra one. I told him thank you, and I was real glad to have it, and I was afraid my father would wonder where I got it, but I could always ask him to ask the foreman. Then the foreman asked me what I was going to do with it, and I said I didn't know. He said I could use it to learn how to write. I said yes. He laughed and said I probably didn't care if I ever learned how to write. After he said that, I wanted to give him his clipboard back. And when he told me that he wouldn't give his son a clipboard because he wanted his son to do something else and not be a foreman, I wished I could get away from him — fast. I already knew what he was going to say next, and he did: the Mexicans aren't smart, and so we do the harvesting, but his son is real bright, and he ought to go be a lawyer; they're the ones who make all the money. He's told me the same thing five or ten times, and I know the words almost by heart. Then he always pulls my shirt collar and says I'm a lot better than most 'Mexican kids,' and that's why he keeps me working for him."

Now that he has explained how he came to have the clipboard, he is ready, even glad, to use its pad of paper, his boss's. The paper is company paper: G. Long and Son, Growers, San Benito, Texas. There is a telephone number too; Domingo immediately crosses it out, but leaves the rest, as he thinks about what he will draw. When he is ready, he draws a black crayon across the word "Growers," then across "Long and Son"; but a change of heart takes place, and abruptly the top of the paper, with all the printed matter, is torn off. "Now I can begin," Domingo says, and he does. He closes his eyes intermittently while he works — as if the person he wishes to represent must first appear in the artist's mind before he can be set down on paper for others to see. Eventually Domingo is satisfied; he turns to other matters — a thin sky, a fragile sun, a line of brown to indicate that everyone has to stand on the ground. (Figure 16.)

Satisfied that he is finished, Domingo pulls the drawing from the clipboard. He puts the piece of paper down on the ground while still cradling the board on his lap. He looks at another piece of stationery. A minute or so later the boy's right thumb moves back and forth, back and forth, over the name, the occupation, the town, the state, the telephone number, until the force of pressure exerted prompts, at the very least, awareness, and maybe a touch of embarrassment — the latter expressed as an apologia of sorts: "I don't know Mr. Long, except to recognize him and try to stay out of his way. He may be all right. He has a bad temper, a real bad one, I've got to say that. The foreman is always talking about Mr. Long's temper. The foreman once got Mr. Long mad, and he near killed the foreman, that's what I heard. The foreman himself told me what happened; he said that he was sitting and minding his own business, and suddenly he heard Mr. Long's voice from the car. He went toward the car, but Mr. Long got out and started shouting, and he kept on hitting one of his fists with the other fist, and saying that everything was going wrong and it was all the foreman's fault. Then Mr. Long really went crazy. He got into his car, and he came out with his gun, and he shot it three times — into the air. The foreman was sure he was going to be killed. He says he just stood there and said to himself: 'This is it.' He kept on saying that. Mr. Long was screaming and shouting, and in between firing his gun. He'd call the foreman every bad word he could think up, then he'd shoot his gun.

"When he ran out of bullets, he told the foreman that he was fired, and so were all the Mexicans who were working for him, the men and women in the fields, and even the old couple he has for his own use and his wife's at home. The foreman started to walk away because he figured there wasn't any reason to stay, and he was afraid maybe old Mr. Long had another gun, all loaded up, in that car of his. The foreman didn't get very far though. All of a sudden Mr. Long was walking right beside him, and shouting and saying he'd get the sheriff, and he'd get

the Texas Rangers, and he'd get the governor. But the foreman didn't stand still. He kept moving. Then Mr. Long got
control of himself, and he said he didn't mean to take it out on
any Anglo, when it was really our fault, the Mexicans' —
that's what he told the foreman. And Mr. Long confessed that
his son isn't much good; he's been arrested a lot for driving too
fast, and he gets drunk a lot, and it's only because the sheriff
is a friend of Mr. Long that the son hasn't ended up being sent
to jail."

There is more to tell. As Domingo talks he continues to keep
the board on his upper legs, sometimes sliding it up and down,
between his knees and his lower abdomen, into which he once
or twice playfully presses the top edge, with its metal clip. He
announces an interest in drawing a picture of Mr. Long as well
as the foreman, but he decides that he'd rather speak about
them. He has heard a lot about Mr. Long's son from Mr. Long's
foreman, and for some reason what he has been told means a
lot to him: "I like to hear the foreman tell what he has overheard, and what Mr. Long says to him when he's had some
whiskey. The foreman once told me it's too bad I'm not older,
then I could be a 'houseboy' for Mr. Long; he has three of
them, and they do errands and help the cook and the cleaning
lady and the others he has working for him. The foreman is the
only Anglo working for the Longs. Mrs. Long tells her cook
that she doesn't like Anglos to work for her. She once had an
Anglo woman who came there every morning and cooked, but
she was fired after a year. Mr. Long told the foreman that his
wife was always arguing with the Anglo woman, so she had to
leave. I have a friend, and it's his mother who's the cook now.
My friend tells me what his mother hears the Longs saying
about the foreman, and the foreman tells me what he hears
the Longs saying about everyone else."

Now he stops, as if to savor all that he has heard. He has a slight, ironic smile on his face; he seems to realize how strange it is for a mere boy like him, a small, quiet, poor, badly educated *Mexican,* to be privy to information, gossip, stories, secrets — a whole array of fact, rumor, and, no doubt, exaggerations if not outright lies. He conveys his perplexity, his wry amusement: "My grandmother used to say that mice bother no one, and so let them enjoy their crumbs. When the foreman starts telling me every secret he knows, he always says that it's only me he can trust, because I don't make any difference, I'm just another Mexican kid. So I nod my head. But I can't figure out why he tells me so much. I get scared. I don't want him to get angry with me. He has a bad temper. He's always saying that next to Mr. Long, he's got the worst temper in the county. But he's never let me see him in a temper. He says it's mostly his wife who sees his temper, and his daughter and his son. His daughter ran away, and she came back without a husband, but she had a baby. Then she ran away again, and she left the baby with the foreman and his wife, and then she came home again with another baby. Now she's gone away again, and the foreman keeps saying that he'll soon have another baby to take care of. When he's had a couple of beers, he tells me he's been 'relaxing,' and then he wonders if the third one will be a boy or a girl. The other two are boys, and he would like a girl. Sometimes he talks about going out and finding the three men — he calls them the three pigs — who made his daughter have the babies. He says it's his wife, and not his daughter, who's taking care of the two; and when he told her to expect a third any day now, she couldn't believe he was right. But he reminded her that he'd always predicted right, and she said she was ready for another baby, and it'll be coming any day now, and she knew it, even before he'd told her."

He wants to proceed, but he is somehow stopped by the words he has spoken; they have compelled him to think about himself and his own family rather than the foreman's. He worries that one of his sisters might in the future behave as the daughter of the foreman did. He is sure, however, that his father would not be so tolerant, his mother so generous and forbearing. The priest would certainly be a person to reckon with; he is not one to stand idle while any of his parishioners do wrong. But Domingo is hopeful about his sisters — and himself. They are poor, and will no doubt always be poor. They will never have the "chances," he calls them, that Anglos have. So what! They will be spared some of the possibilities for tragedy. Life is like that, ironic. All of that he says with a few words, a look or two — and with some crayons, which he now decides to use. As he does so, he reminds himself that his sisters will never have the money the foreman's daughter has. He is, in fact, drawing a picture of the foreman. Not an easy job. The picture, half completed, is thrown out. The point is to balance animosity and compassion, Domingo emphasizes. ("He's a bad man, but once you know him, you feel sorry for him because he tells you his troubles.")

All Anglos are quite hard to figure out, but when one is with an Anglo a lot, he becomes a person — the foreman, who has his moods, but isn't bad all the time: "He wants to talk with someone, he tells me, and he says I'm as good as anyone. I never let him know I'm sleepy, even if I am. I keep looking at him, and he keeps looking at me. He says that his wife falls asleep sometimes right in the middle of a sentence. She'll just lower her head, and he has to pinch her to wake her up. He once was going to get a cattle prod and bring it home, but he changed his mind. I got scared. He said he'd thought of using it on some of the men and women out in the fields, but he might get into trouble, because there are nosy people from the outside who come down here and look for trouble. He asked me if I'd ever say anything bad about him, and I told him no,

I wouldn't, and there wasn't anything bad I knew. He said he didn't believe me. I was scared. I didn't say a word. I just looked straight ahead. He said he knew he was no good. He started calling himself all the bad names; I was afraid to tell my father, when I got home, what they were. My father told me that was the one time I could go ahead and swear and swear, all night, if I wanted, so long as I was repeating what the foreman said about himself. But my mother said no."

At that point he again stops, as if he still can hear his mother's "no." He looks at the second picture he has done of the foreman and decides that he still has not done as well as he might wish. The man is crusty, self-centered, hard to predict, but outgoing, affable, even charming; and such a hodgepodge of qualities isn't easily put on a piece of paper with crayons. Domingo can draw the man as he sees him, but he cannot quite convey how the man talks and how he, the artist, feels in such a man's company. He laments his situation as an artist: "I would like to draw him so that everyone would know him, and then he wouldn't be what he always tells me he is: 'I'm a mystery, here, to those Mexicans, and as long as they don't know what I'll do next, they obey.' I think I do know what he'll do next. I can tell, as soon as I'm with him, whether he's going to ask me to listen to him, or send me on errands. When he wants me around, he tells me not to worry, he'll get someone else to go do the errands; and besides, Mr. Long doesn't pay anyone what he deserves — even him, the foreman. When he doesn't have anything to talk about, he shouts at me — one, two, three jobs waiting. I can't remember them all; and he knows by my look that I can't. He tells me to come back when I've finished all I can remember to do, and he'll tell me the rest for the second time. By then, he may remember something he wants to talk about; so he'll point to the water fountain and say I'm as good as the cattle, and I deserve something to drink, and why don't I go get water, and come back, and he'll try to 'educate' me — it's what he says he does when he talks. That's when I know that I'm finished with my errands for the day, and all I have to do is stand there for a minute or two while he begins to talk, and then find a place to sit on, while he goes on with his talking."

Talk of talking prompts silence. Talk of water prompts thirst. Domingo gets himself an orange soda, drinks it without showing the slightest interest in saying anything. Eventually he does wonder out loud whether he needs another orange soda. The answer is no. He sits in a chair silently for a minute or two. He removes several ticks from his dog. He sharpens the knife the foreman gave him a year ago. As he does he thinks of the day when he received that gift, which he still prizes so very much. He describes the weather — very hot indeed. He was sweating profusely when he put the knife in his pocket for the first time. Again silence. The boy works on the blade with a stone, then folds the knife, puts it away.

He begins to talk again: about the Rio Grande Valley, about the growers who run it, about his own people, who are forever harvesting crops and fighting to keep their heads above water. He is not self-pitying or plaintive. He is not didactic. He is not polemical or rhetorical. He is intent on getting across some of the scenes he has witnessed, some of the people he has heard, some of the thoughts he has had from time to time. He does not go on and on. He stops after a few sentences, looks about the room, thinks about what more he has in mind to speak, then resumes. He is not really interested in carrying on a conversation — or in being helped to get his views across through the intervention of someone older, better educated, and convinced of his ability to organize and give direction to language. He has his own sense of what to say, how to say it, and with what pace or rhythm. He expects his own capacity for silence, his genuine and frequent inclination toward silence, to be reciprocated by anyone within hearing distance.

A man on a horse comes into the field of vision and prompts a shift in the boy's remarks: "That man is going to end up in jail. The foreman doesn't like him; calls him a 'dirty Mexican' — just because he rides the horse of the grower's wife to keep the horse in good shape, and the grower talks to him. The foreman doesn't want the grower talking to *any* Mexican! The foreman complained to the grower, but it didn't do any good. The foreman told me that a Mexican who starts getting big ideas is headed for a lot of trouble; he'll end up in jail. The way it is in this part of Texas, I believe the foreman. My cousin would always say that in the cities of the North, in Chicago, it's different; but he's not too happy up there, I hear. The priest told us that you have to remember that the people on top don't always stay on top. In Mexico there was a revolution, and now the government is better. My father says he doesn't really agree with the priest, though. My father says the Mexican government of today is better than the old government, but it's not so good — if you're poor. My father says that as bad as it is here, if you cross the border and see how our people live in Mexico, you feel lucky you're living in Texas. My mother disagrees. She says we have a better house than our people across the border, and we have electricity and a television set, but this is not our country, and Mexico is, and the people in Mexico have their own country, and that's better than electricity.

"My cousin's friends, they stayed here. They are fighting the Anglos. It's not like it was when my parents were growing up. My father gets very angry at the young Chicanos; he doesn't want to hear himself called a Chicano. He says the Anglos will allow so much and then they'll sweep through the county, with their Texas Ranger cars, the sirens going and the red lights on, and it won't be long before the jails are full, and if necessary, new jails will be built. I've asked the foreman if he thought my father is right, and the foreman said yes, he is sure my father is right. The foreman says I'm lucky to have a father who has his head screwed on in the right way. If you listen to the foreman and believe him, no one is ever going to win against the Anglos. He says that the Anglos are just smarter, and you can't deny it, and that's why they're on top. I was going to ask him if he thought that the grower is really smart, but I decided I'd better keep my mouth closed. He's always calling the grower bad names — dumb, stupid, an ass, and worse. My father asked me to tell him what the foreman says about the grower, but I looked down at the floor. I was afraid he'd punish me if I said some of the words."

The thought of punishment stops his train of thought, or at least, his train of spoken thought. He looks again at the picture of his father, taken when he was in the army, during the Korean War. He looks at a picture of his cousin, sent down from Chicago. It is a small photograph, no doubt taken in a downtown booth for a quarter. He stands, walks toward the window, gazes. He returns to his chair, stopping on the way to look at himself in the one, broken mirror his family owns — a gift, actually, of the foreman, whose wife had thrown it out. Domingo recalls the occasion: "I'd gone with him on one of his inspections. He said I was a big help, because I saw the gas was almost gone, and warned him. We turned around, and we got to the station just as the tank was empty, and the engine began to make noises. He said that four eyes are better than two, and he would have caught a lot of trouble from the grower if he ever found out. He told me that I was a smart boy, even if I wasn't doing good in school. I said I didn't know if I was doing good or doing bad, because the teachers never let us know how we are doing. He said I was a Mexican, so I probably was doing bad. He said his own son had trouble, too, but it's different with an Anglo kid, because he's got to go on to high school, and college, too, so the teachers have to straighten him out; but with the Mexicans, with us, it doesn't matter, because we don't need to go to school at all. (He's always telling me that.)

"A mile or two down the road he suddenly turned the truck around, and I thought to myself that he was real angry, and I was going to get into trouble, but I wasn't sure why or what he'd do. He has a temper, and I didn't want to be on his bad side. I looked out the window, and he drove real fast. All of a sudden he asked me if I ever looked at myself in the mirror. I said no, I didn't. I was wondering what he'd say next, but he didn't say anything. Next thing, we were on the road where his house is, and I was glad, because I was sure that whatever was wrong, it was between him and his wife, and maybe his son, and maybe his boss, and at least he was headed to his home, and if he had to get into a fight, then it wouldn't be with me, and that's what had me scared, that he'd start pounding on the wheel, while he was driving, like he does sometimes, and speeding up the fastest he can make the truck go, and using his horn, and cutting in and out of the cars ahead (and then *they* start using *their* horns), and meanwhile telling me I'm a Mexican, and even if I'm all right now, I'll turn sour. He always talks about Mexicans turning sour.

"He got out fast; he left the motor of the truck running. I didn't know what to expect. I thought he'd left his wallet behind. He likes his wallet; it's new, and his brother gave it to him. It's brown leather, and he carries new bills in it. He can't stand old bills. He goes to the bank and gets himself new ones. He says he'd rather have ten one-dollar bills than a ten-dollar bill; he feels as if he's richer that way. He says when he gets to feeling low, he takes out his wallet and looks at his new bills.

I've seen him do it. He says the noise he makes with them is as good as a shot of whiskey. Sometimes he'll carry a bottle of whiskey around, but he hides it. I thought if it wasn't the wallet, he was going home to get the bottle. But he went to the garage, and he looked into a barrel and started shouting to himself, while he threw newspapers and boxes on the ground, and then he picked out something and came with it back to the truck. I got out, to go clean up what he left on the ground, but he ordered me back. He said to hell with his wife; and he called her bad words, and said she needed the exercise, so let her do the cleaning up."

Domingo looks at the picture of his father again. He gets up, goes nearer to the picture, looks even more intently at it. He glances at the mirror, shrugs his shoulders, goes back to his chair, resumes the narrative account he has been giving: "My father never would talk that way about my mother, or anyone else. It is hard to tell my father or my mother what I hear from that foreman. I cannot use the words I hear, even if my parents say it's all right. I am afraid that my father would get angry and go see the foreman. Then we'd be thrown off the grower's land, and we'd have no place to go, and we'd be in real bad trouble. The foreman has ordered families to leave, and they're gone before the sun sets. He says: 'Git.' If they don't start moving, he calls the sheriff, his friend. The sheriff drives over, and he tells the people that they either leave in an hour or he'll arrest them and throw them all in jail. He'll do it too; he'll take a family and put them all in one cell and give them nothing to eat except the muddy water and dry bread he's always talking about — that they deserve. But he isn't always mean. When he's nice, he's real nice. He'll buy me a Peppermint Pattie. He'll buy me a chocolate bar. He'll tell me that if I'm good, he'll try to get me a job when I grow up; he promised that one day he'll tell Mr. Long that I'm the best

Mexican kid he's met, and I can be trained to lead the rest of the Mexicans. I told my mother what he says about leading people, and she warned me not to tell my father because he'd be very upset."

Another glance at his father's picture, and then at the mirror: " 'That's for you,' he told me. When he came back to the truck he said that and handed it to me. I didn't know what to say. I thanked him. I told him I'd give it to my mother, and I was sure she'd know where to hang it up. Then Mr. Long caught up with us in his car, and he passed us, and he kept using his horn, so we stopped. Before the foreman could get out, Mr. Long was out and walking over to us. He was all upset. Someone was investigating him, and he'd been looking for the foreman and couldn't find him, and what was going on, he wanted to know. The foreman said he was sorry, but his wife was ill, and he'd had to call the doctor for her.

"Mr. Long didn't pay any attention to the excuse; he told the foreman that the federal government, in Washington, is now on the side of the Mexicans, and he'd better watch out, because they're down here, from some part of the government, asking to talk with the Mexicans, and they hadn't called him yet. The sheriff told Mr. Long not to sweat it, because it wouldn't be but a day or two, and the men would leave and go back to Washington, and everything would quiet down. But Mr. Long didn't believe the sheriff, and when the foreman tried to say that the sheriff was right, Mr. Long turned around and walked back to his car. The foreman followed him, but it did no good. The boss just drove off, real fast. The foreman started swearing at him, then he turned and came back, and I was scared; I thought he'd blame me, and I'd be in trouble. But instead he laughed. He said he hoped every Mexican in the county talked to the federal men about all their complaints, and he hoped Mr. Long got called into court, and he might have to go to McAllen, and maybe San Antonio, and he could be thrown in jail, and then everyone would be happy, even Mr. Long's wife and son and younger daughter and older daughter. His older daughter lives in San Antonio, and she is a teacher, and she doesn't like her father, according to the foreman."

Another glance toward his father's picture, followed by an expression of interest in drawing a picture. He announces the subject right off: a jail. He has never seen the jail. He hopes he never will. He has seen the sheriff. He has thought about the sheriff rather often. Domingo's friends threaten one another with the sheriff, with jail: "Watch out or he'll come" and "Watch out; you'll end up there." They, in turn, have been so threatened — by their parents. Domingo knows that his father doesn't want him to go to jail, but he has been told often enough that if he doesn't watch his step, the sheriff will appear, and that will be that: no appeal, no self-defense, no chance whatsoever of defying him.

The boy ruminates as he draws: "I guess you don't study to be a sheriff. The foreman says you have to know somebody, a politician. You need people like Mr. Long behind you. The sheriff works for the growers. They meet and decide who's a good man to carry the gun and arrest people. The foreman said he'd like to be a sheriff, but he's too soft; he said he'd always be tempted to let people off, and he wouldn't want them in jail for weeks and months. The teachers are always telling us that we're bad, and we don't learn the way we should — fast enough, well enough — and that at the rate we're going, we're going to end up in jail, and once you go there, even if you get out after a while, you keep getting put back in. And the principal, he came to our class, and he said he doesn't believe in taking us out of school, to go on tours, but he may take us to the jail so that we'll get to see what it is like, and maybe then we'll obey the teacher and learn more. My friend's father is in jail. They called him a drunk and they said he was a bad troublemaker. He was trying to get the other men to join a union. My father said my friend's father should be up in Chicago with my cousin. There is no room for a union down here, my father said — except if it meets in the jail, where all the members will be put by the sheriff. The growers call the sheriff up and give him his orders, and he goes driving off in the big car they give him, and he has his deputy, and if he needs more deputies, the growers will give him as many as he needs, so long as he does what they tell him to do. And he will."

No more sociological observations and political analysis; Domingo works intently, silently, with his crayons, bearing down with them especially hard. Gradually the jail begins to take shape, or at least its foundation does. The boy decides that his vision of what he would like to draw is too large for the paper he is using, so for the first time he decides to put aside a partially completed drawing and begin again, now using a much larger piece of paper. And he certainly takes his time; he is not about to put up the building through broad strokes of a crayon. He *builds* the jail; he draws one block, then another, each black. When the walls are standing, he turns to the floor, then the roof. For a moment he pauses, as if about to end his labor. Then a new burst of energy comes forth — a lush countryside to evoke. The grass is no mere stroke of a green crayon; the sky is more than a thin blue line; and the sun is not a quickly done yellow circle with a line or two radiating outward. Nor is he content to throw up a casual tree or two with a few flowers nearby. He is painstaking with this landscape and interested in people as well as Nature. Minutes become a quarter of an hour, then a half-hour; he has no interest in speaking, and apparently, no need to stop and rest.

(Figure 17.) Only when he is finished does he realize what has happened: "I guess I worked too hard on this; in school they always tell us: five minutes, and no more — no matter what you're doing. The teacher says you get lazy if someone doesn't watch over you and hurry you up. She says we'd better learn speed now because when we're out there in the fields harvesting, we'll have to keep moving, and if we don't, we'll be in bad trouble. If I tried to work on a picture like this in school, the teacher would come and take the crayons away. She'd say that I was getting silly 'ideas'; she's always telling us not to get 'ideas.' "

He has no doubt that his effort to mimic the teacher, emphasize a word as she does, even speak in a bit of an Anglo drawl as she does, will not quite convey what that teacher has in mind. So he does one final imitation, then goes on to explain himself — and her: "The trouble with us, she says, is that we don't follow orders the way she thinks we should. She wants us to be as quick as can be; when she says start drawing, we should start, and when she says stop drawing, we should stop — and we should be through with what we've been doing. She'll tell us: 'Draw a picture of the Texas flag and the American flag.' Then we start, and she shouts at us because we're not going fast enough, and soon she's saying, she's shouting: *stop*. After that she says that we all have 'ideas': we think we're going to be big shots, and that's not what will happen — ever.

"She wants us to tell her — she wants us to believe — that the Anglos are the best people, and we're no good. My cousin told my older sister to speak back at school. I don't; I'd be sent home. But I say things to myself. I answer the teacher without speaking. I tell her that we *do* have 'ideas,' and maybe one day it will be different here in the Valley. Even my father says the day might come when every one of our people will agree to stay away from the fields and the packing houses. Then how will they harvest the crops, and how will they separate the good crops from the bad ones, and how will they put up the boxes and send them north? But so far the Anglos are on top, and no one gets very far fighting them. That's what the teachers mean: if you get 'ideas,' then you're going to be sent to jail. Jail is where people stay until you get 'ideas' out of your head! My cousin said we should go to jail, all of us. Let them fill up the jails! My mother heard him; she said no, it's terrible, sitting day after day in jail. My sister said she agreed, but we have to watch our steps outside of jail too — so what's the difference! My mother said there's a lot of difference — just go to the jail and see what it's like, and you won't ask what the difference is. She was right to tell us that. The father of one of my friends just got out; they beat him and told him if he gets any more 'ideas,' they'll deport him — they'll send him across the Rio Grande, and if he tries to sneak back, and if they find him, they'll lock him up, and he'll never get out, and he won't live to be seventy, like the priest says it's allowed by God."

Domingo looks at the drawing he has done; it is his largest, he knows. Never before has he put so much time and effort into a picture, and now he is not quite sure what to do with it: keep it where it is, on the table, touching his father's picture, or perhaps pin it on the wall over the bed he shares with his two younger brothers. He is torn between his desire to keep something to which he has devoted a lot of time, much energy, and his awareness that a jail is no joyful scene. Suddenly a smile comes upon his face, and he has an answer: "I will not let the teachers win. If they knew that I had this picture over my bed, they would be happy. They would say that Domingo is a smart one; he is learning and he will not get into trouble. That is a good reason not to have the picture around! I don't want my little brothers to wake up and see a jail, and to go to bed and see a jail. Even if you can't forget the Anglos and their sheriff, you don't need to have their jail in front of you, day and night! The priest once told us that God watches over us, especially the poor; He was poor Himself. I wonder why He doesn't get angry, and hit that jail with lightning, and set it on fire, and let it burn to the ground. He must have the power. He must have more power than even Mr. Long, and his friend Mr. Barry.

"Mr. Barry owns half of the Valley and Mr. Long the other half; that's what the foreman says. My father disagrees; he claims there are more growers than just those two. But God is above everyone, and I can't see why He allows all our people to be run by a few Anglos. My cousin challenged the priest to give an answer, but the priest said my cousin wasn't asking anything new: everyone wants God to come and do something for him. God can't interfere, according to the priest. In school, after the teacher reads from the Bible, I think to myself: I'll ask her what she thinks Jesus Christ, our Lord and Savior, thinks of the rich and the poor here in the Valley. Which of us will get into Heaven? But I don't think I'd get very far. One question like that, and I'd soon be home here, and my mother would be crying, and my father would be very angry with me, and he would have me standing before him, and he would be telling me that I had better stop trying to be like my cousin, or anyone else who has 'ideas.' You see, it's not only the teachers; my father keeps reminding us that if you let yourself get too fresh, the only thing that will happen is that the Anglos will show you how big their muscles are, and how thin and weak you are."

He does not want to regard himself as weak, or be so regarded; he makes that quite clear. He has seen the muscles his father has, his uncles have. He is quite sure that most of the "Mexicans" the foreman refers to are sturdily built men; after all, they do the most demanding, exhausting of physical work for long hours day after day. He knows that there is, of course, no literal connection between the size of one's muscles and the political or economic strength one has. Put differently, he recognizes that his father, like others, has a right to use a simile or a metaphor to make his point. But he is not quite as resigned to the status quo; hence his inclination to quibble, if not disagree outright: "Once the foreman had taken too many beers, he said. I was afraid he'd run us into an irrigation ditch. He kept asking why all the Mexicans don't get together and march to Mr. Long's house, and scare him. I was going to remind the foreman that he's always told me how friendly Mr. Long and the sheriff are, and how all Mr. Long has to do is pick up the phone, and the sheriff will come running over. But the foreman remembered himself. He said that the sheriff was only one man, even if he did have guns; and his deputies were only two or three men, and then there was Mr. Long himself, and Mr. Barry, and a few other growers. 'There are thousands of you,' he kept saying, and he'd pound on the steering wheel, and I'd try to keep looking ahead at the road. Then he told me that there's no great trouble in getting guns. He said we should break in, steal them. If we don't have the money, that's what he suggested: steal. He said he'd be glad to lead us.

"I'd never heard him talk like that before. He was calling himself an 'Anglo-Mexican,' and swearing at Mr. Long, and telling me that the only good grower is a dead one, and how he does all the work, and Mr. Long makes all the money. Then he told me he was sorry that he forgot to mention the Mexicans, including my father and my uncles. He said they do the work, too, along with him, and Mr. Long gives the Mexicans nothing, and he is the foreman, and doesn't get so much, either; and he's up at five, and running everything until seven or eight at night, when he comes home tired, and his wife

— well, he said she wasn't much better than Mr. Long, because she is always after him to do things for her. He told me he wished he had his wife and Mr. Long sitting where I was, then he'd take the car and wrap it around a tree, and he'd be willing to die, if they would also die. He must have figured out that I was scared, because he promised me that I'd be all right, and then he took his foot off the gas pedal, and we coasted, and the cars began to pile up behind us, and he wouldn't pull off to the side of the road, and he wouldn't let anyone pass, either. Every time someone tried, he put his foot on the gas pedal and turned to the left. He said he was going to hog both lanes, and he hoped there were ten growers behind us, and if they wanted some trouble, let them try and have it: he was ready — and why didn't the Mexicans, my people, stand up and fight, the way he was doing then! When we turned off the road to go visit the packing plant, I looked and all the cars were old, and they belonged to Mexicans."

Domingo did not easily forget that moment. He discussed it with his father that evening. The father agreed: if all the Spanish-speaking residents of Texas were ready to stand and die, rather than submit and live the extremely marginal lives of fieldhands or migrants or underpaid factory workers (in nonunion plants), then the Anglos of Texas would, at the very least, begin to stop and examine their alternatives as never before. But the father laughs at anyone who suggests that among thousands of extremely poor and vulnerable people such solidarity and willingness to risk everything is likely to appear — and persist over the long stretch of time needed if a political struggle is to be won. And the father has at least half won over his son: "My father has made my cousin stop talking and listen; when my father would say everything on his mind, my cousin never really answered him back. My father keeps repeating himself; he keeps saying over and over that even if we're stronger than Mr. Long and his sheriff, and even if we could outshoot them, or wrestle them to the ground, there are thousands of others who would come, and we'd be helpless: the Texas Rangers and the United States army and the air force. Suppose the sheriff disappeared; they'd send in some-one to take his place, and if *he* disappeared, they might move in the Rangers, and they'd have helicopters, and machine guns. If we kept fighting, it wouldn't be long before we'd be in jail, and not here in the county, but up to the north, where the Anglos are not few but many — most of the people. I told my father I'd repeat what he said to the foreman, but my father didn't like that idea at all. He said that I'd soon be in a lot of trouble if I did. My father says we should never argue with an Anglo. Agree with *everything* they say, but know what you really believe, that's what he claims we should do."

The boy worries about the conflicting advice he receives. He says so. He knows that his father is a wise man who has lived his whole life as a Mexican-American farmhand in the Rio Grande Valley. The father knows that Valley, knows who owns what, who has the power and who is utterly without any power. He does not want to deny his children a future; he believes that their lives will be better than his — and Domingo is quite aware of that. But hope has to be guarded — and, maybe, balanced by cynical despair. The boy says as much, points out how hard it is for his people to get even the smallest amount of respect from Anglos — never mind political rights or good jobs. On the other hand, there is something to the foreman's point of view; he, too, is shrewd (Domingo knows) and perfectly able to size up the weaknesses of those who dominate *him*. Those who have power quite naturally make a show of invincibility; but the world is always changing, and such change takes place, often enough, because those who are weak and subservient, and realize it full well, are unwilling to

sit back and acknowledge the existing political "realities" of
the day. For Domingo it comes down to this: "The teachers are
always talking about the American Revolution. They say the
English were bad, and finally the people in Massachusetts and
places like that decided to fight, even if they didn't have an
army. And most of the people were against the English, so the
revolution was successful. My cousin said that if we decided
basta — no more Anglos treating us like dogs — we could beat
them. The foreman says the Anglos need us more than they
ever let on. That's why I think he's right; he's an Anglo, and
he knows the bosses, the growers, because he's always around
them, Mr. Long and his friends, and he hears what they say.
When the foreman has drunk too much he tells me what he
has heard Mr. Long say when *he* has drunk too much!

"I don't think the Anglo teachers really count; they will do
what Mr. Long says, according to the foreman. He was once
a teacher himself. He taught football and baseball in a high
school, an Anglo school. He liked the work, but he didn't get
much money. He decided to leave when he met Mr. Long. Mr.
Long offered him the job of foreman at twice the pay he was
getting as a teacher.

"Mr. Long's wife is 'distant kin' to the foreman; that's what
he always says when Mr. Long orders him around, or when
he's told to do something by Mrs. Long or their daughter. She's
funny, their daughter is. She has a room, and it's full of dolls,
and it has pictures of castles. She even has a kitchen for her
dolls, and she can cook with the stove. She jokes; she pretends
she is a princess, and she is only staying with her parents for
a while, because they aren't really her parents. She'll say she's
related to the queen of England, and she is a descendant of
Mary, the queen of Scotland, I think her name is. Once the
daughter told the foreman that I looked nice, and maybe she'd
make me a knight! The foreman told me to watch out!

"Her father bought her a wand, and she goes around with it. The foreman says she's not right in her head; she does a lot of pretending. I like her though. She smiles at me when she sees me, and she doesn't look at me as if I'm no good. She says hello, and she says she hopes I come back and that we can stop and have some cocoa. The last time I was there she talked like my cousin. She said that it wasn't fair, the way her family lived and the way my family lived — the difference. She said if she was 'in charge' (that's how she spoke) it would be different. She'd send an order that everyone in the county should get the same salary, and everyone should live the same. Then we all could be friends, and we could trust each other, and not be enemies. The foreman told her that she'd better watch how she speaks, because if her daddy overheard, he might be plenty upset. She shook her head and said no, he wouldn't be, because he's already heard what she'd just said, and he knows she's not going to change her mind either."

Domingo smiles as he talks about Mr. Long's daughter. He especially enjoys remembering the way she talks about her parents — rather critically; and about Anglos in general — also critically. He likes the rather casual yet forthright manner she presents to the foreman; she doesn't get bossy with him, throw her weight around. She tells him what she thinks, and pretty soon he's agreeing with her, saying that she's the smartest one in the country. The boy decides to draw a picture of the girl, who is a year older than he. The paper is again a consideration. How large a piece ought he use? He holds one size in one hand, another size in the other hand. He chooses the larger. He starts with the girl's hair, an extraordinary beginning, he himself seems to realize, because he stops before he goes on to her face to make a comment: "Her name is Elizabeth; she says that's a name queens have. She is always trying to fix her hair. She has yellow hair, and she told me that it is better than anyone else's. I believe her. I've never seen anyone who has the same kind of hair, *so* yellow. She laughs, and tells the foreman that she would like a crown on her head, and then she could order people to do things; she'd send the sheriff to California, and he could live there. The foreman thinks that is a great idea. But she keeps threatening to tell her father that we agree with her, and we want the sheriff sent away, too.

"The foreman doesn't want her to go reporting on us to her father. Once when she was joking, the foreman pulled me by my shirt. He said we'd better get out of the Longs' house, and we did, as fast as I've ever done anything. When the foreman wants to move, he moves! The last thing we heard, as we left the house, was the girl, Elizabeth; she was leaning out of her window, in her bedroom, and she was calling to us, and she was shouting that we should come back, and to let her know when we were coming, and she'd have her mother's maid around, and she'd give us some real good cookies and something to drink. We could have juice or milk, she told me. And we could go tell her father what is *right*, and what he should do about the sheriff! But I was already in the foreman's truck, and I was afraid to answer her, for fear of what he'd say."

Back to the picture; he closes his eyes for a second, obviously to conjure up young Elizabeth in his mind. He proceeds, draws her face, her features, her neck and arms and torso and legs. Then he wonders what she ought to wear. He is puzzled, is stymied. He moves to another concern — a fit environment for her. He works especially hard on the grass and flowers at her feet. He offers her shade — three trees. He constructs a chair for her: hardly a royal one, simply the kind his own parents have in their large room, which serves as a kitchen, dining room, living room, and storage space. (There are two bedrooms for Domingo's family.) He suddenly has a thought:

his subject should receive some protection: "I'd better give her a rifle. She might need one. If she starts ordering the sheriff around, she'll be in trouble, and he may want to arrest her. Even her father might want to arrest her! If he was against her, and if the sheriff was, she'd be in real trouble. I don't know if a rifle would do her much good. I wish that the 'magic' she talks about would work. I wish I could give her a real magic wand. Then she could use it. She could get rid of the sheriff. She could tell the growers to stop pushing my father and my uncles and all of us around. She could tell the foreman that he can go back and be a teacher, and she will give him ten times the money Mr. Long does.

"I think the foreman would rather be a teacher; he might be the best one we have here in the Valley. He's always saying that if you believe in God, you can't see one person, one type of person, as better than another type. 'You're one type, Domingo,' he tells me, 'and I'm another type — but we're both here because the good Lord has some reason in His mind.' When I told my mother what he said, she said that sometimes she'll be trying to figure out what we're going to have for supper, and she hasn't much for us, and the growers won't let anyone take home any of the crops, just pick them and pick them — well, it's on days like those that she asks herself why God decided to put us here, and it makes no sense. But then she feels bad for thinking like that, and she confesses to the priest later."

The boy feels distracted. Why not go back and finish the drawing? There is no point getting endlessly preoccupied with sociological (and even theological) matters. His mother's advice, often the priest's, is to *accept*: the world cannot be fathomed, only endured. The boy is quite shrewd and terse when he chooses to summarize such a philosophy: "My mother talks with the priest, and then she tells us that we cannot ever

ESKIMOS

FIGURE 1.

FIGURE 2.

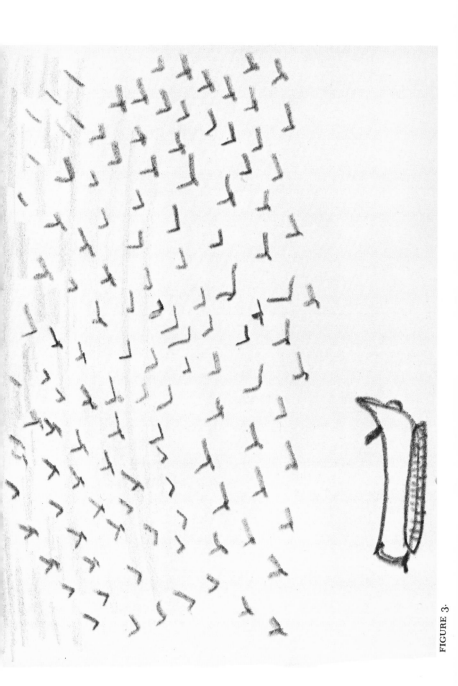

FIGURE 3.

FIGURE 5.

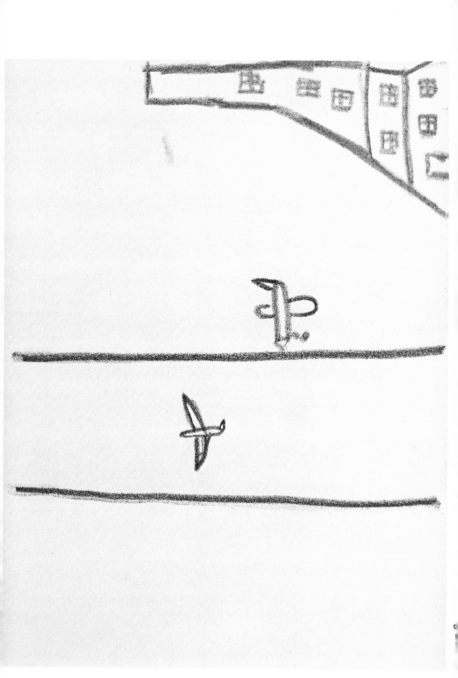

FIGURE 7.

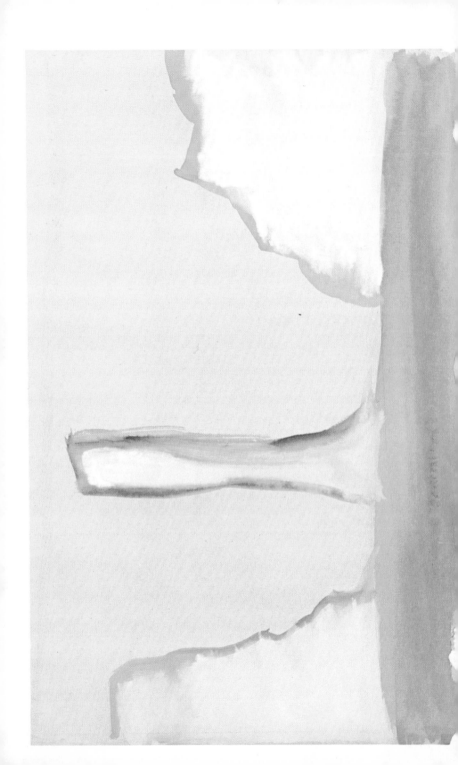

FIGURE 9.

FIGURE 10.

CHICANOS

FIGURE II.

FIGURE 12.

FIGURE 13.

FIGURE 14.

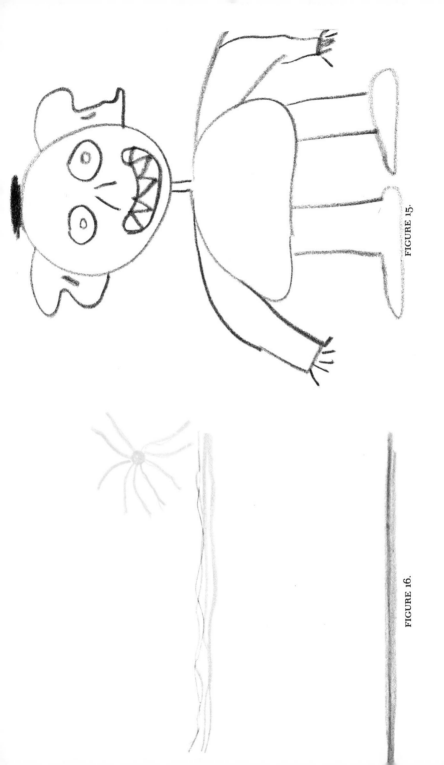

FIGURE 15.

FIGURE 16.

FIGURE 17.

FIGURE 18.

FIGURE 19.

FIGURE 20.

INDIANS

FIGURE 21.

FIGURE 22.

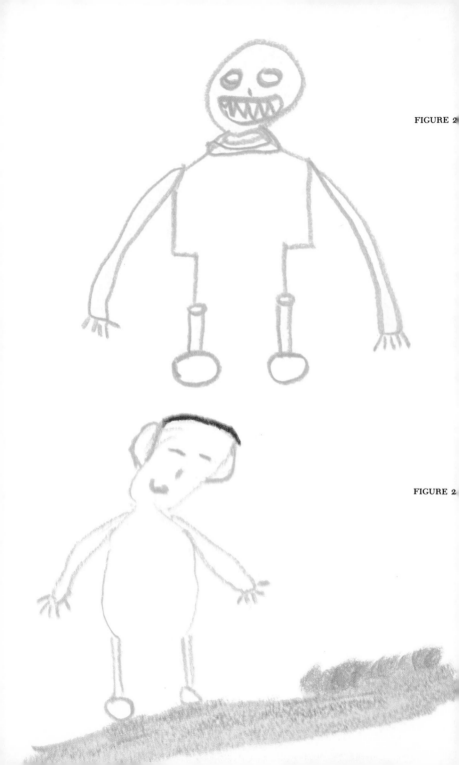

FIGURE 2

FIGURE 2

FIGURE 25.

FIGURE 26.
FIGURE 27.

FIGURE 28.

FIGURE 29.

FIGURE 30

FIGURE 31.

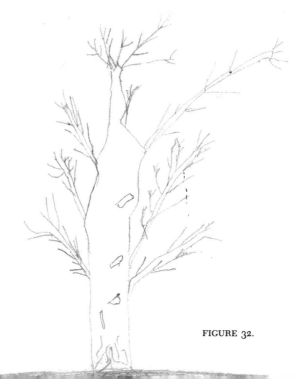

FIGURE 32.

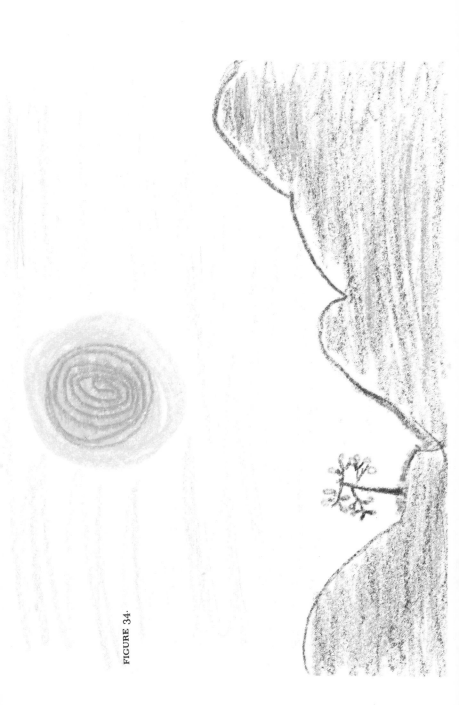

FIGURE 34.

FIGURE 35.

FIGURE 36.

FIGURE 37.

understand why God has made the world the way it is, and it is best to keep our faith in Him and not question His decisions." Not her husband's way of seeing things; he is more combative by instinct, the boy knows, but he has learned to restrain himself rather carefully: "He would like to shoot a lot of Anglos, I know it. When my mother says that we have to love our enemies, my father says *no*, we have to obey them, if they have all the guns on their side, but we don't have to love them, and we shouldn't." Domingo is in no position to reconcile those points of view, at least not explicitly. But he does decide to do something else with his drawing. He announces out loud that he is going to make himself part of what he is using his crayons to evoke: "Mr. Long's daughter would like to change the world. That's what she says, and I believe her. I'd like to help. Maybe she needs some people to follow her."

He stops abruptly his observations on the nature of social change and political activism. He attends to himself, it can be said. He puts himself at the edge of the paper, makes himself a good deal smaller than Elizabeth, who in life is just his height, maybe a half an inch shorter. By no means does he make a real effort to represent himself, as he did with Elizabeth. He comes across as blurred, a makeshift addition to the picture. His presence seems to confuse and trouble him — and eventually, cause the drawing (Figure 18) to be declared finished and put aside: "It's never going to happen; I mean, I don't think Mr. Long is going to let his daughter grow up and do the things she says she'd like to do. The foreman says that Mr. Long keeps complaining that his daughter has all kinds of 'crazy ideas in her head.' The foreman told Mr. Long that all people do, and then Mr. Long got angry and he asked the foreman if *he* does, if *he* has 'crazy ideas' — and if he does, what are they? The foreman said he sat there and didn't know what he was going to answer, but finally he heard himself telling Mr. Long that he was only a foreman, and he was too busy to do much thinking, not when he had to make sure that hundreds of people did their work and didn't sit around drinking wine all day, while the crops rot.

"Mr. Long said he was glad the foreman spoke that way. Mr. Long told the foreman that the trouble with his daughter, and with his wife, too, is that they don't have much to do, and that's why they sit around and have all these 'crazy ideas.' The foreman said, 'Yes, sir.' The foreman changed the subject; he got Mr. Long thinking about something else by telling him that they needed some new shovels and new clippers, and the sooner the better. Mr. Long sometimes tells the foreman that it's all his doing, the money that's made on the crops. I heard him tell the foreman that he should get a bigger salary, but if he did all the other growers would be unhappy, and there'd be trouble. Later the foreman told me that if Mr. Long started increasing salaries, or if he paid attention to his daughter, and gave bonuses to everybody, all the Mexicans, then the other growers would run the Longs out of the county; they'd be called traitors. The foreman agrees with Mr. Long's daughter; she says that the growers are as scared of each other as my parents are of the sheriff, and there's no one who can really get his way because everyone has to be careful. That's why Elizabeth Long is right; she says it'll take magic to change the world, and my mother says *right*, but only God has it!"

Domingo likes Elizabeth Long; she may be a source of annoyance or anxiety to her father, but to him she is a thoughtful, attentive person who never fails to pay him attention — even a kind of deference. She tells him that she likes "his people," that she is troubled by the injustice and inequality she sees around her, and that one day, she hopes, there will be changes in the Rio Grande Valley. The foreman who can be so surly toward and demanding of "Mexicans," a word he can sometimes virtually spit out, is the same foreman who listens to Elizabeth Long with obvious interest and, not rarely, exuberant satisfaction. Domingo is as taken with the foreman's flexibility of thought as he is with Elizabeth Long's extraordinary social views.

For a second he contemplated adding the foreman to the picture he worked on so long and hard, but he decided to talk about what he had in mind — and reserve, perhaps, the right to do a separate drawing of that constant companion (and educator) of his: "If you're on top of others but below the real boss, then you're in between, and you have to keep on your toes all the time. When Mr. Long's daughter talks to the foreman, he begins to smile. He doesn't smile much. He tells me *never* to smile, especially when Mr. Long is around. He says that if you smile in front of the growers, they think you're up to something tricky, and the next thing you know, they'll fire you. If you smile in front of the Mexicans, according to the foreman, they'll think you're easily fooled, and they'll walk all over you. We'll be in his truck, and he'll hear something funny on the radio, and he laughs, and then he explains it to me, but he always tells me to forget what I've heard, because I might remember, and say something that makes him laugh, and somebody might be near and see, and he'll get into trouble.

"Once we were talking with Mr. Long's daughter, and she said she wanted to enlist the two of us in her army, and the three of us should try to make the Valley a different place. She told him right to his face that she knew he was scared of her father, and she didn't like seeing people scared like that. Then she said *I* was scared, too; she looked at the foreman, and said I was scared of him. I told her no, I wasn't. She said I *was.* The foreman told her she was wrong, and she shouldn't tell people how they feel, she should ask them. But she wasn't going to listen to him. She told him some more; she said that the foremen were the ones who made everything work, and the grow-ers made all the money, and she was sure that no foreman really liked being a foreman, he just *had* to be, or else he wouldn't have any money to bring home to his family. And she said it was her *mother* who told her that, and her mother had even told her father that, too. The foreman said: 'Are you telling me the truth, young lady?' And she said she was, and she would never lie, and she only wished more people told the truth, and that was what the trouble is — everyone telling lies, and not the truth. The foreman decided he should sit down after she told him that, and he told me I should sit down, too — and I should say anything I want to, and not worry about what he might think of what I say, because it's a free country. Then Mr. Long's daughter said I should call her by her first name, and she would call me by my first name, and she wasn't sure about the foreman — how she and I should speak to him, by his first name or his last."

He smiles and looks again at the picture he had completed; once more he contemplates finding in it some space for the foreman — but no, he had best keep things as they are. The foreman is older, as he and Mr. Long's daughter reminded each other that day. It is hard for people of different ages to speak candidly in a conversation. Not that Domingo was able to be all that frank and discursive with his age-mate, Miss Long. The fact is, he reminds himself, he could not heed her suggestion and call her by her first name. He can't even *think* of her by her first name. Domingo insists that he was too shy even to suggest his own view, any view, pro or con, on the subject — then, when in the company of the girl and the fore-man, or afterward, when alone with him. She is "Mr. Long's daughter," and that is that.

Suddenly he makes a leap, though; he is willing to talk about the most extravagantly hypothetical situation, and enjoy doing so: "I could picture myself in Mr. Long's house — his son. If I was his son, I'd talk like his daughter does, I'd have the same ideas she does. I'd try to convince Mr. Long; I'd tell him what I believe is right and what is wrong. If I was the foreman's son, I'd tell him too — but I'm not sure he'd listen. I don't know Mr. Long; I don't know whether he listens to his daughter or not. She says her father is busy, and she thinks that if she tried to tell him something important, he would tell her that she's a wonderful girl, but he has to go talk on the phone, or see somebody.

"I don't think Mr. Long would do anything bad, even if his daughter did tell him everything she thinks, and everything she's talked about with the foreman and me. If I was in his house, and he came in, and I was his son, I'd go up to him and start talking; I'd say that I have something on my mind, and I want to get if off my mind. The foreman says that Mr. Long doesn't like to hear anyone's ideas, only his own. But I've seen him listening while the foreman explains what's happening to the crops, and Mrs. Long and her daughter, they both do a lot of talking, and the foreman himself said that Mrs. Long has more to do with what her husband believes than anyone else. He would pay attention to his daughter. She would cry, if he didn't, and then he would apologize and let her talk. I know that is what would happen. If one grower changed, the others might follow him. You need to have hope. You can't always expect the worst."

He begins to draw, but does not say who or what he has in mind to represent. Soon a large woman appears holding a ruler: his teacher. He wishes that Mr. Long's daughter had such a teacher. He is sure that a word from daughter to father and from father to principal, and that would be the end of the teacher's tenure. As a matter of fact, he muses, wouldn't a "word," spoken by a girl like Mr. Long's daughter, be something of a miracle? No doubt such "miracles" are rare; he does not believe that he will ever be in a position to say something to somebody of such telling import that a teacher, or anyone else, would lose a job. Yet his cousin had said often that changes do take place, that what seems quite permanent and unassailable one moment turns out to be a deteriorating set of circumstances a bit later. His father, in contrast, has no such vision of the world; his father laughs at the optimism he has heard from his nephew.

Domingo is not one to disagree with his father. Domingo remembers various and contradictory appraisals of society espoused by relatives, friends, teachers, his boss, his boss's boss, the daughter of his boss's boss, and tries to pull together all he has heard: "My father says we should expect nothing to change very much — but he tells me that the teachers are getting a *little* better. They used to insult us all the time; now they are more careful. My teacher is always complaining that *Anglos* aren't being treated right by the government in Washington. She says that if you're colored or Mexican or Indian, the federal people are for you, but if you're an Anglo, they're suspicious of you. The foreman says that the country is still run by the Anglos, even if the government is trying to help the Mexicans. He says it'll backfire, all the help given to Mexicans. I asked him what kind of help, and he said he didn't know of any, but he was sure there was some. He said they had inspectors come from Washington a year ago, and they said they wanted to look at the farms, and see the houses where everyone lives. But Mr. Long drove up, and he had them come over to his house, and they never went much farther.

"According to the foreman, no one can make it any different here unless troops came in. But the troops would be on the side of the growers, not my father and his brother and our friends who pick the crops. My cousin says it's always hard to fight when you're poor, but you can win if you keep fighting and if you get help from people all over the country. My father says we shouldn't listen to him; and his own father, my uncle, says his son has dreams, and he believes in them, but they are not going to come true. My uncle wishes my cousin had stayed here and worked with him in the fields, but my aunt is glad he has left us. She cries for him, but she prays that he stays away. She would like to see him again, but she hopes she never does if it means that he comes back here, and gets arrested. The foreman says that if my cousin sets foot in the county, he'll be arrested, and they'll keep him there in jail for years, until he grows old. I don't know what I'd do, sitting in a cell all day; and the food is only water and old bread, I was told, and rice sometimes.

"I'd like to grow up and have the state of Texas become different. I'd like Texas to join Mexico, but that won't happen. Maybe if Mexico, the whole country, became part of this country, the United States, there would be more of us here, more Mexicans, and then we would be listened to, and we would get some respect, and then we'd be able to walk anyplace and say what's on our minds, and not be afraid that we're going to get into trouble. That was what my cousin once told me — that we should be as free as the Anglos, and be able to take a walk, or say something, and not always look over our shoulders afterwards. I still remember him saying those words to me; he had his hands on my arms, and he asked me to look up at him, not down at the ground. I kept forgetting, but he kept asking me, over and over, to look up, look up, and finally, I did, and he said that someday we'd both be 'free men,' and I hope so."

He is ready, at last, to draw a picture of his cousin. In the past he has worried that he would be inadequate to the task — how to evoke the young man's boldness, courage, willfulness, lively spirit? A modest boy, Domingo senses that his cousin is a hard one to characterize. The artist begins with the environment; he draws the ground, a sky with a plane or two crossing it. At last the cousin himself is begun. (Figure 19.)

This is no ordinary person, the artist seems to know. This is a person who has to be acknowledged as quite special, important, forceful of character. The face is wide-eyed, commanding; the boy talks about it as he draws: "My cousin has ears that can pick up noise far away. He knows when the Anglos are whispering and what they are saying. The foreman told me that the trouble with my cousin is that he listens too much; and he won't just forget what he hears. My cousin has good eyes; he told me to look at people and try to figure out what they're after. I wasn't sure I knew how to do that; but he said you can be five or six and know what's going on, or be seventy-five and know nothing. My father said my cousin thinks he knows more than he does, but I think he does know a lot, and he never learned anything from the schoolteachers, only from himself, and that's what he kept telling me and my brothers and sisters — we should be our own teachers. He said that once in front of my parents, and my father left the room, went outside. Then my mother smiled. My father came right back in, and he told my cousin to leave, and my cousin did. But he came back right away too — and then my mother said that we should all stay right where we are, and no moving in and out of the house, because we all belong together; we are from the same family, and we belong to the same people. My cousin thanked her, and said she is right, we come from Mexico, but we're here, and we won't go back, and we have to *claim* this country, he said, and make it ours, as much as it is the Anglos', and my father nodded his head."

Domingo often wonders whether he dare ask the foreman to come visit his house. He has discussed the subject with his parents: why not? They answer rather briefly: No. If the boy persists, and he does sometimes, they ask with equal brevity: Why? He is at a loss to find an answer. He summons his cousin's spirit, if not actual words: the Anglos are bosses, and we had better get to know them and come to terms with them — and here is one Anglo with whom we might begin such an effort. The father is skeptical; the mother is troubled, uncomprehending. How can an Anglo be a friend of theirs? Why is their child so naive and trusting? Even if they said yes, what would they all have to say to each other? And this Anglo, who can be so brutal to Mexicans — why does he favor their child, talk with him so much, confide in him, it seems, more than anyone else?

The father thinks he knows: the foreman's own son is a strange, difficult, hard-to-control child, and so what is missing within a family gets found at work — a child for a companion. Though unsure of herself, the mother comes up with observations full of nuance and irony: the foreman is a Mexican to Mr. Long, who is a Mexican to the huge company from hundreds of miles away that wants to buy his land, everyone's land; and the foreman is a lonely man who finds Domingo a source of comfort — a boy to whom he can express some of his various and contradictory opinions, or sentiments, and from whom he can obtain a certain kind of quiet, reliable, and, most important of all, sincere reassurance: I am a mere Mexican, always heedful, never demanding, quite anxious to go along with the ups and downs of your moods.

"My mother told me once," Domingo remembers, "that I will know I am a grown-up when I have become as free and strong as my cousin said I should become." He offers his version of his mother's words: "When the foreman asks me if I want to listen to him, and when I tell him that I will listen, some other day, but not now, because I'm busy. My mother wishes our people owned the land and grew crops, and there was no foreman over us, and no Mr. Long around here. But when I ask her if she will live to see the time, she says no, and she is not sure we will, or our children either. When she talks like that, I feel sad. I want to run away. I don't know where I'd go, though. My cousin has not found the freedom he wanted in Chicago. In Mexico our people suffer. The people who live in the villages across the Rio Grande are worse off than us. My uncle describes those villages — very bad, he says. We have to stay here, and maybe we will become stronger, and maybe one of us will become a foreman. Even my father says that miracles happen, that the rich lose their power and the poor take over. But Mr. Long's daughter won't be the one to change the Valley. I would like my cousin to return in a few years. I'll be older then. I'll be ready to follow him. I would give my life to *la causa.* The foreman would be ready to shoot me if he heard me say so, but I *would* give my life if it meant that the Anglos stopped shouting at us — if it meant that we could go to school and not be called all those names.

"The other day a teacher said all of us 'Mexicans' should go to the ocean and get cleaned off by swimming there for a whole week. Then she stared at us, and when she stared at *me,* I didn't lower my head; I stared right back at her, and I kept staring, and I was afraid, because my father would hit me, if he knew I was staring back like that, but I kept it up, and then *she* looked down, and she got red and she said we are *brazen,* the young Mexicans, and she was sure that we called ourselves *Chicanos,* and there was going to be a lot of trouble one day, and it would take the Rangers to teach us our place. She went to her desk and began hitting it with her ruler. She said she didn't even want to hear us *breathe.* Then she pulled out one of her books, and read us the Alamo story again, and told us that Texas would be just like Mexico, just like all the towns across the Rio Grande, if it hadn't been for the Anglos, and they are the ones who are smart, and they brought civilization with them, and we must never forget that.

"I stared right at her. Then I looked around and saw my friends; they were all looking down at the floor. I wanted to stand up and tell them they are wrong to look down; we should look up. But I was afraid myself. I saw the teacher's eyes, reading the book, and I was sure she was going to stop, and look right at me, and then I'd be in real bad trouble. She'd give me the ruler, ten times, twenty times, on my hand, and she'd send me home, and my mother would start to cry, and my father would curse my cousin and curse the foreman and curse Mr. Long and his daughter and all the Anglos, and then he'd even curse God, and my mother would run out of the house and go see the priest."

If only — he wonders — if only the priest would come back with his mother (with other women) and tell his father (other men) and their children that they ought to fight as well as pray. But that is not the priest's job, the boy dutifully reminds himself. Priests pray; his father works for the grower planting and harvesting; the foreman orders fieldhands here, there — anywhere he deems wise; and he, Domingo, must go along with the particular rhythm of his life — up early, to school, home, a stint of work as the foreman's helper, supper, and to bed. A day will come, though. A time will come. The future will arrive, and his present life will recede into something called his memory. He keeps making such observations; it is as if he has to remind himself that there is *some* hope, that the endless hours, days, months ahead will not be without variation, without a moment or two of hope. "A year may come when I will lead a garrison to the Alamo and take it for us," he says. Or another time: "I'll catch a ride, and another, and ten more, and end up in Canada. I'll find land and make it grow crops. I'll be away from every grower in the Valley. I'll be in a different country. No sheriff will be watching me. I'll forget about sheriffs and the Texas Rangers."

And as an afterthought, even if expressed a month later: "This is not the only country in the world. The priest told my mother to remind us that we are part of God's kingdom as well as the United States. I would like to stay in Texas, but I wouldn't like to have the teachers and the sheriffs here in the Valley standing over me for the rest of my life, telling me I'm 'just' a Mexican. Yesterday in school a friend of mine spoke back to the teacher. She told him to sit up straight, and he said he *was* sitting up straight, and she said that he had no right to talk back, and she'd have him thrown out of the school and thrown into jail, if he didn't watch out — and he was just a Mexican anyway. He stood up and shouted back at her: 'Just a Mexican!' He didn't say anything else. I felt like standing up and shouting something too — but I didn't. I knew I'd get into trouble. I knew I'd be thrown out with my friend. He looked at me. He looked at others. We all kept silent. I wondered what my cousin would have done. But if I had said one word, the teacher would have put me on her list. She makes a list and goes to the principal with it. He calls the sheriff if he needs any help. The sheriff isn't very far from the school. My friend is now with his father in the fields. Sooner or later we all go there — that is what the teachers say. I hope Mr. Long's daughter figures out a way of putting the teachers and the principal and the sheriff in that jailhouse so that the rest of us won't have to worry about the Anglos."

Mention of the Anglos causes Domingo to do something quite unusual — close his eyes in midday. For a full minute he does so, sits and holds his head bowed, his eyelids firmly shut. Then he simultaneously opens them and stands up. He insists that he is *not* "just a Mexican." He is a Mexican; he is living in Texas; he may end up fighting for the United States just like his father did. He wonders once more why his father ever surrendered his rifle when he left military service. Surely there might have been some way for that gun to have been kept. Surely those who risk their lives on the battlefield deserve to keep the weapons they used as infantrymen. What happens to all those guns once a war is over? His cousin used to wonder aloud what would happen if every "Mexican" in the Rio Grande Valley had a gun and was willing to stand up and call attention to it when the Anglos called attention to *their* guns; but Domingo's father did not like such talk, and the boy understands why. Violence begets violence; the priest says so, but so do others less committed to Christian ideals — the very cousin who brought up the issue of guns: "My cousin told us that he knew it was foolish to think of fighting with the Anglos. They outnumber us; it is their country; and we are not the kind of people who want to brag about how many guns we have anyway. The foreman has seven guns; Mr. Long has a large number of them, I don't know how many, maybe twenty. He has rifles and pistols. Some of them are very old; some are new. The foreman likes to go shooting; he has targets. He, too, has both rifles and pistols. Of course, he always has a pistol with him, in the truck or on him. He says that you carry a pistol so you don't have to use one. If he didn't have a gun, people would think he was an easy one to laugh at. He is a deputy sheriff, and he can carry all the guns he wants. When he has a beer or two in him, he tells me that he'll teach me how to shoot; but he never has. He told me once that he didn't want any Mexicans getting 'gun happy.' He told me that we're not going to have any trouble in the Valley, the way the colored people caused in east Texas and in Louisiana.

"The foreman comes from there; his grandfather came to Texas from Louisiana about the time my father's grandfather came to Texas from Mexico. He says we're both not Texans the way some Texans are Texans, but Mr. Long wasn't even born in Texas, and the foreman says he's a *real* Texan. Mr. Long was born in Oklahoma, I think. He came here with his father, and his father made a lot of money. His father was the one who brought in Mexicans, a lot of them, and got a lot of machines to help them harvest, and became rich. One of his sons, an older brother of Mr. Long's, left Texas, and the foreman thinks that he may have killed himself. The foreman is always saying that if only his father came here and did what Mr. Long's father did. I told him I wished that someone in my family was rich. He said that Mexicans don't get rich, only Anglos. My father says a few of our people have made a lot of money."

The foreman has asked Domingo whether he wants to make a lot of money. Domingo says no, not a lot, just "some," just "enough." The foreman always has a forecast for the boy: you never will, no matter what you may have in mind to do. But the boy has his own idea of what the future may hold, and in a quiet, unself-conscious way he speculates, dreams: "I'd like to be a foreman; no, I guess I won't be a foreman. I'd like to go to San Antonio. I could get a job there. I could work in a store maybe. They say it's not a good place, San Antonio; you can't find much to do there. I wish I had some money; I could buy land, and then I could grow some vegetables, and sell them, and the money would be mine. My little brothers could have jobs; my cousin could come home and be a partner. Mr. Long told the foreman that he's glad he doesn't have a brother around to bother him. The foreman said that Mr. Long's younger brother never comes here to visit. If I went to San Antonio, I'd want to go with my brothers and sisters. The foreman says the trouble with Mexicans — it's that they stick too close to their families and they don't try to go out on their own. When he asked me if I had anything to say about that, I said I didn't know as much as he does, I admit, but I was glad we stick together, because if we didn't, there might be real trouble, and there'd be no one to help out. The foreman laughed and said I was a Mexican all right.

"One of my brothers said we should both go to Mexico — to the capital, to Mexico City, and see if we can get jobs there. My father heard us talking and laughed. He said we'd get lost, and we'd be in trouble, and we'd want to come back here to the Valley. The United States is our country. Mexico can be worse for us than here. An uncle of my father's went there; he said he was tired of living in this country, and he wanted to die in Mexico. But he came back very fast. It is much harder there to live. There are no jobs at all. You can starve, and no one seems to care. Here it is bad, but the Anglos, as bad as they are, have built the country up so there is work for us, like the foreman says. My father told me last night that I pay too much attention to what the foreman says; but my mother reminded him that the foreman is my boss, and I have to keep my ears open when he is talking, and I can't really forget what he says, or I'll be in real trouble. The foreman told me once that I should 'get wise' when I grow up, and figure out a way to make money out of my own people. The Mexicans are poor, he said, but even poor people have to eat, and they wear clothes, and someone sells them everything they have. If I had a store, I wouldn't like to take all the money away from the people who came in to buy."

He seems ready to go on; he seems ready to explain why he would be reluctant to make a great deal of money at the expense of others — his neighbors, his own people. But suddenly he quits sitting and talking. He moves toward the door, pointing toward the outside. And there, across the sky, moves a jet plane. It is flying low, and he had heard the noise. He stares at the thing as it moves almost cumbrously across the flat Valley. When there is nothing more to see or hear he returns his eyes to land, glances at his family's dog. It is an old mutt, and the boy wants to be reassuring: the plane intended no harm. The fact is, however, that jet planes don't come that low and near so often: "Maybe it crashed nearby. If it was very near, we'd hear the crash, and see the flames. I hope no one got hurt. Or it could be that they're sending planes on different routes. The foreman was in the air force. He says I should go into the air force. I don't think I'd like to fly, though. I'd be afraid. Those jets go everywhere. They can carry atom bombs. They can drop one on people and before they know it, they'll all be dead. In school they told us — the teacher said: 'One bomb to a city.' A girl asked what about the Valley, here, where there aren't big cities, just people scattered all over in camps. The teacher said she was asking a stupid question and to shut up if she can't do any better. But the girl asked the right question, because you can't just go and drop atom bombs on a hundred people here and two hundred people there. You have to have a lot of people in one place. I checked with the foreman, and he said he agreed with us, and the teacher was dead wrong. He said we shouldn't pay much attention to teachers, anyway, because they don't know a lot of things, even if they think they know everything and they try to pretend that they do. The teachers tell you to listen to them and to repeat after them, but you could be repeating the wrong thing! The foreman is right, they're out to prove themselves smarter than anyone else."

Again he stops for no apparent reason. No plane is in sight. He looks intently at his parents' house. He makes a half-hearted lunge for a butterfly. He is glad that he missed: "Even if I caught it, I'd let it go right away. One of our teachers collects butterflies. She kills them. She is tough. Anglos are tough. We can't win against the Anglos; they have jet planes and atom bombs. If Mexico tried to fight on our side, the

United States Air Force would take care of Mexico pretty fast. My cousin has given up, from what my aunt and uncle say: he used to think he was in a fight and he'd win, and now he just hopes it might get easier for us in this country after a while. I would never want to be like Mr. Long — rich, while the people who work for me go without any money. I wouldn't want to steal from others. The Mexican who owns the store, he is a crook; he is like Mr. Long, even worse than Mr. Long, because it's his own people he is stealing from. My cousin said that it's not only the Anglos; it's our people too — a lot of them would be as bad as Mr. Long or the foreman, if they had a chance, and maybe worse. If only we could help each other, all the Mexicans in the Valley, then we wouldn't be like the teachers in the school, or the sheriff, or Mr. Long, none of us would.

"The foreman, he's a little different; he's bad, sometimes, to the men and women out in the fields, but he tells me later that he hates the shouting he does, and he wishes he could stop. But he would soon be out of a job. Mr. Long expects *results;* that's what the foreman tells me, and I believe him. Once I went with both of them, and Mr. Long told the foreman to stop being so *nice* to all the Mexicans. He must have said that ten times. He told the foreman that it's all right to be nice some of the time, but you can't let people run all over you. You have to get tough when they start cheating you by not working hard enough. The Mexicans in the field seemed to be working *very* hard; but I was afraid to say anything. Mr. Long asked me if I would do an honest day's work for an honest day's pay when I was older, and I said yes. The foreman spoke up for me. He said I was doing a lot of work now, helping him out, and he was glad to have me with him, and he wished that all the other Mexicans did as much work as I was doing. Mr. Long said he knew I was 'the best of them.' He told me that again later on.

When he left to get into his car, he put his hand on my shoulder, and he squeezed it, and he told me for the third time that I was 'the best of them,' and that maybe the day would come that I would be their 'crew leader,' and I would report directly to the foreman, and carry out his orders, and since he carries out Mr. Long's orders, I'd be working for Mr. Long and I'd be helping him and doing a good job. 'Everyone needs a leader,' he said. The foreman said, 'That's right,' and he looked at me, he stared at me, until I knew I'd better say the same thing, and I did. I said, 'Yes, everyone needs a leader.' "

Silence, several minutes of it; Domingo has no further comment to make about either Mr. Long or the foreman. He looks sullen. He decides that he will draw another picture. As he begins to do so, he remarks, once again, how much he dislikes school: what is the point of going there, day after day? He is thankful, that in a year or so his parents will stop insisting that he attend. Even his mother, who tells him all the time that she wishes he might one day read as well as the priest does, never has mentioned high school as a possibility for him. And he is glad; if he went on to the seventh grade, the eighth, there would be a good deal of trouble. He would have to go to an Anglo junior high school where he would be one of a handful — maybe alone, for all he knew. And how would he get over there, to Anglo territory? And where would he get money to buy the books and other "incidentals"? And what would he have to say, day after day, in such a situation? It is preposterous, the very thought of being at school with people like — well, Mr. Long's daughter. Still, *she* would like him to be at school with her. There can be no doubt about that; he heard her say so a few weeks ago. "One tomato does not make a crop," his mother had observed when told by her son of the Long daughter's hope, and Domingo had not felt inclined to disagree.

But now he is drawing; he stops talking. He seems utterly preoccupied. It is as if he no longer cares to waste his time thinking about teachers and bosses and growers and sheriffs — the assortment of Anglos who, he realizes full well, control his life and will continue to do so, most likely, as long as he lives. The crayons are there, and he has a vision of sorts to set down, on a large piece of paper. He begins to lay down some soil, some grass, a mound or two, and one large tree. Next comes a horse, a large chestnut mare whom he works at assiduously. The legs are disproportionate — too long — the nose is more pronounced than it ought to be; the tail is certainly too long, too thick. And the eyes — they are quite large and fiercely prominent, to the point that they call attention away from the horse as an animal, and tend to dominate the entire picture. On the horse he seats a man with blond hair — who has a gun on his back. And the horse is reared, markedly so. The picture (Figure 20) is done; Domingo has nothing more to add. He puts the paper aside, then has second thoughts; it should be folded up, and kept someplace, otherwise it will disappear — and besides, maybe he will want to add something to what he has already drawn. Come to think of it, yes; he picks up his crayons, uses them knowingly and quickly, looks at what he has done with a certain satisfaction, and then folds the drawing twice, puts it under the pillow on his bed. During that afterthought he had added a few men, all with black hair — small in stature when measured against the size of the horse, which looked as if it was going to go right toward them and crush them with its front feet.

Each afternoon the foreman comes by and gives Domingo some errands to do — or simply tells him that it will be "easy" that day: just sit in the truck and listen to the driver and respond to him by picking up whatever cues he throws out. Maybe that is all Domingo will ever do, as the years become decades of his life: work for some foreman. The boy wonders out loud as he waits for the truck to arrive: "He'll want me to count the baskets the men have filled. He'll want me to go and remind some of the men that they're slow, and the foreman won't give them too many more chances. I hate going up to the men and saying that to them. But I guess they can't blame me. They look over my head to his truck, and they curse him. I do too — but I tell them to smile while they're speaking, because he might be looking, and he'd catch on. Once I was talking with the men, maybe ten of them, and they started kidding me. They said I was beginning to look like the foreman. They said I was beginning to sound like him. They said I was an Anglo in sheep's clothing. I guess I started to cry; I didn't realize I had until they started patting me on the back and telling me that it was all right and not to take them so seriously. The foreman had his back turned to us; he was shouting at one of the men — there are always reasons for him to shout. I remember thinking to myself that we could rush him; we could tackle him; we could all be on top of him; we could throw him into the irrigation ditch, and if he came up for air, we could push him down, all of us, and no one would know what happened to him, even the sheriff. He'd stay down, maybe. He'd stay down if we filled his pockets with heavy stones.

"I know it's not his fault, all the trouble Mexicans have in the Valley. He told me once that if he went away, and Mr. Long did, there'd still be trouble for us, the Mexicans; and I believe him. If only you could get all the big, rich Anglos together, and we could round them up, like cattle, and lock them up in a corral, and keep them there until they promised to read the Bible and obey Jesus Christ, not behave like the bad people Jesus Christ kept running into; then it would be better around here. I'm afraid that the Anglos are too fast, though; we'd try to round them up, and they'd run for their airplanes. Mr. Long doesn't own one, but some of the growers do. They have their own jet planes and their own landing fields. Mr. Long has an old plane; he uses it to spray the crops. He couldn't get too far in it. We could ride after the plane until it ran out of gas, and we could get him. But I don't think we'd get away with it. The other Anglos would be after us."

A minute or two later the big Anglo in his life drives up, makes repeated noises with his truck's horn, even though the boy is sitting in plain view on the ground right in front of the house. Just in case anyone has any doubts about anything, the foreman guns the motor several times. As soon as the boy gets in the truck, it is off — and even though the sun is out on a warm midafternoon, the red light Mr. Long has installed on each truck for each of his seven foremen goes around and around, as the wheels plow through the Valley's mud and inside a boss tells an attentive boy "what's up" for the day.

III

CARLOS: A BOY'S CLUES

W HEN SHE believes herself pregnant she tells her husband. She is not one to keep careful track of her periods, nor do they come regularly. She has never practiced any
kind of birth control. She "lies with" her husband often; men
are like that, demanding, and she obliges, not so much with
reluctance or even resignation but out of respect to "God's
wishes," which she further characterizes as "what is natural":
men with their demands, women with their sense of obligation. Not that she is a cold person, uninterested in sex. She
wishes that the priest did not condemn sex as he does sometimes during confession. She had once admitted the exhaus-
tion she feels at the end of the day: eight children, and a ninth
on the way. The Father had scolded her for self-pity, a kind of
pride, he reminded her, the sin of sins. She became, to her own
surprise, terribly upset; she fought back, defended her right to
complain about her life, and even wondered out loud how well
the priest could manage her daily responsibilities.

He had, of course, responded — denounced her in no uncertain terms. How dare she defile confession with such arrogance? Didn't she know that she was speaking to God; he was
merely an intermediary between her and Him, "a simple ves-
sel." She said nothing, but he would not let the matter drop.

She was contrite, but to no avail; he became agitated, determined, apparently, to make sure that he would never again be so challenged — and in the very bastion of his authority. Why did she keep becoming pregnant if she felt her children such a burden? God did not establish any particular number of children as ideal. God sends us souls — puts them in the bodies of infants, which eventually get born. But we are under no obligation to *seek* children; that would be a kind of lust, a kind of pride: the notion that with each child we have additional evidence of God's good favor. It may be that a family with one or two children has been graced by Him as much as a family of eight, nine, or ten children. If she is not happy with her children, if they weigh her down too much, *and* cause her to become rude and insolent in a church, when speaking to a priest, perhaps she ought examine herself very carefully then and there — and later, too. Perhaps she and her husband enjoy sex too much and really don't have in mind what sex ought be a mere prelude to — conception, birth, the presence of a child, who has to be nourished both physically and spiritually.

It was a fearful confrontation, one never forgotten. Now, two years and one child later, the mother can still recall the chilly mid-January morning: "I went to confession early; we had all been up with the sun, and it was exceptionally cold. We don't usually have such severe weather here in the Valley. I had a sore throat, and I was afraid I was getting pneumonia. I would cough up thick green stuff; I was barely able to stand on my feet for longer than five minutes. My husband told me to stay in bed; our oldest daughter could manage the other children. I said no. I told him I had better go to church; maybe a prayer and confession would help. He did not like that idea at all. He told me I would use up all my strength going to see the priest, and then he would tire me with his talk, and then I would come home even weaker. I laughed. My husband is a fine one to talk; when he meets the priest he is all smiles, trying to earn his entrance to Heaven! And when he left for the packing plant he made sure to tell me to send his best to the priest. I laughed and asked if he meant for me to be as truthful as possible. He laughed and said to be as truthful as I dared be!"

The visit to the priest did help. She came back feeling stronger. She came back to those waiting: a baby she is nursing, a toddler who is up and down all day long, and a three-year-old who can be still and reflective one minute and a tornado the next. The mother makes the comparison often: "He is like a weathervane, or like one of those Anglo growers — sometimes quiet, but other times not so: then we have to dig in and expect the worst. I worry about the boy. What will he be like when he is grown up? Will he be able to settle down and take orders and do what his father does, or will he be one of those men who are very unhappy, and go to the bars at five in the morning, before the pickup trucks come to carry people to the fields? My husband wishes they would close those bars down, but the growers own *them,* too. Whatever happens, they win; they get work out of men like my husband and pay them practically nothing, and if there are men who don't bow their heads and kneel before the Anglos as if they are sent by God, then the bars are waiting — and the drinks cost a lot. My husband's older brother is married to liquor. When he was a boy he was like my three-year-old son Carlos. My mother-in-law shakes her head when she sees Carlos; she says he will cause us trouble, because he will be like chili in the mouth of the Anglos, and they will get very angry, and they will 'spit him into jail,' she says. Well, first they'll spit him into the bars, I'm afraid. They don't want anyone in jail until he's either so beaten up he can't tell you his name, or he's become like a sour pickle in a jar — drowned in wine and beer.

"The police chief of the town used to drive my brother-in-law home sometimes. He took to him; he would tell my mother-in-law that her son was too smart for his own good — that was his problem, and that was why he drank. My mother-in-law didn't know what to say; she was afraid to say anything. He didn't care whether she spoke or not, though. One day (I was there) he told her that it's better that her son be drunk than be shot dead for trying to stir up a revolution in the Valley, like some 'smart Mexicans' have got it in their heads to try and do. My mother-in-law broke down. She cried so hard that the chief left right away. I started crying too. I wanted to be stronger, but I couldn't. My husband just stood there; he didn't say a word. Then he left, and I heard him working on the fence, cutting the wood with the saw. A little later he came in with the saw, and he said he'd like to cut off the police chief's head. My son Carlos was two then, and he heard his father, and he said, 'Yes, Daddy' — no more.

"Carlos wanted to play with the saw; and my husband let him! I was terrified. I was sure the boy would hurt himself. I pleaded with my husband; but he would not listen. The boy must learn how to use the saw, that's what he kept saying. And he taught him; he has been very patient with Carlos, and the boy looks up to him. When the boy sees his father, he stops whatever he is doing and waits for his father to pick him up, or take him by the hand to go do something. When my husband has no time for the boy, I know it's going to be a hard hour or two for me. My husband says that God has spoken to us through Carlos, that someday the child will be a strong man who is afraid of no one. I believe that he won't live long — if that is the kind of person he is going to be, he won't be spared. They will beat him up. They will drive him to the county line and dump him on one side of the road, and then the police from the next county will come and pick him up and they will finish the job. We won't even see him — the body will be thrown away, and we won't know where."

She shudders as she finishes her awful prophecy. She is surprised to hear herself talk like that, but she is also quite unrelenting. She has definite opinions about each of her children; she can't put into words what it is that prompts her to reach the various conclusions she comes to, but she is quite willing to take the significant step of putting her thoughts and intuitions into spoken sentiments: "I shouldn't say some of the things I do. My mother tells me to seal my lips, but my mother-in-law says no, go ahead and tell others what crosses your mind. I am not trying to persuade anyone. Carlos is Carlos; I had him inside me for many months, and when he was born, when my sister took him out of me, I looked at him, and I heard his cry, and I told her: He will be a handful of trouble, I know it. My sister thought I was delirious, but I wasn't. I have a child now in me, just beginning to grow, and I think it will be a quiet one. The last one, my little daughter — she is quiet too. In life there are periods of quiet, or suddenly there is much noise. So with children: quiet ones and noisy ones. A mother cannot expect that each child be the same. I look at some of my children, and I wonder how it can be that each of them has the same parents. But that is what the priest would call 'a mystery of God's.' "

Her eyes move quickly to the door; Carlos has wandered outside, and now he is back inside. She talks to him: has he seen anything worth looking at? No, he has not, he tells her silently with a shake of his head. Then he runs for his stick, which his father has made to resemble a sword. He waves the stick about and laughs as his little sister begins to cry. His mother does nothing to stop him or soothe the girl. She turns to her washing. She has an old-fashioned scrub-board, and she uses it with a vengeance. She interrupts herself occasionally for a second or two to stare at a picture of the Virgin Mary, which she has pasted on the wall in front of her. The Virgin's head is tilted slightly as she regards the Infant Jesus, and as Carlos and his sister continue a struggle of sorts, their mother tilts her head a bit. A sign, a sudden turn, a glare directed at both children, and she is back to work; meanwhile, Carlos has decided to stop showing his sister how wildly he can wave his sword, and instead is making machine-like noises and running his right palm over the floor, as if he wanted to dust it, yet not touch it. The girl is entranced. She is holding on to a chair and following him as if the chair means nothing; but were he to leave the room, she would fall flat on her face. Carlos stops after about three minutes and asks for some orange pop. No, that is for supper. Orange pop costs money, is not something that one fetches from the nearest irrigation ditch; he had better learn that.

The boy has gained what rest he needed by standing there, making his request for a drink, listening to his mother's refusal. He resumes, now with more noise, more energy, more activity. His sister begins to laugh, and doing so, forgets to keep her left hand on the chair. In a second she is on the floor. Carlos stops immediately but does not rush to her assistance — or begin to make noises of self-justification. The mother continues her scrubbing, but again tilts her head slightly, surveys the scene behind her, and in no time is staring fixedly at her husband's dungarees. The little girl had begun to cry when she hit the floor, but stopped almost before she started. She picked herself up and caught hold of the chair again. Carlos walked over and told her she deserved a carrot or a piece of celery — and he was going to give her some. The girl didn't have the slightest idea of what she was being promised, but seemed to know that her brother meant well, and so smiled. He, in turn, resumed his noise, and told the girl for the first time that he was harvesting crops with a machete of sorts: "Here I go, and soon all the celery will be cut, and you can have some. It's not as good as orange soda, though."

The mother smiles. Now she is ready to be interrupted. She lifts her hands out of the pail and holds them up in the air to dry — and begins to talk: "I don't care if you ever eat celery. I hate the sight of celery. I'd sooner eat a branch from the tree." Carlos is quite excited by his mother's remark. He walks toward her and tells her that she shouldn't say what she did: "A lot of people like celery." His mother forgets herself for a minute; rather than say what she later felt she ought to have said — that everyone is entitled to his or her preferences — she shouted out something quite else: "The Anglos are the ones who eat celery. None of us do around here. We get sick at the sight of it; we are reminded of all the sweat we lose taking the celery crop in. Sometimes I would be on my knees, cutting and cutting and cutting, and I'd see knives, knives: each of the celery plants becomes a knife as I cut it. With tomatoes, your father would think of hand grenades."

She is surprised that she has passed on that kind of information to her children. She tries to cover her tracks: she is only being funny; she is *certainly* not serious; she thought they would like her to play make-believe. Carlos became quite attentive when his mother spoke. She, in turn, watched him carefully. She was a touch unnerved by his silence, his watchful eyes, which would not leave her. Finally she had an idea: why not distract the boy and end an impasse that confused her. She picked up his sword, told him to resume playing with it — outside. But the boy did not want to go. He had visions of a field full of knives, a jungle of red hand grenades: maybe it could happen; maybe the celery could turn into knives and the tomatoes into grenades. Why not? Isn't it true that God works miracles? Isn't that what the boy has been told —

by his mother, more than anyone else? And if the miraculous should happen, what would they all do — his parents, uncles, aunts? The mother wants to tell her son to stop entertaining such fatuous hopes, but she is also intrigued with his questions and his implied conviction that there was some point to entertaining a military dream or two: "Oh, Carlos, you are like your grandfather. My father used to tell me, when I was a child, that there would come a day when all of us from Mexico, the Mexican-Americans of Texas, would stand up and tell the Anglos that we are leaving, we're going home, or else we're going to stay and be their equals, if we have to fight them to prove it."

The boy listens, then goes directly for his sword. He is not quite sure that he has understood every word his mother has spoken, but he is ready to join up with his ancestors, his contemporaries, his descendants; he is ready to act, if only someone will give him directions. As he starts marching, his sister again becomes his audience, his fascinated observer, his willing accomplice. She moves toward him, falls once more, but manages to crawl back to the chair and pull herself up in a matter of seconds. The boy turns to his mother and addresses a question to her: "We're ready to attack. When shall we begin?" The mother smiles, goes over to the boy, and pulls his head toward her legs. She holds him and says his name repeatedly: Carlos, Carlos, Carlos. She lets him go as she turns her head toward the Virgin Mary again. Then she moves back toward the pail. Her husband's pants are done, and she must take them out to be hung in the sun. The boy offers to help. He would like a pair of dungarees like those. He will have them, soon enough he will, his mother tells him. She is sad as she makes the promise, and in a half aside, addressed to everyone and no one, to the child, his father, the priest, and Jesus Christ Almighty, she laments: "So soon that I want to cry."

She crosses herself immediately: she has no right to self-pity. There are people who are much worse off — so why the melancholy and sense of foreboding? Besides, Carlos is such a vigorous, imaginative, resourceful, and, most of all, entertaining child. He will surely find his way; he is surely not doomed to the life his parents and grandparents have lived. Have not things changed in her lifetime? Her children will by no means have the same memories she has, and cannot shake off. As they walk outside, the sun strikes them: the baby crawling; the boy walking briskly, sword in hand; and she hesitantly, the pail of wet laundry held with her right hand and resting on her right hip. Even their dark eyes require a second of accommodation, so (as if graced with an excuse to do so) she stands still. She makes oblique mention of her volubility before it becomes apparent, then gives way to it: "I should not say anything. There are days when I wake up and promise myself that I will not open my mouth at all except to have some coffee and bread. But then one of the children gets me going; Carlos lately has been the one. He frightens me. He has such energy, and he knows too much for his age. He will soon be four, I keep reminding myself, but that is not an age of wisdom. Every day I seem to worry about Carlos. I find myself asking the good Lord what will happen to that boy. Now, look at him — how he waves that sword, and shouts at the sky, at the heavens, at the good Lord, for all I know. Carlos asked me yesterday if I knew any Anglo boys his age he could play with. I did not even know how to answer him. I should have said no, and let the child go on to his next question. But I hesitated, and he saw me hesitating, and I was lost. I told him that there aren't any Anglo boys near here, that the nearest are the sons of the police chief, and of Mr. Haynes, who owns the food market and the tractor company, and a lot of land besides. Carlos wanted to know if the day will come that he will go to school with them. I told him that I doubted it, that the Anglo children go to a separate school, and we go to our own school. Carlos asked what would happen if he showed up at the Anglo school, and had a few hand grenades on him, and threatened to throw them. I told him to stop talking like that. He laughed, but I was very upset, and I told him why."

She is not sure that she has the strength of mind and spirit to repeat what she said to her son. She wants to do it, for she became quite agitated when she talked with him, but she is afraid that even now, when the incident is a thing of the past, she will lose control once more. She has not, however, put the issues that came up yesterday entirely behind her. She hesitates, stares at several of her children playing near the house, resumes her account of the challenge Carlos is to her these days: "I can't really keep my hands on him the way I should. His father is the only one he respects; his father blinks, and Carlos stops in his tracks. I scream, and Carlos continues on his way. The boy's trouble is that he listens too much and sees too much. I divide my children this way: those who ignore a lot of the sadness around them, and so are happy, and those who don't, and so are unhappy. It is my own idea; I told the priest what I think, and he said I have a point. I told my mother what I think, and she said I had learned my idea from her — she used to say the same thing all the time. I told her I don't remember her ever saying that, and she said she used to say that to me all the time! Well, if she did, she was right!

"I worry about Carlos; he is not like his father. The boy loves and respects his father, but he is not like him. His father has never caused any trouble; he knows what will happen if he does. Two of his father's friends tried to tell the other men to join the union and fight the growers. They are both in jail. The welfare people cut them off too — their families. We all help; I bring some food over when I can spare it. This world is not very good. My husband tosses in his sleep; when he wakes up, he is covered with sweat. I ask him what the matter is. He tells me that he has had a bad dream. I ask him what the dream was about. He says nothing, nothing. I coax it out of him, though: the police have arrested him, as they did the others, and they are questioning him, and finally they start kicking and punching and slapping, and his hands are behind his back, locked up, and all he can do is take it, take it, and finally he is knocked out, and then he wakes up. The man who sweeps the floors in the jail, the janitor — he is one of us, he is a cousin of my husband's. He has told us everything that goes on. We all know the price we have to pay for speaking up. My husband knows; I know; but Carlos doesn't know. And I am afraid that when he does, he will want even more to fight the Anglos."

She looks at Carlos and shakes her head. But he does not at all appear to warrant such serious, even foreboding, concern. He is running in circles, chasing a bee. His mother decides that she must speak to him: Does he need to use the nearby outhouse? No, he does not. Why does she bother him with that question? He is old enough to take care of himself, he lets her know. But she disagrees, reminds him of his repeated "accidents" — which she also calls, lest he be too sure of himself, "mistakes." He frowns, makes for a tree, whose bark he has been systematically stripping. His back is toward his mother. He talks to himself: He will, eventually, cut the tree down; it is half-dead anyway, and it deserves to be done away with. His sister has crawled to his side, is enjoying the role of encouraging spectator. He gives her the bark, once it is removed, and she holds it for a second or two, then throws it as far as she can manage, a half-foot or a foot away. Her mother, so anxious to have her three-year-old son use the outhouse, makes no effort even to dress her little girl; it is hot out, and she is naked. When she wets herself, the mother may dry her with a cloth — or may not. Soon enough the skin will dry on its own.

The baby sleeps on a towel, which in turn rests on an old mattress, which is on the floor near the parents' bed. The mother washes the towel every day: "I try to keep the children clean. It's not something to worry about, though; children should be allowed to have fun and not worry about getting dirty. When our children grow up, life will be hard enough. Carlos is a little man now. When he was two, I told him that he must stop making me wash that towel every night. I told him I'd make him go without clothes until he learns how to control himself. He learned very fast. We had a cold spell, and he shivered. He begged me to give him clothes, and I did. He made no more messes. My mother was the one who taught the older children. She is very strict. She would spank them until they learned to do what she wanted: keep their clothes clean, lower their heads when spoken to, move out of the way when a grown-up comes near. My mother still wants to bring up my children; she has delivered three of them, and they are hers, I often catch myself thinking. The children are afraid of her; they think of me as an older sister of theirs. Not Carlos, though; he is the only child of mine who won't even obey his grandmother. He is old enough to obey. My other children obeyed me when they were younger than Carlos. But he will be running, or throwing rocks at the tree or out toward the field, and if his grandmother tells him to stop, and come over to be kissed, he races toward her, stops before he gets to her, then races away. I think she is afraid he will run her down one day."

The boy is racing again, right before her eyes. His father is approaching; the boy wants to be the first one to greet him. When he reaches the father he looks up at him, says hello. But soon he lowers his head because his father has gently but firmly reminded him not to run quite so fast when approaching someone: the person may become frightened. After the father has stopped talking, the boy feels free to look up again, walk by his father's side. But not for long: he moves away, shouts the word "Indians!" several times, runs off — only to return and quiet down considerably. The mother explains the child's interest in Indians: "He wants to be an Indian. He has told me several times that Indians are strong people, and they have horses, and they ride them fast. He was told by one of his older brothers that the Indians still have not lost all their land to the Anglos. Carlos has not forgotten that. I think he pictures himself, even now, owning a horse, and a gun, and defending all of us against the Anglos. That is why I worry about this boy; I am afraid that he will keep thinking of himself as an Indian — an Indian who fights with the Anglos and beats them. No one beats the Anglos."

Carlos, meanwhile, begins jumping, circling the house. He speeds toward a tree, tries to climb it, fails. He begins to sulk, brightens up, goes running after a chipmunk, to no avail. His father tells him that chipmunks are harmless animals, undeserving of a child's (or adult's) persecution. The boy is not quite ready to live and let live. He chases another chipmunk. Now his father raises his voice just a little, and makes the same point. The boy has caught the emphasis, has no further wish to carry on a discussion, never mind an argument. He walks toward his parents and stares at them. They are busy talking. He sits down on the ground. He seems lost in thought. Suddenly he is up and running again; he is jumping again and moving fast — an Indian on the move again. Every minute or so he looks at his parents for the smile or nod of approval they offer. Eventually he tires, of course; but he has had a good, active time of it, and he has prompted a few thoughts in his father, and his oldest brother, who is thirteen. The father is brief: "He is a boy who has fiery blood; but he will learn to be quiet. Let him have his fun now."

The brother is willing to comment on Carlos. "He is a fast one; he is always on the move. I wonder if it means

that he'll move north with the crops. I wonder if he'll get a
car and go from farm to farm — and do a lot of drinking.
They leave here drunk and they come back drunk. They
go to the bars before they are picked up by the crew leaders; or they go to the stores and buy as many bottles as
they have money for, and then they start drinking while
they sit in the trucks or buses. The way Carlos is, he'd go
out in a field, take a few tomatoes, go to the grower's
house, and throw them at his windows and go running off.
That's what we all should do. But my father is right; we'd
end up going to jail. They might even kill us. I'd like to go
into the air force. I'd like to learn how to fly. I wouldn't
mind being in the air force all my life. With a uniform, you
can be the equal of the police. No sheriff is going to push
you around too much if you have an air force uniform on.
Maybe that's what Carlos will be — a pilot. He's as fast as a
jet fighter already, and so he'll probably want to get a job
where he can move a lot — and not always be picking for
growers and being cheated out of everything by them."

Carlos is not so sure; even at three he has his own ideas. He
would like to be a policeman. He would like to have two
pistols, wear them all the time, even when going to bed. He
would like to own a rifle, also; that, too, would be kept constantly near him. Who would threaten him, prompting resort
to that substantial firepower? He knows exactly. He takes pain
to indicate who are and are not his enemies. His brothers and
sisters, no; they fight with each other, and he with them, but
he would not want to shoot them. In fact, he has designs on
no one he actually knows. The enemy is distant, yet real, and
not the stuff of imagination: "The white man has guns, and so
will I. I would shoot the white man dead, if he came to bother
us. If he started kicking, I'd kick back. If he drew his gun, I'd
draw mine. But I could tell if he was going to pull the trigger,

and so I'd be first. That's the only way; be first when they come after you."

He has heard others say what he says: his older brother, his father, his uncles. He has the determination, even fierceness, they can feel and show to each other, but not yet the melancholy guardedness that they also know enough to express, yet struggle with inside themselves. He both delights and alarms those older people; they smile and even urge him on. They pretend to be "white men"; the boy goes after them; the father falls down and plays dead. But he quickly stands up, tells the boy that it is all make-believe, that in real life the Anglos must not be spoken back to, never mind be shot. The boy, of course, both understands and doesn't understand. He looks puzzled, disappointed — the game is over, though why he is not sure. His mother takes up where her husband has left off: "The Anglos have the guns. They own land. We work for them. If we get into a fight with them, we will lose. There is no point standing up to them, when you know they are sure to win in the end."

Carlos isn't able to comprehend all the implications of his mother's admonition, but he does see the look on her face — no smile at all and eyes wide open; he also hears the gravity of her concern in the voice she uses on such an occasion. And he has the additional benefit of his older brother's rather shrewd way of making social and political judgments: "I tell Carlos that he'd better learn to hide his guns because the Anglos are careful; they keep their eyes on us. They even steal from each other; there are only a few rich Anglos. If you are an Anglo and you don't own a ranch, or a factory, but work for someone else, then you have to be careful. Carlos goes bang, bang, bang all the time. But when I give him a look, he knows I am annoyed with him. He tells me that I'm his brother, and not an Anglo, so I shouldn't be afraid, because if I was an

Anglo, he'd go put his gun under the bed, and hide there. I don't like to see my brother getting ready to hide; I'd rather see him afraid of no one. But if that's what he learned — to look everyone in the eye and to speak back, if anyone insults him — then he'd be in jail before long, and they don't treat you well there. Jails are the places Anglos use to remind us that we'd better watch our step."

Carlos is not altogether impetuous; he watches his step, even at the age of three. When he goes to the store with his mother, he is quiet, obedient, obliging. He stares at the Anglo sheriff quite intently. He talks about that sheriff only later, in the privacy of home, and even then in hushed awe: the sheriff's pistols; the bullets one can see on the sheriff's belt; and most impressive of all, the sheriff's car, with its roof light and siren. Carlos is still not as knowing and cautious as his older brother, though. For the brother, the prospect of becoming a policeman or sheriff is absurd; Carlos, however, believes that there is for him a very good chance, someday, of obtaining a position of power: "Even if it's not allowed, I might become a sheriff. I could make friends with one, and he could give me his badge, and his guns. He could go away and do something else. My father said that the sheriff would like to work for the growers; then he'd make more money. Maybe all the Anglos will leave here, and then we'd get the jobs. We'd be the sheriffs, and we'd have the land for our own."

The boy looks to his elders and receives from them the patronizing smiles of those who want to oblige a child's fantasy but who know better — and are made nervous by the discrepancy between a child's sense of what is possible and their own all-too-solid appraisal of the world around them. Carlos's mother describes how she goes about helping her young children become fully conscious of who they are — and are going to be: "When my children are small, I try to keep them as

happy as I can. Sometimes when I am holding them and feed-
ing them, I say to myself: it won't be long before this little one
has found out about Texas. These days, it is Carlos who must
learn the important news — that Texas is not only where we
live, but something more. I don't know how to say it —
Texas is what Carlos will have to bow down to! I teach our
children to respect older people, and to respect our priest, and
to respect Texas. 'What is Texas?' they ask me. I try to tell
them. I try to say that it is a country, or part of a country, and
it is owned by people, and those people aren't like us, like our
people. And if you don't own something, and others do, then
you are poor, and they are not poor. A young child doesn't
know about money, and a young child doesn't know about the
sheriff. If the rich growers don't like a sheriff, they get rid of
him. The crew leader told my husband that, and my husband
said that it made him feel good; he didn't know why. I think
it is good to imagine the Anglos fighting with each other.

"The worst time is when the children start asking me *why*.
I discourage them. I tell them please, stop coming at me with
questions. I don't know why the Anglos are on top and we are
on the bottom. I don't know why we are so many in this
country and they are so few, and they control everything. I
don't know why we all don't get together and start marching
down the road. One child tells me that we could win, if we
only fought. Another child says we wouldn't have to fight, just
stand up and shake our fists, and teach them that we are going
to be our own bosses. That is fine — the talk of someone who
is not old enough to work, not a man or a woman, but instead
drunk on a dream.

"Let them have their hope, though. I do not want to crush
my children with too much of the knowledge I have picked up
over the years. There is a nun I know who has helped me a lot;
she has made me a better mother. She will tell me what to say,

how to answer questions. I used to argue with her. I used to
say that I shouldn't say anything. But she won me over. She
made me see that I can't ignore my children and hope that
they stay out of trouble. After all, my mother always took me
aside when I was a small girl and told me things. I recall her
lowering her voice, almost to a whisper; and I would go away
and think about what she said. Now I do the same; I call Carlos
over to me, and I tell him that he is a strong boy, and he will
be a strong man, but he must not say bad things to the Anglo
foreman when he walks near, and he must not wave his toy
gun around and promise to kill people — the sheriff. There is
a good chance that the sheriff would laugh, if he heard Carlos
threaten him, but there is just as good a chance that the sheriff
would begin to wonder what is going on. He and his police
come through here once or twice a year; they go from house
to house, 'just checking,' they tell us.

"I remember a year ago, the sheriff saw a toy pistol, and
picked it up, and pretended it was real. He asked the children
to put their hands up. They saw he had the toy in his hand, so
they laughed. He repeated his order. They still laughed. Then
he got angry. He threw the toy on the floor and shouted at the
children to get against the wall and put their hands up. They
did too — right away; even Carlos, only two then, knew that
he had better do exactly as told. I was afraid the sheriff would
pull his guns, but he didn't. He just kept his hands on them and
gave us a lecture: don't we know who's boss, and don't we
know how to obey the law, and don't we know how to stay out
of trouble, and from now on he's going to keep a special eye
out for us, and we'd better be ready at any moment for him
to come around, or one of his deputies, and when they do,
we'd better not get fresh, or we'd all spend the night in jail,
and he'd put us in one cell, and we could stay on the floor and
have bread and water, and nothing else, because he doesn't

believe in spoiling prisoners. Then he told the children that he was 'only kidding!' "

She stops, not because she has nothing more to say but because she can still remember the terror (and rage) she felt that day. It was not the first time she had been afraid that the sheriff would hurt her; but it was the first time he had stood there, right in her house, and lined up her children as if they were common criminals. Until then the police and their boss, the sheriff, were men who showed up while she and others were on their knees, picking vegetables. The mere sight of them was enough to keep everyone in line for a good long time. Now she wondered if her home would be invaded again.

A spurt of labor-organizing activity (it failed) had prompted an assertion of the growers' power — as a result of which a thoroughly uneducated woman, with no interest in political action, no urge to organize her neighbors and friends, was moved to point out what she thought the police had in mind when they paraded themselves ostentatiously up and down the land of various growers, or entered a home like hers: "The police are scared too. Everyone is scared. I don't tell my younger children that. My older children, yes; I want them to understand, because if you do, you will be less likely to get into trouble. If you know that the sheriff is afraid that we might one day all turn on him and that even a whole room full of bullets won't be enough to stop us, then you will take care not to get him nervous. When he gets nervous, he starts using his siren and carrying a rifle. One of my daughters asked why he carries a rifle and wears two pistols on his belt, when he only has two hands. I told her that even pistols and rifles don't give one an easy conscience. That is what the priest has taught us, and he is right. My daughter is ten; she could well understand what I was trying to say. But Carlos, all he knows is that the sheriff has both rifles and pistols, and he has a radio in his car that sends messages all over the place, and he has a light that goes around and around, and a badge, and a club. I think Carlos would give up his soul to the sheriff (the way the priest talks about selling your soul to the Devil) if in return that club was left here just one night. Once the boy asked me if there wasn't some way I could persuade the sheriff to let us have that club of his, and I told him no. Then Carlos said it must be because we're bad, and the sheriff doesn't trust us — that must be the explanation.

"Well, I went to the priest. I did not want any of my children, even one so young as Carlos, thinking we are bad. The priest had no patience with me. He reminded me that we are all sinners, and it is foolish to expect that we will forever be able to persuade our children that we are as perfect as Almighty God. But I was worrying about *Carlos,* not all of my children. I thought it was too young for him to feel so disappointed in us. I think he is too young to see the sheriff come into our house and treat us like animals, like mice or rats. Carlos would go around 'making believe' he was shooting at the sheriff and bragging to his friends that he had killed the sheriff, if I didn't make him stop. I had to tell his father, and he had to take Carlos by both his hands and look him in the eyes and warn him: No more. Later Carlos asked me in a whisper: why don't we 'really' shoot the sheriff? Didn't he come here and tell us he'd shoot *us?* Yes, I said, that is true — and that is the reason you can't play as you do. He might come here again, and hear you, and the next thing we will all know, they will come and take the whole family to prison.

"They will call us 'suspicious.' They will say we are union troublemakers. That will be the end of us. Once they arrest you, they never leave you alone. They watch you. They keep scaring you. What they really want is to send you to the next county, or back to Mexico — to any place out of the state of

Texas, that's what they've told people. They drive you to the county line, and say good-bye, and say *stay away!* Carlos has got to understand that he can't just pretend to shoot the sheriff, and laugh about how dumb the sheriff is because he has three guns on him but only two hands to use. Some children can play a game like that, but not ours. We all have to seal our lips; the Anglos keep a close watch on us, and they look for clues: the words of our children! I hope the sheriff's sons have a good time saying they'll aim their toy pistols at their father! I have heard Anglo children say things that I wouldn't believe any child, anywhere, would ever think to say!"

IV

FORBIDDEN PLAY

CARLOS'S MOTHER has heard those Anglo children say various things because for a time she worked in a grower's home as a maid. She obtained the job because her sister has an even better job; she cooks for that same grower. Soon Carlos's mother quit because her niece wanted to work with her mother. The niece works hard: helps cook when there is company or on a holiday; dusts and sweeps. The niece's name is Francesca; she is twelve years old. She dropped out of school at the age of ten. The girl was encouraged to leave school, as she vividly remembers: "I was told that it's a waste of time to be in school. The teacher said so; the principal said the same thing when I went to her office. They told me I should only go to school if I thought that I was going to use my education. But I wouldn't be doing that, they said; I'd be in the fields. I fooled them though; I'm in this house, and it's a good place to be. The lady is nice to us. She lets us eat all we want. She buys special food for us. She says she doesn't want us eating Anglo food — milk, fruit, meat. She wants us to eat chili and Cokes and all the bread we want. I have tasted some of their steak; it's good. They can't keep track of their food; they eat so much, and throw away so much. Once a week the lady tells us to throw away everything in the refrigerator, all the leftovers. She says they are good for the dogs; but if we want them, she tells us, that's okay too."

The thought of her boss's inconsistency troubles Francesca. She remarks upon it — the lady's claim that she doesn't want to "force" Anglo food down the throats of her "servants" and her rather casual weekly offer of the refrigerator's food, any food on the shelves. What sense is a twelve-year-old to make of the grower's wife? Francesca shrugs her shoulders, laughs: Anglos are, for her, "a funny people." But she knows that she doesn't really feel like laughing at either the Anglos or her own involvement with them. There are days, actually, when she wants to run from the grower's house, from the town in which she lives, from the county, from the Rio Grande Valley — from the United States of America: "My mother tells us that we are young, and we must be grateful for the life we have, and look forward to the years ahead of us. But I will hear her crying to herself. If I try to ask her what is wrong, she turns away. She does not want to talk with me. She points to the door, and I leave very quickly. Once I just stayed there. I didn't say anything; I stood and waited. But she did not want me there. She pointed again and I left. I decided to go peek, though. She would have been very angry, but I had to see. For a few seconds I thought she was going to go to the chair and sit. She kept staring at the chair. But no, she didn't want to sit. She went toward the wall, where the picture of Jesus Christ is, and she got down on her knees and prayed to Him. It seemed forever; she must have recited the rosary over and over again. Finally she got up, and I was happy. Her knees must hurt, really hurt, I thought. But she seemed to feel good; she went back to the stove, to cook.

"All of a sudden, she picked up the long wooden spoon she was using to stir food and started hitting the table with it. I was about to rush in when she stopped. I was afraid to move. I was afraid she'd find out I was there. I was afraid someone would come, see me, say something, and then she'd hear. I started praying to the Lord myself. But no one came; and in a minute or two my mother seemed her old self, so I pretended to be out of breath, and went back in. She wanted to know where I'd been, and I said I'd chased a squirrel for fun, and she said she hoped I didn't capture it, and I said no, it's impossible. I began helping her, and we made supper. When we were almost finished, she took hold of me and kissed me, and said she was *sure* my life would be better than hers, and I said I was sure, too, and then I tried to clean up the dishes we'd used. I knew she didn't really believe what she said, and I didn't believe what I said, either. But the priest is right when he tells us that you are a very big sinner if you lose faith. God can always change the world if He wants to. I don't believe He is going to interfere. I guess He is sitting up there, waiting for all of us to join Him. I hope that when the growers and their wives get up there to Him, He gives them bad marks and tells them that they're selfish people."

Francesca has learned with Anglos, all Anglos, no matter their stated intentions, to be quiet, even demure. Even when she talks with her parents about Anglos, she has to watch what she says. Her mother has taught her to be polite toward Anglos even when they seem to be far away. At home, as a young child, Francesca was punished for cursing Anglos: there is no telling when they might show up by surprise — and besides, when one gets into the habit of cursing people, a moment of dissatisfaction or anger can turn into a serious confrontation, with the winners and losers all too certain from the outset.

She can remember those early lessons: "I was nine and I was ready to go and march, when the union people came here. I was ready to go tell the grower and his foreman that they are bad people. My father heard me talking with my brother. My mother did too. They were listening in. I was swearing. I can't remember the words. I only remember my father's words: 'Don't let me ever hear you talk like that again!' I stood there, and I waited for him to go. I stared at the floor. When I heard his feet moving and the squeak of the floor, I knew I could look up. And there was my mother, ready to give me one of her lectures: 'Oh, Francesca,' she always begins. Usually she starts crying after a minute or two, and stops trying to say anything to me. I wait for her to stop, then I ask her if I can go, and she nods her head. But this time she didn't cry. I know I wanted her to; that way I'd be able to get away fast. She meant business, though. She told me how she has learned to smile at the Anglos, when she hears them speaking insults about us. She told me that she was *not* a coward; that she had the same hatred for Anglos others have, the same hatred the Mexicans had who fought the Americans a long time ago here in Texas; that she knew how to curse too. 'We have to lock our mouths'; I remember her saying that, and raising her voice, and coming toward me, and holding my shoulders with her hands."

Francesca has been moving her own hands, raising them a bit, letting them drop to her side. She notices her gestures, decides to stop; the arms go to her back, and her hands get firmly clasped. For a minute or two she seems to be obeying her mother's orders. She has nothing to say. Remarks meant simply to break silence, to make conversation, are answered with a nod, a shrug, no words. Suddenly she begins to talk. She is full of questions rather than comments, but she is not really asking anything of anybody — save herself. She is giving voice to old arguments and new realizations: Why should we keep silent? How long will it be this way? Will it ever be any other way? Is there *any* chance we will be able to get a better break here? Before there is an opportunity for reply, she shifts into quite another mood. She wonders what life is like elsewhere, and for others. Would she be going into high school soon, where she living in San Antonio? Would she end up becoming a teacher or a nurse, were she an Anglo? Do people like her always meet with scorn, or are there some parts of America, some foreign countries, where it goes better for those who speak Spanish?

She has heard, for instance, that in Mexico there are many people, millions in fact, who fare even worse than her family does. She knows that thousands of those Mexicans struggle to enter legally or slip across illegally into a nation she, as a young American citizen, already has severe doubts about. Nor can she understand why her own people are sometimes cruel to one another: the Mexican-American crew leaders, several of whom she knows and hates. And then there is the whole nation of Mexico, which she has heard described critically by a priest who goes back and forth across the Rio Grande: "The priest is always telling us not to be so hard on the Anglos. I want to spit in his face, but that is a terrible thing to want to do. I confessed to him once my thought, and he laughed and said he could understand how I feel! Then I wanted to go hug him! He said that the Anglos run Texas; they own America. But he said there are a lot of Anglo people who aren't much better off than us. And he says that in Mexico it's the same thing: you have the rich and you have the poor, and it's always the poor who outnumber the rich.

"Mexico is bad for a lot of Mexicans, and I don't think the Valley here will ever be a real good place for us Mexicans. I used to think that so long as there's one Anglo left in the Valley, we'd be in trouble. But now I accept the priest's words. If the Anglos left, all of them, a few of our own people would take their place. The crew leaders would run things; they'd push on us and shout at us, just the way the Anglo boss and his foreman do. The other day I heard one of our crew leaders fighting with a man; his name is Sanchez, and so is the crew leader's. And that crew leader, he called the man Sanchez who was cutting lettuce a 'dirty Mexican,' that's what I heard. I wanted to go kick that crew leader and spit at him and throw a rock in his face. I was standing there with my little brother, and I was going to leave him, and run toward the crew leader and at least say something, but I decided I'd better stay out of trouble. There was a big rock near me, and I stood on it; then I wouldn't be tempted to pick it up!

"My brother is only three, so what would he know. But he began crying. I couldn't figure out what was wrong. I asked him, and he cried harder. He wasn't wet. He didn't hurt; he said he had no pain. He must have seen how upset I was. He pointed at the two men and he looked at me. I think he was worried that they'd stop arguing with each other and come and bother us. I took him and started going away, but he kept looking back, and then I knew he'd been frightened by them. The crew leader was pushing the man Sanchez, but he didn't fight back. The crew leader was drunk. I was glad to get away from them and I was glad when my brother stopped crying. It was really strange though; my brother picked up a rock himself, once the men were out of sight, and he threw it in their direction. I couldn't figure out why he wanted to do that — unless they scared him. When I got home and told my mother what had happened, she shook her head and said no, my brother also knew what was going on, and he had the same idea I did, only he didn't know enough to put the trouble out of his mind. 'But Mother,' I said, 'I didn't forget what I'd seen either!' She said she knew that I didn't, because I never forget anything!"

Her three-year-old brother doesn't easily forget the incident either. As his sister talks with his mother, he takes a piece of wood in his hand and holds it up and aims it and makes his noises: bang, bang, bang. Silence; then he repeats himself with the triple fusillade. Now the mother and sister take notice. The mother tells the boy to stop. He does for a minute or two, but resumes with a longer outburst than before, as if to make up for lost time. The sister steps in. She does not rely on words; she walks over, smiles at Eduardo. She kneels on the floor. He looks right at her and she at him. He smiles; she does too. "Hold your fire," she says to him. He both knows and doesn't know what she means. He knows that she, also, wants him to stop shooting, stop making noise. He knows that she is more earnest, direct, affectionate with him — that, in certain respects, she is his mother, the one he spends a lot of time with, the one who cares for him, feeds him, tries to keep him clean, and now, as is the case so often, tries to get him to behave. His mother says *behave;* his sister comes to him, smiles, tickles him, promises him a later reward. If his father is there, however, neither his mother nor his sister asks much of him. His father says *Eduardo,* raising the voice just a bit, and the boy knows that it is best to stop what he is doing and, usually, leave the room.

The father is not there, though; the mother is the one who now goes out to fetch the clothes drying in the midday sun. The sister feels free to go on at some length, even if she is by no means convinced that her brother actually understands her words: "Don't keep shooting, Eduardo. It makes people nervous." The boy listens but is not impressed. He gets ready to shoot again. But he hesitates — as if waiting for his sister to intervene, if she wishes. She doesn't, however. She stands still, says nothing. So it is bang, bang, bang, again. The boy is triumphant; he has won his sister over and shot the enemy dead. He says so in his brief but pointed way: "We killed them." The sister is both delighted and worried: "Yes, we did; that's good. But there will be more of them, you know, Eduardo, always more." The boy can't at all figure out why she talks like that. He looks at her quizzically. He doesn't say anything, but his eyes scan her face: tell me what you know that not only prompts you to make a factual prediction but obviously affects the way you feel. She responds — not sure the boy will understand her every word but anxious to let him know of her apprehensions: "Eduardo, you will grow up and learn who has guns and who doesn't. Guns cost money. Even if we had the money, we'd have the sheriff and his men here, if they thought we had guns. I once heard the foreman telling his boss that he doesn't like to see any Mexican with a gun, even if the Mexican just wants to go hunting. The foreman said he doesn't even like the crew leader to have a gun because he's a Mexican. But the crew leader does; he carries it on him all the time."

The boy has had enough. He is not quite following his sister, though he realizes she is speaking seriously and therefore it is best to keep quiet, pay attention. Nevertheless, there are limits to a child's patience. Eduardo races across the room, pretends to hide behind a chair. His sister is a little confused: why that act? He soon enlightens her; he asks her to come over there with him. She refuses. She asks him please to come back toward her because she has a piece of candy she wants to give him. No, he has every intention of keeping his distance, of staying exactly where he is. Bang, bang, bang, he goes; then silence from him and his sister — a struggle seems to be going on between them: who will speak first? The boy does. He asks his sister whether she is mad at him. No, she is not. She simply wants to know what he has been shooting at. He is quick to tell her: the sheriff! She breaks into a strong laughter. She abandons her previous point of view; she is with him, completely. She says *good,* and she starts pretending with him: "Eduardo, did you get him, did you?" Eduardo is quick to join her in this new phase of a game. Yes, he did get him, but he's not sure

that the sheriff is dead, so he'd better shoot again. His sister
becomes a military ally, or tactical adviser; she also becomes
a shrewd teacher — someone who helps the young boy realize
the seriousness of his struggle: "Eduardo, we had better go
outside and hide; the sheriff won't just sit someplace, waiting
for you to come and shoot him again."

The boy doesn't need any further explanation. He runs outside, followed by his sister. They silently cross the field, headed
toward the dusty, unpaved road. The boy says the sheriff may
be in his car, nursing his wounds. ("He's trying to get better.")
The girl says that he's used his radio, called for help. They had
best keep moving, see what happens next. The boy goes along,
happy and excited by his sister's willingness to be a partner of
his. They stop eventually near a tree, circle it, stand behind it
— huddled and serious. The boy is ready to shoot again, but his
sister puts her hand gently but firmly over his mouth; they
must hold their fire. A car can be heard approaching. They
draw even closer together, hold each other. As the car comes
nearer, they begin to pull apart, each curious about whose car
is actually approaching. It is the foreman's. Eduardo is again
ready to shoot, but his sister asserts her authority. She kneels
and tells the boy that they can run from their hiding place and
pretend to ambush the man driving the car, but they must
under no circumstances let the driver feel that they actually
mean to hurt him "in real life." She takes his right hand and
begins running slowly, fast enough for him to feel that he is
exerting himself strenuously against the foe. The car draws
closer, and they approach it, do their shooting, seem almost to
become Indians doing a dance. They hop about, make a circle,
keep up their fire — a cascade of bangs that vie with the noise
of the car. Suddenly they halt and stare at the road; the foreman has stopped his car and is getting out! They search his face
apprehensively. Should they turn and run? Should they ap-

proach him? They compromise, stand frozen. Their eyes have narrowed.

The foreman is soon by their side. He has a broad smile on his face, but the two children do not relax. When he reaches them he says hello, even tells them that the weather is especially good, and, receiving no comment from them, no gesture of acknowledgment, even recognition, he looks back toward his car. But he is not yet ready to leave. He pats the boy on the head, smiles at the girl, asks her whether she has seen the crew leader. She shakes her head. He takes out a cigarette, lights it, draws heavily on it, tells the children that there is no particular reason for them to have seen the crew leader. He adds: "If you do see him in the next few minutes, tell him I was around looking for him." A nod from both the boy and the girl. For the first time they each move — the boy to let drop his stick, the girl to change positions, inch forward, let her right arm hang loose, so that her stick is in front of her rather than held awkwardly to the rear. The foreman asks them what they've been doing. They are silent. He laughs, says one word, "playing," as if to answer for them, and turns to go back to his car. As he begins to walk, they begin to relax. The boy moves from his previously fixed position. He picks up his stick. The girl scratches her forehead with her left hand, glances at her shoes, resumes her intent stare at the man, who is now entering his car. When he is inside, but before he has started the motor, he lets down the window fast — it is electrically run — and puts his head out. He smiles at the children, tells them to have a good day, says he hopes they weren't interrupted by him, drives off — very slowly though.

The children follow his car with their eyes until it is out of sight. They say nothing to each other for a minute or two. Suddenly they begin an extremely active shoot-out. The air is full of their guns going off, aimed at the empty road. The boy doesn't stop until his throat is dry and has begun to hurt. The girl says she could go on longer but is also thirsty. They go back home, hand in hand, the girl telling the boy that she regrets that they had to stop. Next time she will bring a jar of water! The boy says he hopes the foreman *does* get shot someday. The girl says he won't — that the chances are he'll shoot some-one else, a Mexican instead. The boy asks why he'll do that. The girl replies that all Anglos are "gun happy." The boy again asks why. The girl says she will tell him later — but it is best, for now, to stop talking. The boy does not comply. He starts to answer his own question. He says that the foreman is bad, that he hits people, that he shoots them if they don't obey orders, and that he, the boy, might one day get shot by that foreman or some other foreman. The sister stops, just before their house, and says no, it will not happen. The boy either does not hear her or does not choose to indicate that he has. He starts repeating himself; he will die at the hands of a gun-man — perhaps the very foreman he has just met. The girl will not put up with such talk any longer. She grabs her brother, covers his mouth with her hand. He struggles to get free. She will not yield. His muffled noises soon stop. His kicking also stops. She lets go. He stares at her; he is at once angry and fearful. She turns away. She starts to turn around and walk away from her home but has second thoughts. She opens her arms. The boy quickly moves to her, and in no time she is carrying him inside — where she tells her mother that they have been playing, have had a good time, and are hungry.

As they drink a Coke, the boy opens his mouth, but suddenly closes it. He has noticed his sister's nervous talkativeness; she goes on and on, telling a series of stories about the people they have just seen, the play they have just had together. The boy knows that his sister for some reason is using her imagination rather freely, but he also knows to keep quiet. Soon he has obviously forgotten the immediate past. He is playing with his favorite toy, a Coke bottle. He makes it go around and around. He sets it up straight, then stands near it, throws pebbles at it, hoping each one will go inside. Slowly he stands farther and farther away, testing with great determination his ability to throw accurately. Meanwhile his sister has begun to relax. She stops talking, begins to sweep the floor. Every minute or two she casts a look at her brother: is he still engrossed with his solitary game? Yes. She can take for granted that her mother and, later on, her father won't hear what happened.

They have been told, she and all the other children they know, never to risk any conversation with an Anglo, never to let themselves play near a place where Anglos might spend time. The next day, when the sister was a good distance outside the house and her brother well inside, she reminded herself of her father's repeated warnings: "He has said that he'd punish us very hard if we ever spoke back to an Anglo — if we ever had anything to do with them. He doesn't even like us going to school: the Anglo teachers are mean, and they can get you in a lot of trouble if they don't like you. They can report you; they can pick up the phone, and the next thing you know, the sheriff is there, and some other Anglos, and they are looking at your house, and saying it's dirty, and your mother and your father, they're dirty, and no good, and you have to go leave. That's what happened to our cousins; they were taken away, and their mother cried and cried, and our priest tried to get the children back, and he couldn't. He went to see the bishop — he lives far away — and I think he helped out. They brought our cousins back, but they told my aunt and uncle that they should be careful, and not cause trouble, and not join a union, or it could happen again. My uncle works with my father. They both pick the crops. My father says: no one is safe as long as he's one of us — not an Anglo. That's why I was afraid for my brother to tell our parents about the game we played. If we told them that the foreman had discovered us and had kidded us, then I think we would have been punished very hard. I *know* it.

"It is bad listening to those teachers in school; but you have to watch out wherever you are. One of the teachers used to tell us that we could never fool her because she has an eye in the back of her head, and she can see us even when her back is turned. I believe her; I believe she has eyes all over the county, and she might suddenly show up here, and we'd be standing and shaking and pleading with her. One of my uncles decided that he had enough of the Valley; he woke up and got his family together and told them that they were leaving, right away. He stopped at our house and asked my father to come along. He is two years younger than my father, and he is still very respectful. He lowered his head when my father said no, he didn't want to leave. My uncle never tried to say more; he just put out his hand and shook my father's hand and said good-bye. My father told him to go see the priest before leaving. The priest told him to go see a priest in San Antonio, who helps people from the Valley. That was the last time I've seen my uncle and aunt and my cousins. I will go visit them, I hope — someday when I have money and can go to the bus station and buy a ticket. I wonder if my cousins are all right. I wonder if they can play games, make believe they are shooting Anglos without worrying. I wonder if it's forbidden for them to play — because the Anglos might see or hear."

V

A BARRIO GAME

HER COUSINS aren't doing so well in San Antonio. Francesca wants very much for them to be prospering, and unashamedly she acknowledges why: there would be hope for her too. But they have exchanged one form of hard life for another, as the uncle, Antonio, who insisted that they leave willingly admits: "Up here, no sheriff rides up and down checking on you; it is different. We are left alone — so long as we stay to ourselves. The police don't want to come here if they can help it. The storekeeper calls them when he is robbed, and they take half the day to show up. When they do, they give the storekeeper a lot of trouble. They threaten to close his place down because it's a fire hazard, they say. The poor man, he ends up pleading to be left alone. He'd rather be robbed than threatened by the police! He slips them a few dollars, and they go! That's justice in the city! I walk the streets here and wonder why I ever left the Valley. My brother was right. He is always right. I thought I'd show him what I knew, but I'm afraid that I didn't know very much!"

He pauses, seems about to resume, then indicates by his lowered head that he has nothing more to say. He has been in San Antonio for a year and has not found a job that lasts. He worked for three months as a short-order cook, but the restaurant closed. He has applied for many other full-time jobs, only to be turned down. He has resisted welfare with vehemence, turning instead to the church. He gets odd jobs that enable his family at least to eat. If only there were some large farms near San Antonio; then he could work at harvesting crops but live in the city, where (he feels) his children are getting a better education than they would have received in the Rio Grande Valley. He takes exquisite care of the house he rents. He weeds the lawn, hovers over the flowers, frets about a semitropical vine. When he can find no more work to do around the house, he volunteers to help the priests at the church; their garden needs the kind of affection he has for grass and plants. His wife will soon work; when their baby son becomes a toddler, she will try to become a maid. Then, at least, there will be a steady if small income.

The barrio where they live is, of course, not near the well-to-do section of the city, but there are buses, and she will be glad to take them, even if she will have to be away from early in the morning to rather late in the afternoon: "I wish I could find a good job," says Antonio. "I don't want my wife to work. She doesn't want to take care of anyone else's house. She wants to take care of us. But there is no choice. She will be glad to find work, and we can only hope that she finds a boss who is a good person. The Anglo women can be mean and spoiled and selfish. The Anglos have too much for their own good. My neighbor's wife works for a lawyer's wife. She is a big Anglo woman; she eats cake all day long. She goes to a bakery and buys a cake — after her husband has left for work — and she eats it up before he comes home. Once she caught my neighbor's wife eating a piece after telling her to eat anything, *anything at all.* The Anglo woman went crazy. She screamed and told my neighbor's wife that she was fired, and she had to go home right away. Then she changed her mind and said that she should stay, only she must never tell the lawyer about his wife's habit.

"The poor Anglos — they have more than they know what to do with. But ask them to give up a dollar for one of us, and they are ready to fight at the Alamo again! That lawyer's wife, she is always telling my neighbor's wife how lazy and spoiled the poor are. If the poor really wanted work, she says, they'd go find it. Instead, the poor demand welfare checks, and sit back and cash them and eat to their heart's desire. She is swallowing a big piece of her cake when she talks like that! Then she goes to the bathroom, gets a diet pill, and announces that she's going to lose fifty pounds in the next month. An hour later, another slice of cake goes down to her stomach. I am sure that she could swallow all my children, and there would be plenty of room for them to breathe and move around. I remember my oldest son coming home with a story he'd heard at school — a big whale had swallowed some people, and he had been tickled, and he coughed or sneezed them up, and they swam away. The Anglo woman must have a stomach that big, to listen to my neighbor's wife. But the fat Anglo lady has gone away now, to a resort in Arizona. She will come back thin, she says. She has already ordered dozens of new dresses. Our neighbor is sure it won't be good; the lady will hide food in Arizona. The lady buys crackers and eats them in front of her husband, but she knows where the cake is. He has his own life; he has a girlfriend. So he doesn't care. That is the rich for you up here in the city! I miss our grower and his foreman; they are tough people to work for, and when they get mad, you are in real trouble. But I think they are more honest. The Anglos up here, even the lawyers and businessmen — the priest tells us that they are all scared of each other, and they don't trust each other out of their sight. And I came here to improve myself!"

But Antonio is sure that he will do just that — hence his refusal even to consider (seriously, at least) a return to his former home. There are some people in the barrio who have fairly good jobs, by his standards. And no doubt about it, the city offers a certain privacy, a certain sense of remove from the immediate and overwhelmingly assertive political and economic authority of the Rio Grande Valley. Nor does he forget what he left "down there," though to his own surprise, at times, he manages to come up with nostalgia: "I wake up in the morning, sometimes, and I say to myself that this is no place to be. But before I am ready to go back to the Valley, I stop and remember. I remember the foreman with his guns. I remember the grower, driving up to us, and spitting, always spitting, while he leaned on his car and watched us picking his tomatoes. Then he'd whisper something to the foreman and go drive off — while the foreman stayed and started blowing his whistle and shouting at us: harder, harder, pull in more, pull in more. My back would be almost broken, and my hands covered with blisters, and I'd be covered with sweat, but they'd want more, and if they didn't get it — well, they'd get us. Some men would go back and forth, from the farms to the jail. They'd call them drunk, whether they'd had a beer in them or not. You learn to work as hard as you can; it's better than being inside, behind bars. But the weather is better down in the Valley than up here; not so rainy, and warmer. And you had more room; your children could go and play, and you didn't worry so much that a truck might come and run them down."

His children do indeed find life different. His oldest son is ten; he had stopped going to school at age eight, when he was in the second grade. A teacher had told his parents that he was very slow, that he was, in fact, retarded, and that he would never really learn very much. She had suggested to the parents that the boy leave school, go work with them in the fields. That way, she observed, the boy would learn how to do something useful, would make money, and would be a source of help to others. In school, it seems, he was noisy, overactive, and uncooperative. When the family came to San Antonio the mother took the boy, Luis, to the priest, who in turn took him to a school, where he was enrolled in a special class for older children who have not yet learned how to read or write. Luis began to do well in that class, and his parents were told that he was, actually, a rather bright boy, who had a lot of interesting things to say about the world around him. He was an *expressive* child, and they liked hearing that very much. So did Luis: "Once my mother called me to her. She was sewing. She said she wanted to talk to me. She said the teachers think I'm smart. I told her the truth. I told her I don't like the teachers. I'd rather not go back to school. It's a waste of time — repeating the capital of Texas after the teacher, and the capital of the United States, and the other countries. My friend, my new friend up here, he wants to be a pilot. I wouldn't mind being a pilot. But I'd rather be the chief of police, right here in San Antonio. Then I could give orders to the police. I could tell them to leave us alone here and go bother other people. I could send them down to the Valley, and they'd outnumber the sheriff there and beat him up. He belongs in jail.

"I won't ever be the chief of police. And you can't send the police from here to the Valley. My father always pours cold water on my ideas. He tells me I'd be lucky if I got a job selling in a store, or working in a factory. The chances are, I'll be standing in line for the welfare checks. Or my wife will. I don't want to get married for a long time. I'd like to meet a girl who is smart, and she can get a good job. If you work as a maid for a rich family, and they're good people, then they will help you out — they'll get you a job, if you ask them. That's what I've heard. There's a friend I've met, he's twelve, and he said you're better off looking for a rich Anglo family that needs the grass cut and the garden weeded and dug up than you are sitting in school listening to those teachers tell you how stupid you are."

Luis is, again, not stupid; and he has not been called stupid by his San Antonio teachers. Quite the contrary; they have tried very hard to encourage him about his academic future. A Spanish-speaking woman has given him a battery of tests and found him "superior." Nor does Luis talk as cynically to his teachers as he does at home. His father is quite cynical, and with good reason; he has had serious trouble keeping his head above water in San Antonio. The boy hears his father, repeats what he has heard. He is the first one to acknowledge how much he admires his father — despite all the hardships the father has had to face and has not succeeded in overcoming. Luis has only one criticism he feels willing to state: he regards his father as too kind toward his natural enemies. Luis has asked his father how he would behave toward Anglos if he had all the money and power they have. The father said he would be very kind — he would follow the example of Jesus and love people he knew to be, in a way, his enemies. Luis was quite upset; he told his father that he felt that the Anglos deserved less. The father said nothing. The boy prodded him. The father became angry, said *basta!* no more talk about a fantasy rather than a real possibility. Luis nodded, left for the street, his friends, a game of war.

Those games of war take place every day: us against them, Chicanos against Anglos, the barrio against other barrios, the Chicanos of Texas against the people of Mexico — but most often, Spanish-speaking boys against imaginary Anglo boys. If only the latter were there in the flesh, then there would be a time: "We'd go after them. We'd even give them a head start:

let them make the first move. We'd dare them. We'd trick them. We'd surround them. They'd have to surrender. If they refused, we'd move in. They'd be all through, all through. They wouldn't know what happened to them. Even if we went to fight on their streets, even then we'd win. The reason Anglos are on top — it's because they tricked people, and shot them, and did everything dishonest. That was our mistake. We gave in too easily. We weren't tough with them. My father says we should love the people who spit on us, but my friends say that's the trouble, a lot of people like the Indians trusted the Anglos too much, and it did them no good. They lost everything. That's what the Anglo teachers don't like to tell you. They admit that the Indians lost most of their land, but they tell you it was only right because there wouldn't be the America we have if the Indians had been allowed to sit there and do nothing. One teacher kept telling about 'the trouble with the Indians' and 'the trouble with us,' my people: we sit back and do nothing, while the Anglo, he's always building up the country, and now it's the strongest, richest, best country in the whole world. I guess that's true. I don't like to hear the teachers talk like that, though. They seem to be saying that they're good and we're bad."

He returns to the imaginary game, the large-scale struggle between mortal adversaries that he and his friends play. They picture themselves older, and with guns. They picture themselves in downtown San Antonio. They meet the chief of police, walking down the street. They stop him, ask him to come talk with them. He says no. As he begins to reach for his gun, they surround him, tell him that he either comes with them into their car or he dies immediately. He complies. They drive away, keep driving to a deserted area, stop the car, get out, begin to talk. The police chief cannot understand why they are troubled. He keeps begging that he be let loose. They tell him that the police are unfair to their people; in their own language they list many grievances: a high rate of unemployment; poor jobs; insulting schoolteachers; streets that are unpaved; whole neighborhoods denied adequate sanitation and drinking water. The chief is indifferent; he simply wants his freedom. He makes a final demand: let me go, or there will be a high price to pay. They tell him they are quite ready to die, and will not be intimidated. He realizes they are serious. He begins to agree with them. He tells them that they have a point, several points. He tells them that they are right, that he regrets not acknowledging so earlier, that he intends to repent his ways. He will hire many more of their people; he will try to bring about various changes in the way justice is done in San Antonio. He will, in short, be a friend of theirs and will enlist other friends.

The particular words used may vary, but the drama that Luis and his neighborhood pals go through again and again remains quite constant: "We play 'police chief,' that's the best game. One of us becomes the chief, and the rest of us have got to capture him, then persuade him to join up with us. If you're the police chief, you have to fight back, but after a while you begin to see that you've been wrong, and the guys who have captured you are right. They've got to argue you down, but you aren't dumb, and you're not completely bad, so they get to you after a while, and then you make your promises to them, and that's the end. We used to have the chief escape sometimes, but mostly we don't anymore because you've got to convince him to change sides, and the more he escapes, the harder it will be, and we don't want him to escape. Why should we let him? There are a lot of us; he's only one. If we let him trick us and get away, the teachers would say: You see, you guys are lazy, and you're not quick enough; you're dumb, compared to the Anglos. That's what they say in school, and they give us a smile, and look at the clock: how much more time until we can leave and get out of here and go over to our side of town, where the smart Anglos live?"

Occasionally Luis doesn't want to think about that game. The same holds for his friends of nine or ten or eleven. They are a band of boys who now and then favor what they call "the real thing." They leave the barrio and work their way toward downtown. They walk, or they persuade an older brother or sister, rarely a parent or aunt or uncle or grandparent, to give them money for a bus ride. When they arrive at their destination, they are excited, curious, active, happy. They move fast; they stare intently at a store window, abruptly become bored, move on. They especially are drawn to stores that display men's clothing, musical instruments, posters advertising travel abroad. They are also taken with various automobiles they find parked. They can gaze in windows for two or three hours straight, or examine car after car. They show no apparent desire to enter any store, even the one whose display holds their attention the longest. Finally they decide to go home: they will be missed, and will be punished, unless they appear at such-and-such a time.

On the way home they begin to think of games they might play later on that day or the next. They will, for instance, break into a bank, leave with a lot of money and a policeman as hostage. He, too, will be won over to their side and will help them escape to Mexico, where they all will live in comfort, joy, and self-respect for the rest of their lives. Or, less ambitiously, they will venture into a music shop, convince the owner that they are truly extraordinary musicians, come home with drums, a banjo, a clarinet, a harmonica, some records and a hi-fi set. Their families will rejoice — especially when told that those objects were gifts and not stolen. Or maybe they will go into a clothing store, be promised jobs when they get older:

salesmen. With the jobs, of course, go a wardrobe: suits, jackets and slacks, shoes and socks. Everyone they know will envy them! They will move elsewhere — but return to visit their families. They might even get similar jobs for their brothers, cousins, good friends.

There are other times, however, when they all become moody, distracted, sullen, resentful, and exceedingly quiet. On the way home they speak monosyllabically, if at all. Once, on such a day, Luis said not a word from the moment he got on the bus in downtown San Antonio until the moment, a half-hour later, he got off another bus — back in the barrio. It was then that he muttered, to no one in particular: "It's not fair." One of his friends asked him *what* wasn't fair. Luis shook his head, and could only say: "Everything." No one felt it necessary to ask that he be more specific.

VI

GROWING UP CHICANO

WHEN A BOY like Luis has made that kind of remark, he has indicated a judgment about life in general and himself in particular. He has declared himself part of a landscape of hopelessness and injustice. He has decided that he is entitled to go beyond his own experiences and arrive at a more general statement about the world — *his* world. In so doing, he obviously sets severe limits on the amount of luck that is possible, and he states his conviction that the future is quite predictable not only for the person he knows best, himself, but for others like him. There is a decisiveness to his remark, a lack of qualification that becomes a finality: "everything." Nor would he hesitate to make a few sweeping sociological or psychological generalizations about others. He knows, already, the condition of his "people," the nature of his fate. When challenged, and he has been, the result is a brittle truculence: this I *do* know, and best not to differ with me.

Chicano children are brought up, by and large, in homes that with good reason could be called "authoritarian" and "patriarchal." Nor would any number of Chicano fathers (or mothers!) object to the use of those very words. Over and over again one hears a Chicano father insisting upon his obligation to be "firm," or "strict," or "tough." And mothers more than echo those sentiments. Often Chicano mothers remind their children that there is no escaping "Father"; he is boss, his word is law, and all others must yield to him in the event of any controversy. Not only does the father's authority go unquestioned; it is sought — and when absent, sorely missed. Mothers complain endlessly when their husbands have joined a crew of migratory fruit pickers or fieldhands. What to say to the children, what to do?

Nor do those mothers, with absent husbands, gain and assert their own authority. In homes where the husband and father has become seriously ill or died, an uncle, a grandfather (or sometimes a priest) becomes the moral and psychological paterfamilias. In some instances, when the father is gone and there is no other man immediately available to help deal with a certain crisis, the father's picture has to do — even though it was taken years before, after the marriage ceremony was performed or while he was in military service. The child hears from his or her mother, "Father is over there, watching." The mother may attribute words to the man in the picture; may even say that she has prayed to God that He send a message from the absent father; may remind the child or children of other times, when "he" was there in the flesh — or of the future, when he will be there in person once more. Or the mother may go it alone, speak quite strongly and convincingly on her own — but then, later, collapse in anxious tears: how dare she assume prerogatives never meant to be hers! And not rarely, on such occasions, a child will cast a quick but obvious glance at the father's picture, or politely but firmly ask when, exactly, "he" will be home.

Are the Chicano women in such homes resentful underneath, full of an obsequious passivity that only masks other, less acquiescent, traits? They usually say no; they cite their own reasons for standing back, letting their husbands have the final word — especially when it comes to disciplining the children. Men are strong — maybe foolhardy sometimes, maybe stubborn and all too self-satisfied; but children need such qualities in a parent — or so many Chicano mothers fervently believe. It will be bad enough later, they say to themselves — when the child begins to realize what is in store for himself or herself. Best to learn from a tough, unyielding, imperturbable parent a measure of stability, as a preparation for what will soon come. But why can't women have the same persisting, evenhanded, tough approach toward life and toward their children? Chicano women smile at such a question, however phrased, and shake their heads. No, one hears repeatedly: "A woman is a woman, and a man is a man"; or "a mother is a mother, but a father is a father."

Mumbo jumbo — or so an outsider decides. But Chicano mothers stand by the words, mostly. They also make sure that they exert continuous influence on their children. As a matter of fact, Chicano mothers are extraordinarily close to their children, quite protective of them, and far from handmaidens of paternal authority. The father is regarded as the ultimate arbiter of conflict, but he is only rarely called upon for a decision or to inflict punishment. Mothers do the latter constantly, and with unblinking competence. Mothers may at certain times mention the priest or the child's father as the source of moral standards, but usually they stand their own ground and draw the line of *ne plus ultra* rather confidently: I am your mother and I know; or sometimes, interestingly enough, I am a woman and I know.

There is no provision in most Chicano homes for a father's day-to-day participation in the rearing of the children. Mothers breast-feed their children by preference. In the first months of life the father only rarely spends time with the child. The father often asks the mother when the child will be

able to look directly into another person's eyes: *then* it will be
time for the father to become more interested — only gradually, though. Once a day, perhaps, he will stare at the child in
hope that the child will stare back; if that does not happen, the
father will quickly walk away: too young, still! Meanwhile the
mother is constantly at the child's call. While the baby sleeps,
she will sing to it, pray out loud to God for its health and future
welfare. The baby, it is claimed, understands the seriousness
of the mother's activity because Chicano mothers quite often
insist that their children *never* cry while being serenaded or
prayed for. Well, almost never; if an outsider with his prying
statistical-minded incredulity has nothing better to do than
remind a mother that on X day or during Y month, during a
visit, the baby did indeed cry while the mother sang or spoke
to the Lord, Jesus Christ — then pity that outsider! Perhaps
he needs to hear someone sing to him or pray for him!

Chicano children (one keeps on adding "mostly") are
weaned rather slowly, toilet trained casually, and not hustled
out of infancy or early childhood. The mothers are not especially sensual or indulgent, however; they possess a balance of
affectionate concern and detachment that is remarkable
— and has to be compared with the maternal attitude one is
likely to see in rural black women of the South. The latter
often vacillate between unrestrained emotional generosity
and severe, forbidding aloofness. They have felt terribly excluded and scorned and want to let their children know that
they, too, will feel that way. In contrast, Chicano mothers,
however poor, feel principally desperate and fearful for their
children. They turn to Mexico, and even Spain, in comfort: we
came from those countries and so are not without our quite
explicit national and cultural roots; if need be, we can cross the
Rio Grande once again and escape the sheriffs, though not
extreme poverty. Moreover, they have the Spanish language,

a constant reminder that one is not hopelessly Anglo, that one has one's own words, one's way of putting things and regarding the world, and, not least, one's privacy and independence. No wonder many Chicano mothers, who can speak English easily, if not fluently, and who know full well that their children will be going to Anglo-run schools where English is the only or certainly the preferred language, choose to speak Spanish not just to their young children but, it often seems, *at* them — as if the sound of the language will itself be reassuring. And, too, the language offers the mother a sense of herself to fall back upon, a certain reserve that causes the child to feel comforted and loved, yes, but at the same time aware of "a limit." One hears Chicano mothers tell their infants so — that there is "a limit" — even when the little girl or boy is not able to understand what is actually being said. The mothers, of course, are talking to themselves, reminding themselves that their children may well suffer in the future, but at the very least will not lose their language, their sense of a specific heritage: a religion, a nationality.

Chicano mothers are remarkably uninterested in giving long lectures to their children or punishing them in such a way that they will "never forget." The point is to be quick and, if need be, summary but not to hold a grudge or even belabor a particular issue. Mothers say "no" to their children, then change the subject, or pick them up, show them where they ought go to relieve themselves, and watch with satisfaction as the child begins to get the message. Eye-to-eye contact is especially important, and the child is picked up and held so that he or she becomes an "equal" of the mother's. Some advice, a reprimand, or an exceedingly brief speech is followed by a knowing look, a stare, on the part of the mother, reciprocated by the child. Sometimes the mother shuns all words. She points to what she finds objectionable — a puddle of the child's urine, for example — and quickly, firmly lifts up the child, looks at her or him intently; then, in a moment, down the child goes, and out the mother's arm goes, so that a finger can point to the proper direction and ultimate destination: a toilet bowl in a bathroom or, more likely in the Rio Grande Valley, an outhouse.

Later, at about the age of four or five, when the father becomes more significantly involved in the child's life, there is the same emphasis on a face-to-face contact: a look and a look back, often with few or even no accompanying words. Some parents, to an outsider, sound mystical as they talk about the eyes of their children. A mother says she need only look into her daughter's eyes for a second and "all is known between us"; and also with her son. A father maintains that he talks to himself more than he does to his children; that is, he wants his eyes to "say" what they ought to say, not less or more. By speaking to himself silently, or even, at times, out loud, he can manage to obtain for his eyes the "right look." Will any doctor ever be able to explain what it is exactly that he has in mind when he attempts to prepare himself (mind, soul, body — and, specifically, eyes) for a child by trying to obtain from his two eyes that "right look"?

Moreover, there is the matter of the hands, the uses to which they are put; the matter of touching. Chicano children are not often punished by slapping or being pushed or punched or otherwise hit — with a belt, a stick. An angry mother or father will scowl, frown, glower, will move toward the child, appear ready to go after her or him, but suddenly slow down, stop short of the young one's body, then approach it — but only to seize an arm or a shoulder and stand there, holding on tightly. In a moment the grip relaxes, the parent moves back; the point has presumably been made. And the child has a way of acknowledging just that; the child looks at the parent and, commonly, reaches for him or her. All the while: stillness. An outsider feels noisy, wordy, especially intrusive.

In so many Chicano homes there may be an undercurrent of singing, praying, laughing. A mother is apt to ask her children to keep the sound of the television set low so that she can hear herself. If one listens, she does indeed have reason to want a degree of silence; she is speaking, giving forth with music and laughter — and who better than herself to hear the words, the humor, the entertainment! Not that there aren't grim, sad, anxious moments, or outbursts of temper. But they are frequently more circumscribed than one might believe possible — explosions of emotion, true, yet almost unnervingly controlled, or *ritualized.* A mother leaves the house, stands outside, away from her children's sight if not hearing, and shakes her fist, shouts, asks God to curse someone. A man hits a table so hard that his wife is sure it has been broken. But the children know better. They gather round, say that the table will survive their father's clenched hand. Their father has not spoken a single word, but they know why he is angry. Even a three-year-old child does; she points outside at the crew leader who is waiting to take her father away — weeks, maybe months of harvesting crops. Soon the father is doing his best to say a happy, confident good-bye; and the children are doing *their* best: a hug, a kiss, and, not least, a lingering look.

How do those children learn to be so responsive, so knowing, so trustful — when, at the same time, they have also learned to be guarded and wary when it comes to Anglos, especially Anglo schoolteachers? Not surprisingly, the answer has to do with the transmission of knowledge, both factual and psychological, over the generations. Often it is the grandparents, the "old ones," who help in that regard. The parents are quite candid about their reason for turning to others far more advanced in years. It is a question of pride and, maybe, a matter of concern for the child's future. After all, as many parents quite willingly point out, the person who tells a child about Anglos and their power is also telling the child about Spanish-speaking people and their relative weakness or vulnerability. Better to have an old, highly respected person tell such news in Spanish — a person who has already lived a life and so knows how to put things in perspective, and a person whose integrity and honor have been tested repeatedly. Children are, in essence, told that by their parents, told to listen well when their grandparents speak to them about the world and its various devils. The parent is an announcer of sorts: soon your grandparents will take you aside, talk with you about a number of matters; pay attention, and remember always that they are soon to depart for God's kingdom, so their only interest is in leaving their knowledge with us.

If such a paraphrase seems ornate, formal, a touch overdone or pretentious, then Chicano people would nod and say yes, it is hard to move from one culture, one language, one historical tradition, to another. Chicano children are often surprised, indeed, when they hear Anglos of their age speaking to a parent or a teacher. How dare a boy or girl be so informal, blunt, outspoken with a grown-up! And how dare a grown-up permit such talk, be part of it, really! In home after home, however humble the building and uneducated the inhabitants, one hears Chicano men and women referring to their children as "sent by God," as possessing "the Lord's ears." As a result a mother thinks twice about what she says and how she speaks, as does a father. Yet by no means do those parents tremble at the sight of their own sons or daughters; or become self-conscious, prim, watchful of every word uttered. It is a matter of faith, really — an inner conviction that the child has not simply appeared out of nowhere and for no particular reason, but rather as an expression of a much larger scheme of things: God's grace. "Please God," the mothers exclaim when they are shown their newborn children — and not as a mere exclamation. And when a child first stands, and later on, takes a step or two, the words "thank God!" are meant quite literally, and are often followed by a recitation of the rosary, or when conveniently possible, a trip to church. The point is not to congratulate oneself — the proud and, by implication, successful mother or father — but to affirm a strongly held faith in "Almighty God, the protector of our children," a phrase a large numberof Chicano mothers know well and use continually.

Philosophers and theologians for centuries have discoursed on the polarities of transcendence as against immanence. The latter refers to the everyday life we all live, its rhythms, demands, opportunities. The former refers to those moments in which, somehow, often inexplicably, we exceed or surpass ourselves, reveal ourselves (sometimes to our surprise) as more, in certain respects, than we ordinarily appear to be. For existentialist philosophers (and novelists) who are not especially interested in the Bible and the Judeo-Christian tradition, interpretations of those alternative states of mind or being turn out to be strongly psychological in character. Still, the nature of transcendence for materialistic psychological theorists is at best hard to fathom: elusive if not thoroughly mystical. Theologians, of course, and novelists who are strongly religious in their writings find an immanent God at work in our ordinary, humdrum lives, and also a transcendent God who in unusual, demanding moments appears among us in the form of — ourselves, especially responsive or "called": instruments of an incomprehensible divine will.

Every day Chicano mothers call on God in the most direct and personal ways; call on Him for advice, for support; call on

Him not only for various favors but for the strength needed to help themselves and, of course, their children. Moreover, the spirit that prompts those daily prayers is a spirit that children come to know long before they have set foot in a school building. Mothers of the Rio Grande Valley show children love — however harassed as parents by poverty or fears of Anglo political and economic authority. Under the same circumstances fathers ask of children a respect for certain standards — control of mind and body, in accordance with the family's, the neighborhood's demands. But both mothers and fathers remind their children endlessly that there is a law higher than man's, and that there is a love that does not fit into the usual categories: love of parents, of brothers and sisters, of relatives, of country, of friends.

That love, God's, is also available to His creatures; or so Chicano parents believe, and so they tell their children — all of which makes God part of a child's life in a way that many outsiders might well find hard to comprehend and, maybe, of no interest, anyway. The considerable pride that many Chicano parents have and against great odds transmit to their children simply cannot be attributed to the workings of a "culture" or "ethnic heritage," unless such a word or phrase includes a strong Catholic faith of an especially vivid and tenacious nature. Nor will it do to dismiss that faith as "primitive," "superstitious," or as evidence of the ignorant desperation of a severely exploited people. For thousands of Chicano parents and children, the Catholic Church and its rituals are not an "opiate" or a means of evading "reality" but an important part of the world, an instrument, really, of self-knowledge and self-respect.

When a Chicano child is characterized as "proud," even by an Anglo schoolteacher in the Rio Grande Valley of Texas — a teacher who has no great admiration or respect for

Chicano children — the child's upbringing is, of course, also being described. The boy or the girl has apparently learned to have a healthy respect for himself or herself; has appeared unwilling to feel lowly, inadequate, hopelessly worthless. Nor is it a matter of an overworked denial — pride as a cover-up for self-doubt, if not self-contempt. Chicano children, however impoverished and frightened (when in Anglo-run schools), have a way of both looking down respectfully, yet impressing their teachers (and other Anglo adults) as unnervingly sure of themselves. One hears from those Anglos repeated protestations of confusion, curiosity, apprehension and, not rarely, envy: how is it that such children learn to be so self-contained? Often they are described as "locked up in themselves" by their teachers. One hears about the "arrogance," no less, of the children of Chicano migrant farm workers and the "strange manner" of those same children — as if, in a teacher's astonished words, "they actually believe they are superior to others."

Well, not quite; the imprint of poverty and social discrimination upon Chicano children is obvious and requires more than passing mention, especially when their pride is being discussed. In fact, the aloofness and uncanny self-restraint that some Anglo teachers notice in Chicano children are intimately connected to the attitudes those very teachers have toward the boys and girls in their classrooms. If Chicano children are regarded as poorly spoken, slow, hard to understand, uninterested in learning, not very bright or promising so far as an educational future goes, the children hear that judgment of their teachers expressed — perhaps a remark one day, a gesture or facial expression the next, but most often, perhaps, the everyday indifference of the teacher. A Chicano boy or girl does not need an outsider's confirmation of the state of mind he or she has developed toward schools and those who teach in them. That boy or girl has been listening and watching for weeks, months, years. The result, in that icy, abstract phrase is a certain kind of self-image. But frustration and despair are not necessarily victors, only strong contenders. Quite often the Chicano child fights back — does so, too, in a way that confuses, mystifies, even enrages his Anglo teachers.

The teacher gets cross, the child bows his head, but not low enough to hide completely a slight smile. The teacher makes a point, the child nods, even when the nod is affirming something quite unfriendly or harsh. The child looks back intently, uninterruptedly — a stoic gaze that falls short of becoming a glare. Surely such a child is peculiar, maybe retarded. In no time the judgment is made, not just privately by a particular teacher, but formally, administratively — one more "Mexican" who can't learn because he or she lacks the "intelligence." But how can a teacher who measures "intelligence" in children only by what they say, and how they say it, do so with any hope of accuracy when the children in question speak Spanish, not English, and even more important, though perhaps less obvious, when those same children have been brought up not to use many words, even in Spanish with their parents?

Chicano fathers look at the faces of their children and so come to conclusions about how they are feeling and what they are thinking. Mothers, too; they often remark that "a child's face tells a lot, a child's eyes tell everything." As those children grow up, begin to use words, the parents are selectively encouraging. They teach their children the virtues of silence; teach them to listen carefully before speaking; teach them that at the very least one ought to hesitate before saying what is on one's mind. God addresses us in strange ways, priests tell their Chicano parishioners; His words come to us, yet they are, of course, inaudible. So with Chicano parents; they tell their children that it is quite desirable to have thoughts — but keep them private. The issue, obviously, is one of degree; any child, any adult, has things on his or her mind that don't get uttered. But in the white, upper-middle-class world, children are often taught to "express" themselves, be "open," honest, forthright — meaning, usually, talkative, even insistently voluble. Some Anglo teachers in Texas or Florida or California have had the self-critical awareness to realize that the Chicano children in their classrooms regard silence as a state of thoughtful composure, even a moment of triumph. Let that teacher go on and on with sounds out of her mouth; I will give away nothing. Those same teachers will contrast that attitude with the one conveyed by Anglo children: I think this, or that, and I will let you know just about *all* I think, in no uncertain terms, if you give me the slightest indication of your interest in me and my ideas.

Shyness is part of the explanation for the degrees of reticence in children — *all* children. Some Anglo children, no matter how forward verbally their parents want them to be (or precisely *because* of such hopes on the part of their parents), very much resemble Chicano children — are taciturn, wary, sullenly observant. And some Chicano children are not at all reserved; are quite willing to stand up for themselves, state what is on their mind, shout, yell, blurt out opinions. But those children are usually regarded by their parents as in some way peculiar — though not in the contemporary, middle-class American (Anglo) sense of that word: a "problem" for a psychiatrist to unravel. A mother might go to the priest or to her mother and father, ask one of them why it is that an otherwise good child holds forth so much. Doesn't the child understand that he or she is a member of a family, a community, a people — and that "it is better to feel God's presence than drive Him away with words and more words"? So a priest spoke once, and so his parishioners speak at home, at the table — when food is taken silently, when even grace is a brief statement of thanks, when a child knows to bow the head and get on with the business of eating, and ask with the eyes rather than the mouth to be excused.

There are wonderfully noisy times, too. Children laugh and call each other names. Parents sing, complain, make fun of themselves or their children, cry, get exceedingly angry and make their anger quite clearly known. Again, it is a question of degree, of tone, of emphasis — and, really, of faith. Chicano children grow up to regard themselves as members of a particular community of people, a community under the surveillance of Almighty God, a community, it is to be hoped, suffused with the spirit of the Holy Ghost, a community that is poor and embattled and for the most part weak politically, ostracized socially, but nevertheless a community that is not at all beyond hope and grace, as Christ spoke of people from similar communities in the Sermon on the Mount. Teachers in the Rio Grande Valley often unwittingly tell Chicano children how different they ought be by asking each child to be "independent," speak up loud and clear for himself or for herself, prove to be no one's follower or imitator. The Chicano children listen — not indifferently or in uncomprehending silence, but with the intelligent sense of discrimination they have learned from their parents: how to make that familiar distinction of "us" as against "them."

The elements that make up the "us" of the Chicano child (especially well indicated in drawings) are, as with the lessons of all cultures, an amalgam of consistencies and contradictions — antinomies as well as harmonies. Chicano children are taught to be stubbornly careful, lest they reveal or betray themselves to the feared and hated Anglo boss, teacher, sheriff, storekeeper. Chicano children are taught to give not an inch on crucial matters: better to say nothing and be called dumb or have one's wishes or actions misinterpreted than to yield to the Anglos, give them what they want — words and more words. And then there is *machismo,* that often misunderstood word that is sometimes welcomed by women and daughters as well as fathers and sons: a collective strength of soul (rather than mind) that will, in the end, show those who are apparently weak to be in reality the strongest.

A boy is told that his teacher can call him every uncomplimentary word she wishes to use, but she can't "enter your soul" unless she is allowed to. If the boy were to join battle with the teacher, use her own weapons, and argue with her, try to defend himself with the vocabulary of self-assertiveness that she teaches — then he would be finished. Her might would prevail over his right. On the other hand, if the boy smiles or keeps a straight face — revealing no protest, however strong it is felt to be inside — then he is automatically the victor. He has proven himself to possess machismo; his teacher has talked, talked, talked, but to no avail. And so with girls; a young woman can be told that she is doing something wrong, that she is not behaving herself, yet she will sit still, stare at the teacher with just the faintest touch of a smile, and seem impervious to criticism, almost able to enjoy it. In the girl's mind, all the while, a mother's advice keeps repeating itself — especially helpful when the teacher's words become strident or accusing: "Our people can be stronger than 'they' are." The strength turns out to be a girl's machismo, her proven capacity for a kind of social, cultural, political resistance — the best she can do under the circumstances.

On the other hand, that girl, or a brother of hers, can be silent out of a spirit of resignation, taught by the same parents who encourage their children to be determined, self-protective. How can a child be at once full of determination, yet so resigned that he or she already prophesies what the years ahead have to offer — extreme, chronic poverty, a number of humiliating encounters with various Anglo authorities, early sickness, and, quite likely, an early death. Is the child "cyclic" in personality, given to mood swings that explain the alternation of postures: combative, then yielding; or strong, confident silence, then a mournful eloquence, companion of a growing despair? Or is the Chicano child trying like his or her parents to be simultaneously hopeful and realistic?

As Chicano children become toddlers, they are gradually, gently weaned, taught control of their body functions, encouraged in response to an elaborate system of cues to comply with the wishes of their parents. The father lifts his arm, the child must know how to stop, pay heed. The mother says *basta*, enough, and enough it is. The mother puts her hand down on the table — a noisy touch, but not a loud bang — and the child comes near, looks up briefly, then down: up to get the message, down to show that the message has been duly received, and now is being stored as an important experience, a future memory. But sometimes the signals or cues break down because those who use them are of two minds. A father becomes strangely irascible, even agitated. He drinks wine or beer; lifts his fists up, shakes them at eternity, it seems, rather than at anyone. The child is afraid, but senses that the trouble may well be with the outside world rather than in him or her, or in a brother, a sister. The child may well be told exactly that by a mother who wants very much to emphasize the distinction — a significant one indeed.

Many Anglo parents of more comfortable means find themselves at moments turning on their children unaccountably, or for reasons that scarcely seem to warrant an outburst. But that is life — there are arbitrary, difficult moments for all of us, and children must know of them. If those moments increase, become too frequent and too emotional, the story is different; all children have got to know, from the very beginning (as soon as they can interpret words, gestures, or signals), that their parents have a rather limited private psychological life. Every day there are serious burdens to contend with, and all too frequently there are tragedies. They are actual events, not only matters of symbolic importance; or rather, both at once. When a Chicano child knows that a father is outraged or bitterly saddened by the treatment he has received from a migrant crew leader or an Anglo foreman, an Anglo grower, there is good reason to be frightened: what will come of the father's job, never mind his emotions?

The child has, in fact, been taught to understand that there is a lot in this world beyond anyone's control — anyone in the family, in the neighborhood, anyone Chicano. The child also has learned that parents, that all grown-ups, must keep careful watch over their feelings; must find a safe moment to let them surface. All of which may seem like nothing much — the life of the poor, the life of poor children. But a teacher wonders why that child is so morose. The teacher has just reprimanded the child, perhaps, for being "uncooperative" or sullen. Suddenly the teacher reminds herself that it is a matter of degree; the child is always a bit solemn, somewhat inscrutable — as are, indeed, all Chicano children. The teacher is sure she knows that underneath, below the mind's surface, where we have been taught much of psychological truth lies, there is another child — troubled, angry, full of noisy complaints. It is a misrepresentation — the grim silence and the concomitant pride of "these children." Get to know them long enough, pay attention to them, and their "real" side emerges.

All very nice — for the Anglo teacher. She has simultaneously found herself to be both perceptive and patient and, in a way, quite justified with respect to her everyday behavior in the classroom. (She prods the children, tries to get them to "communicate," become more like Anglos.) But she has missed the point, failed to inquire what has been happening in the child's life, and so construes neurosis, or a "cultural block," from actions and appearances that are, in fact, utterly in keeping with events: no work, no money, the threat of no food — and trouble with a county official as to eligibility for food stamps and welfare. Which county does a migrant family call home? The county official has asked that question of the child's parents — with an answer ready in his mind before he listens to them. His decision: wait, while the matter is discussed; come back in a week. That week is a long one for the parents, and a long one for the child. The child's moodiness is the result: apprehensive concern — accompanied, it has to be added, by a growling stomach. No money means food purchased (at terribly inflated prices, compared to what can be bought for cash) on credit in a small store owned by a prominent grower, the very man who discharged the child's parents. This cycle, at once economic, political, and bureaucratic, has been described any number of times — the way a grower's needs for cheap, obedient, always available labor are connected to the way a county is run. But the profound and disturbing psychological consequences for a family and, especially, for the children of that family, are less obvious. Moodiness for such children is an accurate response to a concrete, ongoing, real-life situation.

No wonder the horse is so prominent a figure in the mental lives of Chicano boys and girls. They are, of course, children of the West. They are, too, living in a rural area or, if in the city, are recently arrived and have fresh memories of country life. Since they are twentieth-century Americans, they see airplanes over them, they ride in automobiles, as their parents move "up the road," to the next farm, and they watch others drive cars or motorcycles. But the horse still figures in their minds and is often used, quite openly, as a symbol of hope or promise, and also as a symbol of gloom. It is uncanny, at times, hearing Chicano children talk about growing up and having a horse. The children are seven or eight and are having daydreams. They would like to escape from the life they are now living. The girls often picture themselves carried off — by a boyfriend, or a favorite brother, or a boy cousin. The boys neglect to mention anyone else; they will ride off on their own. The parents may turn sad when such dreams become spoken: a pity that children should be so dissatisfied with their present life! The child may start with a motorized journey of the imagination; the journey takes him or her well away from others, with a view of hills or mountains, and always with a horse.

The horse is company. If the parents haven't been taken along on the flight of fancy, the horse may well be sole company. The child will feed the horse, give it water, and in return have a reliable, affectionate, hardworking friend. The child will also prove himself or herself quite responsible and self-sufficient; will find good pasture land, build a corral, make sure there is enough to drink nearby. And if, by some chance, any danger threatens, as it well might, the horse will be there, ready and waiting, able to take the child away across meadows and prairies, through forests or swamps, thereby thwarting the Anglos' automobiles and even airplanes. The lesson: one can escape, one can hide, one can be independent and self-sufficient. Very important: if the machine-borne Anglos can't ever really be trusted, and if one's own people can even turn mischievous or treacherous, then the natural world provides the only alternative.

On the other hand, there are dangers and pitfalls in escaping. Children who have good, objective reason to seek refuge don't forget those reasons, no matter how elaborate the escapist fantasy. Besides, the horse is not only a vehicle of flight, liberation, but a reminder of how desperate things were in the first place. Almost always the Chicano children have some reservations about their imaginary deliverance: how long can it possibly last? Not forever, they remind themselves. Eventually the horse becomes the center of the fantasy; it gets tired, becomes sick, proves unequal to the demands of a new life. The food may be scarce, the water supply low, the terrain strange or different. The horse wants to return home; there it may be a hard, even brutal life — but at least a familiar one. Tired, weakened, unhappy, yet strangely relieved, the horse returns to its old "place," once again to be a "beast of burden," as the Anglo textbooks put it.

The fateful, disappointing, but somehow reassuring home-coming does not usually mark the end of the story. The child wants revenge, even as parents do. The parents constantly pray to God for restraint. The children are less clear about the need for such an adjustment to political, social, economic reality. They have been told of the necessity — a million times, it must seem to them. But they are not yet grown up, and they are still unwilling to surrender one of the few freedoms they have, and maybe ever will have — the right to imagine a way out, and if not that, the possibility of revenge.

In the Chicano child's spoken fantasies, one continually hears an extraordinary, stark mixture: best to go home quietly on the horse, thereby letting the entire matter drop; but if this is a surrender, it will be a bloody time. Often there is a moment of extreme violence just before the runaway child and horse get safely back: the violence of thunder and lightning, followed by fire; the violence of a windstorm or a tornado; the violence of an animal run amok. Who experiences the force of that fantasy of violence? Never the child; never Chicanos; always it is an Anglo; or it is an Anglo section of a town, a city, that gets damaged, and sometimes totally obliterated. A Chicano child of seven, for instance, wakes up in a state of excitement rather than horror; calls for his father, not his mother; tells him that he had "another dream" — a ride on a pony toward the hills well to the north of the Rio Grande Valley, and an eventual return. The father shakes his head: why this story in the middle of the night? He is about to go back to bed, but the child's eyes flash a message: there is more. In a moment it is told: an indeterminate number of Anglos were killed by a tornado; the boy, on his horse, saw the tornado strike as they were approaching home — and wonderfully, the observer was spared. The father smiles. The boy bids him a fond good-night. The father tells the boy that he has had a rather unsettling night of it so far and should proceed to a quiet, restful sleep. The boy does.

The next day a visitor hears the dream, asks the child whether he was in any way scared: after all, a tornado! No, he wasn't. And the father is now convinced that the child was having a pleasant time of it. Is it natural, the father wants to know, for a boy in his dreams to like action, noise, excitement? Of course. No Anglo outsider, however earnest and friendly, can make a judgment of what is "natural" for a Chicano child. In any event, it is all in fun, the father asserts. Oh, one day, some disaster might actually strike the area. Meanwhile, his life and his dreaming son's life go on, along with that of the various Anglos they as Chicanos have to come to terms with every day. He looks up to the picture of Jesus Christ, the only one on the walls of the cabin. Did not even Christ — as the priest reminds his parishioners occasionally — strike out at those in the temple? It is not so much a question as a reassuring declaration.

But for the child, no matter how often he or she hears a priest or a parent prophesy, there is only the present: hopes to be expressed, worries to contend with. For Chicano boys there are games of hide and seek, or war between Chicanos and Anglos — very much like those played by others of their age. Parents enjoy hearing about such games, watching them. Parents also inspire them by asking when they are next to take place. But Chicano boys who fight mock battles are often warned afterward: watch your step, take care, speak your epithets in Spanish. The boys listen and for the most part obey.

Girls are quieter, are more cooperative with teachers, not out of friendliness but a certain compliance that they have learned never to shed. Chicano girls are taught that their people have a hard time, but as women they will find it doubly and inevitably hard. Women must learn to shrug their shoulders, keep doing their tasks faithfully. Women have a fate: the house, the tasks of cooking, washing, cleaning up, and, of course, rearing children — as well as, at certain times, working on their hands and knees as farm laborers beside their husbands and, all too often, their children, too. When entire Chicano families pick fruit or vegetables in the Rio Grande Valley, the boys stay close to their fathers, the girls to their mothers. The fathers often point things out to their sons, show them shortcuts — how to work as fast as possible. The mothers tend to be less interested in cultivating speed, competence, efficiency among their daughters. The girls respond by daydreaming or trying to distract their mothers. The mother may periodically stop, look at the daughter(s) a bit plaintively — as if waiting for an excuse to stop work. The boys plod on. They see their sisters or girl cousins playing rather than working, show a certain haughty contempt on their faces, remind themselves that girls are weaker, need to rest.

The girls, in contrast, show no interest in what the boys are or are not doing. The girls seem more self-sufficient, more sure of themselves — for all the braggadocio of the boys, especially prominent after a day in the fields: see how much *I* have picked, earned! The girls refuse to compete, to brag of their achievements. A particular girl may be especially industrious and able, may surprise her mother by how much she has picked, but will refuse to let her brothers know that she, in fact, has surpassed them. The boys, suspecting that, eye her baskets, so full and neatly arranged, but choose not to press the matter. The girl steps back, lets the boys go first, right after their father — first at weighing in, first to receive cash from the gringos! The boys hold on to their money, give it to their father later, at home, in private. A man makes money, keeps his money as long as possible. For the woman it is different; the mother immediately hands her money over to her husband. The daughters hand their money over to the mother, who then gives her husband a second installment of cash. The boys watch, show a slightly smug, condescending look on their faces: oh, yes, that is how it goes now, and will always go — when we are older, for instance. The girls don't notice, however. They smile at their brothers, joke with them, win them over: the boys' faces lose their self-consciously macho appearance.

Such deference has its limits, though. Chicano girls have their way of teasing boys, letting them know how vain, self-centered, and foolish they can be. When the family is on its way home at sundown after a long day in the field, a girl may pull her brother aside, tell him that he is a miracle worker: he has not only filled the pockets of the Anglo grower but made enough money for his father to justify an extra few bottles of beer or wine! The boy does not get angry; he recognizes a shrewd piece of social and psychological observation when he hears it. At other times, when boys and girls are together in the home or outside it, the girls are fond of mimicking the boys, calling attention to insufferable male conceit with deft caricature, imitation, and exaggeration. The boys retaliate, of course. They laugh at the posture of acquiescence, diffidence, self-effacement.

Chicano boys and girls have in common a relative lack of interest in doting on themselves in the mirror. The contrast with middle-class Anglo children is obvious. In many Chicano homes there is no mirror; or if there is one, the children pay little attention to it. They also pay less attention to clothes than do their middle-class counterparts. They are likely to have fewer of them, of course, but even so, they are reluctant to display themselves. As the boys and girls approach ten or eleven, they are quite prepared, in many cases, to leave school before getting a complete "elementary" education, never mind a high school diploma. In the later years of childhood, the years that immediately precede adolescence (ten to twleve), Chicano children warily but pointedly challenge their parents: is *this* the life you have bequeathed us?

The specifically political or sociological content of such questions distinguishes Chicano children of that age from many Anglo children. Chicano girls ask their mothers how they have managed to be so long-suffering, so enduring; the boys want to know whether they will ever be able to take so much on the chin in silence and without protest. Their parents do not by any means become apologetic. If need be there is a confrontation — perhaps a necessary prelude to the child's full realization that in a short while he or she will himself or herself be working full time, and for all practical purposes, be a grown-up. "They" can't be "kept" in schools, Anglo teachers say — quite sure it is a matter of willful lack of interest rather than the demands of a harsh, impoverished life. The parents seldom make much effort to hold their children in school. Why? To what purpose? The children can work, get some money. And there are often younger children to take care of, or a household to help maintain.

But the mind does not easily surrender. No matter how limited the social and economic possibilities may be, a child or a young adult is not going to consign himself or herself to "reality" (as some call it) in toto. Nor is the only refuge one of illusion, fantasy, distortion, or, ultimately, madness. Quite the contrary: most Chicano children, however poor, hold on to their senses, adapt to the terrible, insistent demands of the world, but keep an ear open, an eye out, for a chance, any chance, of escape or refuge. And mostly it is the city that they dream of — at least if they live in the rural, farming areas of states like Texas, California, Florida. Girls wonder what it would be like if they had been born in San Antonio, Los Angeles, Miami. Boys talk of "trying it," meaning a departure for a different life.

However, it is astonishing how sensitively Chicano children learn to gauge the practical choices available to them. A boy in Edinburg, Texas, says that yes, he would like very much to "try it" in San Antonio, *but.* That is the point when the voice loses all authority. The subsequent silence is eloquent: they know full well that even as San Antonio would offer certain advantages, they would not amount to a miracle; life would still be hard. Whence that kind of "wisdom," if such it be? What makes for canny social and political analysis in children? Mental pathology? Budding philosophical speculation? The exercise of intelligence? Maybe all three; certainly Chicano children indicate at eight or nine a certain reasonable gloom about their future. Ambitions casually voiced at five or six are put aside in favor of a ready, candid acknowledgment of what has to be: the same life that parents knew — one that will be handed down yet again, after a while, to one's own children.

Such knowledge generates more than gloom, however.

Children try to make do, buttress their disappointments with expressions of hope; and sometimes, a particular boy or girl will go further, imagine revolutionary changes — a childhood "fantasy," as some would call it. Mexico suddenly looms in the mind. Why not go there, try to become a somebody, a Mexican somebody, as opposed to a nobody, an American nobody or, at best, one of the few who "made it" in Texas or Florida? Such questions start at ages eight, nine, or ten: how did the Mexican-Americans ever get here, in the United States, and why did they come, and what is the point of staying? Parents, maybe for the first time, are confronted with a certain rebelliousness, strange and unsettling. The children don't shout their questions, don't act insolent or brash when asking. The children have learned their lessons well, are mostly demure, a touch grave, quite polite, when putting queries to their parents — usually on Sundays, before or after church, a time when it seems only natural to speculate a bit about "life." But the children are also insistent, not deterred by the effort their parents may make to fend them off, change the subject, turn to more prosaic or comfortably discussed matters.

There are the times when a grandparent, an elderly aunt or uncle is called in for help: they know more about Mexico, perhaps, or they have learned with age how to talk with suddenly and embarrassingly curious children. A people's history is conveyed to growing children — accounts of humiliation, ingenuity, perseverance, and, alas, failure. The outcome is not always satisfactory. The children still dream of a return to Mexico, but maybe halfheartedly now, knowing in the back of their minds that there really isn't any point to such a return for most of America's Chicano families. The children think of America's cities with a bit more enthusiasm, but wonder aloud about that alternative too. Does it make any more sense? Or if the children are already in the barrios of an American city, they begin to look at the more exotic, sinister, or "special" people in that city — those climbing the ladders to success available to the urban poor: a disc jockey, a nightclub owner, a record store owner, a numbers man, a drug peddler, a "fast woman."

Yet the influence upon Chicano children of Catholic ideology is also strong, a consequence not only of a long religious tradition, but their people's isolation. Unlike the Irish or Italians, Chicanos have found it hard, even after generations of American citizenship, to become integrated into the nation's industrial and commercial life. For one thing, they are still heavily rural people. When they move to cities like San Antonio or Los Angeles or Albuquerque, they remain very much to themselves, cut off significantly from the Anglo world. They have clung to their values and language, for instance, much more tenaciously than, for example, Polish people, who were also Catholic, non-English-speaking, and predominantly rural immigrants. Perhaps it has been the Southwest that has made the difference. Like the South, it has until recently resisted the dominant thrust of American urban, industrial culture. And since much of the Southwest was, in the first place, Spanish-speaking, it is the Anglos who were the true immigrants to the region, and who had to make *their* adjustments and accommodations. Nevertheless, the Anglos soon enough obtained political and economic control and now, through radio and television, as well as the influence of the school system on children, are in a position to enter, so to speak, the overwhelming majority of Chicano homes. And the result, for boys and girls, is a number of conflicts — the tension between a rural, mystical, emotional Catholic faith and an agnostic, urban, materialistic culture, occasionally wrapped in fundamentalist Protestantism but, in the clutch, committed to Mammon.

Chicano boys and girls of eight or nine begin to pay close

attention when they hear that cultural conflict put into vivid words, as parents and priests urge one set of priorities or beliefs and teachers, growers, or sheriffs enforce quite another moral and political code. But the parents, and even the priests or nuns, are not without their own mixed feelings. The most devout, pious, and otherworldly priest has to reckon with the cost of maintaining his ministry and with the political authority of the county: building codes, an automobile license, fire regulations, laws that regulate the seating capacity of a hall. As for the higher echelons of the Church, many Chicanos regard, with certain exceptions, even the bishops as the property of the Anglos. By the time a recently arrived, politically liberal parish priest who works among Chicanos (he may well be Irish or Italian himself) has learned to get along with his church superiors and with the people who run the county, there is little likelihood that the Chicano children who encounter him are going to become aroused by a revolutionary zealot.

Nor do their parents, however enraged by the inequities they have to face as a matter of course, show a lack of restraint in the social or political comments they choose to make. It is not always conservatism at work, either. The parents know how unfair things are and know full well what they would like to see happen — a drastic change in the status quo. But what is not possible is just as well forgotten. The children nod, make such knowledge their own. They say their prayers, cross themselves, remember that Christ had a special affection for the poor, repeat for their parents the various injunctions: a "clean tongue," respect for older people, modesty in dress and manner. But they also love the fast, suggestive music they hear on the radio; use all kinds of curses covertly; wonder out loud how old they will be when they are able to have sex as their parents do; and meanwhile are at times quite seductive with one another, always behind their parents' backs, of course.

Chicano children also watch television intently and imagine themselves, as millions of middle-class children do, owning virtually everything they see advertised. Especially the children who live in the cities find it hard to dismiss their own wishes and dreams as impossible. Somehow, they insist, it might actually come about — a time, a world, when and in which they are owners as well as viewers. And in example there are always the rich and successful ones — the "operators," whom a mother or father may despise, speak badly of, but whose big cars and flashy clothes and easy way with cash prompt envy as well as contempt. In the rural areas the child's dreams don't easily get connected to specific stores, countrymen, occupations. Rather, in a touching reflection of their parents' mystical Catholicism, the children of seven, for example, ask when Christ will come back to earth again — this time showing Himself capable of new kinds of miracles: toys, bikes, gadgets instead of the fish and the loaves. If parents can pray for God's favors — for health, for work, for a better life — children feel no embarrassment in asking for a few benefits of their own. They may get reprimanded, by a mother who feels that a child ought not waste God's time with such requests, or a father who hates television because of the self-centered Anglos who appear on it. But they aren't intimidated. They argue their case with God and man alike. They point out what they have heard — that "*every* child deserves" X, Y, or Z. They ask why not them, if others. When told, they ask once more, as if they are unwilling or unable to believe the explanation.

Their parents often get the point, decide to stop *discussing* the issue. The children are greeted by shrugs, annoyed silence, a change of subjects. More often, they are ordered to stop a particular line of inquiry. They may, thereupon, become young theologians, go to a Spanish priest or nun, resume their apparently ceaseless probes. They would like to go to Heaven, like to be the very best of Catholics, but they are also American children and, as such, have their desires. The priest backs the parents up: go play outside; use rocks, stones, wood — anything available and free. The schoolteachers, for quite other reasons, do the same — *assume* that Chicano children wouldn't know how to play with certain toys or games in class, so don't try to obtain them for the children. And if the children ask too importunately for a particular "educational toy," which they have been told on television many schools possess, the teacher is not at all ashamed to take offense: *I* am the final court of appeal.

Under such circumstances the ethical development of young school-age Chicano children becomes significantly complicated. On the one hand they believe, as perhaps few other American children do, in the New Testament promise that for the poor there will be another chance — after death. And death is no stranger to them. They often see people get sick and die. They may well be born at home and die at home themselves. They may well never see a doctor in their lives. The sight of a priest praying near a sick person, or near a mother giving birth to a child, or near an infant who has never really lived — all of that impresses upon children a grave and guarded view of life and its possibilities. The children have reason to be doubly philosophical; because they are taught in church to think about God's mysterious presence, and because in their daily lives they live close to tragedy — extreme poverty, serious illness, unpredictable death. They tend to ask questions about the meaning of things longer, harder, more urgently than is the case with middle-class children.

All children, to a degree, want answers. And all poor children, in one way or another, want to know whether there is any good reason that they, as opposed to others, have to live as they do. But Chicano children (as opposed to many Indian or Eskimo children) have to contend with the Bible's contradictory attitude toward poverty and political authority. Indian or Eskimo children are given an account of how it has come that they live where and as they do. The account is both factual and symbolically idiosyncratic — the naturalistic religion of a particular tribe or "people." Chicano children worship the same God their Anglo bosses (the growers) or teachers do, but the Catholic Church, or certain priests and parents, may well use the Church's teachings to remind a child that the meek and poor of the Bible are him and his brothers, sisters, parents.

Quite early on, when six or seven, Chicano children begin to develop a sense of loyalty to their people, to their *fate,* that distinguishes them from Anglo boys or girls of the same age. They become less and less, rather than more and more, individualistic. They renounce personal ambition, become — a children's version of the poor, huddled masses? — deferential to one another in school, as opposed to their teachers, whom they tend to obey rather than respect. And whether those children use the word *Chicano* or the word *Raza,* they become psychologically part of a people, membership in which, they increasingly sense, offers them what little sanction and support they are to find in their dealings with the Anglo-dominated world. The fact of that domination, it can be argued, exerts a major influence on their moral and ethical development. Psychologically they feel defenseless, victimized, ashamed; ethically they feel no real loyalty to the laws or rules of the Anglo world, only a practical sense, slowly acquired, that it is best to bend with the oppressor rather than to challenge him.

But invisible challenges are quite another matter. A child can talk of killing Anglos, can make pictures of them not for an interested visitor but for himself — the familiar "objects" children take aim and fire at. A child can dream of seeing a dead Anglo foreman, then wake up glad rather than guilty. When a parent reminds the child that he best be careful and not tell the foreman of the dream, the child smiles: yes, of course — but one has to have hope! The father knows that, is glad his children have hate and murder on their minds. Christ must have felt the same way when He fought religious bureaucrats or a whole empire's power. And murder was the outcome then — Christ on the Cross.

Murder figures prominently in the life of the oppressed and those who fight on their behalf. Priests say so, mention the killing of Christ; and parents connect the Christian faith to their own experience: we have a right, even an obligation, to distinguish ourselves emphatically, angrily, from them. By contrast, white children from southern segregationist homes don't make that kind of clear-cut distinction while young: that is, at the age of seven or eight. Rather, at that age they are likely to be playing with black children. And even when teenagers, certain white Southerners may look down upon blacks, treat them with contempt or callousness, but not quite regard them as Chicanos regard Anglos — a people utterly apart, a people toward whom one has not mixed emotions (as white Southerners or black Southerners have toward each other) but a consistently distrustful, aloof, calculating, and objective attitude.

There are subtleties and refinements of involvement, admittedly, between Chicano and Anglo individuals, including Chicano children and Anglo teachers, foremen, sheriffs, growers. And those children don't *only* suspect (or, deep down, hate) the Anglos they happen to spend time with; one senses in a given child awe, envy, admiration of sorts, reluctant but real. One senses, at times, even camaraderie. But such children don't seem to let go, allow themselves to become swept up in the entanglements of friendship, however much the Anglo may signal his or her wish for it. How different from its southern counterpart, this tough, austere, self-possession of the Chicano child!

How and why does such a psychological stance become the preferred one for Chicano children? There is practically never one explanation — not when the complexities of the human mind and, perhaps, the soul of a people, are involved. Chicanos are obviously a badly ostracized and exploited people. They are predominantly poor; they have, historically, been kept out of schools, colleges, jobs. They were conquered, subdued, put to menial work, taught systematically to regard themselves as ignorant, docile, inferior. They were segregated, kept out of certain residential areas, whole towns, in fact — kept in rural or urban slums. They are Catholics in a predominantly Protestant country — especially in Texas. When they have been numerically the stronger religion — as in, say, the Rio Grande Valley of Texas — they were still the far weaker society. And they are darker than their Anglo bosses. They have memories of being called, among other names, "light-skinned niggers" by Anglos whose rudeness, ignorance, and brutishness (and endangered sense of worth) thousands of Chicanos have had to contend with for a lifetime. But finally, and perhaps most important from the viewpoint of child development, they have their own language, to which they have clung tenaciously, uncompromisingly, in the face of the Anglos' open insistence or temptation.

The Spanish language has given Chicano children a refuge, a sanctuary, that is hard for any Anglo outsider to appreciate. It is not simply the obvious matter of emphasis or tone, and it is not so much the "structural-linguistic" differences; no doubt those factors do indeed influence the way Chicano children

think about the world, view it, and then put into words what
they see, hear, feel going on. Unlike Indians or Eskimos, whose
languages often lack words and concepts that are important in
the English language, the Spanish-speaking people of the
Southwest speak a tongue akin to English — developed and
used in a Western nation whose history for centuries has been
tied up with that of the British Isles. Almost any word or idea
available to the Anglo growers is available to their Chicano
fieldhands. But the private world that Spanish provides
Chicano families is quite another matter. The Anglo foreman
can shout, scream, rant; the laborers listen with apparent respect, then chatter away in Spanish as he leaves. They call him
every name they cannot summon in English. If their children
are nearby, they tell them how important it is to be silent
while the gruff, arrogant, cocky Anglos carry on with their
stream of words. But don't listen too closely, the children are
told, because every Anglo has the same basic message for
Chicanos. Accordingly, English-spoken reprimands, admonitions, advice, exhortations are taken with a fistful of salt
— and followed, inevitably, with Spanish-spoken scorn,
amusement, rage, promises of eventual vengeance. And many
parents explicitly tell their children that there is, finally, one
possession no Anglo, no matter who he is, can take away:
fluency in the Spanish language.

Often the language is regarded mystically — as something
handed down by Almighty God for at least a few of His people
to treasure. And the child is taught to be very much aware of
the privilege he or she has — a separate way of being alive,
virtually. No wonder Chicano children have been so reluctant
to learn English, have not at all yielded their language for
another. Better to leave school altogether than to speak English so well and so often that one begins to falter at Spanish.
They have had no desire at all to speak English exclusively in

school, and, and, as a consequence, they have either maintained a rather persistent silence or gradually left school well before adolescence.

Even when bilingual education has been offered, a development of recent years only, there is great suspicion and fear among Chicano parents and their children. What is the Anglo devil up to now? The Anglo teacher who now encourages the use of Spanish is regarded as wily, manipulative, out to do no good. The Chicano teacher, newly brought in, is often regarded as a traitor or a collaborationist. But even for those Chicano parents and children who are more willing to move toward and become part of the dominant Anglo world, there have been reservations — a sense that one loses as well as gains something. What is lost? Do poor people treasure their privacy, their particular cultural heritage, so much that they are tempted to turn down the blandishments of the well-to-do and stay to themselves? The feelings in question are complicated, contradictory, and hard to categorize conveniently.

Consequently, a list of psychological "attitudes" held by or characteristic of Chicano children lacks the consistency that an Anglo observer, trained in the social sciences, might want to find. Chicano boys can be noticeably peaceful, to the point of apparent lethargy or indifference; but they can also be quite cynical and truculent, especially when they live in the barrios of the larger cities. Even in rural areas, where Anglo sheriffs are so arbitrarily powerful, a group of Chicano children can find a deserted field, safely away, they are sure, from Anglo scrutiny, and begin to pour forth their resentment, their outright fury. When they are through, ready to return to their homes, or to school, or to work alongside their fruit- or vegetable-harvesting parents, the change in behavior is dramatic. Faces once more become impassive; voices sound obliging; gestures, if any, are restrained. They are "nice" children, if somewhat "dull," one hears from Anglo foremen or shopkeepers or teachers.

The word "nice" is meant to describe an accepting person — a child who goes along with things as they are rather than speaks out sharply, bitterly, pointedly. But the same Chicano child can be both accepting and bitter, both yielding and active, both self-effacing and self-regarding, even proud; he or she can be energetic as well as slow, nostalgic as well as strongly interested in the future. As some psychiatrists might want to put it, such children have a good sense of "reality testing"; they know when, where, and with whom to say what. But they are not confidence men (or women), and they do not endlessly manipulate the world. They react and respond by instinct; they have learned their lessons well — and those lessons exert their influence quietly, unconsciously. The Chicano child not only fears and distrusts the Anglos who bear down on his or her family's life but *knows* them, to the point that their reflexes become the child's too.

A child may anticipate with deadly accuracy the reaction of a particular Anglo. In dreams or in games Chicano children live out, play out the social and psychological analysis they have learned to make of American society — including, of course, their position in it. Over and over again certain Chicano children ask about, get told about Texas. They get prepared, as it were, for an encounter with Texas — with teachers, bossmen, store clerks, the police. By the time that encounter is about to take place, the child is ready — with words or a stolid silence, with gestures or postures, with a gradual withdrawal or an immediate flight. The preparatory or anticipatory aspect of the child's responsiveness to Anglo life is the result of an inner immersion in the ways of the powerful. A Chicano child imagines himself the landowner, grower, or police chief. A Chicano child imagines herself going to an Anglo "beauty shop," having an Anglo hairdresser wait on her. Chicano boys often dream of a military career; but they also have other dreams — being an Indian, for example, who ambushes the white man. The Chicano child's Indian is an Apache or a Sioux, bent on revenge, rather than a Pueblo or Hopi. In daily life, of course, the Chicano child must react to white people as the Pueblos or Hopis do — politely, decorously, acquiescently. Indian children, unlike Chicanos, rarely imagine themselves joining the military when grown up. They belong to their own "nation." Chicano children are supposedly (and mostly by rights) Americans.

And then there are the Indians, whom so many Anglo children play games of attacking, surrounding, wiping out. Chicano children often take another view of the Indians: comrades, people who have suffered similarly at the hands of armed Anglos; and people who, as a matter of fact, have done better than Chicanos have — because a reservation, however impoverished, is a place of seclusion, a hideout, and, very important, proof that the white man has stopped short of total conquest. Many Chicano children in Texas, New Mexico, and Arizona ask their parents why they, too, don't live on a reservation, where Anglos would be absent, or admitted only at the pleasure of the residents. The cowboy, with his fast horse and blazing guns, is no hero to Chicano boys.

The pride those children feel in their imagined status as Indians and the anger they direct toward Anglos tell a lot about the continuing struggle Chicanos must wage within themselves. It is a struggle that never really ends; a struggle most dramatically, poignantly, and explicitly waged by young people who have a way of enacting mental conflict more vividly than grown-ups do. On many occasions, parents become alarmed by the words they hear from their children. On the other hand, those same parents have their limits as obedient, fearful employees. If they cannot speak out loud to their bosses, they can drink a beer or two and speak out loud at home. It does commonly take some beer or wine, or a particular, desperate experience on the job, for a mother and father to let their children know — without qualification or omission — what the world is like.

Chicano parents may keep their silence so long that, ironically, their children are made even more curious: why do *we* live like this when *they* do so much better? There are dozens of such questions asked and left (for a while) unanswered by men and women who don't know where to begin. In the middle-class Anglo world, parents wonder how to answer the questions their children ask about sex or wonder how to curb the noise, the truculence of those children. In Chicano homes parents rather easily learn to exact restraint, tact, quiet from their children, and rather casually tell them to "wait, wait" for a discussion of sex — but become quite anxious, fearful, sad when they contemplate a discussion (inevitable they know) about the Anglos. "What shall we say of the Anglos to our children?" The question is asked repeatedly, in home after home, and never answered satisfactorily. It is the one question a mother reports asking herself all the time and never knows how to answer — let alone go on to the next step: the actual conversation with her children. A father insists he can take anything, *anything* — except a talk with his sons and daughters in which he has to tell them exactly what it has been and is like for him as a Chicano migrant.

The children sense the reluctance of their parents, become all the more seriously interested in their future fate — but at some point learn decisively to keep their questions to themselves. Many times, in many homes, one hears the proviso: a child will be told or has been told — but never again will the message be repeated. In a way the explanation given Chicano children of their almost certain future is not unlike the explanation of sex given white, middle-class children — an important and usually unforgettable moment. It may be that the Chicano child doesn't understand every detail he hears, just as children hearing about sex don't always absorb all the implications of a parent's exposition, because the mind takes in only so much and discards what is, at the moment, beyond comprehension. Chicano parents know all that quite well — know to wait until their children are eleven or twelve, say, before they sit down for a talk, for *the* talk.

After that moment is over various fantasies no longer get spoken: ideas for vengeance upon Anglos; thoughts about amassing money and power, using both against sheriffs or school officials; dreams of acquiring large homes like those owned by Anglo growers and large, air-conditioned cars, like those that foremen use, when they are not driving the grower's truck. After that there is the final loss of faith — an acquiescence that delights Anglos, who are quick to appreciate what has happened. A "boy" has "grown up and settled down." A "girl" has begun to "grow up and come to her senses." *That* about children who are fast becoming men and women and who are giving up whatever hope they have managed to nourish about their future lives! And the Chicano children hear what Anglos say about them — not rarely, right to their faces. The response? The silence, the politeness and exquisite forbearance, the valiant effort at cheerfulness — all a "face" for the Anglo.

How does one describe such a "face" psychologically? Is a child consciously contriving, or is it a matter of unwitting compliance? The children don't know themselves, nor do their parents. Of course they *do* quite explicitly realize how important it is to get on with Anglos, talk to them in a certain way, say what is expected, do one's "duty." But upon reflection

Chicano children and youths find themselves puzzled, surprised, enraged; they had not meant to be *quite* so cooperative. How to survive in an Anglo-dominated world, they wonder — and hold on to one's self-respect? How to be so constantly watchful of what one is about? How to avoid "forgetting"? How to avoid doing "everything" the Anglo wants — as opposed to "only enough"? Such questions are not explicitly asked often, but they do come up. They are questions that priests hear in confession, that Chicano children ask their parents — having listened to their parents speculate themselves in just such a vein: survival and its psychological risks, costs, penalties.

At twelve and thirteen, especially, as Chicano young men and women begin to develop active sexual interests, those issues must be met head-on. In rural areas the young men and women have commonly left school already and have worked in the fields, alongside their parents, for several years. They are no stranger to the status quo — its never-ending demands. But when a couple, however young and poor and under an alien yoke, begins to leave the authority of parents, even to a limited degree, and begins to think ahead of a lifetime, a new psychological crisis often arises. Anglo growers or their foremen remark all the time upon the "speed" with which Chicanos "grow up and come to their senses." Yes, indeed; in no time, it seems, mere "kids" have become working men and women, who show up early in the morning for agricultural work, or "loaf" in the barrios of various cities, where the unemployment rate for Chicano youths, as with blacks, goes as high as 30 or 40 or 50 percent. The prejudices that certain Anglos have about Chicano children begin to be confirmed; they do indeed stand idle on street corners, love "strange" music, seem "full of sex," and appear mute, sullen, on edge, to outsiders who happen to be driving by.

A number of Chicano activists have recalled the difficulty they had for years of putting into words emotions like rage, envy, shame, bitterness, awe, confusion — the everyday psychological tribute that the rich and the powerful exact from the poor and the weak. Chicanos who have become political organizers, who have learned to speak out on their own behalf and on behalf of their people, never for long stop struggling against the reticence of those being enlisted as fellow combatants in a tough social and political struggle. Why, one often hears organizers asking, do Chicano children, "our children," grow up so silent, so long-suffering, so indifferent, seemingly, to the burdens thrust upon them?

The questions are familiar to all political activists — the so-called apathy of the exploited ones, an apathy that has a way of yielding rather quickly once a real revolution or a significant change in the existing society actually takes place. Until then, the poor are skeptical indeed and a source of frustration (sometimes unacknowledged) to those bent on "uplifting" their countrymen. In the case of Chicanos there is, arguably, special cause for that frustration. Chicanos often tend to deny to themselves, never mind others, the depths of their anguish. Chicano children learn early on to bow their heads not only to their parents but to the Anglos and, indeed, "life" in general. Those children do not feign resignation; they live it out. In the Catholic Church, moreover, their parents do not shout and scream their outrage, do not pour out their fury (and passionate hope for a different future, "a new Heaven and a new earth") as blacks do in the fundamentalist rural Protestant churches of the South or the storefront churches of urban ghettos. In the Catholic churches of the Southwest Chicanos sit quietly, pray solemnly, go to confession with no intention of "catharsis"; in those churches an old, conservative kind of Catholicism dominates clergy and parishioners alike.

Children sit still — in awe of the power and splendor, the rituals and ceremonies of an institution that is, like the Anglos, not without influence and wealth. The Catholic Church is no fragile, idiosyncratic, evangelical "prayer group," here one day, gone the next. Chicano children come home from church reminded once again of the authority of those priests who are "above" them, even though, quite possibly, friends or supporters. Mothers and fathers remind their children that there is no direct access to God — that He is approached through a church and its hierarchy, even as the city or the town or the county or the farm has a hierarchy: foreman, grower, banker, sheriff, state police chief, and so on. The direct dealings that take place in the South between blacks and their God, between blacks and a particular white plantation owner or "bossman," are often missing in the Rio Grande Valley or in the towns of New Mexico. Children get the message: best not even to try to fathom things out, never mind aim for a confrontation of sorts. A confrontation with whom? And over what? And for how long, before a terrible day of reckoning comes?

Chicano children are not only full of the contradictions and ambiguities that others, all over the world, possess, but have a right to be granted their own special psychological territory. The "sadness" an Anglo teacher sees in a Chicano child may well be a curious kind of detachment, an ironic, wry way of looking at an alien land, the Southwest — in which, nevertheless, some five million Spanish-speaking people happen to live. The stillness and even the apathy of a Chicano child may be the wise and shrewd and adroit behavior of a boy or a girl who has made a judgment — of the prospects at hand and those in the future.

If that kind of judgment, at once an act of social appraisal and self-appraisal, is considered by Anglos of whatever background or educational achievement to be too sophisticated

— beyond the ken of *any* child, and certainly a poorly educated Chicano one — then perhaps it is not only Chicano boys and girls who require "study" and "analysis" but Anglo grownups, and not only those explicitly unfriendly to Chicanos or exploitative of them. The worst Anglos, some Chicano children have learned, have dared to say, are those who pity Chicanos. Better an out-and-out enemy than a condescending "supporter," "interested party" — or "researcher." And better silence, Chicano children have been known to observe, than compassonate tears or slogans that make no difference, change nothing. "Best to wait, work — and pray that one day the waiting will end, the work will be better"; a Chicano child of nine gave that as his father's "advice" to him, but the father said no, he had never said such a thing to his son, though it sounded "good" to him. Nor had the priest spoken thus; nor the boy's mother. Finally, the boy acknowledged the source: an Anglo teacher's description of how the cowboys felt as they worked on the dry western Texas prairies decades ago. A child, it appears, can make his own synthesis, use just about anything to come to terms with the world — and thereby prompt surprise, respect, and, one hopes, a touch of modesty in an outsider similarly anxious to comprehend what is going on.

PART FIVE

INDIAN CHILDREN

I

PUEBLO CHILDREN
ON THE BOUNDARY LINE

I N A PUEBLO between Albuquerque and Santa Fe, Rose, a girl of nine, talks to herself. From a distance her mother watches and smiles. Overhead a small, single-engine plane slowly approaches. At first it is a silent object in the sky, a welcome addition to exceedingly sparse terrain. But gradually the plane becomes something immediate, noisy, commanding, intrusive, distracting. Rose does not hesitate to register her disapproval, her outright annoyance. She gestures impatiently; she waves off the plane rather than waving at it. Almost simultaneously her mother also expresses how she feels: a frown upon her upraised face. Soon the plane recedes from view, and the girl resumes talking; the mother's face again shows a smile.

Ten minutes go by. The mother withdraws. She has chores to do. Rose keeps talking sporadically to herself; a minute or so of words, a couple of minutes of attentive silence. The girl's sister appears; she has been playing elsewhere but has become bored and curious: where is Rose? Sally, aged eight, picks up a stone and throws it. The stone lands where it was meant to — near, but safely not-too-near, the older sister. Rose acknowledges the kind intent, but appears upset — as if Sally is an airplane that has been moving along the land, preparing for a long takeoff, and now has chosen this spot, of all places, from which to lift up toward the sky. Soon Sally finds out why Rose has looked so impassive, surly even. An injured jay, able to hop, skip, jump, but not to fly away, has been chirping nervously, incessantly around Rose — neither leaving her altogether nor coming close enough to warrant a rescuing grab.

Rose wants to feed and care for the bird. She has been intermittently talking, singing an improvised song, standing rather still, hoping that the bird would get the message: here is someone friendly but not pushy — someone without ulterior motives. Rose's mother has been delighted that her daughter can feel such concern, can demonstrate restraint, such a continuing and respectful sense of control. When Sally learns — rather quickly, in fact, and without any instructions — what has been going on, she too takes her position and tries to be, at the very least, an impassive, earnestly neutral figure. For several minutes longer they split roles — the older sister actively beckoning, the younger one almost transfixed.

Finally the scrub jay is enough won over to stand still and be silent — at a distance. The three of them now form a triangle. For another few minutes there is not a movement, not a sound. Then, Rose gently signals Sally with her right forefinger to edge over. Gradually, step by step, with periods of stillness in between, the younger sister moves toward the older one. When they are together they say not a word; they stand still, then slowly sit down. The bird is by now interested in them. It does not move away. It stares at them, and they at it. An impasse, it seems. But the bird relents, moves toward the girls, and soon is busy eating. Rose has been furtively surrounding herself with small amounts of grain, and the bird could not resist. Finally, Rose swoops and catches hold of the bird. With great skill she seems to persuade it — most likely by the assurance her hands convey — that she is up to good rather than harm. The bird has not frozen in the girl's hands and does not make a lot of noise — but rather, nibbles some food that is offered.

Like a skilled but tender and respectful surgeon, Rose examines the bird; it continues to be strangely compliant, quiet. The girl talks to the bird, reassures it, tells her younger sister what the problem is: a damaged wing, most likely. They must go home, the two of them, and find a place for their newfound friend. The girls walk silently toward their house. They are ordinarily capable of, prone to, continuous chatter. But they worry that their talk would frighten the bird. When they reach their house they have second thoughts. Without saying a word, Rose starts to make a detour, and Sally not only follows but registers a knowing look: what will their mother say if she sees them entering the house with the bird but with no resting place prepared for it? Soon they are ready for their mother's possible objections; they have some of their pony's hay, are fashioning a nest, and smiling at the bird — and, with a certain satisfaction, at themselves.

Their mother, who had gone inside to prepare food before the bird was caught, stops cooking and joins their silent company. She motions with her head toward a corner of the room; the girls go there so that they can attend to the nest. The mother examines the bird, lingers attentively with the wing, thereby concurring in the diagnosis her daughters have made, and walks over to them. In a minute or two the bird is in the nest, with some water and grain nearby, and the mother and her daughters are outside the house, their eyes eagerly searching the sky: is there another bird up there circling, circling in vain? Satisfied that such is not the case, the three feel free to resume the rhythm of their lives. The mother has her cooking to complete, her washing to do. Rose and Sally want to help her, but she says no, they have been very helpful to the bird, and now ought to play.

Sally spies her cousin and runs to say hello. Rose is feeling a little reflective and nostalgic: "My father told me once that his uncle used to ask him a question: 'Do you know whether the sheep were put here for us to use, or whether we were put here to be of help to them?' My father would kill a coyote, then he would think of his uncle's question, and if one of us was with him, he'd ask the question again. I would say that I didn't know, and my father would always say that I was right, and he hoped I never answered any other way. Last year a coyote killed one of our sheep, and we killed a coyote later, and my father said it was probably the same one, though he wasn't sure. Then I asked him about the coyote: Why is he here? My father said he didn't know, but he was glad I was asking. Then when I was in school I decided to ask the teacher. She said it was a foolish question. She said that coyotes are a nuisance; they kill our sheep, and they should be shot on sight. She said animals are for us to use; that's what the Bible says. Then she told the class that sometimes the Indians worry too much about animals and birds and plants; and if you keep on worrying all the time, you'll never build a country, like the white people did here in America. When I came home and told my mother what the teacher said, she was very sad. She told me to feel sorry for the white people and for that teacher of theirs. She said there's nothing we can do to change the way white people think, but we at least can shake our heads and think to ourselves that coyotes aren't always as bad as we may think they are when we see a dead sheep. She told me to tell my father what I told her, the story of the teacher, when he comes home later in the day. I did, and he looked very serious, and he thought to himself; finally, he called me over and he told me that long ago our land was a young sheep, and then the white people came, and they built the country up, like the teacher said, and now we are living in a pool of the sheep's blood."

She looks upward, notices a large puffy cumulus cloud racing across the sky, predicts that it will narrowly miss the sun, is proven right, feels pleased with herself. When she was younger her father and an older cousin would stand with her and watch intently as the sun struggled to break through a cloud. Sometimes they would venture predictions: yes or no. She would always say maybe, until one day her father with some seriousness, and a touch of disapproval, indicated that henceforth she ought to stop hedging and risk a choice. She remembers how afraid she was to do so. She remembers her cousin trying to let her know the basis for his decisions — the size and thickness of the cloud, the speed of its movement, the heat of the day. She has never really taken those various considerations into mind as she makes her predictions, at least consciously, but she has made a lot of them, and apparently with a good deal of success: "I look at the cloud, and I may decide right away that nothing, not even the sun, will break through. So I say no. Or I may be unsure; then I say yes. I'm never really positive, but if I'm doubtful, that means the sun will probably shine through to us. I worry about the broken clouds — all the pieces scattered. My grandfather heard me asking my mother if it is painful. He said no, there is no pain, there are no good-byes. The small clouds are on their own, and they just keep moving."

She decides to draw the sun, the sky, a cloud. (Figure 21.) She starts with the cloud rather than, as white or black or Chicano children almost invariably do, with the sun or the sky. She works very carefully with a pencil; she is anxious to convey a mixture of fragility and strong presence. When she is satisfied with what she has done, she takes a black crayon and goes over the pencil lines ever so gently. Then she is ready for the other crayons. But the sky, too, is a demanding task for her. Unlike American children of different ancestry, who tend to draw skies quickly, often as an afterthought, she works slowly, painstakingly. She muses aloud as she works her way across the paper: "I hope I am being fair. The sky never stops watching over us, and I want to show my appreciation." As for the sun, it is, as she often observes, "the mother of the earth." She uses a pencil first, slowly makes one circle after another, until she produces a size that strikes her as right. She wants the sun to be prominent, but not too prominent.

Why that struggle — the circular lines put down, then erased in favor of another broader arc, or smaller one? She is quite sure of what she has in mind, and why: "If you look at the sun when it is trying to break through a cloud, but so far hasn't, you wonder how it will ever break through *any* cloud. But if you look at the sun on a clear day, you might be blinded. The sun is the most important part of our world, but you could forget about that and never remind yourself — if it wasn't for your mother or your father. Once I brought a picture home from school. I was just learning how to draw, and I drew our house and the tree next to it. My father saw the picture and he didn't like it. He called me over, and said that something was missing. I didn't know what to say. I looked carefully, and then I noticed that I'd left out one of the windows to our house. He became even more upset. He told me that he didn't care whether I had any windows in the small house, or whether I drew the house so that it looked like one of the big houses rich Anglos have in the city. It was the sun I'd left out! How could I do that, he kept asking. I stood there and wished I had crayons like those the teacher gives us to use, so that I could do something right away to make the picture look good to him.

"I told him that I'd like to go buy some crayons, but I didn't have the money. He asked me why I wanted to do that. I told him what I was thinking. He didn't like me at all for saying that I wanted to please *him!* He was even angrier. He said that I owed it to the *sun,* not to him, to be more careful. We owe the sun our lives, and so does everyone else — he kept saying that every day for a week or two, until I could tell when he was going to mention the sun, by the look on his face, and I started saying what he was about to say before he opened his mouth. Then he decided that I had learned my lesson; and he was right, because I've never since drawn any picture without first wondering where I should put the sun, and how big it should be, and whether I should have the sky clear or cloudy."

When Rose has sketched the right outline for the sun, she is ready for her crayons. She does not quickly apply yellow, then go on to something else, as most other children from other parts of the country are likely to do. She works slowly, deliberately — with the same care some children give to pictures they draw of themselves or friends. When she is through with the yellow crayon, she takes the orange one, and gently touches the sun with the darker color. Still not completely satisfied, she uses a touch of red. Then she hesitates, considers whether she wants to do any more with the picture, and decides that she is indeed through: "I will call this picture 'The Sky'; it is my favorite subject. It is my mother's and my father's favorite. My uncle likes me to draw the ground; he says I should show where the sun's light falls. But that's what I'll do in another picture. I would rather draw two than one!"

She is quick to prove herself a person of her word. She takes another piece of paper and picks up a brown crayon, as if ready to proceed, but looks at that paper's emptiness for a minute or two, a rather long time for a child of nine — especially one who has a clear idea in her mind of what she intends to draw. When she does begin she again shows herself different from many other American children. She starts her view of the ground from well below its surface. In fact, she begins by outlining a rabbit's burrow. Then she uses a heavy application of brown to illustrate some worms. The sandy earth is made light brown. She is very careful with the roots of plants and small brush, which she indicates with strokes of her black crayon. The above plant life also gets close attention. As she works along she reflects: "If this was the desert, it would be different. We're at the edge of the desert here. We're near enough to the Rio Grande, so there is a good water bed. I went with my father to Arizona a year ago, and there I saw the true desert. Even here we have cacti, and to someone from the city, who has never been to the southern part of New Mexico or Arizona, this looks like the desert. Our teachers at school say it is semidesert. My father said that before the white man is through with his tricks, all the rivers will flow to the cities, where the white people live, and on the reservations we will have no water at all. But the teachers say no, the government in Washington wants to be fair. The teachers work for the government, and they are sure they know what it's going to do. My father says he knows the history of our people, and it's not the same history they teach us in school."

As she concludes her drawing (Figure 22), she makes remarks about the land she has pictured, and she freely acknowledges their source: "My mother used to punish me. She would see me kicking the earth, or pulling up some brush, and she'd tell me to stop. We'd complain that we were just playing, but she didn't accept our excuses. Once I brought some water out, and I was making mud-bread, I called it. She didn't like that idea too much. She said I should be more careful. She told me to go in the house and think about what I could do that was better. I told her I didn't know why it was so bad for us to make forts or cook food — with the mud we made by bringing water to the outside earth. She said it was the *way* we were playing; she had been watching us, and we were digging in one place, then another, leaving ditches and holes, and not bothering to fix up what we'd done to the land after we were through. Instead, we started a new game further down the path. She told us we were acting like white people. She told us that a lot of Indians learn to act like white people. They learn in school, and they learn in their jobs. She said we'd better watch out.

"Then my father came home, and he told us off. He was upset with my brother. He told my brother that he's thirteen, and he should have stopped us, instead of going along and helping us. My brother had an old tire from a car, and he'd put water in it, and was making it go round and round, up and down the path. My father made him return the tire to the car. My brother said the car was just a pile of junk; it had been left by some white man near the reservation. My father said the white man had been very successful; he not only spoiled the land, and got rid of something he had no use for anymore, but he managed to spoil *us,* too!"

She stops abruptly. She looks out at the path that leads from her house and takes in her hands another piece of paper, as if she were about to make yet another drawing, this time of that path. But no, she puts the paper down. She has remembered her father's remark. She has, she acknowledges, spoiled nearby land upon occasion — the path, for example. If left to her inclination and that of her brother or her sisters, the path would be even more rutted than it is. But she has learned. She has been told repeatedly that even if Indians are weak and vulnerable, with respect to the white man, they are a thoughtful and intelligent people, who treat with respect what they do own, what they have left. And what they own is, actually, not theirs. Rose is careful to distinguish between her own sense of property and the lessons she learns at school: "We are here, and we will stay. But a day may come when we leave. A day may come when the white people have to leave too. That might be in the future. My brother once asked a teacher if she thought America would change — if the white people would always be here. The teacher thought he meant that someone would attack the country and drive all the white people away. She asked my brother if that's what he meant, and when he said no, she decided that he was asking her a 'stupid question,' that's what she told him. She said there are over two hundred million people in the United States, and most of them are white, and they'll just stay here, and the country is changing all the time, because it's a free country, but that didn't mean it's in any danger of disappearing.

"My brother decided not to argue with her. He came home and told us that all he was trying to say was this: there was an ice age, and a tropical age, and there were the dinosaurs, and then they disappeared; and it could happen that people would disappear, too. And he was trying to tell her what our father always says: that the white man keeps on winning victories, but he may lose the war. He may end up turning his land into a big pile of junk. He spoils everything he touches, our father says — including us, the Indians! So it's our fault; we've become like the white man. That's what my father wants all of us to remember — that we should fight the white man right here, in our house and outside, on our land, by being different from him."

On the other hand, her father was pleased to be given an old television set by a white man he knew. The man was going to throw it out and asked her father whether he wanted it. Yes, of course, he did. The set works well; it has a small screen, however. Rose cannot fail to wonder about that set — and the pleasure her father and mother get out of it. Not that she, too, doesn't like very much to sit and watch one program after another. But it has been her teachers, the whites who are at the school run by the Bureau of Indian Affairs, who denounce most television sets — in the same vein she hears her father speak of other gadgets. Once she talked with her brother Tom about the apparent incongruity. Ought they not talk with their father? No, the boy said; if they were going to anyone, and he recommended against it, they should approach their uncle, their mother's brother, because he is more outspoken and tends to influence their father. Moreover, he knows white people quite well. He worked for a time in Albuquerque for the Bureau of Indian Affairs; he was a clerk, a person who ran errands, and later he was in charge of a pool of cars. Now he works for the state of New Mexico; he helps maintain and protect a series of irrigation ditches and helps with plans to develop the state's roads.

Rose speaks of the uncle with a certain awe: "He has been around. He knows the state of New Mexico like I know the front and back of our house, like I know the lines on my palms. That is what he tells us; he shows us the lines on *his* palms, and says he knows the roads just as well! When we decided to ask him what he thought of the television set, we were a little worried. He might think we had no right to ask any questions of him. He might send us back to our parents. He might become angry. He can give someone a look, and he doesn't have to say a word afterwards. Once we saw him walk away from a friend. They were talking, and suddenly our uncle turned and walked away. His friend followed, and tried to say something, but our uncle wouldn't recognize him. He just kept on walking. He had his head fixed; he wouldn't turn it to the right or to the left — only straight ahead. I felt sorry for the friend, but our mother said the man must have offended our uncle in some way, because he's very polite, except when he feels you've bothered him with a stupid question or said something that doesn't make any sense at all, and then he feels that you've insulted him, and the only thing he can do to let you know what's happened is to walk away. According to our mother, he is trying to teach the other person to be wiser."

She stops to think. She wonders out loud whether the person so confronted actually learns the lesson. She has, on several occasions, brought up that question with her parents; they have answered guardedly; maybe no, in some cases, but certainly yes in others — and one must be grateful for the latter. Rose is often told that there is good news and bad news every day, that one has a choice: emphasize the one or the other. She has not by any means been told to laugh away the most obvious worries. The point is to add one's energy to the more hopeful side of things. She recalls her mother's advice: "Our uncle told our mother to take us outside and show us the land; part of it is without grass or bush, and the rocks are broken and crumbled; part of it is good for grazing. The sheep don't stop when they find land that is no good for them; they keep looking until they come upon the good land, and then they eat. When our mother told us that, my brother Tom said that we aren't sheep because we keep thinking about what has happened before. My mother told us to go tell our uncle that! We were afraid to! But she made us do it. So when he came to see us, we asked him if we could talk with him, and he said yes, and we did.

"He told Tom that he was right, we aren't sheep. But he said we must eat too; and if we trouble ourselves all the time with thoughts of regret, and more regret, then we won't have time to find food for ourselves. And then he said it; he said that the white people think sheep are dumb, all animals are dumb, and even a lot of people are dumb — the people they have conquered. But sheep know how to find food, and they do the best they can. At least they leave the land alone that doesn't offer them food; and they leave other animals alone. The white man won't leave anyone alone, and he'll take land that is no good, and before he's through with it, there's even more trouble. The white man could learn from a sheep because he thinks he's made things better, and they're actually worse, while at least the sheep doesn't add to the world's troubles, and doesn't pretend he's better or smarter than he is."

She is not quite sure of the value of her uncle's, her mother's comparison. Her father and her mother and her uncle stress the hypocrisy white people are capable of, but she and her brother Tom, who is thirteen, have seen their own people deceive or exploit one another — and have heard their parents or uncle call attention to that fact. Moreover, sheep can be willful and destructive as well as innocent. Rose calls upon her brother's observations: "Once Tom and I went to see our uncle, and he was very angry at white people. He said they have hurt us Indians a lot. Then he said they don't think for themselves. They are like sheep. Tom was going to remind our uncle that he once said sheep are better than white people. But we were both afraid to speak. On our way home Tom said that when he is bigger, he will argue with our uncle, even if it means trouble, and even if our mother and father are upset.

"Tom likes the teacher he has this year. The teacher tells Tom he is smart, and he should stay in school, and he should go to college later on. Tom says Indians can be unfair to white people; Tom says some of them even lie to each other, and steal from each other. And didn't they do that before the white man ever came here! The Navahos and the Pueblos fought hard all the time. The Hopis and the Navahos also fought hard, and they still do. The white man didn't bring us *all* our troubles. Tom says we should be fair. He tells our mother a little of what he thinks, but she says he should keep his ideas to himself, or else he'll get into trouble with our father and our uncle, and the spirits of our grandfathers, both of them, will be made restless, and they will come to visit Tom.

"Our mother says that she knows when she has said or done something wrong; she gets upset, and she walks up and down, and she can't stop walking, for an hour she can't, and that's because the spirit of her mother or her father has heard what she said or found out what she did, and is unhappy with her, and she can feel the unhappy spirit inside, and she has to walk and say to herself that she will not repeat her mistake if she can help it. Then the spirits leave her, and she can go back to cooking, or something else she was doing. Tom wouldn't say it to our mother, but he told me that he's never had any spirit visit him, and he doesn't think any spirit ever will visit him. When you die, you say good-bye. The teachers say there aren't any spirits. If you know you've done wrong, then you try to say to yourself that it won't happen again, if you can help it. That's what the teachers tell us in school — to try to learn from the mistakes you make and not worry about spirits."

Rose cannot let it go at that, however. The teachers, too, make mistakes — spirits or no spirits. And then, even more explicitly in defense of her people, she reminds herself out loud that there are crimes and crimes, that Indians have never been quite as successful at dominating others as white people have. Her brother has acknowledged that also; like her, he can go only so far as a critic of his own people. On her own, Rose has come up with a theory about the difference between white people and her own people. The former, she believes, are fast-moving, restless, all too worried about themselves and what the future has in store for them. She watches the white teachers in school, watches white people when she goes to Albuquerque, watches them when they get out of their cars, near the reservation, to look around. They can't stay still; they walk faster and talk faster than Indians, or so she believes.

She is willing to express what she feels with crayons; she is willing to sketch a white man she knows, who works for the federal government, and an Indian she knows who does the same. They often come to the reservation together, and Rose is convinced that if she were blind, she could still identify the one as opposed to the other. She draws the white man first. (Figure 23.) She explains why: "If I draw the Indian first, I won't want to draw the white man. It's best to draw your favorite picture last. You can look forward to doing it." She has no interest in putting the white man on the ground, or in showing a sky or the sun or clouds over him. She starts with his feet rather than his face, a rather unusual point of departure. She works her way rather rapidly up to his knees, his hips, his chest. Finally his face begins to take form. She gives him wide eyes but no ears. His arms are added at the very end, and they are quite long, simian, really. The last touch is the mouth, which she says out loud that she has forgotten. It is wide open, teeth bared.

As for the Indian, she needs another sheet of paper for him, even though there is plenty of room on the one she has just used, and even though when she sees the two men they are almost invariably together — "inspectors," she calls them, "from the bureau." (Figure 24.) The Indian is done from top to bottom — his face first, and it is a contrast with the white man's: hair quite slicked down, ears rather substantial, eyes mere slits, mouth firmly closed, head turned slightly down. The neck is shorter than the white man's, the torso thinner, a touch smaller, the legs and feet also thinner and also smaller. When she is through with the body, she prepares to stop drawing. She begins to gather her crayons together and puts the two drawings side by side as if to look at what she has accomplished. Suddenly she has an afterthought. She decides to put ground under the Indian. In fact, she ends up locating him on a slight incline, barren but with some desert grass nearby. No sky over him, no sun. As for the white man, she feels no inclination, it seems, to do anything further about him. The Indian is put on top of him, and the crayons on top of both of them.

But they are not so easy to put out of one's mind. Rose remembers the last time the two men visited the reservation: "They were curious about our water supply. They did some tests, I think. They had test tubes, like in school; they were going to send the water to a laboratory. The white man always smiles at us; he smiles too much. He likes to pat us on the head. He told the Indian that we are good children. My brother filled up a bag of water; he wanted to throw it at them. My mother said he mustn't. An Indian can get into trouble with the government. The Anglos say it is our land, our law; but they run everything. The Indian man is the one who knocks on the door; he's the one who asks if he can come in. But it's the white man who carries the notebook and he drives the car. My brother said if he was older, he'd pull the Indian to the side and ask him if he knows how to drive. If he said he couldn't, I'd tell him my father would be glad to give him lessons. Tom says the teacher told him at school that the only way that white people will ever get to look up to Indian people as equals — well, according to the teacher, the only way is for us to *prove* we're equal. Tom and Sally and I will prove we're equal when we're older. It will be hard though. My mother says the Pueblos have to walk on a boundary line — one foot on the white man's land and one foot on our land. You shouldn't go too far in either direction. You can get into trouble."

II

KEEPING AN EYE
ON THE WHITE MAN

ANOTHER STUDENT of the teacher Tom quotes so often is less impressed with what he hears — and less inclined to worry about boundary lines. Sam is Tom's second cousin; he is also Tom's age, give or take a few months. He won't tell Tom his birthday; or rather, he likes to move his birthday around, one day claiming to be Tom's junior, the next his senior. He has his mother's sanction for such evasiveness or forgetfulness; she long ago told him that she isn't quite sure herself of his birthday and doesn't especially want to be, either. Sam can be defiantly her champion in that regard: "I don't care if I'm twelve or thirteen today. It's all right to keep track of the years, but why bother with the month and the days? My grandfather says it is the white man's madness, birthdays and wedding anniversaries and the candles on the cakes. He says he doesn't know when he was born or how old he is and he's tired of being asked by white people. They look at the lines on his face. They ask him his birthday. He smiles and says nothing. He tells us that once he was a child, and then he became a man, and then he became a husband, and then a father, and now he has us grandchildren, and two of his grandchildren have their children, and he is old, and he will die one day. He says it is only white people who spend most of their time calling themselves twelve, thirteen, fourteen, or sixty, seventy, eighty.

"Once he took me on a walk, and we walked very far, out to the mesa, and then to another mesa. We talked a lot. He kept pointing out birds to me, hawks, eagles. He showed me where snakes hide. He told me about the rocks, which ones are soft and which ones are hard, and how to tell without picking them up. He remembers when the bureau came and when they built the school. He told me about his grandfather, and how they would walk together on the reservation, and how his grandfather would be with white people: he would look at them and not say anything, but if he had to talk, he would think to himself first how to say what was on his mind in the fewest words.

"I told my grandfather that in school the teachers want you to talk a lot if you're giving an oral composition. He smiled. He said I was right; you can't make anyone's life the guide for your own. He said that he knows many ways to walk to the mesa, and it's up to both of us, when we're walking, to decide which way is the best one. But he said one thing I must never do is stop every other minute and ask myself: how far have I gone, and how far do I have to go? All the signs on all the roads, telling you that there are twenty miles between here and there, and a few minutes later, eighteen miles — all those signs are the white man's, and they are his way of stopping himself all the time, to ask how old he is and how far he's gone and how much he has to go until he gets to — the next sign!"

Sam laughs. He can recall the impatience and scorn in his grandfather's voice as he talked about birthdays and road markers. He can recall the smile that came over the old man's face. There are times when Sam worries that his grandfather belongs to another age — that his strong convictions are hopelessly outmoded. But there are other moments when the boy realizes that he has been brought up short by the old man — and that it is all to the good: "My grandfather is from the past; he belongs there. When he grew up there weren't any automobiles. No one thought of traveling from home to work (over thirty miles) in a half an hour; you couldn't move like that. Those signs just let you know how fast you're going. But he makes you stop and think. It's true, people aren't like they used to be. He wishes they were. But if you're young, you don't have his memories. When I go see him, he tells me what happened in the First World War and the Second World War. He sounds like the teacher, when she reads from her history book. He's talking, a lot of the time, about white people who aren't alive. The white people today aren't the same as the white people were fifty years ago. The Indians aren't the same, either.

"I'd like to have a car, and if it could go real fast, I'd really be glad. And if I was driving along, I'd want to know how many miles I'd just traveled, and how many more until I hit Albuquerque. My grandfather doesn't drive, so he laughs at the signs. And he makes me laugh too — because when I walk with him I see what he means: it's nice, like he says — just using our feet and not worrying about the state police or the traffic signs or lights. He walks half the day, then he rests. He worries that we don't walk as much, his grandchildren. My father says it's the same with birthdays — in the old days you didn't have to worry about when you were born, the day or the year; but now it's different because the teachers and the government people, they all have to know, and the reason is that it's the law. The government has to know when you're old enough to go in the army, or when you've reached the age you can collect money because you're too old to work."

He has been quite serious, but suddenly he smiles. His

grandfather has again come to mind: such a proud, strong man — and so wise, so kind. A few seconds later the boy is less relaxed. His grandfather is intransigent, irreconcilable, pointedly scornful of "progress." He reveres the old man, indicates that his words also mean a lot to many on the reservation — but that many others are all too caught up with the white man's world. He begins to draw a picture of his grandfather. (Figure 25.) As he draws, he tries to give voice to the old man's, to his own, ideas about contemporary life on the Pueblo reservations of New Mexico. He was prompted, as he indicates, by his desire to do justice to an old man's apparently frail, yet ever so lithe, strong and certainly well-practiced legs: "I can't do it. If I was the best artist in New Mexico I still couldn't do it — draw his legs right. If you look at them they seem ready to fold under him, and never carry him anyplace. But he stands up and starts moving, and it's a miracle. He talks to his legs, especially when he is getting started. He thanks them for all the carrying they've done. Once I asked him: For how long? He said he doesn't know. And what difference does it make? I laughed. I said I know, I know. He joked with me. He said he didn't know if he was seventy-five or eighty — so he couldn't tell me how long his legs have been going! He said he has never kept track of his age.

"My uncle's legs have moods; one day they feel bad, and they don't want to leave the bed. The next day they are full of life. They want to keep going, even when he says no, he is ready to stop. That is when there is a war going on, between his legs and his chest. He coughs, so he wants to rest; but he can feel the itch in his feet. He sits down and holds his feet and talks to them, and then they quiet down, and he is smiling again.

"My uncle tells me that I should learn to do what I want to do, and think what I want to think, and not be taken in by the white man. I say yes, yes; but he gives me a look, and tells me that he knows that I am young and he is old, and I don't agree with him. When I tell him no, I do, he laughs and says I must stand up to him and say what *I* believe. Then I do. I try to argue. I repeat what I've heard others say. He listens. He says yes, yes. I think I've won him over. But no, he is following me, but not agreeing. He is saying yes to let me know that he sees exactly what I'm telling him. But he's heard it all before. And he has the answers. If you give in to the white man, then you are not yourself any more — that's his reply to me. I don't understand; so he goes on. I'm *still* not convinced. Finally, I'll say it: we have been conquered — a long time ago. Then he'll smile some more and give me his long speech.

"He'll say yes and no; we were conquered, that's right, but we can still fight for ourselves, and the best way to fight is to stay away from the white man's habits. Once you start counting time like him, and miles like him, and coins like him, then you've been trapped, you're beaten. At least we can live according to our own beliefs on the reservations. The white man has cornered us but not trapped us. There's a big difference, he says. Even my father agrees — and he will defend the white man sometimes. I'll be driving with my father, and he'll want to know what time it is, or how many miles to Santa Fe, and I smile, and then he does too because he knows that I'm thinking of my grandfather and what he would say, and suddenly my father is thinking of his father too."

Sam says that he knows one thing for sure: he will never live to be as old as his grandfather, nor will he be as strong as his grandfather — physically or mentally. Any effort to cast doubt on that conviction is regarded as meaningless and ignorant reassurance. Hasn't Sam's father said essentially the same thing — about himself, of all people: that he is soft, that he has been "corrupted" by the white man? Sam remembers those words, "soft" and "corrupted," as he draws his grandfather's face: strong features, lines and more lines, large and knowing eyes. As for the arms, so strikingly stretched, the boy offers an explanation: "He loves to call the land ours; he says it *is* ours, and no one will take it away, not while he is alive. If white men come from Albuquerque to invade us, he will walk in front of their cars or trucks. They will have to kill him. When I try to say that I'm sure no white man wants to touch our reservation, he says that may be true today, but tomorrow might bring different news. Then he will laugh and say that I am the wise old one and he is the small child; he says that every time we talk about the white man. No, I try to tell him, but he shows me why. He holds his arms out wide and says the land *is* ours, and the white man can't take it away from us, even if he drives up and down every road, with his trucks, and even if he sends his planes to cover us like a big cloud, and even if he hoists his flag over every building on the reservation. I'm right, he tells me: there is nothing to be afraid of. He bends over and picks up some of the soil, and says that it's inside him, not just there, beneath us. And soon he expects to die, and then he'll watch over the reservation, and no white man will dare try to bother us."

It is hard to argue with that line of reasoning. The boy has been told that he is right, but he isn't sure that he is being considered right for the right reason. The boy puts aside the drawing — puts aside his grandfather, it seems. The boy even admits that upon occasion he has thought of joining the white man's army and traveling all over the world. He would, as a matter of fact, prefer the navy or the air force. He has watched old movies and followed serials on television, and taken a liking to the planes and boats used in World War II. Might there be some of them left? Might he get to travel on an old destroyer across an ocean, or fly across America on an air force plane? As for the new jets, to be a pilot and fly them, one requires a college education, he has been told. He will never get that far in school, never be a pilot. There may be other air force jobs available, but he doubts he would be found suitable for them. As for the navy, why should it accept someone like him — an Indian who knows nothing about the water?

He wonders out loud about other Indians. Have any of them been in the navy, the air force? If so, as pilots, as members of a submarine crew, or in less interesting and attractive positions? Suddenly he turns on his own train of thought; it is foolish for him to think of going into the air force or the army, and for precisely the reasons his grandfather would suggest: "My grandfather knows many Pueblo Indians who have left the reservation and gone into the city to live. He knows men who have gone into the army, and men who have even tried to leave the country, and live in Canada — anyplace to leave here and try to get work and make some money. But they come back. They are not happy away from home. If a place is your home, you never will stop missing it. Our ancestors, they call for us, wherever we go. My uncle says he can feel the pull; he will wake up, and he will be thinking of his mother or his father, and he gets out of bed because his mother always wanted him to get up as soon as he's awake, and he checks on the horse and the dog and cat, because his father always said: Animals before people! When we're walking, he passes a tree or a shed, or the store, and he lowers his head, and I'll think he's talking to himself, but he isn't. He says it's the spirit of his mother or his father — inside him.

"My father and mother are a little like my grandfather. They talk to people who have died. My father gets angry with himself; he says that he has made a lot of mistakes, and he is sorry, and when I see no one nearby, I know it's his mother he's talking to, and his mother's brother. The teachers tell us we've got to forget a lot of the beliefs our people have, but we don't agree. We keep quiet. We say yes, but cross our fingers — that way we are really saying no. I don't think I could stay away from my people for too long. I don't talk to my ancestors, but my grandfather's voice — I do hear it a lot of the time, when I'm wondering what to do. He taught me how to ride his horse, and he taught me how to care for the chickens, and build a shelter for our dog, so the sun doesn't beat on him all the time. They used to have horses in the army, but no longer. I guess an Indian belongs on land, not the sea or the air, if he's going to be in the military. There are Indians at the air force base in Albuquerque, I believe. They are janitors."

That observation stops him short. He stares out the window — up at the sky. It is a clear, sunny day in April, not too warm, a bit breezy. He has never been out of the state of New Mexico, and only rarely has he ventured to cities like Santa Fe or Albuquerque. His father is a janitor, not at an air force base, but another property of the federal government, a Bureau of Indian Affairs school. And his father considers himself lucky indeed to have that job, any job. Sam has five uncles, two on his father's side and three on his mother's, who are without work and have been for several years. Sam breaks his silence by making reference to one of his uncles, his father's younger brother; he wanted to join the air force, dreamed of being a pilot, or a navigator, watched any television program that had to do with aircraft, got as far as a recruiting station and a medical examination, was told he had tuberculosis, spent two years in a sanatorium, almost died, managed to recover, has never been able to find any permanent job, drinks excessively, tells his nephew Sam that he ought to go to Denver or California, and try to find work and lose himself among white people, but has also told the boy it is impossible to do that, and so he may one day be in the same predicament as his uncles are and will be for "all the years to come."

The boy repeats the phrase when talking about the sky he has been silently gazing at: "Up there it is always the same. For all the years to come there will be the sky. When it gets very cloudy, I wonder how deep the clouds are, and I think that maybe they have won their battle with the sun and will keep it from us every day. But soon there is only the blue, and the sun and the moon and the stars. My mother is sure that the stars talk to each other. When they flicker and twinkle, she says they are gossiping. My father says no, we will never know the secrets of the heavens. I told them what we learn in school; and when the white men went up to the moon, I told them that one day there would be landings on other places up there, but my mother said that the white men landed here, in New Mexico, too, but they didn't really know what to look for. My father said that some white people are good, and they mean well, but they don't live in the same world we do; they go driving through their world, and we're walking through our world on tiptoe! That's what his father told him when he saw the first automobile come to our reservation. His father knew that a million more would follow (that was the number he predicted) because the white man does everything big."

He has averted his eyes from the sky toward the road, but now he again stops talking and again regards the big sky. He decides to draw a picture of that sky. (Figure 26.) He works carefully and without feeling the need to say anything. Soon he has covered a large piece of paper with blue. He uses his yellow crayon cautiously, subtly. He will have no part of conventional yellow circles with radiating spokes — the white man's sun his schoolteachers have portrayed and handed out in their illustrated storybooks. He infiltrates the blue with the yellow, manages to give the light he has evoked a somewhat vague, ill-defined appearance. He is offering an impression, a suggestion of what he senses going on above him. A child who has never heard of French Impressionist painters, or their predecessor, the Englishman J. M. W. Turner, struggles hard, and knowingly, to escape the tyranny of form. As he turns to a black crayon, holds it poised, he decides to clarify his intentions: "I wish I could see a cloud when it is born. We used to watch chickens being born, and my uncle would say that trees are born and clouds, too, and once, a long time ago, the sun and the earth, they were born; but we can't just go out and see things like that happening. My grandfather used to tell my father that everything has a life; the sun will die, and when that happens there will be other suns being born. Everything comes and everything goes. The years to come are the only things that stay; they aren't the white man's years, though; they are just light and dark in the world."

He acknowledges his deep sense of awe at the mysteries of being — of time and space, of beginning and end, of life in its various manifestations. He approaches the paper with the black crayon; it has been suspended from its task for a while. Just before the crayon touches the paper the boy tightens his hold, moves his hand in a circular fashion over the drawing — as if wielding an instrument. Suddenly he stops his hand, he moves the crayon from a slanted to an upright position and lets it touch the paper gently, then firmly: a black dot. He makes another, another. He talks freely about what he has in mind to create: "I'd like to show the start of some clouds. A cloud must be very small in the beginning. There must be a place in the sky where (if you could only be near there) you could watch clouds begin to form. They told us in school that clouds are moisture; but my mother said that clouds are *clouds,* not moisture. There is moisture in clouds, I guess you can say that. The reason I'd like to go up in a plane someday is that I'd like to see the clouds from the other side, and I'd like to see rain falling from them, and I'd like to see how they bump into each other, and become bigger or smaller or disappear."

He is done. His last gesture is a determined, brisk move of the palm of his drawing hand over the picture — as if to insist that he wants things blurred rather than precise. Then a new drawing (Figure 27); possessed of a new surge of energy and enthusiasm, he decides to take on the night.

Sam is a great one for the evening. His mother loves that time — after supper. She asks her children to go outside and sit with her. She asks them to be quiet. She asks them to look at a particular segment of the sky. There is no apparent method in her nightly inclination to scan the stars. She simply follows her whim — one night that spot over there, the next night another spot somewhere else. The moon comes first though — at night, as well as in the drawing. The mother and her children smile at it, or lament its absence — in which case, however, they always remind themselves of the near future: a full moon will come sooner or later. The mother often tells her children what she calls "sun-moon stories," which she heard from her mother and grandmother.

Sam tells his favorite story of the evening while he wields his crayons: "Once it was a very cloudy day, and my mother saw the sun trying to break through, but it never succeeded. Then it rained. Then it stopped raining, but still no sun. Finally evening came, and no moon, either. Early the next morning everyone woke up, because there was much thunder, lightning. It was one of the worst hailstorms we'd ever had: large stones all over the Valley and up the Sandia Mountains. By the time my mother got out of bed, my grandmother had made cereal, and was singing away. My mother asked her why she was singing so much. She didn't like the question at all. She said she always sings in the morning. But my grandfather said that some mornings she hardly sings, or doesn't sing. And he said she'd never sung as much as that morning! My grandmother smiled and said she wasn't going to argue. 'You are the

listeners,' she said, 'and so you must be right.' Then she said
that she'd jumped out of the bed, with the first strike of thunder and lightning, and that she'd been watching the rain and
later the hail fall, and that all of a sudden the sky cleared, just
before sunrise — and there was the moon. And a few minutes
later the first light came over the sky, beyond the mesa: the
sun slowly rising.

"She said the hailstones sparkled in the early morning sun,
and she went out and picked them up and looked at them in
her hand. Then she noticed the shadow of the full moon, and
she decided that she would ask the moon and the sun what had
happened. She made herself coffee, and she brought a chair
outside, and put it right in front of the house, and she sat and
drank her coffee and looked up at the sky. That's when she
decided the sun and moon had been fighting, and they'd been
chasing each other, and finally they stopped, and threw stones
at each other; but only for a while. The sun decided to stop,
and the moon said yes, it was time to stop, and they made up,
and the next thing everyone knew, the sky was as clear as it
could be, and the sun was warming the earth up, and the moon
could hardly wait for the evening, when it would come out a
full moon, and all around it would be the stars. That evening
the moon was low, and there were more stars than anyone had
ever seen, and even the white men, the Anglos, stopped on the
road, at the high point to the north of the reservation, and
got out of their cars and looked at the sky. My mother thinks
the hail might have been small stars that fell. The moon and
the sun used the stars to fight each other. When they made up,
the stars celebrated; they were brighter than they'd been before."

He has no memory of the actual evening, for he was a baby
of two or three. When he asks his mother whether he *ought*
to remember the event, she says he *does*. She tells him that

once in school they showed the children a picture of a microscope, whereupon he came home and said that he wished he
could put a hailstone under the microscope because thereby
he would be learning more about the fights that go on up in
the sky. Sam doesn't remember *that* either; he does, however,
remember quite well the various times, more recently, that
his mother and father have sat down with him and his brothers and sisters and talked about the sun and the moon, the
clouds and the rain, the hailstones and thunder and lightning
— and about the mesa, toward which they look so often and
about which they think and wonder and talk. The boy wants
to finish his drawing of the sky. He works intently. He falls
silent. His moon is very much like his sun, indistinct yet luminous. His stars are glowing, anything but remote from the
viewer. His sky is dark yet inviting, intriguing. He takes the
unusual step of mixing paints and crayons — a splash of white
paint to give a phosphorescent quality to the evening clouds,
which (he patiently explains) have caught a moonbeam, hence
their virtual sparkle in the night sky. A splash of blue to lighten
the darkness — a promise, maybe, of the coming morning. He
acknowledges that he is glad to be finishing this particular
drawing. It is not easy to do an evening sky; he is sure he gets
too easily and too much distracted by his family's strong and
continuing interest in what happens (and what might be happening) in the world above them.

But that difficulty, that "problem," is nothing, he is quite
willing to assert, compared to the challenge of drawing the
mesa. For Sam, and for other Indian children who live near
him, this mesa is both nothing and everything. It is a mere
elevation of land — as his teachers have time and again reminded the boys and girls in their classrooms. It is no rarity;
mesas are a fairly constant feature of the southwestern landscape. It is also, however, a distant place that one might reach,

given the energy and will, but which one is by no means anxious simply to use or enjoy (for games and rest). The mesa, actually, is something to *see;* it is also something that literally enables vision — and most broadly, a certain perspective.

Sam struggles hard to say what he wants to say, no more and no less. He is anxious to indicate where physical appearance ends, psychological significance begins. He is anxious to indicate the challenge that the mesa as an artistic object presents to him and to his crayons and paints. And as he speaks, he makes clear, also, his conviction that those crayons and those paints are not inert. "I remember my father took us to the mesa. He said he didn't want us to go there all the time, but he wanted to show us that we *could* go there. So we did. When we got halfway there I told my father that it wasn't the same mesa we'd been looking at; and he said that was true. And when we got all the way there, it wasn't a mesa at all. I mean, it was, but it wasn't. When we were on the mesa, we looked at our reservation. It seemed different — almost as if we were in the sky, looking down at the earth. You start thinking when you are on the mesa. You don't talk. You look. I was glad to be there, but I was glad to leave. I was glad to get back home; then I looked out, and there it was, the same mesa we'd always had. My grandfather used to talk to the mesa; he'd say that when he woke up and he didn't feel too good, he'd sit down and keep looking out toward the mesa, and he'd ask it for some of its strength, and after a while he'd begin to feel better.

"I hope the crayons know that they're doing an important job; and the paints, too. They can be a help; sometimes I feel they do all the work! In school, my little sister says she doesn't like to draw at all. But at home it's different. She says that when the crayons are here in the house, they're our crayons, and they do the right thing. But in school you're doing something for the white man, and the crayons are his. My grandfather used to tell us not to bring home a lot of rocks from the mesa. That's a white man's trick, he kept reminding us — to take things and move them around and dig up everything and change the whole world around, and soon nothing is the way it was meant to be."

Sam has been working carefully with brown, green, and gray, trying hard with crayons to evoke the arid semidesert of north-central New Mexico. As he approaches the mesa itself, he stops talking and switches to paint. He does not, interestingly enough, look at the mesa while he paints it. He had glanced at it repeatedly while on his way to it, so to speak, but now he gazes intently at the image that is slowly, stroke by stroke, emerging in front of him. Only when done does he sit back for a moment and look outside. It is good that he does; he realizes that he has by no means completed the job. The paints are again mobilized, this time for the sky, which becomes an extension of the mesa. When he is satisfied with his work, he puts it aside. His sister had wanted the picture, but he says no, it belongs to no one and everyone. He will leave it on the table, and there it will be the family's. He wishes he could go and visit cousins of his who live to the north in another pueblo. They have a rich choice of mesas; they have mountains too; but his cousins are near the Rio Grande at its full, stormy, swift best. Farther south (where Sam lives) the river becomes weak, tired, dissipated, a ghost of itself.

As the boy talks about his cousins, he provocatively evokes the meaning to himself of the land about him: "I like to sleep outside, even when it's cold. I don't like ever to sleep with the windows closed. My father says that when you cut yourself off, all the way, from the outside world, you are headed for trouble. Most white people live in buildings, and they don't care if they ever leave them. Even our teachers tell us that the Indians have always liked the land. Well, the white man likes the land, too; he wants to own all he can get. Our land is good; even if we don't grow much, it is good land. But my relatives have better land to walk on. My father tells his sister: You had better watch out, you'll lose what you've got. Some Anglo will come there, and he will wave dollar bills under your nose, and say take them, and if you say you won't, he will smile and go to some judge, or call up the people in Washington, D.C., and the next thing you know, you'll be pushed back into a smaller reservation, and they'll be telling you that you shouldn't worry because the United States takes care of the Indians. My aunt laughs; she says that the Pueblos know how to take care of themselves, and the days of the white man are numbered, anyway. That's the way my cousins talk, too; they say we will be here as long as it is meant for us to be — as long as we are sent here by our ancestors to stay awhile, then return to them. But the white man, he could get into bad trouble, and he'd be gone. The Anglos could destroy themselves with their bombs. That's a good reason for us to stay away from them — or at least to keep an eye on them. Sometimes I like them, but then I remind myself that I should watch every white man I see very carefully! My cousins have a lot of hiding places up north. We could get there in an hour."

III

INDIAN DEER

A N HOUR'S RIDE to the north and they are indeed "there." The two cousins Sam knows best are a girl aged nine and a boy aged ten. Sam and the girl, Joan, are quite fond of each other. She looks up to him but also exacts compliance from him when he is on a visit. Her brother, Jack, often defers to her. She is a little taller than her brother and quite independent of him. She explores the surrounding countryside more eagerly and knowingly. But she is no tyrant; nor is her older brother without his own force. Their father is an active, intelligent, outgoing man who served in the army, thereby going to Europe. He feels quite comfortable with white people. He works in a store in a town north of Santa Fe, drives a four-door Oldsmobile, is proud of a recently acquired color television set, and has wondered from time to time whether he ought not move his family to Albuquerque and try to make it there on his own, away from the various psychological, social, and economic supports of reservation life. His two children listen to the argument he and his wife wage with themselves as they weigh various pros and cons. The parents make a point of discussing with them what the various issues are.

Joan is especially anxious to take part in those family talks; Jack tends toward cynicism: whatever the parents want to do, they will end up doing, and there is no point in saying much to influence them one way or the other. Joan attacks Jack when he thinks like that; she is more outspoken, and she wants him to be so. He smiles and shrugs his shoulders: will it make any difference? The more he expresses his inclination to sit back and let fate, circumstances, his parents' collective will combine to decide where and how and with or near whom he will live, the more his sister speaks up: "I tell Jack that Indians aren't always people who sit back and let others tell them what to do. He tells me that I'm a white woman; that there's a white woman in me; that I'm under the spell of my Anglo teacher. Once we had a bad argument; we were ready to hit each other. My mother came just in time and stopped us. She didn't like the sound of our voices — too much noise. She'd been listening. She said we're *both* white; we talk too much, and we raise our voices the way the Anglos do, especially in the city. My father says that if you say one thing an Anglo doesn't like, or if you disagree with him a little, he'll come after you as if he's ready to kill you. My father says he feels their voices hitting him, and he wants to duck, but he can't; he'd be fired. I don't know why it is that Anglos talk louder than us; I've tried to shout, and it hurts my throat. And the teacher said to me once that I spoke the best of everyone in the class! My friends started telling me I was Miss White!

"My brother agrees with my friends, I think. He says I worry too much about everything. Maybe he's right. When I see the people on television, I wish I could live like them. I like our people; but I think that if you live in a big city, in one of the apartment buildings or in a hotel, then you have a much better life. I saw one Sunday a program about Indians, on how we live; and the man said that we're the poorest. My father said the whites have money, a lot of them do, but they don't live right. I said that if we could only get money, then we'd live much better. He nodded his head. My mother asked me what I'd do with a hundred or a thousand dollars, if someone came here and gave me that much. I said I'd buy myself dresses, and I'd get a bicycle, and I'd get skis, and learn to ski, like the Anglo girls do, and I'd buy some good shoes. And I'd go into Albuquerque, and look through the stores, and if I got an idea, then I'd have the money, so I wouldn't be dreaming and knowing all the time that I'll never be able to have what I want."

Joan looks at the television set, as if to emphasize that she, for one, is not at all uncertain about her desires, or indifferent to the larger American world, of which, she knows, the Pueblo Indians are a small and not typical segment. She teases her brother about that set: why does he sit before it if he finds so much of it "silly"? He replies that he can find better programs to watch than those she likes. When challenged to go ahead and do so, however, he invariably refuses. When she turns the set off and leaves, he will often switch it on again, without changing the channel. He doesn't mind watching Anglos look ridiculous, he lets her know, when she begins, with a look on her face, to scoff at how inconsistent he is. It is one thing, he insists, to sit back and watch the Anglos making fools of themselves and enjoy it; it is quite another matter when one pines for a life that others, far off, are pictured living. But they are not so far off, she answers. True, the television programs come from New York or California; yet she has been to Santa Fe and Albuquerque and watched the Anglos — their way of dressing, talking, and in general, living. Why don't Indians try to copy the white man? She suggests that to Jack. She asks that of her mother. Nor does her mother respond immediately with a rebuke.

The mother is a strong-willed woman, who has upon occasion argued with her own three sisters in the same vein as her daughter does with Jack. The three sisters regard the question as wrong and sad — and a reflection of what happens when Indians begin to lose faith in their own people and their destiny. The boy Jack is quite able to talk about this and with no prodding from his sister: "It is not fair that our aunts accuse my father; they say he makes my mother talk the way she does — but that means they don't know their own sister. Their mother, my grandmother, used to tell us — she still does — that our people, the Pueblos, have always had the most in common with the Anglos, here in New Mexico, and we have lived with them, and with the Spanish who came here, and we understand each other, and there's no trouble between us. And she'd say that we should learn to respect others, even if we want to keep apart from them. She persuaded my mother and my mother persuaded my sister to pay a lot of attention to the white people. My father always agreed with my grandmother, but that doesn't mean it's been his ideas that have won over my mother. She has her own mind. And no one can say that my sister doesn't have her own mind!"

A faint smile — he does not wish to be sarcastic, only ironic. At times he likes to leave his home, have as little to do as possible with his mother and sister, or with his aunts on both sides of the family who are likely (at least one or two of them) to be visiting. He has a friend whose name is also Jack. The two Jacks, about the same age, leave the cluster of homes in the pueblo for the surrounding countryside. In particular they seek out some high ground that affords them a wide-ranging, spectacular view of the whole reservation, and beyond it, one of New Mexico's northern towns. They could see the sun rise, move across the sky, and set, if they were willing to stand patiently and long enough. However, they usually arrive on weekends, in the late morning, or, on schooldays, in the late afternoon; and though they usually vow to stay "forever" — most especially when they are fleeing some unpleasant situation at home — it is at most a matter of an hour or two.

One boy gives an account of what happens: "My friend and I tell Joan we'll see her tomorrow. She wants to come along, but we won't let her. We tell her to go see her own friends. Then we leave. We take water, and a jam sandwich or two. My mother says she can always tell where I am, if she sees the jam opened and on the table. When I don't want *her* to know, I put the jam away! While we're walking we try to figure out what we're going to do. We mostly go exploring. I'd rather go exploring than anything else, but my friend likes to play cowboys and Indians! He likes to be a cowboy! I tell him that we should both be the *Indians,* since we *are* Indians, but he laughs and says no, we should both be the cowboys because they almost always used to win. He likes to watch the programs on television, and he's gone to some cowboy movies. He says the Indians were always bothering the cowboys, and all the cowboys wanted was more land for their cattle.

"My friend and I fight! I let him be a cowboy; I'm an Indian. He pretends there are other cowboys and I pretend there are other Indians. Then we start. He keeps going on the path we know, and I stay behind. We agree to wait until we can't see each other. That takes time. He has to go up and over a hill. Then I follow — but I don't just walk to the top of the hill, because he might be waiting there for me and take me by surprise and shoot me. I try to sneak up on him. The one who shoots first wins. We keep shooting; we aim at the other guy's men. I'll say: there's a greedy cowboy, and go bang, bang. Then I'll say to my Indians: we got him all right! Meanwhile, my friend is shooting at my Indians. I know a way to ambush him. He always forgets about a path my father showed me; it leads to the side of a hill, above the path he walks on. He thinks he can spot me before I get up the hill, but I know a way to walk that takes me there without his being able to see anything — until, all of a sudden, I come at him, with both guns shooting. The poor cowboy!"

He wonders whether Indians ever felt sorry for the cowboys they ambushed, or whether cowboys showed kindness and concern for the Indians they hurt or deprived of their land. He is sure that Indians hesitated to kill white men; he regards the white man as the intruder, the conqueror, the profiteer. His friend argues the other side; the Indians fought each other, never mind the white man, and were capable of doing some killing of their own. They don't carry on long debates nor do they take each other too seriously. Ultimately they join forces, become two Pueblo boys in search of a common enemy: "My sister Joan will ask us if we had a good time, and we always say yes because we always do. After a while we stop our fights! We become explorers. We go all over until we hit a highway or the edge of the reservation. Once we got lost, and I was really scared. Suddenly we came upon some white people; they were camping out. It was our great chance: an ambush! We'd circle them, and come at them with tomahawks, and they'd run away, leaving everything for us! We'd take all we could carry and bring it home! If Joan asked me where I got everything, I'd say from some whites — and they ran off before we could hit them with our tomahawks! She'd say we're no good; that's what she calls Jack and me when we tease her. But we'd show her the tomahawks and the things we'd captured, and she'd want to go get something for herself, so she'd come back with us."

Joan has her own friends, her own interests. She goes on her own expeditions. She likes to climb trees, much to her mother's chagrin. She rides on a pony that belongs to an uncle of hers and his children, one of whom is a girl of her age. The cousin won't climb trees, however: conduct unbecoming a girl. "Why do people have these ideas that they won't change?" Joan asks, then goes on to become specific: "I like to climb trees; I like to ride a bike — the faster the better. My mother says no, I should sit with her and learn to cook, and learn to sew and mend and dust and wash. Even the teacher in school — she has two children — told us that it's all right for girls to play the same games at recess that boys do. She said it's wrong for boys only to play sports, and girls only to sit and watch and cheer them on. That's what my mother says I should do: help Jack, help the other boys. Help, help, all the time help.

"I feel like running away sometimes. I saw a program on television about California, and I said to my father: Let's go there. My father laughed; he said he'd never left New Mexico, but I could go if I wanted. I said I do. My mother became upset. She said there was some bad spirit that was bothering me and wouldn't leave me alone. She said she would start going to church again. My father doesn't like to go to church, and so she doesn't go either. I told her not to go just because of me. I told her I would be a good daughter and that I didn't care about California; I was just curious. But she said that's the trouble, I'm always trying to find out about something. She says I am looking for trouble. I'm not; I'm trying to have fun. If Jack and his friend can go exploring, why not me? We are not the same Pueblo people we used to be. When I tell my mother that, she shakes her head. She says I am becoming a white girl. My father smiles and says he thinks my mother may be right."

She does love to draw and paint. Her parents approve of her artistic activity. Her mother is herself an artist; she does quiet landscapes or portraits of her children. Her mother also makes pencil sketches — on impulse, she is quick to say. Joan sketches, too, out of whim, and uses paints to show what she thinks of people, as well as, more neutrally, to represent them. She will be talking about a person, then decide to draw a picture of him or her. She keeps her work for a few days, then abruptly and for no reason that she can or cares to specify, discards what has been, usually, left on a table near her bed. Her mother has asked her to keep some of her work, but Joan says she will not. She has seen pictures she would gladly keep and hang up over her bed, but not things done by herself.

The issue is not modesty, as she makes quite clear: "I'm pretty good, I guess. I always get A in art, and the teachers say I have 'talent.' But I don't care to get up and look at what I've drawn — not when I can look outside and see our land. I try to draw what I like most to look at: the hills at sunset. I try to paint too — the shadows falling on the land. But it's not like stepping outside and using my eyes. Once the teacher told us that we should all learn to use a camera. I think she'd heard me tell Ann that nothing I drew, or anyone drew, could be the equal of what my eyes saw every day. She lent us her camera, and I used it; all I had to do was take the picture, and it came right out of the machine. I was disappointed; I liked my own drawings better than the one the machine made! When I told the teacher, *she* was disappointed. She told me she was sorry that she'd even suggested the idea. I told her not to feel sorry; I was grateful to her: she taught me that the white man's inventions couldn't do better than the hands we are born with."

She becomes immersed in her thoughts, but not for long. She takes note of the weather; it is warm; the sky is clearing after a brief rain. She is moved to draw: "Sometimes I really think I can do it — capture the hills and valleys the way they are with my crayons. But I never succeed. I'm going to try again. The sun is over halfway through its journey across the sky. The sun is beginning to get old. Every day, my grandmother tells us, we can step outside and watch a day get born, grow up, begin to get tired, then slowly say good-bye. We read a book in school — a story about boys and girls in the city. The author said that when the people had nothing to say, they talked about the weather. One of them looked up at the sky, and said 'nice day'; or another time, she looked up and said 'a bad, rainy day.' I didn't say anything to the teacher, but I thought it was sad, the way white people live. They don't know that you can enjoy rain as much as the sun. My mother stops us from complaining to her or arguing by telling us to look at a tree, or listen to the rain. She points to the clouds blending into each other. They don't fight, she always tells us; they know how to settle their differences quietly and to live as part of the sky."

As Joan thinks, talks, listens, she looks intently toward the distant hills and begins sketching with a pencil what she sees. Though the sky is clearing she notices the dark rain clouds in the distance and chooses to start with them. She is less interested in form and structure than in conveying a mood: the thick, heavy, welcome blanket of clouds carrying and disbursing water; the grateful land. She knows that she cannot do justice with a pencil (or with crayons or paints, either) to images and feelings she has within her, so she talks about what she is trying to do, to evoke: "It gets so dry for so long; the earth cracks, and when you walk over it, you can hear it cry for water. Even a cactus plant seems to be saying that it would like a little drink. I could have cloth over my eyes and know if I was walking over some very thirsty land: the noises, the feel of the earth under my feet. It is like rubbing your skin with your hand when you've hurt yourself and the cut is just beginning to heal. I want to run away and leave the poor soil alone, or come and bring it water — but there is not enough for all the miles of dry land. Only the clouds can heal the land on our reservation, my father tells us, and it is wonderful when the clouds come and pour their water down upon us. The cracks in the land — thirsty mouths, my father says they are —

get filled. Sometimes it is sad, though; the land has become so dry, it doesn't know what to do when the rain starts falling. And either there is no rain or too much, too fast. We watch the water run off: the gullys are full, but the poor soil has not had all it needs."

When she has finished her sketch (Figure 28), she decides to start over again, with paints. She has essentially used the pencil to indicate degrees of gray — as if rain represents, among other things, a movement of gray from one height to another. Another child, perhaps a child who is not an Indian, might see things quite differently, might want to turn the sketch around and regard the dark clouds as the earth, and the thinly drawn, almost fragile land as the clouds. She is aware of that possibility — has been made so by one of her teachers: "In our art classes, I try to draw what the Anglo teachers like, but I don't succeed. They tell me that I don't make pictures that they can recognize. One teacher said I should go to New York or Paris; the artists there would like what I draw or paint. I tried to draw a picture of my friend; the teachers keep telling me to concentrate hard on a person's face and draw it. I don't like to draw people; I like to show our teachers what our reservation looks like — in the winter, or in the summer, when it is hot and dry, or when we have been visited by rain. I tried to show them a strong wind, and they couldn't understand what I was doing. When I draw the rain falling, they turn the picture upside down, and they say 'maybe this way.' I say no, the other way. They tell me, again, they don't understand! In my mind I say: 'Yes, I know you don't!' But I just look at them, keep my mouth shut, and wait for one of their suggestions. A teacher is someone who always has suggestions for you; but if you have a suggestion for her, you had better keep it to yourself."

As if to show how good she is at doing so, she says nothing for a few minutes. She wants to do a drawing of the wind, and she works hard with her crayons, looking up only once or twice toward the land outside. Gently, almost unself-consciously, she murmurs a bit, blows air from time to time upon her paper. She smiles a little at the scene she is busy creating. She breaks her silence with: "I remember my grandmother telling me that there is always a message in the wind — many messages." As she continues, she comments on the various ones that are possible: "For the tree, the wind is a reminder to get exercise. The tree can stand there, lazy as can be. The wind makes the trees bend. The wind makes the branches go up and down, up and down. My grandmother says the tree is much stronger after a strong wind has blown. The tree loses its weak branches. A tree can get old and be ready to die, and the wind tests the tree, and if the tree can't meet the test, that is the end: the tree falls down. For the dry earth, the wind is not so bad; it blows through and moves small stones or leaves or twigs. Sometimes the wind is like a comb going through hair — the ground looks so clean afterwards. But nearby, where there is a bush or a wall, all the loose things have been dumped. When the wind comes and we are inside, our mother and father always tell us to go outside and say hello. My little cousin opens her mouth and breathes out very hard — her wind against the sky's wind. We like to run out toward the hills, and sit down near the grass and the bushes; the wind excites them; they sing, and so do we. My mother laughs and she sings, too; she calls one song her wind song. She made us learn the words a long time ago: 'Come and be strong/We can be strong/We welcome you/We will miss you/We will wait for you to return.' "

The picture is done, a subtle and elusive effort. (Figure 29.) Though it is now sunny outside she thinks of the winter wind as well as the summer breezes she loves so much. She decides to add an afterthought to her series of pictures, made over the months, on "wind." She has pictured snow before but never a windy snow; so she begins. Snow is for her something beautiful, magical, comforting. She has an explanation for snow — for its purpose, its meaning: "When it gets cold the world tries to be brave and strong. After a while it is rewarded; the snow comes and covers everything, and the world looks clean and new. Only the streams up the mountain or the Rio Grande remain uncovered — unless they freeze. Then the snow covers them. My grandmother says she can feel the spirits — our ancestors — telling the clouds to do their work, and the wind to help out: bring peace to the reservation, cover it with a blanket and tell it to stop and rest.

"We don't like to go to school when it snows. My father doesn't like to work when it snows. We don't want to build snowmen, the way the Anglos do. We don't want to push the snow all over. We are not like the New Mexico Highway Department. My father says the Anglos won't let anything alone, even snow. Here in the valley, the snow is a visitor who leaves quickly — a day or two. Up the mountains, the snow stays much longer. The Anglos even push it and clear it from the steep roads. They worry: has enough fallen for their skis or sleds? We like to walk and look. We don't mind the Anglos clearing a road, so all of us can go to school, but my father says that when we stay at home we can learn from him and our grandparents and uncles and aunts."

Her picture is meant to show what she has learned at home, rather than in school. (Figure 30.) She concentrates on a few snowflakes, makes each of them something to appreciate. She doesn't show any interest in the ground, or for that matter, the sky. She is not interested in the accumulation of snow, in snow as a building material, or even as a source of fun and games

— at least in her picture. Snow in the air; snow on its way someplace; snow quite wondrous to behold? She has no title. She likes what she has done: "I'm glad I used the black paper. I asked the teacher once if she had some blue paper or black paper so that I could draw a snowstorm. She said no, they only had white paper, but I could use a light yellow crayon. I said I'd try to think up another topic. My father asked a friend of his who works in Santa Fe if he knew where there was any black or blue paper. The friend said yes. The Anglos prefer white paper, of course! I like white too: snow! But white is not the only color!

"I guess I wouldn't mind living in Taos and skiing there every day in the winter. My cousin says you can go south to the Sandia Mountains, outside Albuquerque. I've been near both places. I've looked at the mountains and not seen anything but the snow: no people skiing down the sides. My father laughs; he says you can be in a car and look up a mountain and not see the goats, the deer, the birds, the people walking and climbing — all that goes on. So, of course, you wouldn't see people skiing either. We don't see things if we're not looking for them. A lot of white people don't pay any attention to Indians. We could be climbing the mountains, and they could be nearby; they want to see the summit, not us! I told my brother once we are deer, Indian deer. He didn't like what I said."

She has seen television sports documentaries and in school has been given pictures of ski resorts: men, women, and children gliding down the slopes. She has, however, imagined herself skiing alone, and, in her mind, she does not appear to be the same kind of skier that others see on film or in photographs. It is, of course, a matter of differing perspectives, as she once tried to make clear by making yet another drawing. She chose to call it "Skiing," rather than a picture of a particular skier. And she chose to emphasize the landscape rather than anyone in it. In fact, she labored hard to build just the right kind of hill, steep enough but not too steep. She supplied plenty of snow, but also insisted on the presence of trees, hawks, and yes, the wind; then, one skier — a dot, virtually, in the midst of a rather grand winter landscape. The skier is well down the hill, and the artist has some thoughts about the scene: "It is not me; I would be frightened. It is my cousin. He is thirteen, and afraid of nothing. He is the bravest person I know. He would climb a mountain, carrying the skis on his back, put them on, and laugh while he went down, or sing our grandmother's song about the mountains. The song goes: 'They reach high up/They stretch the land/They point toward clouds or the sun/They remind us of our height/They tell us that there are always surprises/They make our eyes dance/They say hello to our ancestors: Please come here anytime/Our ancestors say thank you, we will.' "

She wonders what her cousin would do when he came to the bottom. He would, most likely, walk away. He might even leave his skis behind. She has little interest in the mechanics of the sport, the tows and poles, not to mention the various kinds of skis. She has no interest at all in ski clothes. Her cousin would wear a leather jacket and dungarees and his good winter shoes, and somehow, she is not sure how or where or when, he would put a pair of skis on, get up a hill or mountain, slide down it, divest himself of those skis — and walk away, she makes clear. "My cousin wouldn't want to go up and down, up and down. He might want to stop right after he started and take off his skis and walk down the hill. Once my brother asked him if he would like to fly, like a hawk or an eagle. He said no. He said that an eagle has no wish to fly. An eagle just flies. The same goes for us; we shouldn't try to be anything but ourselves!

I think my cousin wonders if white people are the same as us. He once said he couldn't understand why they spend so much time speeding down our hills. Maybe they are different — like eagles."

IV

PUEBLO RIDER

THE thirteen-year-old cousin's name is Gerry; he lives on another Pueblo reservation, farther north in New Mexico. He is one of four boys, and the oldest. A younger brother, Joe, is twelve, and then there are Larry, aged nine, and Mike, aged eight. Two sisters, born after Mike, died very young, one of pneumonia, the other of diabetes, or so the parents were told. Gerry and Joe are quite good friends, besides being brothers. They have worked together, too — as errand boys in one business, as laborers in another, as shipping clerks in still another. They have been fortunate to have such jobs; their father has helped secure them. He works for the state of New Mexico — helps keep the roads in good repair, helps clear them in the winter. His oldest son has occasionally gone out on state trucks with him, has become familiar with the Anglos who give orders to his father and with their children. An outgoing, friendly, active youth, Gerry has a self-mocking side to him, which he knows appeals to white people.

He claims he "really knows" those whites rather well, though he does not mean to boast — merely state the nature of his involvement and, maybe, the necessity for it: "Some friends I have on the reservation, boys I've grown up with, have never talked to white boys, only to the Anglo teachers, or tourists who come poking around, looking for Indians with bows and arrows and wearing feathers on their heads! One Anglo tourist asked me last year: 'Where are the Indians?' I said I was one. He said I didn't look like one. I said I was sorry. He thought I was getting fresh, maybe — or he thought it was strange that I was apologizing to him, so he pressed the button in his car, and up went the windows, fast, and away he and his wife went, fast. The poor road, I thought to myself: our land being treated like that! He made the largest cloud of dust I've ever seen from a car. I could hear the earth saying that it hurt. The dust tried to catch him, but of course he had air conditioning in that tank of his. I spoke to the dust: Don't waste your energy on them!

"My father, a long time ago, would take Joe and me aside; we would go on a walk, and he would show us how to smile at the white men. Joe would pick up a rock, and say he'd like to throw it at them; but our father would take the rock from Joe and put it down on the ground, right in the place Joe found it, and ask us to think about the *rock* — have respect for *it*. If we throw a rock at someone, we are doing what the white people do: use anything for their own purposes. They are too many and too strong to fight. We tried when there were fewer of them, and they weren't as strong as they are now. It is not in our blood to fight with them. It is not in our blood to fight with other Indians. My father says we should be proud that we would lose every time if we tried to fight with the Anglos of New Mexico, or any other state! That is what the Anglos do best: fight. I was going to put my father's ideas in a composition for our teacher at school, but I decided I'd better not. The teacher would call me to her desk, and she'd ask me to 'explain' myself. She does that sometimes with us; she admits to us that she doesn't understand what we are thinking, and she asks us to 'explain.' I try to 'explain,' but sometimes I only succeed in making more trouble for myself."

Memories of "trouble" interrupt his chain of thoughts. He begins to recite some of his sad and comic experiences — the misunderstandings that, he realizes full well, Indians are bound to have with white people. He finds it especially hard for his teachers to appreciate his love for squirrels, hawks, fish — and not least, the various kinds of stones and rocks he has noticed, casually gathered over the years but not brought together into a "collection." One teacher of his discovered his geological interests — his "aptitude," she described it — and asked if he did indeed have a "collection." No, he did not. She suggested that he ought to start one; he compliantly agreed. A month or so later she asked about the "progress" he was making as a collector. He replied that he hadn't yet gotten around to beginning — whereupon she was quite stern with him: he must not continue to be as indifferent or outright lazy (and intellectually unresponsive) as he now seemed. He again went along with her — nodding, when he knew full well that he would never really act on her plan for him. But the more she praised and admonished him, the more he tried to appease her: yes, yes, I will, I will.

Soon boy and teacher had become hopelessly entwined in a mixture of pleas, requests, promises, and deceptions — until Gerry summoned the nerve to come clean: "I told her. I went up to her, and I said I'm sorry, but there won't be a rock collection because I can't do it. She interrupted me before I had a chance to explain why: she *asked* why. But I could see by the way she was asking that there was nothing I could say to make her see my reasons. All she had were her reasons; she told me I'd never go to high school if I didn't learn to be a good student and study the way other American boys do. She said that her brother used to collect rocks, and he had a coin collection, and she collected stamps, and so did her brother. I didn't say anything. I decided that the best thing to do was shut up. I did. After a while she asked me why I wasn't saying a word. I still didn't say anything. Then she turned real *white* on me! She told me to go back to my seat and stay there. She said the Indians don't know how to build themselves up the way 'other people' do. I don't know what she meant. I wanted to ask her: What do you mean, build ourselves up? We have homes that we've built. We have a reservation, and we take care of it. We have built a life for ourselves here. We've been here for a long time, for a longer time than any white people, and our ancestors had built up good villages, and no one was bothering them — even other Indians, who were envious of the Pueblos — until the white people came. We lost to the white people. But everyone loses to them. They have conquered the whole world, not just us. Does that mean that we are no good?"

The answer for him, needless to say, was no, it does not mean that he and his people are no good. But he knew full well what his teacher's answer was and always would be. He knew then and there that he was facing the same kind of conflict his ancestors had long ago faced with other Anglos. He is quite able to put this into words: "You can't tell the Anglos, the white people, to think the way we do. My father used to tell me that, and I didn't know, at first, what he meant. But I do now. I learned. The white people demand that you think the way they do; and if you don't, you'll get into trouble. They call you bad names, or they punish you, or they try to push you out of their way. My father says that at work an Anglo will come up to him and ask him to do something. Even if my father thinks that he has a better idea, he's going to smile, though he doesn't feel like it, and he's going to keep quiet. If he doesn't go along with the Anglos, he'll lose his job. With me it's the same way; if you don't get the teacher to think you're on her side, she'll consider you an enemy, and it won't be long before she's shooting you down, ambushing you, trying to get you sent out of the school.

"My teachers want us to be good, and they want us to be like their own children, or their nephews and nieces; that's what they say, and I believe them! The principal, he's a big skier; he goes to Taos, and he's fast, and he never falls. He told us he was going to go to Switzerland and ski there. He substituted for our teacher a whole week once; she was sick. He told us we didn't know anything about geography. He made us memorize the capitals of a lot of foreign countries. He said Switzerland never gets into a war, and they have good skiing — the Alps mountains. I wish he'd go there and stay there. When our regular teacher came back, and she asked us what we'd learned, and we told her, she said that Switzerland was also a very rich country because a lot of rich people send their money over there. When a girl said that the Anglos who come to ski at Taos, they're rich, too, the teacher said it's a free country, and anyone can ski, the rich and the poor, and there's no dictator telling Americans where to live and whether they can ski or not. I told my brother Joe and our father, and we had a laugh! The government told our people a long time ago where to live, and then if the Anglos decided to change their minds because they wanted gold or water, they did. And sure, all you need is a few hundred dollars; *then* you can go to Taos and stay in one of the places there, and you can ski until you have pains in your legs and you are hungry. There are nice restaurants, and you can rest and eat plenty — for more money!"

His father comes home occasionally with food. A friendly storekeeper has aging bread, for instance, and gives it away rather than throw it out. Gerry and Joe like jam sandwiches, like chocolate milk and cupcakes, like Coca-Cola. They have heard from their grandparents about other times, when Indians ate differently: bread they made themselves, vegetables and fruit, fish they caught themselves, if they lived near mountain streams. The two boys cannot imagine that kind of life; they are given to the sweet, inexpensive, and not especially nutritious food they eat. They have numerous cavities. They do not suffer from gross vitamin deficiency diseases, but they have episodes of colic and diarrhea. In school they get instruction about food, a balanced diet; about the importance of yearly visits to doctors and semiannual visits to dentists; about the need for a proper amount of exercise, plenty of rest, at least six to eight glasses of water a day, not to mention a quart of milk.

Gerry listens and wonders to himself: "There aren't any doctors or dentists for us to see. We have to drive to Albuquerque to get to see a doctor in a hospital. Sometimes they'll send a doctor up, but he's only got a few hours for the whole reservation. We can't buy the food the teacher says we should. My mother says the teacher is probably right, we should eat different things, but we can't afford to buy what she says is good for you. My mother says our ancestors ate better food than we do. Our ancestors knew the right things to eat; they just knew. I told our teacher that our ancestors ate the right way, and she said that is probably true. Then she asked the class why we don't follow our ancestors' example. No one raised a hand, and I was about to, but I didn't dare. Then a girl did; she said she likes to cook, and she and her mother go shopping together, and her mother says that the white man has conquered the Indian, when it comes to food. The Indians buy the same food the white people do, and they get sicker than the white people because they weren't born to eat that way, but white people seem to be able to eat anything they like, and if they get sick, they have a doctor to tell them how to get better. Besides, the whites have more money, so they can eat *more.* The Indians should stay away from a lot of store food, but they can't. The reason is that they don't have the farms they used to, and they've forgotten how their ancestors used to cook food, and what they liked to eat. That's what the girl said, and the teacher said no, it's not true."

The teacher's way of putting the matter did not escape the boy's notice. The teacher pointed out that Indians aren't compelled to give their children Coca-Cola, potato chips, candy. Let Indians return to the ways of their ancestors. Let them stop *talking* about their ancestors, stop venerating them, and instead actually follow their lead. Such a challenge, made forcefully, if not stridently, humbled (perhaps humiliated) many of Gerry's classmates. After school was over they wondered aloud as they went home why, in fact, they don't try to live the way Pueblo Indians once lived. None of the boys Gerry walked with had an answer that satisfied him. They all agreed that it was difficult, living at one time in history, to resume habits and customs prevalent under different circumstances. For Gerry the conversation was hard to put aside; he came back to it frequently in the days that followed: "We didn't like what she said, but I told my friends that she had a point: why don't we try to forget about the white people and build our own world? My brother Joe had a good answer: you can't, not now. Anyway, if you've got the kind of land we have, you can't grow much food. The white man has taken our water away. He beat us a long time ago, and we're not going to be able to win, if we start something now with him. Some Indians in South Dakota and places like that are trying to fight the white man, but I notice they ended up in jail. They sure didn't win! My uncle always says it is a miracle we are still here, some of us Pueblos. A lot of Indian tribes have disappeared. Many tribes are much smaller than us. We have tried to keep our heads up, and look straight at the white man, and not with our heads down, and we will keep trying. But we'll always belong to his country, America; it's our country, too."

He wants to make clear that the land around him does not really belong to anyone, not even his own Pueblo Indian people. The land is part of the world; he spells out with a good deal of passion what he has in mind: "I don't think the Anglos, the white people, know that the land is like the sky. The land is all over. It stretches for miles and miles; it meets the sky. The teacher keeps saying that California is less than a thousand miles from here, and that the land ends there. I raised my hand once and said that the water begins there, but the land doesn't end there. She told me I wasn't being very helpful. A little while ago my mother saw my little brother digging a big hole; he'd poured some Coke into it, and he'd thrown some candy wrappers into it. She called him over, and asked him why he was doing that. He said he was only playing. She explained to him that he wasn't only playing; he was digging up the land, and throwing food and garbage on it, and making it hard for us to enjoy that little spot on the reservation.

"I remember when I was little my mother talked to me the same way; my brother Joe and I had cut down a couple of branches from a pine tree, and we were using them to make a fort. My mother asked us where we'd found the branches, and we told her. She was very annoyed with us. She was going to send us over to her father and mother, and have them tell us how bad we'd been, but she changed her mind. She took us down the path to a pine tree — not the one we'd been taking branches from, but another one. She asked us to sit down on the ground and look at the tree. I wasn't sure what she wanted us to see. I was about to ask when she started talking about trees, and the grass, and the plants, and how they are children of the earth, and how the sky and the earth are their parents: the sun touches the earth, and the seeds grow, and there are meadows of grass, and trees rise up and cover the land. Then we come along and start hurting the earth's children! She told us we weren't going to be punished, but we must do one thing: every day look at the tree we'd been cutting, and at some other trees. Joe and I obeyed. Joe was upset; he said people cut trees down all the time. My mother said yes, they do, and they also kill and steal from other people all the time! She was very tough with us, and we decided to stop talking. She told Joe that she'd speak with him in a week or two after he'd thought about what she said to us."

He decides that he will use crayons to draw a tree, but he has a change of heart before he actually undertakes the project. Why not do the sky? He can watch it for hours. Like other Indian children, he has memories of staring and staring at clouds, as he makes clear when he begins to talk about the drawing he is doing: "Without the sky there would be no earth; and without the earth there would be no people. The sun brings us life. The sky sends us light and water — and the night for resting and sleeping. When I was smaller and I'd get into trouble fighting with Joe, my mother would make me take Joe's hand and go outside and sit down and look at the clouds and follow them, while they ran into each other. She'd ask us to come and tell her when the sun was halfway across the sky. We'd be really excited when the clouds would build up, and they'd begin to look like a mountain, and some would be low in the sky and some high in the sky. Joe and I would wonder if it might rain soon. There might be lightning, but no thunder and no rain. There might be thunder, and we'd miss seeing the lightning. There might be a drop or two of rain, but no more. The poor land, it would be as excited as us. The wind would come, and the trees would bend and the leaves would talk to the sky: we're waiting. But there is a lot of land in New Mexico, and the clouds probably have a hard time figuring out where they will let the water fall. It never once rained over us while we were little kids, watching. We picked the wrong times, maybe. We could see rain falling once in a while, but far away. We don't get much rain here."

He has been working patiently on drawing the clouds — as if they were a vertical building of peculiarly amorphous architectural design. As he begins to feel that there is no more work to be done, he stops, seems to be caught in a reflective fantasy, smiles to himself, but says nothing. He stares at the picture. He puts it aside and looks out at the sky: a cloudless day. He closes his eyes, as if to conjure up what he was trying to draw. Then he picks up a black crayon and makes with it a relatively small spot, to which he adds a pair of wings. A bird — an eagle or hawk? No; it is an airplane. (Figure 31.) He smiles again — and speaks: "I have seen the big planes flying through our clouds. The principal told our school that we are under the route used by jets that fly from New York or Washington to California. None of us has ever been to those places. I wouldn't mind traveling. My mother says it is dangerous and a waste of time, but it would be fun to see other parts of the world. The clouds travel, so why not us! When I said that to my mother, she smiled and said all right.

"There are some of our people who have gone to the cities, not a lot, but some. I have a cousin — he is much older — who lives in Albuquerque. For a while he lived in California. My mother promised us once to take us to see him there, but she never did. Then he came back to New Mexico. He said that he missed being near the reservation. He said he would look up at the sky and wonder if the clouds had been here, then crossed the desert, then showed up in California, where he was staying! I asked the teacher once if that happened, and she said no. But my mother told me it was wrong to ask white people such questions, because they don't look at the same sky we do!"

With that thought Gerry is ready for a few remarks about what it means for him to be an Indian boy. He begins by making clear how, a while back, he never gave the matter any thought at all. But his teachers have said things that have prompted surprise, anger, pity, envy in him; and of course, he watches television: "I'll be looking at a program, and I think to myself: the white people aren't like the Indian people. When the white people are in a plane, they watch a movie, like it shows them doing on television. If I was up there, I'd be scared — so near the clouds. I'd be excited. I'd want to be on a *slow* plane so that we could pick a cloud and follow it. My mother says the white people are always moving from place to place. They get the itch to go someplace, and they go. Their ancestors were eagles, according to my aunt. White people will be flying and suddenly they'll swoop down because they see something they want, and the next thing you know, they've got what they want. You can't beat them. They're too fast and too strong. The Indian — he's no match for whites in a war.

"I'd like to own a horse when I'm grown up. I'd like to ride the horse a lot, every day. My aunt says maybe my ancestors were horses because I love horses, and she says that when I run, she thinks of a horse. I was taught to ride when I was just learning how to talk. I remember my father saying that I had to hold tight with my legs, and I'd squeeze as hard as I could, and I wouldn't fall. My father was watching carefully — I now know; but I didn't realize he was, and I felt strong. Then, when I got bigger, I learned how to take care of the horse. My father made sure I was a good friend to the horse before I was allowed to go on rides by myself. I'd wake up and all I wanted to do was go feed the horse, and get water for her, and ride her, and I'd forget to feed myself! My father took me out one day with him; he borrowed a horse, and I was on mine. He told me that I'd better watch out because the horse would be very sad if I stopped coming around all the time — and if I got sick, then I'd no longer be able to care for the horse. That's when I started having my breakfast again!"

He will draw a picture of the horse, he decides. He begins, stops, begins again, stops. It is hard to draw the horse, almost as hard as to draw a person. He has never wanted to draw anyone, himself included; he will not draw the horse either. The horse is to visit, feed, water, ride — not depict on paper. He wonders what the horse would think of such a picture. She would probably whinny! Then she would run off; and when he caught her and tried to ride her, she would reply by throwing him. All he will do is talk about her, portray her with spoken words: "I talk to her before anyone else in the morning. She moves toward me when I go out, and her eyes are looking at my hands: the water or the food. She is very quiet. She is not a nervous horse. Some of them are very hard to live with! They think too much of themselves! But not our horse. She is *not* ours, my mother tells me; she belongs to the world, and we have been lucky enough to have the duty to care for her. When the teachers give us little bags of candy to bring home, we give them to our brothers and sisters; our grandmother tells us not to hold on to presents because they can take you over: soon you're not yourself. You've become the boy who has a bag of candy and doesn't want anyone else to have any! That's the first step in the direction of becoming the man who wants the whole world and won't let anyone else have a share of it."

Even if the horse is not *all* his, but part of everyone's world, he does indeed have the responsibility of caring for the animal, and he is the one who rides her most. He grooms her, cleans her hooves, keeps her mane and tail at a pleasing length. When he goes for a ride, it is usually a long one. He takes with him a bottle of Coca-Cola, or some water, and occasionally a jelly sandwich. He rides to one mesa, then another. Or he heads for the Rio Grande and follows it as best he can. He knows trails and never gets lost. That is to say, he always allows the horse to help him, if he thinks he may have gone too far and if he is not quite sure how to get back.

As he rides he looks carefully ahead, the way a good rider should; but he also admits to letting his mind drift: "I wait for places that I remember; there is a tree I love, and I always stop so that I can let its shade give a rest to the horse. I have some of my Coke. When we start moving again, I remember my father's words: always thank the tree for all it has given you. So I do. A few times I've let the horse graze, and I've climbed the tree; I've gone halfway up. When I hear the branches speaking to me — telling me that I am hurting them, and please, won't I stop — I know it is time to go back down and to apologize. I climb the tree because I like being up in it; my father says sometimes he wishes we could live in a cottonwood tree like that, especially when a wind comes and shakes the leaves. That's when the tree talks back to the wind. The horse lifts her head up when a wind comes, and her ears, too. She's waiting for a message. If there's a storm coming, the wind brings the news. You have to respect the wind; it has messages for everyone!

He decides to draw that tree with a pencil; he speaks of "the tree where the wind rests, and my horse rests, and I rest, too." He can see the wind coming toward the tree, sweeping the land here, combing it there, pushing bushes one way or another; then the encounter with the tree, which is too strong and large to yield easily. The leaves shake a bit, chatter noisily, then stop; the wind has moved along. Once on television he saw a documentary devoted to ships — merchant ships, navy vessels of various kinds, sailing boats, and luxury liners. What he most remembered and wanted to talk about was the path a ship makes as it moves over the water. He was reminded of the wind and what it does on the land he knows so well.

At times he becomes restless, as he indicates in the comments that accompany his effort to draw the tree: "I would like to ride the horse a day or two, so that I could sleep away from home. I would like to go a great distance, and then I could come back and tell everyone what I saw. I would remember everything, I hope. I don't want to get to the ocean; I only want to explore Indian land; there is a lot of it that other Indians have, and I am sure they wouldn't mind a visitor. I have an uncle who married a Hopi woman. They live in Arizona, on the Hopi reservation. I would like to go to visit them. I would like to test the horse; she lets me know sometimes that I am not giving her much of a challenge. I turn around and want her to go home, and she obeys, but I can feel her words in her muscles: we haven't even *begun* to ride! And it isn't that I'm tired. I'm just not old enough to ride harder. My father is old enough, but he doesn't care to ride; he says some of us are born to be riders, and some of us aren't. I'm a rider! In the old days, there were hunters, and those who grew crops, or took care of the pueblos — protected them, or kept the water supply working. My father has told me that one day he'll let me go on a long trip, though he thinks the Hopis are too far away for the horse and me to get there. He admitted he may be wrong, though!"

The tree is finished, and he likes what he has done. (Figure 32.) He has not offered the tree a sky, or the sun, or even ground. He decides to work on the last of those, and does so in silence and without interruption: no gazing off, no sip of Coke, no look toward others as they come and go. When he is satisfied that the tree is rooted firmly, he stops, resumes his talk about travel: "I would first go to the tree and say good-bye. The tree's branches are its arms, and the tree will pray sometimes; I'm sure it would say a prayer for me if I told it I was leaving and wouldn't be back for a month, maybe. When I see the tree on the rides I take, I think of my grandfather, with his arms stretched out, saying his prayers outside: 'Please, may we all be good to each other, everyone and everything under the sky;' that's what he always would say, and we would repeat his words. Then I'd move on; I'd go down the trail until I reach the edge of the reservation, and I'd be headed for the Anglo towns.

"They don't bother us now, the Anglos — so long as you don't get in their way. If you try to let them know you don't go along with their ideas, you'll get yourself into a lot of trouble. My father said that his grandfather used to say: Lower your head and keep moving, and the white man won't bother you. I don't like lowering my head because of them; I just *turn* my head, and I think of something important. I'll look at one of the smaller trees that's trying to grow, just outside the school, and if the teacher tells us we're not doing something right, I'll pick a tree, and go sit under it.

"My mother told me a long time ago, when I first started at the Bureau of Indian Affairs school, not to talk back to the white people, or to the Indians they have working for them, and not to mind if we hear bad things said about us. She said we should try to catch the sun's light on a tree, or keep our eyes on some shadow, and think of how welcome it is to the ants and worms, to the grass. Even the cactus plants don't mind some relief from the sun; some of them will bloom if it gets cloudy and stays cloudy. And they love the snow so long as it doesn't last too long. The funniest sight is the Anglos fighting the snow. The weather turns cold, and a few flakes

drop, and they get all their trucks and machines out. More
flakes fall, and they're scattering sand and salt all over the
roads, and pushing, pushing to keep the roads open; and in
front of their homes they shovel, and they make paths all over
the place. Then the sun comes out and melts the snow, and
what's left is sand and salt and the earth that's been cut up by
the plows. And you'll also see the last of their snowmen melting away. They won't leave the snow alone; they like the snow
because they can make snowmen or forts out of it, or snow-
balls. Our teachers at least give us credit for this: they say that
Indians enjoy the snow, but white people fight it — and white
kids fight *with* it!"

He can be a fighter too. He runs races with his brother Joe,
with cousins and neighbors and friends. He recalls a dream he
has had more than once: he is running as fast as he can, trying
to keep up with his mare; but she outdistances him, he runs
out of breath, falls down on his stomach, goes to sleep —
whereupon he wakes up. The dream is pleasant rather than a
source of frustration or apprehension. In another dream he is
riding his horse; his school's principal is on another horse. The
other horse is supposed to be a thoroughbred and very fast.
There are a number of people watching as the two of them set
out — his brother Joe, for one, who wishes him good luck. It
is to be a race, and he is determined to win — even though his
mother asks him, at the last moment, not to take part. He tells
her that he must, however; he tells her that he wants to teach
the principal how to behave himself, and be a decent, thoughtful, considerate rider who gets the best out of his horse without
hurting it or punishing it arbitrarily, unnecessarily.

In the race the principal seems to have an easy edge and to
hold on to it right along. The boy begins to get worried, urges
on his horse, gets nowhere, tries harder, kicking his horse to
get up speed, fails to gain ground, begins to despair, finally

gives up. He decides that he will lose with dignity and grace; he tells his mare that they will lose and even pats the horse as they keep moving along. He says a prayer of thanksgiving; at least both of them have been permitted to ride as well as they have on that occasion. Suddenly the principal and his horse get in some trouble. The boy passes them, wonders what has happened, finds himself the winner, but is quite concerned about the white man and his elegant, swift horse. Suddenly he wakes up — curious, still, about why he has ended up first, and what happened to his competitor.

He does not speculate about possible reasons; the dream is over, and that is that. But his view of what a dream is, and why such a dream ends as it did, tells quite a lot about who he is and how his mind works: "You dream because an ancestor is reaching out, wants to talk with you; or because you should have talked with someone and didn't during the day, so at night the person catches up with you. You wake up and you go and tell your mother and father who you saw, and they ask you if you learned a lesson, and you did. Sometimes, though, I'm not too sure what I've seen or heard in the dream. Usually, if that happens, I'll have the dream over and over, until I remember more, and I can tell people what it was like. Never try to force yourself to remember a dream; my grandmother used to tell us that, and she said you only make your ancestors angry, because a lot of the time they just want to keep visiting you, so that they can get to know you and you can get to know them before they tell you something that you won't forget. When they do, you'll wake up and it'll be right there on your lips to speak, what you heard, and you can see the dream, even without closing your eyes, when you tell someone what it was."

Even so, knowing and believing all that, he can't help wondering what happened to the principal because he has *also*

been taught to believe that a dream can be a prophetic statement as well as a visit with others, dead or alive, older or
younger — even those yet to be born. (He once dreamed he
was giving a ride to an infant; a little over a year later his
mother gave birth to a girl — after having had no children for
four years, and after having said that she hoped she didn't
have any more because her patience was wearing thin and she
feared that she would not "honor" her children enough.) Perhaps something ill was about to happen to the principal. Gerry
asked his mother and father what, if anything, he ought do.
Try hard to have another such dream as he lay in bed waiting
for sleep to come? Ask others what they know of the principal
and his present life, so that the boy and his parents might
figure out what the dream meant? Go to a teacher and let her
know that there might be some trouble ahead for the principal? None of those alternatives made any sense at all to the
boy. He considered the first an arrogant, manipulative effort;
the second a sly and insulting one; the third a gesture that
quite properly would be scorned and rebuked by the principal. Anyway, Indians can't go and talk with white people about
dreams because (as the boy knows quite well) most white people don't look at their dreams in the same way that many
Indians do.

How does an Indian boy learn about the way white people
regard dreams? And by the same token, how does he acquire
a notion of his own about dreams? The answer to the second
question supplies much information about how the process
implied in the first question gets under way. Gerry knows
quite well how and when he began to take an interest in his
dreams and report on them to his parents: "As far back as I can
remember, I would have dreams, and I would tell them to my
mother and father in the morning. Sometimes I'd forget, but
they would ask me — if I *kept* forgetting — and so I didn't

forget for too long. Once in a while I'd have a bad dream. My parents would hear me shouting or crying in my sleep, and they'd come to me and wait until I woke up. Or if I didn't wake up, they'd wait until I was quiet again, and then leave — and tell me in the morning that they were there, waiting for me.

"The worst dream I ever had, I still remember it, was one I had a couple of years ago. I was trapped by a mountain lion. I'd seen one on television — about a month before I had the dream. In it the mountain lion comes right toward me and is going to eat me up, I guess. I tried to climb up a tree, and I was almost out of its reach, but it got my foot. Then I woke up. I told my parents the dream; they were standing over me. My father told me not to worry; he said I had to learn how to take care of myself. He said that Indians aren't the ones who run America, and we're a few among many: the white people outnumber us over two hundred to one. So it's just as well that I learn how to run fast, climb fast, and be on the lookout most of the time! I've dreamed of that mountain lion a few times since then, and usually I get away without getting bit or clawed. My father tells me that our people, the Pueblo Indians, have never tried to attack others; all we have wanted is to be let alone. But no such luck! The Anglos won't leave anyone alone; and the Navahos aren't much better. It's hard to be a Pueblo — or a Hopi. The other tribes, the Navahos and the Apaches, used to be as much trouble as the Anglos to us and to the Hopis."

He repeats his interest in going to Arizona, visiting the Hopis. He goes on to tell another dream he has frequently had — short and to the point: "I was walking and I saw a mesa, and I climbed it, and on the other side was a river, and I crossed it, and I walked, and soon there was a hill, and when I got to the top, there were Hopi Indians, and they said we should live there, because we could see for hundreds of miles, and we were too high up to be in the way of the Navahos or the white people. So we started building houses, and then I woke up."

His father was especially delighted with that dream; he told the boy that he was doing quite well educationally, no matter what his teachers said. If the boy could realize that the Navahos are preoccupied with land for one reason, and whites for another reason, then he was on his way to being a worthy Pueblo. In the boy's words: "My father said the dream showed that one of my ancestors was keeping watch over me, and was teaching me everything that is most important for me to know. My father told his uncle about my dream, and his uncle came to see me. He said he didn't want me coming to see *him* any more; he wanted to come see *me* — because he was sure his own uncle, and maybe his great-uncle, too, had been the ones who spoke to me in the dream. He told me that I was proving myself to be a good son of our people, and he thought that some day I would realize even more that a dream like the one I had is a sign: the ancestors are taking an interest in the person they decide to visit at night."

The boy had a few mischievous questions to put to his elderly visitor: might not he, Gerry, even if a mere child, pay someone else such a visit? Ought the living, that is, not try harder to keep in touch with each other through their dreams? Do whites have the same kinds of dreams that Pueblo people do — and if so, might he try to give his schoolteacher a scare one night? The great-uncle smiled and told the boy that no one knew exactly and for sure who dreams what and why, or who speaks to whom through dreams — and when, under what circumstances, to what effect. But there is no doubt, the old man agreed, that white people need to be told rather a lot of things, though rarely do they let themselves be put in a position where that begins to happen. Perhaps white people have dreams like Pueblos do, the old man continued. Who can know for sure, given the barriers between "them" and "us"? But if that is the case, he added, they probably keep their dreams "a secret from themselves."

The boy remembered that phrase particularly well. He once considered asking a teacher he liked and trusted better than the others — but not all that much! — whether white people have the same kinds of dreams Pueblo Indians have. But the boy also cringed as he imagined the scene: an enraged teacher, quick to order him to stay home for a given length of time — until he could return and "behave himself." One night he had a dream about that teacher and himself: "I guess I thought so much about asking her if she dreams a lot, like my mother, that I finally *did* ask her — in my sleep. It was a long dream. She stood beside her desk and told me that she was sure she had seen our entire reservation from the window of an airplane, and she thought she could make out the school. I asked her if she'd noticed the mountain I like to look at. She said yes, she had. That's when we had a fight. I spoke right up to her. I told her she was lying. She picked up an eraser and threw it at me. I laughed and left the school, but she came running after me. I think it was then that the dream was over; I was awake and staring at the ceiling. The next day I felt strange when I went to school, and there she was; I thought she knew I'd dreamed about her, but I remembered what my father's uncle said: most white people keep their dreams 'a secret from themselves,' and they certainly aren't going to know if they are in our dreams."

He is not scornful of white people, or proud of his own people's attitude toward dreams. He has learned in his relatively brief life that his interests, choices, hopes, and fears or animosities are not by any means shared by white people. He knows, for example, that when he goes to bed and thinks of a

tree or a mesa or a cactus plant in spring bloom, and hopes
thereby to have a dream in which his thoughts become nighttime visitors of sorts, he is not at all thinking like white boys
of his age. When he compares himself and white youngsters,
he shrugs his shoulders and smiles; he also draws upon his
grandfather's counsel: "I was told by my father that his father
used to say that, just as there are all different kinds of plants
and trees and animals, there are different kinds of people. It's
best to remember that the white people aren't all the same,
either. Some of them are friendly and easy to be with, some
of them are dangerous and greedy. The same goes for Indian
people. My grandfather used to tell us that he knows many
white people born with Indian skin, and he is sure that some
white people really are Indians, even if they look white. My
grandfather knew a Hopi who told him that he was sure the
Navahos are really white men! My father laughs when he tells
us that. He says that some Navahos might say the same thing
about us Pueblos, and they might also say that the Hopis are
stubborn and crazy, like white people!

"I hope when I'm a father I can explain to my children all
the differences between the Indian tribes, and between us and
the white people. My father says he can't tell us everything we
want to know because a lot of our questions have no answers,
and a lot of them would be answered differently by other
fathers. When the teacher told us we should kill all the coyotes
we can, my father said no, we should try to keep the coyotes
from hurting our animals. My father thinks the coyotes make
the noise they do because white men live in them. Some white
men, when they die, visit animals like the coyote; that way the
Anglos keep up their bark, and keep howling at us, and make
us as worried as they did when they were men and women,
here in New Mexico!"

He always follows mention of New Mexico with an expression of curiosity about other American states. He will even go further; he has studied geography and learned the capitals of various European nations, and some day he hopes to visit them. Pueblos are not all that interested in travel, or at least his parents' and grandparents' generations don't seem to have been. But he has watched television, and thereby has already seen much of the world. And the BIA schools have made a point of letting children like him know about how others, elsewhere, live. His travel agenda starts with Albuquerque and nearby Arizona and Colorado. Later on, he daydreams, a time might come when for some reason, and in some way, he will manage to visit "the East" (of the United States) and even farther east, countries like England and France.

He especially thinks of Paris as a city he would like to see. He is quick to explain. "The best teacher we have teaches geography, and he told us that he was in France while he was in the army, and he used to go to Paris a lot, and he has a brother who went to school there, and another brother who worked there for a while, for an airplane company, I think. The teacher showed us the tower they have in Paris, and the rivers, and the buildings, and we saw a movie, and the French cars seemed much better than the American cars because they don't leave you in a cloud of smoke and they aren't big, like a tank. You could probably drive one of them, and it wouldn't frighten everything it went near, and it wouldn't leave holes and marks on our trails.

"The French don't talk like the Anglos. They don't speak Spanish, like a lot of people in New Mexico do. I told my grandfather that in school we heard a record of people speaking French, and they sounded different, a lot different, from the white people we know here. He said he was sure they *are* different; according to him, there were some white people who would have fought on the side of the Indians if they had a chance. I don't know if the French are that kind of white people. Even if they aren't, they're not like our Anglos here, and so I'd like to go see them. And Paris didn't look like any city I've seen pictures of. I had a dream a couple of nights ago; in it I was on my way to Paris. I was on one of those big airplanes. We landed. A man spoke to me in French. I told him that I couldn't speak French, but I wanted to live in Paris for a while, and see the tower, and the church, and the river, and the market, all the places we'd been shown in school by our teacher. The man said he'd help me. He showed me his car, and he told me he was a brother of my teacher's! And then I met his wife, and she cooked all the French food we heard about in school, but I didn't know what the food was. The dream ended with the French woman telling me that there are mountains in France, too, just like the ones we have in New Mexico, and she was promising to show them to me. I guess she meant the Alps; we heard about them in school too."

The dream made him somewhat uneasy; it was almost as if he'd actually left America, visited a foreign land, met the strangers he evoked for himself at night. When he went to school the next morning he took a rare initiative; he asked his teacher for the atlas so that he could look up France, and he also asked for a book about France, preferably with pictures. The teacher had, of course, given the children a few facts about France — but was quite taken aback by the boy's request: why would he be *that* interested? Having questioned him and received no real answer, the teacher produced the atlas and a geography book with pictures. The boy in good time returned them, but the teacher would not let the matter drop there; he asked the boy if he wanted to write a composition on France. The boy said no, he did not. Later on the teacher asked each child in the class to write a few sentences about any subject, and the boy obliged: "I would like to go to visit the Hopi people in Arizona. I would like to go to France, and while there I would see Paris, and the Alps. There are mountains here in New Mexico, and there are mountains in Arizona, where the Hopi live. I know people who have visited the Hopi, and some Pueblo Indians have gone to France during a war, when they were soldiers."

He is quite candid about his chances of getting to France: zero. But he fully expects to leave New Mexico one day, visit Colorado and Arizona, perhaps California. His father and mother have had no such interest in travel, and he dwells a bit on the difference — the one way, actually, he chooses to distinguish his own hopes or expectations from those of his parents. He does not want to *live* off the reservation; he has no interest in living in Albuquerque, never mind Denver, Phoenix, or Los Angeles. Quite simply, he wants to see how other Indian people live, and if possible, how white people live in various parts of America and Europe: "I would like to see the ocean. I would like to fly over the ocean. I would like to see the tall buildings in the big cities. Then I would come back here and tell my parents that they are right: this is the best place to live! My mother says the only thing she worries about is the Hopis; I might like to stay with them. No, I tell her — only a visit."

His mother says she doesn't really believe that he would prefer the Hopis to the Pueblos. She is sure, for instance, that there are Hopi boys who occasionally feel quite anxious to leave the reservation and see how others live. But she emphasizes the constants, the universals, to her son: the sun, the sky, the clouds, the land, the rivers and streams, the animals who, like men, women, and children, are also allotted a time of life on this earth. Once, as she and her son talked, a large cloud suddenly blocked the sun's light, not a rare event. The mother turned to her son and reminded him that the cloud came from someplace, that it was not only their cloud but belonged to others — among them, perhaps, the Hopi. The boy said nothing for a while. Then his eye caught sight of a plane that was moving in and out of clouds. The plane seemed so small, compared to the clouds, and so vulnerable — at least in the boy's mind. The white man is foolish, he insisted, to put so much faith in machines, when the clouds are there, the equal of anything or anybody; and surely, the boy added, all Hopis would agree with that judgment. The mother, somewhat aware of the Hopis through friends and relatives who have spoken of them, took that occasion to suggest that her son not only would, but should, go visit the Hopis. He might, she felt, find in them people to admire a great deal.

V

HOPI GIRL

IN A Hopi settlement in northern Arizona a mother stares at the sky, nods toward a cloud, turns her back on the sun, bends down toward her daughter, who is one year old and learning how to talk. As the mother does so, her older daughter, aged nine, also leans forward. The older daughter reassures the infant as she steps, falters, sits down, crawls, lifts herself up, moves more confidently, but alas, falls down, now a little hurt. The infant cries, softly but persistently. The mother looks down with a kind and not alarmed look, as if to say: this, too, shall pass, and the worst thing I can do is become too preoccupied with the quite natural and inevitable effort on the part of yet another child of mine to stand and move on her own. But she does smile, tilt her head ever so gently toward the baby. The older child, whose name is Miriam, begins to sing words of encouragement to her sister: "You will go/nothing will stop you/soon you will be tired/of walking, walking."

The words and music turn out to be Miriam's. She has heard her mother and grandmother, her aunts and older cousins sing songs — brief, unspectacular, not especially melodic messages, chanted with a rise and fall of the voice that indicate an earnest, lyrical conviction on the part of the speaker: I will speak to you, and you will hear, and we will join hands spiritually, *be*. Yet Miriam may in truth have no such intent. The girl's continuing encouragement to her little sister conveys some very concrete suggestions, as well as what anthropologists call "a world view." When, for example, the baby gets up to walk, Miriam kneels down, blocks the probable point of departure and line of travel, looks into the child's eyes, holds out two arms parallel to the ground, though without touching the child: they are there, to be called upon, leaned upon, if need be. Miriam begins to sing, then speak: "Do not run/do not run before you walk/do not walk/do not walk before you stand/When you stand/you will be one of us/the Hopis. That is for *you*, little one. Just look about. Just move with your eyes. You can go far with them. Later you can use your feet; rest them now. They will get strong, and they will hold you and carry you — until you leave us here. See my arm; if you try to walk, and feel like falling, hold on to it. Hold on to both arms. I will help. I will stay with you. Don't worry. The day will come that you are running with me, and after me, and away from me; and the day will come that you will be standing here, right here, and you will have a baby at your feet, and you will be singing to it and talking to it and you will tell it that you were once here too — crawling and trying to walk. To walk is for us what to fly is for that bird."

She stops to point toward the sky. The baby has watched her, listened intently, even if unable to understand the specific words. The baby has remained still for a few minutes. Now the baby lifts her head upward, tries to capture with her eyes the moving bird — but no luck. The eyes, too — the head, for that matter — are not ready. The baby sits down, at the same time lowers its head. The older girl sits down, also begins to look at the ground. She spies a small, flat stone, picks it up, feels it in her hands, holds it tightly between her palms, moves the palms toward the baby's face, holds them transfixed, almost as if in prayer, in front of the little girl, and suddenly: "Here you are! This is one of many; this is a Hopi stone. Do you see the lines on it? Someone made them. I do not know who it was, but they are here to remind us that before us there were others."

Again she pushes the stone toward the baby. Finally, she places it in the baby's hands and sits quietly to the side while she enjoys what white people would call a toy. But for Miriam the stone is no toy. She wants her sister to learn something about the land that she is trying so hard to walk on. While the mother continues to say nothing, the older daughter gets up and surveys the immediate vicinity for other stones. She finds them, including a rather sizable rock, and gathers them before her sister. She begins to point them out to the little one and talks for a few minutes about the wind, the rain, and time — how large rocks erode or get broken up over the centuries. She does not speak as an authoritative scientist or naturalist but rather as a philosopher: "These stones may have come from a mountain; we do not know. They are here for us, and we will leave them for others. I used to ask our mother if I could take them into the house and save them. I liked them. No, she told me; they are for you, here. They were for others before you, and they will be for others after you. Now it is your turn. I am glad I did not take them away when I was younger."

As Miriam makes her pronouncements, utters her prophecies, comes up with observations or interpretations, the baby leans slightly forward, reaches out with her hands, picks up the stones, holds them up high, drops them — one after the other. Then the last, big one — she puts both hands on it, apparently wise enough to know that an obstacle confronts her. No luck, though. She decides to push. What she cannot lift she can indeed cause to tumble over. She is delighted. She smiles *at* the rock, then looks toward her mother and older sister for approval. They nod their heads but say not a word. The baby seems to take their silence as a cue: if they do not resume their singing and conversational companionship, she had better find some momentum within herself. And she does; she crawls, begins to stand, succeeds in her effort, sets out, moves away from the two older people, and walks, walks.

Not a sound from the mother and Miriam; they pretend indifference, preoccupation with other interests. When the baby decides to turn around and announce to them, standing up, her triumph, they seem involved in another scene: the sheep grazing a mile or two down the hill. The baby feels free of them. She changes her direction, walks off at an angle to her previous course — in the direction of the sheep. She is walking at an incline and, one would think, is taking an unnecessary risk. But she does exceedingly well. She walks thirteen steps, abruptly stops, then decides to confront her mother and sister once again. Now they are quite willing to respond; they smile, they stand up, they say "good, good," but they do not move toward her. Miriam breaks the impasse by pointing to a rock that rests on the ground between them, and the baby dutifully and respectfully moves toward it, leans over, falls down, quickly stands up — with the rock in her right hand. She moves her other hand toward it, forms a cup with both hands, cradles the rock, peers at it, then throws it — her body swaying — in the direction of the other rocks. As her mother and sister look at this addition to the small collection, she moves toward them and stops only when she is right beside them. All of a sudden she sits down, right on top of the stones.

The baby's mother and older sister are delighted; they clap their hands and virtually exclaim to the world beyond them — as if a thousand people were waiting nearby to hear — the news that a little girl has claimed her heritage. The mother says: "She has made them hers, and they will be hers.

She belongs to us, and we belong to her." Miriam says, far less grandly, but with no lack of serious appreciation: "She is beginning to understand. Soon she'll be walking all over, and she'll know the best places to stop and rest."

One such place is where they are, on top of a gentle but barren hill, at the edge of a virtual desert. All around them the land, their Hopi land, stretches. After a few minutes the mother decides to intervene directly for the first time. The mother draws close to the baby, fondles her, then gently lifts her up. The baby is glad to be standing again, smiles, looks up at the mother. But she wants the baby to look elsewhere, and she conveys her wishes patiently, quietly; she looks with her own eyes not at the baby, but out toward the rising hills, and she points in that direction with her forefinger. Soon the baby's eyes leave the mother's face; soon those eyes scan, a bit unsteadily, to be sure, the Hopi reservation. The mother, as if it were bedtime and a lullaby were in order, recites, with a slight singsong inflection to her voice, a series of reassuring predictions: "You will walk from here to there, to the highest of those hills/You will walk to that tree down the road/You will sit under that tree and say thank you, tree, for the love you give to the Hopi people/You will run so fast that the sun will draw sweat from you/You will find the valley and the water/ Then you will not be a baby, but a *Hopi.*"

Miriam nods with each assertion, moves her eyes across the land slowly, deliberately, thoughtfully. She looks at the solitary tree longest. She watches the sky, follows a cloud across it. She sees some Hopi men walking in the distance, smiles at them. She seems ready to point them out to her infant sister but apparently has second thoughts. She points them out instead to her mother, who shows no great interest. The mother has only one more sight to urge upon her younger daughter, and it is a rather subtle one, which seems beyond the grasp of a one-year-old child: "The sun is breaking through the cloud; it is light over there, and darker here. Shadows don't always last. The sun. The sun." The baby does not look at the sun, but the mother is nevertheless pleased; she has made her point. Miriam reinforces it by cautiously moving her sister's face in the direction of the sky, and more precisely, the part of the sky the sun occupies at the time. The baby quickly wants to look away and, of course, is allowed to. But a moment later, on her own, she is bending her neck, peering over the heads of Miriam and her mother toward the sky.

They leave shortly thereafter. Miriam holds her sister for a while, then without saying a word hands her to their mother. The baby is hungry and is given the mother's breast. Miriam smiles as the baby works away, stopping occasionally for rest or to burp. Back at the house Miriam is delighted to tell her older and younger brothers that their sister is getting to know the reservation and even laying claim to some of its stones and rocks. They pass the baby around, each of them holding her, cradling her, congratulating her on her new acquaintance with their reservation. Soon the baby yawns, is put down to sleep. The children scatter — the boys to run and vie with other boys (who can throw farther? who can jump higher?) and Miriam to her mother's side: clothes to wash, food to cook.

An hour later Miriam has some spare time; she is in the kitchen, and has just taken a Lorna Doone cookie. She sits munching at it very slowly and starts a drawing. She will draw the entire reservation! It is easy! She scratches the paper lightly with the brown crayon, then with the blue one, and makes only slightly more restrained gestures with the green one. She is done! An afterthought, however; she picks up the yellow crayon and draws no sun, but rather scratches the entire picture with that crayon too. The result — a sun-drenched

version of the Hopi reservation, as seen from the hill where
the baby had just been. (Figure 33.)

She attempts another drawing. She loves a nearby valley,
tightly held in by red and brown clay hills. She sketches those
hills — is now quite concrete with her crayons. She is especially interested in a solitary clump of grass and a small tree
in its midst — on the side of one hill. She works at the tree with
painstaking care, then moves on: the sun, the sky. When she
is done (Figure 34) she has a few remarks to make about the
scene: "I am waiting for the day I can take my sister to the
valley, and we can sit on a rock there and look up at the tree
and be near the grass. My brothers like to stand on the rock
and jump; I like to sit on it and listen. Almost always a few
stones come tumbling down the side of the hill — our ancestors running about! I don't hear them speak words, but I know
they are there, and they love the tree; it is the place where
they can rest. There may be an underground river nearby. My
father says no, but my older brother says the teacher told him
that for the tree and the grass to grow, there has to be water,
and there's not enough for grass to grow on any other part of
the hill, so maybe there's a well there, if there isn't the river.

"My father laughs: what do the teachers know? He's always
saying that. He says the teachers sometimes have come in here
from far away; they want to be of help to us, and they don't
know how to understand us when we tell them no, we don't
need their help. My father says that once people came here
because they thought there was gold. They looked and looked.
They looked very hard near the tree; they were going to cut
it down. They were sure that there might be some gold underneath the trunk. Our people came and stood next to them and
prayed that they would stop trying to hurt the land. They said
they'd kill us if we didn't stop bothering them. Our people said
they would stand there, even if they were killed. They

wouldn't leave. They were ready to join their ancestors. The white people kept looking, but they didn't find anything. They were going to cut down the tree, just to make our people feel bad; but one white man got scared because the wind started blowing very hard, and the sun hid behind a cloud, and then hail began to fall; it was getting toward winter. So they left fast. My grandmother will tell us the story when the moon is full, and then we go out with her and say her prayer to the tree: 'Stand there/Bend toward us/Your green reminds us of the brown/Your height makes us know our size/Your shadows whisper to us/We are Hopis/We are Hopis.' "

She has memorized the words and sings them to no particular tune, only with the slightest of inflections. She has been told at school that she is a bright girl, but her parents are not all that impressed. They wonder what difference the schooling will make in her life — and they express their doubts to her. She speaks of what she has heard with an air of authority: "My mother says that at school we learn a lot, but what we learn doesn't help us here on the reservation. The teachers want some of us to leave and try to live someplace else, in a city maybe. My father says this reservation of ours is the whole world, and he never wants to leave it; he never wants to go live in another world. Last week I went with him; he was leading the sheep to a field where there is grass. We came to the big rock; it suddenly is there, when you turn the corner of the path. The rock looks like three fingers pointing up to the sky.

"My father told me again the story his grandmother used to tell him — about three Hopi men a long time ago. They were very good friends, but they didn't help others, only themselves. They left their families, and they met some white people, and they joined up with them. They all looked for gold, I think. The three Hopis stopped being Hopis. They became lost; they belonged nowhere. They went to the West, on their way to California. They got into trouble; they were caught stealing. They never got to California. They turned around, and came back to us, the Hopi people, and asked to be taken in. Our ancestors said no, we shouldn't do it. But the three men begged, and their mothers were still alive, and they came, and they asked the other Hopis to be good, and to take the three men back. There was a vote, and most Hopis said yes. But before the men could come to a ceremony and be welcomed back, they died. Then someone said that the bodies should be taken to the Three Fingers Rock, and the bodies would rest there, and they would be among us, and we would not forget them. And we haven't. My father says at night you can hear sand falling down from each of the fingers, and it's the spirits of the three men, moving up there. When some of our Hopis have gone away, they go to the Three Fingers Rock right away when they come back, and the three Hopis up there welcome the travelers back. My uncle went to Phoenix, Arizona, then to New Mexico, and when he came back he went to the Rock, and he said he thought he heard some noise up there, so he asked out loud if the three Hopis were there, and just then the wind rose, and it didn't stop for a long time."

She uses crayons to convey that rock and the surrounding land: a few trees, some sagebrush, a path. As she puts the colors brown, red, and orange on the paper, she makes clear her sense of inadequacy: no one, she is sure, can really draw or paint that towering, mysterious, somewhat frightening rock as it really is — because it changes its appearance so often. She apologizes for her attempt. (Figure 35.) She stops painting, drawing, talking. She looks at the Rock. It is late in the afternoon; the Rock glows from a distance as it catches the setting sun's rays. Some Hopi children have gone rushing to their parents, uncles, aunts, grandparents to tell them that the Rock

is on fire. All who hear go to a place that affords a view and
watch silently — until, as Miriam's mother puts it, "the night
will put out the fire." In a few days there will be the sight of
the Rock lit up by the moon — an eerie luminous color that has
prompted various legends. The one Miriam likes to tell has to
do with the three men. They express the regret they feel for
wandering so far and for abandoning in their minds the conviction that they were and wanted to be Hopis. The glow of
the Rock is the result of the intensity of their sadness, their
self-accusations, their fervently spoken remorse.

In broad daylight and under the sun's unremitting intensity,
the Rock seems to glow with the heat. At times the Rock seems
to have captured the sun itself; the Hopis shun looking at it lest
their eyes be hurt. Stories have been made to go with that
brightness: the three buried Hopis, still greedy for gold, have
set a trap for the sun, convinced that it is the prize of prizes
— full of gold, blazing yellow rays. But they succeed only in
scorching themselves; the sun, of course, escapes. And finally,
there are the shadows that clouds bring. Miriam is not sure
that she likes the Rock at that time. She has been told that for
the Rock, as for people, shade offers relief from the scorching
sun. But she worries that the three Hopis who dwell there may
well feel cold, shut out from the world, condemned to something akin to the white man's hell.

She is not too talkative about such matters, but enough so
to reveal the awe she and other Hopi children accord that
rock: "My mother says I worry too much about the Rock, and
the three men; but she says she is glad that I do. Some Hopis
have tried to forget about the Rock; they laugh and say we
make too much of the place. But why is it there, and why does
it change its look so often? I don't know how to paint it. My
father asked me why I bother. I said that we have a Hopi
teacher, and he says that we should try to close our eyes and

think of the Rock, then draw it or paint it — and that's a way of going there on a visit. I've gone there in the morning, in the middle of the day, and at night. The Rock looks different at different times. The three Hopis are like everyone else; they have moods. My mother tells us to look very closely because each time the Rock looks different. I like to look from far away: the three fingers practically touch the sky. Once we were far, *far* away, and the sun was going down, and the sky was red, all over it was red, and the Rock was a shadow, and it looked as if, any minute, the shadow would go away — it would disappear into the sky, and there would be nothing for us to find if we went near except some tumbleweed. Tumbleweed will run away from you, or it will bother you, if you've been doing anything wrong. My mother says tumbleweed is the wind's hand; if the tumbleweed comes after you and hits you, that means some spirit is telling you something and you've done wrong; but if you're walking and the tumbleweed gets out of your way, then you've been doing good, and you deserve an easy walk."

VI

HOPI BOY

MIRIAM has a cousin who is two years older, a boy with whom she often plays and whom she admires a lot. His name is John, and he argues with her about the Rock, about tumbleweed, about the sky and the land. Not that he disagrees with what Miriam and her parents believe; it is a matter of having additional thoughts and ideas. He has heard Miriam talk, has heard his mother say similar things; but he insists that his mother has told him that he can come to his own conclusions about the meaning of objects around him and events that he sees taking place. He makes clear his loyalty to others, to their beliefs and often-stated values; but he also insists upon his capacity for more or less independent judgment: "When I was younger my mother told me not to climb the Rock. Now Miriam says I still shouldn't climb the Rock because the spirits of Hopis live there, and I should respect them and not bother them. My father said I should respect every part of the reservation; it's all right to play near the Rock. If there are spirits of our ancestors there, they may leave, then come back. My grandmother told me that sometimes there is a struggle between the earth and the sky, and that the Rock is the earth's hand lifted to the sky: let us have peace. The earth would like to be friends with the sky; the sky is often good to the earth.

But sometimes the sky turns into an enemy. The wind blows hard on the land, and we all have to go inside.

"Once, during a windstorm, my grandmother looked outside and said she was sure the Rock was going to be blown away. We were all sad. But she laughed and told us we were foolish for believing her. When I looked out of the window, I thought the Rock was the only part of the land that wasn't in trouble. The sand was all over, and the tumbleweed; but the Rock was the same. My aunt told us she was sure the Rock was shaking its fist at the sky. My father claims he was told when he was a boy that the tumbleweed fight until they reach the Rock, and then they stop; and the Rock stops the sand, too, when the wind blows it. I like to see tumbleweed coming across the land, and first one in front, then another, then another. Finally they all land against the Rock, and they are as still as can be. You have to look with your own eyes; they may see things others miss."

The Rock may be a mediator, a pacifier, an umpire, or, at the very minimum, a place against which the various elements of the natural world hurl themselves, but John wants to make clear that for him the Rock has a personal meaning. He approaches the Rock not with veneration, not with fear. He does move cautiously and quietly, and only in spurts, followed by periods of solitary watchfulness; some sandhill cranes stay there from time to time, and he wants very much to observe them without prompting them to leave. And in the early spring, or late in the summer, migratory snow geese will often stop on that rock, survey the landscape, rest a bit, and proceed north or south. John likes to observe them too. The boy has been interested in birds and in their home, their place of respite, for a long time — as long as he and everyone he knows can remember. Many of his friends and relatives regard his interest with a certain awe: "I don't know whether John has ever told anyone about all he learns when he goes to meet the birds. He will ask all of us please to leave him alone. He never says why, but we know. Then my aunt puts her hand over her mouth, and that means we should be quiet, and not bother John, and let him leave for the Rock. I asked my mother last spring, when John went to greet the geese, why he goes. She said no one knows; she said that maybe the geese wanted one of us to come say hello after their long trip, and John is the one they chose to call."

John knows that if he approaches the birds in a certain way and alone, they don't flee. They do take notice of him and send messages to him. He speaks of this without pride or boasting, but matter-of-factly, descriptively: "The first time that I saw the birds there, I stopped and went no farther. I was with a friend, and he was younger by a year, and I held my hand to my mouth, and he stopped talking. We just stood there. My friend wanted to get closer, and so did I, but we both must have known not to move anymore. The birds were just about to leave; they had begun to open their wings. I saw one begin to lift itself up — the length of a few stones above ground. Then no, it decided no; it decided not to go, but to take a chance and stay. It turned half away from us. I thought for a second it was ignoring us. It wasn't, though; it was trying to see if we'd come closer. We still didn't move. I blinked and expected the birds to fly away. I swallowed, and thought a waterfall was at work inside me. My feet could feel the ground, and wanted to move, but I wouldn't let them. The birds didn't move either. I wondered what would happen next. My friend looked at me; he could see on my face: don't move, *don't.*

"At last the birds moved — first the one who had half turned away from us; it seemed to be the leader. It stepped forward, toward us, then plunged its beak into the ground, looking for food. Once that happened, the others followed; they began walking around and looking for food, too. We stayed where we were. Then we began to walk backwards! They looked at us, but didn't seem worried. My grandfather had taught me to walk backwards, and I was grateful to him. He said that there is no reason to turn away from something you want to keep looking at! I told my friend what to do: first one foot back, then the other — and don't look down. The birds must have wondered what kind of strange people we were! My grandfather said afterwards that the birds may be used to the white man; all he wants to do is kill birds or capture them. The teacher said my grandfather is wrong. I spoke about the birds in class, and the teacher said I shouldn't talk like that before a white teacher, or I'd be in trouble. But I wouldn't anyway, I told her. She said she didn't agree with me or my grandfather; she said she is a Hopi, and she has no great love for the white people, but they don't all hunt down birds, and some of them love birds. I hope she is right."

He believes she is right; he also believes she isn't right. The highest authority for him is his mother's father. They go on walks together. The old man points out birds, trees, sage, various grasses, rocks of different colors or consistencies, cacti. The old man talks about the land, the sky, the horizon, the mesas, the hills, the valleys, the canyons; about Hopi land, Navaho land, the white man's land. The boy estimates: "My grandfather knows the whole world. He will say to me sometimes that a walk down the path toward the Rock is a walk into the whole world. He is sad when he hears that a Hopi has left the reservation. He says that people start in one place and walk and walk, and think they are going someplace else, and end up back where they were to begin with. Every afternoon my grandfather walks halfway to the Rock; he sits down on the ground and looks at the Rock and then at the sky. Usually the sun is getting weaker; he looks toward it, then away. He always watches the sun set, every afternoon that there are no clouds between it and us. When there are clouds, he talks to them. He tells them that they are being stubborn and foolish; the sun will win, and they will be no more."

But the most important times with the grandfather take place in spring when John and the old man take a long walk to a nearby canyon, find birds resting on their way north, a stream full of nearly melted snow, and the first flowers of the season. The old man will be speechless for many minutes; the boy expects as much but admits to nervousness: will he *ever* say anything? The boy knows when his grandfather would welcome a word or two; he sends a wordless "message," and it is not itself something that can be described with words. "I can tell by my grandfather's face that he would like a little more silence, or he would like to talk. It's not his eyes, exactly. It's not his mouth or cheeks. Maybe it's his forehead. I don't know. If his forehead has a lot of wrinkles, I say nothing. If there aren't too many wrinkles, I might start talking — but not always. A few times I am wrong. I begin to talk, and I can feel it that I am wrong, and I stop. But I've never been called wrong. He will listen to me anytime, I know that. I don't want to speak with him, unless he wishes to listen and talk. Otherwise he is a prisoner of mine!"

He has been taught to think like that, to use that imagery. The old man has told him many times that to be free is to know how to be at ease with the natural world and be part of it; to be a plunderer — an excessive talker, for instance — is to be a prisoner. White people, the boy knows, move all over, tear up land, divert rivers, cut down forests, and talk, talk; white people own and run America, surround the Hopis, have control over much of their lives, certainly the boy's education. But many white people, though not all, are prisoners, and many Hopis, though not all, are quite free and independent. The boy elaborates: "My grandfather worked for the government, for forest rangers. He helped them take care of our trees. Some parts of our reservation have trees; some parts have no trees. The rangers told him that the Hopis aren't very smart because they don't want to see any trees cut down. The rangers say some trees are no good, and they should be removed. The rangers are trying to make sure there will be no fires. My grandfather says he is sure the rangers know best, but they don't understand how the Hopi people want to live.

"The white man is always taking something away from the world. White men fight with other white men. The Hopis only want to live quietly. My grandfather says that the white man can't be quiet and can't sit still. He's always in prison. He's always trying to break out of prison. He's always up to a new project! He comes to us with an idea, and then another one. My father and my uncles ask my grandfather for advice, and he tells them to listen to every word the white people speak, and don't look away; look right at them until they look away — and they always do. Then when they are through, keep looking at them, and nod your head, and say yes, I've heard you — but don't say anything else. They'll think you're in need of more of their schooling, but they'll be worried, and they'll leave you alone. They'll say they can't understand the Hopis!"

He smiles. He wonders whether he ought go on talking about the way Hopis get along with whites when one of them is right there listening. The boy decides that he'd rather talk about the physical world. The walks with his grandfather have been the most satisfying single experience of his life. There is so much to see, to learn. The old man is such a good teacher. But John knows that death takes everyone, that his grandfather is likely to die soon, and he struggles hard with that knowledge, even as his grandfather has encouraged him to do just that: "My grandfather told me the other day that he ex-

pects to leave us soon, and he will try to let me know which
walk we take will be our last one. I didn't like to hear that! I
told him no, he would be here for a long time, for as long as
there is time, even if he wouldn't be here as my grandfather,
taking a walk with me. We come here, then we leave our
bodies, and others get born into their bodies. But we never
leave the reservation, and we never stop being Hopis. My
grandfather told me that on the day he says good-bye to his
body, I should go on the same walk we always take. I promised
I will. And he hopes he will say his good-byes at night, and that
everyone will be asleep, and that in the morning they will see
that he slipped away a few hours ago, and they will know that
he is quite happy and is someplace nearby. We will go outside
and call to him and say we are glad he is in our world, and
watching us, and we are glad that he spent the time with us
that he did, and now that he has left his body, we will put it
in our land, and we know he would be very happy if we gave
his body a place near the path he liked to take, the path of
flowers."

That path and its flowers, which blaze out in spring, mean
a lot to the boy as well as to his grandfather. The old man has
taught his grandson to enjoy the sight of flowers, but also to
find them a source of reassurance as well as of beauty: so long
as the cacti and other desert flowers bloom, the world remains
a benevolent place. Often as they walk the grandfather asks
the child to shift perspective, imagine himself an ant or a fly:
how do they regard the flowers? Often the grandfather speculates: why are flowers put here on the earth or, for that matter,
ants and flies — or people? His answers are not really forthcoming: "He asks questions sometimes, but he doesn't expect
me to answer them. He won't answer them, either. I used to
try to give answers, but he'd shake his head and tell me he
wasn't a teacher — one of the white BIA people, or one of

their Indians. My grandfather says he always knows when an Indian is becoming won over by the white people; he will begin to ask other Indians a lot of questions, one right after the other, and he will look very unhappy if he doesn't get answers."

The old man will sometimes get down on his knees, examine a cactus or a spring flower, call upon the boy to do likewise, then turn his head up to the sky and express his delight, his gratitude. The boy isn't always sure precisely why the man should feel so thankful. He will say that he, too, liked what he'd been looking at, but he stops short of an announcement of prayerful indebtedness. One day the boy asked his grandfather why he was *so* enthusiastic. *That* question the old man welcomed and answered: "He took me to a place he likes; we went up a path until we were on top of a hill, and we could see far off. A plane flew over us, and I wanted to point it out, but he'd seen it, and he said: 'The white man.' I said yes. He said Indians can be found in planes, too. I thought we were going to talk about planes and the other machines of the white people, but he said he wanted to explain to me why he is so happy when he sees a flower that wasn't out yesterday, or the sun scattering itself all over, before it leaves us for the night. The flower is there for us; and we are here for the flowers. We're all part of the Hopi world; he kept on saying that to me — his answer, I guess, to my question. Then he said we'd come back and talk some more, but I mustn't forget: the flowers, the Rock, the sun, a cloud, me — we're all part of the Hopi world. I promised I'd keep remembering what he told me.

"The next day we started walking, even though we'd had rain. I wanted to collect some of it in bowls. He brought out some bowls. We started walking and got wet. He didn't mind. In school, the teachers won't let us come into the classroom if we're wet, or if we have snow on us. My grandfather takes off his shirt and washes himself in the rain, and puts his shirt on the ground, and is glad that the shirt gets as wet as he does. Sometimes he holds his hands out, and makes a cup of them, and collects the water, and drinks it. He loves to eat snow too. He likes to lie down on the snow. He says snow feels better to him than clothes, especially the shirts we buy at the store.

"That day, when it was raining and we were walking, he reminded me that soon there would be flowers: the rain does that! I said yes, and we sat down to wait. But suddenly he walked away from me. I was worried. I thought I might have done something wrong. My mother and father always tell us that an old person is a very special person, a person who has been asked to stay with us, so that we can learn from him. I was afraid my grandfather was sick, and he might die. I was afraid I might have said something wrong. He came back in a few minutes though. He'd been staring at the sky by himself, but he wanted to talk as soon as he was beside me. He said I should know that big and little are equal: the ants and the sheep are equal; a snake and a horse are equal; a big rock and a small one are equal; the sun and the moon, the earth and the sky, an old man and a baby, a large cactus and a small one, they're all equal. I said yes, I know. Then he asked *me* a question! Did I ever think that an ant or a flower might want to look at him as much as he wants to look at them? I said no. He said he feels the flowers asking him to bend down and say hello — or the sky asking him to raise his head. So he does."

The boy decides to stop talking and instead draw a picture. He excuses himself, reaches for paper and crayons, sets to work. At first he is exceedingly wary of revealing his intentions as an artist. He lightly scratches the paper with brown, then a touch of green, then a touch of blue, but seems loath to do so in an organized fashion: land, vegetation, sky. For a while he seems to be mixing the colors — so that nothing definite or coherent will emerge. But no, he has his own view to construct. He has heard his grandfather talk about the *connectedness* of the various parts of the world, and he seems to want to remind himself of the old man's philosophy as he goes about his work: "I used to wonder what he meant, when he told me that the sky was in the ground, and the ground was in the trees, and there was nothing in the world that was separate from anything else, but my mother would explain some of what he'd say to me. A lot of the time he'd say that he didn't really expect me to understand his every single word. It had taken him all his life to begin to know that he was understanding, at last, what he used to hear *his* grandfather say. My mother says that my grandfather means that the sky gives us the sun and rain and snow; and the sky feeds the ground — where the trees are. We wouldn't be here if the sun said it was going to leave us, or if the ground that holds us got weak."

Having said that, he resumes his drawing, now satisfied that he has provided a rationale for his artistic approach. It is obviously important for him to be loyal to his grandfather's teaching and to the Hopi values and principles he has heard expressed by those whom he trusts and honors. He works in silence for a good five minutes. He calls upon other colors, yellow and red and purple. He constructs an enormous rainbow, which eventually dominates the entire picture and makes its rather sketchy, amorphous quality seem exactly the right "background." Not that the rainbow is made distinct and imposing. It, too, is subtly drawn, in keeping (the boy knows and says) with its "nature."

As he uses the crayons, and afterward as well, he recalls what his grandfather has told him about the rainbow: "The first time I remember seeing a rainbow my grandfather was taking a walk, and I was with him. He was very excited. He made sure I saw it. He explained to me that I would never, in my whole life, see anything more important. I wasn't old enough then to understand all of what he was telling me. I knew that the rainbow was not something I'd see every day, so I should stop anything else I was doing and look. He said that the rainbow is something we take as a sign of hope — that when a rainbow appears, it means that the Hopi world is smiling and happy. Since that first time, we have seen several rainbows, and each time he has cried, he has been so happy. I feel like crying myself. The tears fill my eyes, but I try not to let them come. My father says it is all right to cry, but some of my friends say the Hopis have to learn to be tough, or the Navahos will take us over, and so will the white man. In school they say that all over the world the strongest win over the weakest. My friend's father was in the war, and he came back and told every Hopi man he met that if we don't change — stand up and fight for our land and our rights — we'll end up disappearing. But my grandfather believes that as long as there are rainbows, the Hopis will be strong and will live as they want to, and no one will win over us.

"The last time we saw a rainbow, he told me that he wasn't feeling too good, and that he may leave us soon. He spoke to the rainbow; he said that his father and his grandfather used to come get him and take him up a hill where they could all see the rainbow better than in front of their house. His grandfather wanted to die on the day a rainbow came; he thought it would be the best day. My grandfather feels the same way; he tells us, every time a rainbow comes, that he may not be with us the next day. But so far, he still is with us. When it rains, I know that he'll be coming out from his house, looking for me: come on, let's get high up the hill, so we'll be ready for that rainbow. I go with him, and he walks so fast, he makes me feel like *his* grandfather!"

The drawing is done. (Figure 36.) The boy looks with pride

at the rainbow. His grandfather has told him much that is important. But so have others. There are schoolteachers, and friends of his, some of whom have parents less loyal than his own mother and father to the Hopi traditions and beliefs. One minute John declares a rainbow to be *caused* by the sun's rays, as they encounter rain or mist; the next he refers to the *meaning* of a rainbow — its symbolic function, as a reminder of the *wholeness* of the natural world, its intactness. His father encourages him to listen both to his grandfather and to his teachers at school; they don't disagree, the father insists, they simply are looking at the world in two ways. It is best not to say that anything anyone says is the last word.

In the boy's words: "There isn't one rainbow; there are a lot of different rainbows. Even my grandfather admits that one rainbow is just the rain sending us a greeting: hello! But another rainbow is the sun and the clouds and the rain holding out their arms to the earth, and the earth saying how glad it is that rain fell. My grandfather says that rainbows speak. I've never heard them speak. Our teachers say a rainbow is the sun's rays, and they go through mist, after a rainfall, and we see different colors. The teachers are right, but so is he. The whole world is under the rainbow, and everyone sees it and everyone stops whatever they're doing. Even at school, they let us out, and they tell us that it's beautiful, and that in a lot of places they never see rainbows, but here we have the biggest ones, and according to the principal, when you look at our rainbows, you can't help believing that all of us — the Hopi people, and our land and our water and our sky and our hills and our trees and our rocks, even our tumbleweed and cactus plants — we are all part of God."

John is not all that sure about the details of Hopi beliefs — nor about the white man's Christian faith. John does know, however, that white people have a personal god and that his family possesses a deep reverence for the world around them. He also knows that his grandfather's religious preoccupations are, to a significant degree, private: have not been shared with others. The same goes for his parents. Actually, they seem far less interested in matters of faith than in living better lives, in making as good a living as is possible, in his education and that of his brothers and sisters. He has his own way of distinguishing the difference between an older Hopi and younger ones: "I like to run. We have races — in school and here, near our houses. I've won a lot of times. My grandfather doesn't like to hear me talk about winning. He says I should learn to go as fast as possible, but if someone else goes as fast as I do or even faster, then I should be doubly happy — for myself and for him. My father says you can't always be like that; you have to keep an eye out for the next guy. For a long time we've let the Navahos come on our land, use it for their sheep. My grandfather says the Navahos are here, just as we are here, and he laughs at the people who want to divide the land, and make sure each side stays where it belongs. He says we are part of the world, like the sheep, and rabbits, and the birds, and it is foolish to argue over a mile of land here, a mile of land there. But my father doesn't like to hear him talking like that. The eagle will swoop down and kill a rabbit; so will the hawk. The rabbit had better watch out! We have been too generous, my father says. My mother agrees; she told us that the Hopi have to learn from the white man, or else there won't be any Hopi left. She says that it's good that we learn some of the white man's ideas; then we'll be able to stand up and defend our land, and we'll be able to keep alive. Otherwise, we don't have a chance!"

The boy is convinced that the Hopi have a tough road ahead, that they must learn to be strong, agile, forceful, competitive, even defiant. He says so, actually, by drawing upon the qualities of various animals, as well as upon the descriptions of the natural world his parents and grandparents and others have come forth with over the years. The rock is strong, impassive, will not yield to the seemingly relentless wind, the driving and corrosive rains or snows, the pounding sun, which can make dust of the earth, and a pool of sweat, it sometimes seems, of a person, even amid the dry air of Arizona. The rabbits are quick, always on guard. True, they occasionally get caught by an even more alert and swift bird of prey, but there would be no rabbits at all if they walked along, sniffing here and there, welcoming anyone and everyone. And the sky has its tough, combative side too. So vast and reliable and protective and nurturing one minute, it can rather suddenly, surprisingly turn into quite another phenomenon: dark clouds, with the sudden gusts they bring, and thunder and lightning.

The boy stops with mention of the last; he decides to sketch a grim, cloudy sky. As he does so he speaks of lightning, thunder, the Navahos, and the white people of the United States of America: "I've seen lightning strike the Rock. I've wondered how the Rock remains the same afterwards. But we are not the Rock; we would be killed. I've seen trees fall: the lightning. My grandfather loves to watch a storm. He tells us that the lightning *dances;* the spirits of our ancestors are having quite a time. They want us to remember them! When it thunders, he claps; when the lightning strikes, he holds both his hands up high. My mother is worried; she has seen lightning hurt our land, block roads — the trees across them. She has seen the sheep run wild, get killed. And she is afraid of the lightning. She says that even if there is nothing to be afraid of, she is afraid.

"She's afraid of the white people too. She says we have to protect what we have. The white people only respect Indians who stand up to them. The Navahos outnumber us, and they are fighters. My mother sees the clouds coming, and they get dark, and she calls us in, and tells us we shouldn't keep running around: this is our home, and we're safest in one place — away from the big tree up the road, or the Rock, or the white man's electricity wires. She holds her ears when it begins to thunder, and she looks to the floor so she won't see the lightning. And she will say: 'Navahos, white men—the sky is full of them!' My father laughs and sometimes even my mother laughs — at herself! But my father tells us later that our mother has a lot of good advice to give us because she's right: the Hopi could be cut down like a tall, strong tree that is proud of itself and that everyone thinks will last forever. One stroke of lightning and there is no longer a tree, just some wood on the ground, and it will soon be cut up, and later it will be burnt up — used in the winter for the fires in the homes."

A glance at the hearth in his own house, then a new intensity to the application of his black crayon; he wants to stress the sky's forbidding quality. Still, he will not leave the drawing without providing a glimmer of hope. He puts down the black crayon and takes up the yellow one; he provides a sharply defined clearing in the sky: the sun and the blue sky. He remarks upon what he has just done, tries to explain a little more than his artistic purposes: "I left part of the sky empty at first. I was going to make the whole sky dark, but if you're on a hill, you can always see the light clouds as well as the dark ones, and if you wait long enough, you'll see a break in the clouds and maybe the sun and the sky. I wish I could draw the thunder! That's what I like about a storm; I close my eyes, and listen to the sky talking to us. My mother says to us that the sky gets angry, and then comes thunder. The earth gets angry, and you'll have an earthquake or a volcano shooting lava. We don't get them here, but in school they tell us about them. My grandfather knows about earthquakes and volcanoes, and he never went to school. The old Hopis know a lot that we don't know about, and they know a lot that we learn from our teachers. We're sometimes sure our grandfathers and grandmothers don't know what we learn in school — until we find out that they do."

When he is through with his drawing (Figure 37) and through talking about the sky and the events that take place in it, he thinks about play. After all, thunder and lightning are not only serious events. Thunder and lightning, he recalls his parents and grandparents saying, are also expressions of playfulness: the clouds colliding, racing, speaking, grumbling, vying with one another for possession of the sky's terrain. What happens in the sky is what happens on earth, he reminds himself. The chickens he helps care for, for example: one of them is always looking for trouble — to the point that he calls it "black cloud." Then there is a gentle, pleasant, appealing chicken, which he calls "light cloud." The two have their encounters upon occasion. The other chickens stand aside, both fascinated and frightened. During a storm the boy often wonders how the "other clouds" are doing — those that are a bit removed from the scene of noise and "spears of light," the grandfather's sometime term for lightning. It is the kind of term a Hopi child often learns *not* to use in school. The point is to speak more or less as white people do, get one's education.

VII

A NEW HOPI BOY

HIS FATHER'S WORDS have become his. His grandfather's words are also his, but he is hesitant to accept them fully. James has learned at home and at school that today's Hopis are not yesterday's. He has learned that if he is to be a Hopi, he must be a new kind of Hopi — perhaps like the children of a friend of his father's, who are mostly older than he and quite determined to be "new Hopis." That is an expression those children use. James is twelve, almost thirteen, relatively tall, athletically built, and forceful. He used to be called Jim, but he now likes to be known by his full name. He is a favorite of the teachers, and they have become, in a way, friends of his; he acknowledges that, is proud that he can have friendly, informal conversations with them after school. James does not, at first, seem ambitious; he may be a vigorous and appealing person, and he may be a rather successful student, and he may even say things that strike an outsider as almost evangelical or messianic. Given enough time he reveals himself as a Hopi — and he very much wishes to do so: "I will never forget the stories I've heard from my grandparents, and from a great-grandmother who lived until she was so old that my mother said she had lived one life and was in the middle of a second life, and she would live a long time, even though she seemed ready to leave us every morning when we got up — but there she was, sipping hot water and eating a cracker. She was the one who told me not to chase the chickens and not to kick the dog. I kicked the dog once, and she got up and held me, and said she was going to kick me! I can remember her hands on my shoulders; I was surprised at how strong she was. Her fingers hurt me, and she wouldn't let go! She said that to others the Hopi are chickens, dogs, rabbits, snakes, birds. To others we are weak, and if we try to say what we believe in, they laugh and go and do as they please.

"She wouldn't let go of me, even after she stopped talking; and I got scared. I began to cry, I think. She let go. My mother came and told me there was nothing to be afraid of. Then my mother told me that I should think about the dog, and how afraid it was — of me. Then my great-grandmother went back to her chair, and she called me over to her. I must have still been scared because I didn't move. So my mother took my hand in hers, and we walked over, and the next thing I knew, the old woman was kissing me and telling me that her husband sometimes would get angry with his dog, and he wouldn't kick the dog, but he'd shout at it, and he'd tell it to watch out, or there'd be no food any more. But he would soon feel bad, and he would ask the dog to forget what he'd said. Then my mother told me that I could try doing that. But now I am glad I can remember the old woman; no matter what the Hopis do that she might not like, I agree with my grandmother that we should never forget her because she was a very good person, and she believed that the Hopis are different from other people, and even if we have to become like other people, we can be different, too."

He has heard others speak like that repeatedly. His teachers have acknowledged the special virtues of the Hopis, but have insisted that in the last third of the twentieth century they must yield to the demands of others. He is not at all unaware of what those demands are. He has thought of leaving the reservation, going to Phoenix, trying to live there and work there. He wants to get all the education he can on the reservation, then move elsewhere. He has met lawyers, who are arguing on behalf of the Hopis in the land dispute they have (and have had for centuries) with the Navahos. Perhaps he will one day become a lawyer. His grandparents can't understand what a lawyer does, and his parents aren't all that sure either, but he has some definite ideas on the subject: "There are fights, and lawyers step in and try to stop the fights. A lawyer knows what the law says. A lawyer tries to help the people he's working for. If the Hopis had a lot of lawyers, we could prevent the Navahos from taking our land. A lawyer has gone to school a long time, and he has read a lot of books, and he knows what to say when there's an argument before the judge in the court. One lawyer came to visit us in school; he spoke to us. He said the Hopi are good people, but they haven't been smart enough. He said we have to do more than we used to do — we have to fight.

"I told my father what the lawyer said, and my father was ready to go to the school and get into a fight with somebody. He said that we can stand up and say we won't leave our land, but that doesn't mean we have to fight. I almost got into a fight with him! I said that if you fight for what you believe in, then you're doing right. He asked me how I'd fight against the white people. I said I'd have lawyers go fight them. He laughed. He said I don't know what I'm talking about! He said the white people make and break laws, depending on what they want to do. If they wanted our land, if they *really* did, they'd figure out a way to come and take it. I said that the white man isn't the same white man he was a long time ago, and my father laughed even harder. He said I'm lucky I'm a

Hopi, and not someone else, living in Asia. He said that the white people don't have to worry about Indians any longer; so now it's other countries that the United States keeps its eye on and attacks.

"My mother told him to stop and leave us alone. I had a friend with me, listening. He said my father sounds like the young Indian men who are fighting with the government all over the country. But my father said no, he doesn't want to fight with the government; he doesn't want to fight with anyone, *and* he doesn't want *me* to fight, either. He told my friend that he just wants to be able to hold his head up high, and have enough food for his family, and he wants his children to be able to do the same. That's why he thinks it's good that we go to school, and learn to become lawyers! But he doesn't want us *thinking* like lawyers — like 'white people and their lawyers,' he says. Then he'll laugh, and say that even if we *do* think like them some of the time, we won't all the time, he's sure."

The boy is sure, too. He knows that he is and always will be a Hopi. He does not want to be considered "an Indian" by his teachers; in a rather sweeping fashion they talk about "the Indians." As a matter of fact, he feels closer to certain white people (whom he knows as teachers) than to the Navahos, none of whom he knows at all. Navahos are not only public enemies, so to speak, of the Hopis, but in his mind they have become personal enemies. As such, he imagines them (he has never seen them in the flesh) as grim-faced, truculent, rifle-carrying, and extremely demanding. They do not only want a little more land for their sheep; they want (he believes) anything that their eyes see, their ears hear of, their minds have learned about.

James has no particular interest in drawing a picture of a Navaho — or for that matter, of anyone. But he has his own way of showing the difference between the Hopis and the

Navahos. The Hopis have land that, in drawings and paintings, he makes both appealing and favored by the sun; the Navahos have land that he portrays stripped, barren, a stretch of utter desert under a dark, cloudy, sunless sky. And as if determined to be consistent, he is unwilling to change things in the evening landscapes he makes. The Hopi sky is graced with a rather rich and haunting moon, and a host of stars. The Navaho night seems dominated by Satan himself; it is black and rather portentous.

The boy is quite willing afterward to put into words what he has conveyed as an artist: "We are trying to be careful here; this land has been given to us, but it doesn't belong to us. When I was little, and I'd be digging a hole, my mother would come out, and she'd say to me that she saw me, and she was wondering why I was digging. I'd say for fun, and to show my friend how deep I could go. But she'd shake her head, and she'd ask us both to come inside. She'd give us one of her lessons. She'd say that the most important thing in the world for us to know is that we are here to honor the land, not use it as if we bought it in the store. I remember another time; we were pulling tumbleweed apart, and we'd cut branches from a tree and were throwing them around too — they were spears, I guess. My father saw us. My father said it was all right for us to play and use the tumbleweed to throw back and forth and make spears, but he wanted us to know that we are Hopis, and that means we must look around us, and be thankful for the land we have, and that includes the trees and the tumbleweed and the cactus and everything else. He said that a tree doesn't talk the way we do, but it can be hurt and it can cry."

He will not forget that episode in his life. He is now old enough to talk about his parents' values, their strongly felt ideals, which he has slowly acquired as his own — but also has had occasion to modify, as he realizes quite well: "I'm not going to live the same kind of life that my parents and grandparents did. My father knows that. He tells me that the Hopis try to be loyal to our ancestors; we try to live as they did. But he admits that he's unable a lot of the time to talk with the old people because they will tell you to turn away from the white people, and you can't do that if you want to live in the America of the 1970s. The white man has given the Indians schools and hospitals, and he helps us prevent the land from drying up, and he helps us plant trees. My grandfather thinks we've made the white people our gods, and we follow them around as if they are the ones who make thunder and throw lightning at the earth. That's not true.

"When I tell my father about the atomic bomb, and what the white man can do with his hydrogen bombs, then my father gets very upset, and says I don't realize that the white man has already destroyed half of his own country, and he'll soon destroy everything, in every country. His grandfather used to tell him that the only hope for us, for the Hopi people, is to stay away from the white man, and stay away from the Navaho, too. They are alike; they are hungry for what other people have. But the Hopis couldn't stay away from the white man, or from the Navahos, either. Who can? My father says: no one. When he hears about the atomic bomb, he wishes we'd tried harder. Maybe if we'd gone farther into the hills; maybe if we'd found some caves; maybe if we'd marched north, farther and farther, toward the mountains, up the canyons; maybe, maybe — but my father knows that there is no chance because the white man has planes and helicopters, and telescopes, and he can see everywhere. Americans have landed on the moon, and they've sent rockets higher and higher into the sky.

"I agree with my father. It's dangerous; the whole world

could go up in fire and smoke. There could be a big explosion. There could be dangerous gases, and we'd all die. The white man himself must be scared. Even our teachers say that everyone could be killed because of a nuclear war. But if you can't turn your back on the white man because he'll find you anyway; and if you can't escape during a nuclear war because everyone might die, then you have to try to live with the white people. Some of them are just like the Hopis, one of our teachers said. They want to protect the land here in Arizona and New Mexico from their own people. A white man came here, and he asked my mother how she takes care of the plants she has. They were given to her by her older sister, and she loves them. So she has grown more and more of them — cactus plants of all kinds and some other plants. The man worked for the BIA. My mother said he was very nice. He was worried about the land; he wants to help us bring in water — for irrigation. He thinks he can get some trees going here.

"He was very polite; and when he'd left, my mother said he was a Hopi. I thought she'd been looking at the sun too long! But she explained to me that her old aunt used to say that the Hopis are all the people in the world who love the world and want to protect it, like a mother and father want to protect their child. That's what she always says to us: the world is our child, and we must love it and be on guard so that it is not hurt. I try to tell my father that it's not hopeless: look at that white man who wants to help us with water and trees. My father says yes; but then he says no. He says the white man I met isn't the United States government. He is sure that in Washington, D.C., the people aren't like that man. I'd like to go there and see. I'd like to talk with the President or a senator and with the people who make the laws there. I don't really think I'll ever go there."

James asks out loud where he will go, what he will do when

he gets older, how he will live. He likes being on the Hopi reservation, but he has to admit that he is curious about the outside world, and he thinks that his curiosity may, in fact, constitute the chief distinction between him and his parents, his grandparents, and others of their generation. Nor does he attribute his cast of mind to the schools and their young teachers; his father used to tell him when he was younger that he must have a Navaho "spirit" watching over him, whispering words into his ear. The boy wasn't content to sit back, look, listen, be glad of what his ears were picking up. He was too combative, too restless.

Of course, other Hopi children fought and loved to explore, but this son teased ever so gently, developed a certain sense of himself and, just as important, a notion of what the Hopis were struggling — in vain, it seems — to uphold: "I used to fight with a friend; we'd push each other until one of us seemed to be stronger and the winner. My mother saw us doing that once; she must have been watching for a long time. All of a sudden she came toward us, and she was unhappy with me. She asked us to stop. She said I should have let my friend go because I was stronger. I was angry. I said how can a person ever really win if he's always supposed to get ready to lose! She laughed, but she became serious right away. Later, my father told me that he heard I was behaving like a Navaho again, or a white man. I knew what he meant!

"I told him that I wished I was born a long time ago. The white people weren't as strong then, and they left us alone because they were busy trying to find gold and build railroads, and we weren't in their way. And the Navahos were pushing in the direction of the Pueblo Indians, I think. Now the white man has every Indian tribe on a reservation, and if you leave it, they tell you that you have no rights; you're just like anyone else. The Navahos want extra land from us, but they have to get the white man to say yes. In the old days we could just go hide. I guess we can now. But the government is here, and they offer to help you. And besides, we're used to living better than we did when my grandparents and *their* grandparents were young. I don't know if I could live like they did; even my mother and father admit that we've all been spoiled — by the white man. We're no longer Hopis like the Hopis once were. I don't think I'm the only white man here on the reservation! Some Hopis say they want to fight the Navahos, even if they outnumber us. And if we did fight, we'd fight to win, and not give up if we were just about to win!"

VIII

A NEW HOPI GIRL

J AMES realizes that there is no answer to the kinds of dilemmas or problems, even riddles, he and other Hopis are struggling with. He turns to his sister Betty, a year older, nearly fourteen. She has thought about the issues he has found difficult to comprehend, and her relative detachment and sense of ironic humor pleases him, even if he does not leave the discussion satisfied that he now has everything quite clear in his mind. Betty is the first one to acknowledge that it is and will be different for her, as opposed to her brother. She is a girl, about to become a woman. She does not have to face the prospect of joblessness, idleness. She will be a mother, she hopes. But she is alert enough to understand that then, as a mother, she will have a child or two, quite possibly, to worry about, as well as a husband.

The girl also insists that her life will differ from the kind of life her mother lives. She is, after all, a child growing up in the late 1960s and 1970s — on a Hopi reservation, yes, but on American soil: "I'm like my brother. He says we're *both* going to be different Hopis than our parents were. We would like to leave the reservation. We wouldn't mind seeing how Indians live in cities. A lot of Hopis say you stop being a Hopi when you go into a city and live in big buildings and forget about our land, and our hills, and the sky over us. Maybe; I don't know. The Indian can't just sit and think of his past. My mother says it's a pity; our people were happy here for so long. Now, a lot of us want to leave. But she admits that we are living better than we used to live. And she says we can still be Hopis, even if we get the white man's knowledge, and spend some of our lives living in his land, not ours. We're not going to have cities here; we're not going to let the white man come and tear our land up, like he's done elsewhere. But we have to live so that our children don't get sick and die, when they could live if there was a doctor and a hospital near. And we have to live in houses where the children don't freeze in the winter. Our mother said her old mother and old aunt didn't like the house we live in at first; they said it was a white man's house. They didn't like the electricity when it was first brought in. But now they do; they wouldn't know how to get by without it. That's why I tell my brother: it's all right to be a white man, and you can still be a Hopi."

Betty says that she has liked watching television, that she hopes someday to visit a television studio, be part of one of the audiences she sees. But she realizes how inconsistent or contradictory her family's attitudes are toward television and what appears on it. Her parents smile at the people who vie for money, who dance and laugh and shout and embrace one another at the sight of an electric appliance or automobile or sum of money. At the same time, her parents value the refrigerator they have, the stove, and of course, the television set. They even acknowledge that if they were given a car, and a supply of gas to go with it, they would enjoy themselves. Their daughter talks in a similar vein, especially when she is with them; but she also is more aware of and more explicit about the various confusions she experiences.

She declares herself torn by her situation, and she comforts herself with the counsel of her parents, not to mention her ancestors: "I wish sometimes I was born white. My mother heard my cousin say that once, and it was terrible. My mother cried. My father told her she was wasting her tears; he said that a Hopi child is entitled to make a mistake or say the wrong thing. My mother answered him; she said that she'd never heard a Hopi girl talk like that. I am glad that I don't say everything that my mind thinks. My aunt is very fond of me. She asks me a lot of the time what I will do when I grow older. Will I stay in school? Have I thought of someone I'd like to marry? Questions like that. I have always confided in her. I told her once that I wouldn't mind going away for a while and living among white people. She wasn't as upset as my mother would be. But I don't think she really believes I'm going to go — and I'm not sure either. She said it was all right to want to know about the white man and his cities. She said it's because of school; we learn so much. When she was young, she didn't go to school. She is right about schools. They show us pictures and movies and we read books. I read a book about France. I would like to go to Paris. I read another book about England. I would like to go to London. I would also like to see California. I would *not* like to visit Washington, D.C. That is where the BIA has its office.

"My old aunt always asks me the same question at the end of a talk: would you come back if you traveled far away? I say yes, and she is happy. But I'm not sure. What would happen if I traveled far and liked living where I was? Would I come back then? I don't know. The white people live a different life than we do; and my father is right, they kill each other in automobile crashes when they travel, and they are always starting a war or trying to end one. And our people have lost so much to them; our men still fight in their wars, and a long time ago, they were making war against us, and we lost a lot of people then. But the Hopis never fought the whites the way the Navahos and the Apaches did; the teachers told us that in school, and my father said they are right because we have not been fighters. My father tells us that to fight is to admit that you are weak and without control over yourself — wilder than any animal.

"But white people aren't just fighting all the time. They can be friends of the Indians; some white people are volunteers; they try to help people — and they even work for the same federal government that sends us the BIA people. My father admits that even a few of the BIA people are getting better. I think in the future Hopis and white people will become friendlier, and the Hopi people will travel more. I wouldn't want to get married as young as my mother was; she was seventeen. I want to see the world first. I told my aunt that I'd like to marry when I am over twenty, maybe twenty-five; she said I'd be an old woman then, and I wouldn't have as many children as I could. I told her I don't want a lot of children, just two. My aunt was very upset!"

So upset, in fact, that she asked her niece to leave; and the memory of that request lingers. The girl had never before been confronted that way. The aunt had turned her head away, had stood up and walked toward the window, had begun to stare out at the nearby scrub brush, and beyond that, the gently rising hills. When the girl was outside they caught a glance of each other; the girl chose to walk past the window, and the elderly aunt looked right into her face, then raised her right hand in a half-salute — but no smile, and no movement from her lips, and certainly no effort to raise the window. The girl did not go directly home. She walked toward the hills her aunt had been looking at; she walked faster than she usually does. Soon she was out of her aunt's sight — out of everyone's sight, she hoped.

Two hawks circled lazily; they would come swooping down, she knew, quickly enough if there was anything to catch and eat. She remembers fixing her eyes on them for several minutes, remembers wondering why they didn't move on, remembers wondering whether, in fact, they weren't waiting for her. But they did leave, and she moved her eyes from them to a nearby trunk of a tree — the remains of what her aunt had told her had once been a haven for her and others, who would come and sit in the shade and praise the sun while congratulating themselves on their relative comfort. The girl decided to approach, climb the trunk, and soon she was perched on top, scanning the horizon. She saw dust rise and fall — a wind. She watched shadows appear and disappear — the sun in its eternal struggle with clouds. She watched a couple of cars work their way across the largely barren but dramatic land; they seemed like toys, wound up by children and on their way to nowhere.

She pictured her aunt in her mind; tried to picture her aunt as she looked when she was a girl on the verge of becoming a woman. Then, lonely and hurt and troubled, she reached into her pocket and took out a harmonica. She had been given it by a teacher — a prize for doing consistently well in spelling and composition. She knew no songs, only the fun of moving her lips along the instrument and hearing the noises it made. Her aunt had liked the harmonica, and as the girl remembered the pleasure the noises had once brought to the elderly lady's face, she played a little more energetically — and smiled to herself. Finally she stopped; her lips hurt a little. She was getting ready to tuck the harmonica into her pocket when she decided to look at it: Made in Hong Kong. Where is Hong Kong? She had no idea — though it sounded like Asia, she knew. What about the Chinese and the Japanese — did they get along well with white people or not? Would she ever leave the reservation, leave America, see a city like Hong Kong?

She knew she wanted to do so, but she also knew that it was unlikely she ever would. Suddenly her thoughts turned to winter, and what an especially severe one might bring: "I had put the harmonica away, and I was getting ready to go back home. The wind I'd seen way off, carrying the sand with it, arrived; I felt the sand coming at me, and I tried to protect my face. I thought in a few minutes everything would be quiet again. But no; so I sat down and waited. That's when I pictured a bad winter storm, so bad that the white men came in their planes with food; so bad they decided to get us out. They had to take us off the reservation because the snow was heavy, and we were running out of food. Even my aunt left the reservation. I imagined her in some city; I don't know which one. We looked at the tall buildings, and we went into the stores, and we had a good time; my aunt, even though she was old, was very glad to go walking. We went into a restaurant, and we went to a movie. We saw a television show being made. When it was time to go, she said she wouldn't mind staying longer. She'd liked going to the stores and seeing all that you can buy there. We came back home — that was almost the end of my daydream! My aunt said she still wouldn't live anyplace else, but she didn't mind my talk any more about traveling, and she said she'd like to go on one more trip before she leaves us."

With that reconciliation in her mind, the girl left for the village where her parents live. She knew that when she went back to see her aunt, there would be no hard feelings. She knew that she was a Hopi and that she had few prospects of leaving the reservation. "I'll bet my aunt would leave the reservation if I learned how to drive, when I'm older, and offered to take her for a ride. She would trust me. She has never had a chance to go anywhere. She is too old to sit and dream of the future, like I do. She thinks only of the past. A few days after I made so much sorrow for her, she was a different person with me. She took me and hugged me. She told me that it is always hard to be a woman because a woman has to suffer for others, for her children; a man works, and leaves the family to his wife, or he doesn't work, but goes off with his friends. When she told me that, I was ready to tell her that maybe women would have better lives soon.

"She said she was no fool; she said that she'd been listening to the young people, and had even gone to a few homes where there is television, so she knows what we are all thinking. If I were her; if I were her age, I'm not sure I'd be as willing as she is to understand people much younger. I told her that recently, and she said that white people make too much of age — who is what age and who is another age — and that some Hopis do too. She remembers when her grandfather told her and her sisters that we are all here on a short visit, and to brag about being old, or about being young, is to be a fool. The years between the oldest Hopi alive and a Hopi baby just born are like a yawn or a swallow, and we should always remember that.

"I can see how an old person would agree; but for me each day is a long time, and I can't imagine what will be happening to me next year. I know I'll be old eventually, but it seems a long way off. Maybe the Hopis will be living someplace else then. Maybe the government will take all our land away and tell us to live in another state. We'd be upset, but I think we'd go ahead and try to do the best we can. The teachers say that the people who came to this country from England and fought in the Revolutionary War — they didn't want to leave their homes either; but they did, and they ended up thinking of America as their home. I guess the Indians lost their homes though. I guess the Indians didn't do too well."

On that thought she stops talking and looks down. Her sus-

tained attempt to be hopeful seems to have ended in failure.
She looks at a brown pony nearby and wonders whether she
ought to take a ride on it. Her brother is rather possessive
about the pony, but she has made clear her intention of riding
it whenever no one else has made a prior claim. She puts on
some boots her father has bought for her, for her brother too.
She looks at the sky: will the weather hold? Yes, she is sure it
will be a long, slow, hot afternoon, ended by a brilliant sunset
— the kind that makes her feel that the sun will never come
back in a mere eight hours or so: the departure has been too
insistent, too flamboyant. ("If I said good-bye like that, I'd wait
and wait to return.")

She moves toward the horse, is affectionate, thoughtful, talkative with it. Does it really want to go on a ride, under such
a hot sun? Has it ever wanted to rear, to buck, to run and run,
as fast as possible, to throw off restraint forever? She answers
for the animal. She changes her voice slightly. She doesn't
want to pretend, however, that ponies talk and that she is
privy to their thoughts. Years ago she half-seriously thought
along those lines; she told her mother that when the pony
snorted, turned its neck, whinnied, more than sounds and
gestures were being made. After all, to the pony, human
words were no doubt puzzling and mysterious noises! Now she
is learning how to read rather well, and she has no intention
of denying man (and woman) a unique ability: the gift of words
and the reflective capacity that goes with it. But she knows
that she can convey rather a lot to the pony and receive back
a good deal, too: the animal's judgment about the weather,
about its own strength and its needs with respect to food and
water, as well as its response to a particular person — affection, suspicion, outright distrust, thorough dislike. She uses her
voice to indicate that the pony is not her or, really, a person.
She believes, however, that she is a little privy to the pony's

habits, inclinations, likely responses. She also believes that the pony and she, for all the barriers between them, will by and large be satisfied with and helpful toward each other. She is attentive to its needs; she receives from it a thoughtful, discerning, as well as brisk, ride — a creature's care that no sudden holes, dips in the land, soft spots, result in a fall.

Once her aunt told her that when she looks into the eyes of the pony, she is looking into the eyes of the whole world, but that when she is looking into her own eyes she is in danger. The girl is not literally convinced of the truth of that observation, so far as the pony's eyes go, but she knows that it is best to reach out to the world rather than spend a lot of time finding that world in oneself — all of which she says, by attribution to the pony, as she mounts it: "I've been *waiting* for you to leave yourself for an expedition with me." It is a remark she has heard her aunt make, a touch facetiously, when they have met and gone for a walk. The girl once thought the old lady, at moments like that, plaintive and herself self-centered. But not recently; the girl is proud of her aunt's humor, spirit, energy. The girl who wants to leave the Hopis for a stretch of time is also a Hopi and no one else.

IX

GROWING UP INDIAN

ALL CHILDREN have to learn respect for themselves — even a kind of self-love that psychiatrists refer to as "narcissism." Of course a child can for one reason or another go too far, become a captive of his or her self-regard — immersed so deeply in private fantasies as to be cut off divisively (sometimes fatally) from others. The so-called narcissistic child has usually suffered a lack of affection from others. But there are shades and textures of "narcissism" — a robust sense of oneself that enables rather than discourages involvement with others, or a consuming self-centeredness that turns any outsider into a mere foil for the mind's egotism. The rest of us, including our children, happen to fall in between these extremes.

Parents, needless to say, make a big difference. Within any culture there are to be found mothers and fathers who hold their children too tightly, or hold them off too consistently. A parent's own personal experiences as a child or a combination of fateful events make for apprehension and fear on the part of her or his children — so that they can find confidence in the future only by fending rather insistently for themselves. But cultures vary with regard to the emphasis placed on a child's individuality, or the importance of neighborhood, family, school, friends. In an Appalachian hollow, parents make sure that their children not only go to school but become thoroughly part of the community of boys and girls in a particular schoolhouse. In American upper-middle-class suburbs, large numbers of children learn to attend school faithfully — and pay attention, get along, "do well," even if in pursuit of the most narrow kind of self-enhancement.

Chicano children learn quite a different attitude toward schools. So do Indian children. Chicanos, by and large, are indifferent, or even antagonistic, toward their teachers; their classmates, all too many crowded into inadequate rooms and buildings, are fellow sufferers rather than competitors or comrades. Indian children are not always as bitter and cynical as Chicano children are when talking about schools and teachers, though the teachers who work for the Bureau of Indian Affairs do come in for a substantial amount of criticism from some Indian children. Mostly, Pueblo and Hopi children appear detached, bemused, uncannily watchful, compliant in an aloof, austere way — but quick to smile if such a gesture will placate (and get rid of) a white woman or man. Some white teachers who have tried hard to "reach" those Indian children, "work" with them, "understand" and "help" them, have thrown up their hands in confusion and despair: what is *wrong* with the Indian people, with their children, and why the "attitude" of the latter in school?

The "attitude" teachers notice, find enigmatic or disturbing, now and then complain about loudly, is not unrelated to the "attitude" a girl has learned toward a horse, toward the land she lives on and considers her own, toward the sky, the clouds, the sun, plants, trees, rocks. When a girl mounts a pony and imagines it welcoming her, she is reminded that she has left herself, so to speak, to be with an animal; or when a girl recalls her aunt's greeting her with the same words of welcome as those attributed to a pony, then she reveals something about the way she views herself. An Appalachian child surrenders herself to a community of children; in their collective strength she finds a personal (emotional, psychological) fulfillment. A Chicano child says "nothing doing" to school and withdraws angrily. A suburban child of the white upper middle class says yes, I will try my best, hoping thereby to feather my cap, bolster my pride, obtain my parents' love, my friends' respect — even if that respect takes the form of envy, scorn, and spite. An Indian child in the classroom, in contrast, is likely to watch more carefully than he or she listens, and not rarely frustrate the school's principal and teachers, who keep wondering why young Indians seem so absent in a private world. It is as if Indian children have a mental reservation that is as important for them to claim as the various territorial reservations are for their parents.

Indian children don't confine their emotional "departures" to the classroom. They are taught to watch lest they become "lost" (as their mothers or fathers sometimes put it). Lost where? Lost in their own private world, with all its pitfalls. Indian parents encourage their children to reach out for others, have more psychological contact with particular people, become involved with various external situations and opportunities. When Indian children withdraw from their teachers, they are doing so only temporarily. On the other hand, they are taught not to immerse themselves indiscriminately in the world. A child who learns to "leave" himself or herself for someone or something else is a child who has acquired a distinct sense of self. The departure from that self is quite deliberate, even announced publicly upon occasion. In time there is a return to self, though never for too long, lest self-infatuation, and maybe megalomania or paranoia, sets in. Those who teach Indian children occasionally talk of the "cyclical" quality of the Indian child's temperament: quite cozy, intimate, cooperative one minute, and hard to fathom, even speak to, another time. Indian mothers can be quite interested in and amused by such accounts of their children. It is quite true, the parents acknowledge, that they tell their children to be doubly careful: don't yield to the temptations of vanity and conceit, but don't forget how important it is that an Indian child grow up precisely as a Pueblo, a Hopi, a Navaho, even one who lives in the twentieth century, and so differs from all those ancestors who (the child also must remember) are very much alive in their own way.

What makes for Indianness? The outsider is prompted, with some desperation, to keep on asking himself this. What specific psychological qualities or characteristics distinguish Pueblo and Hopi children, for example, from Anglo children in Albuquerque or Phoenix? It seems especially important to determine because the Indians themselves appear intent on making the point: themselves as *against* others, themselves as a *refuge* from others. In the very first years of life the Indian child gets taught certain psychological boundaries. Both casually and insistently an infant is told by its parents that the skin is an outer limit, as are the ears and the eyes. There is a mystical side to those explanations. The child hears that when a particular scene is viewed by the eyes a capture takes place — the mind, the person, absorbs a given landscape. The child also is told that when words are spoken, they become the property of the person listening; they change hands, so to speak. Indians or not, all who speak and listen understand, at some "level" of their minds, that an exchange takes place, that something is offered, that something is received. But when Indian parents comment on that development, when they make it a matter of repeated feeling as well as fact for the child, they are making their children more self-conscious, emphasizing what might be called *definition.* Some phenomenologists might call it the particular person as against the "other."

As toddlers many Indian children are often reminded that a rock nearby belongs to the earth; that the clouds are the sky's property and never "visit" the land; that the wind came, touched the skin, but did not stay. An outsider has every right to emphasize the dramatic, "projective," figurative aspect of such pronouncements, but they also convey statements about the meaning of life and about the structure of things. No wonder Indian children are often regarded by outsiders as strangely "philosophical," as almost preoccupied with "existential" questions. Indian mothers feel awe and wonder within themselves as they look upward at the sun, the moon, the stars, or across the desert toward a given mesa; those mothers make sure that their children feel the same. They are not permitted to take *any* sights and sounds for granted.

How many American boys or girls of four, five, six have their attention called, day in and day out, to cloud formations, to shadows upon the land, to the movement of grass, trees, flowers — and then hear their own lives connected to those various sights and sounds? A girl may, for instance, feel tired, weak, sick to her stomach. Her mother tells her that she has stopped being the person she was, because sickness makes one different — "a new person" — even if only for a while. And next, the sky is brought into the discussion — for comparison, for clarification: a clear sky that seems to be clouding up, a lively day that seems to be getting uncertain. In similar fashion, the body changes, sends out signals, goes through cycles of growth and attrition. It is well, the child learns, to know all that, to have that "context"; it is well not only because the world ought to be regarded closely and understood, but because to be an Indian is to pay heed to the reality, to the textures and contours, of the outer world as a means of coming to grips with an inner world, which is, forever, one's private self.

And *forever* it is — or so Indian children start believing when they are six or seven, an age when many other American children grow skeptical with respect to immortality. The white man has his preoccupation with time; naturally Indian children living in the white man's world have to learn to reckon with the importance of the clock, the calendar. But they also learn to think of themselves as part of a never-ending chain of people who constantly are in touch with one another. White children from the American middle class learn at six or so how to tell time; it is an abstraction, one that has to do with numbers, with hands working their way around a circle, and with eating, sleeping, rising, viewing television. Indian children hear about time in quite another fashion: an uncle who once walked the reservation and whose spirit still does; a storm that took everyone by surprise and still appears in dreams or nightmares; the anticipation of a spell of rain or snow; the sun's daily power, but the inevitable approach of evening; the moon that gradually alters its shape and brightness over the days of the month, only to say good-bye; the shifts of daily temperature; the eloquence of an old person's wrinkles — "so many summers, so many winters." That phrase is, of course, a way of giving an account, but the intent is to acknowledge endurance and to suggest that endurance does not end in a void.

The white man is quite capable of doing likewise — praising an aged person's capacity to triumph over the burdens of the years or asserting the immortality of the soul. But Indians link what the white man thinks of as "age" to the natural world. They intend to describe rather than exalt; indeed, some Indians freely acknowledge that when they start *praising* an old person, they have shown the white man's influence over their minds. One looks up to a baby, looks up to a young mother or father, looks up to an old man or an old woman. Time happens rather than progresses — a distinction that is embodied in concrete illustration rather than wordy explanation. The distinction cannot, however — not after all these years of white rule — be clear-cut. The white man's view of the world is now part of each Indian child's heritage, but there are shades of preoccupation, subtleties of interpretation, mixtures of vision. It is linear time, the hours and days as a finite and measurable progression, that many Indians tend to ignore. An Indian child is told about a certain event; the child listens, nods, smiles, or frowns, depending upon what has been said, but does *not* ask the question white children often do: what happened *next?* At least in the beginning those children don't ask such questions. After a year or two of school Indian children certainly do make adjustments in their way of thinking. They are asked questions they haven't been asked before, and they learn how to answer them — and later, at home, ask them. Most of their mothers and fathers have gone through the same experience and smile with recognition of the white man's mental outlook, with its constant emphasis upon whys and whens.

Silence is not so much a virtue encouraged by Indian parents as a state of affairs gradually appreciated by the young. Children don't naturally, inevitably chatter, or ask one question after another. Children can be brought up, starting at ages one and two, to take the world in and respond to it, without trying to take control of it, or claim an awareness of *how* it works, or how it can be *made* to work. Indian mothers often sit quietly with their children — smiling, staring at a tree, a mesa, a particular day's sky, without words. The infant or young child may be made a companion through a nod in a certain direction, a finger pointed at an object. If the child is squirming or irritable, the mother (father, older brother, sister) holds firm, waits for the opportunity: another nod, another effort with the forefinger.

One rarely hears Indian parents asking their children what is "wrong" with them, or explaining things at great length to them, never mind telling them that it is *time* to do this, or that *soon* they must do something else, or that in a few minutes (hours, days, weeks, months, years) a certain event will take place. Not that Indian children or youths don't know how to talk at great length, to tell gossip and recite stories. On the contrary, they love to repeat "lessons" they have heard from their parents, grandparents, uncles, and aunts — descriptions of past tribal experiences, generalized prophecies of what is to come, wry and ironic comments about "life." But those same children become extraordinarily quiet when their own particular lives are the issue at hand — when a teacher asks a personal question, or a mother makes a decision that has strong implications for a boy or a girl and his or her sisters and brothers. Put differently, Indian children seem less self-centered and less noisily insistent upon standing up for themselves, making their presence felt, than is the case with other American children, black as well as white, poor, rich, or in between.

Indian parents from the very beginning direct their children's attention outward, toward the land, the sky, the tribe and its history, its customs and traditions. Indian mothers and fathers don't respond to cries or demands in the direct and immediate fashion of most other American parents. This is not a matter of distraction but a matter of conviction — the parent's belief that a child is not the property of a certain family but belongs to a tribe, a people, and, just as important, a given landscape, a visible segment of the natural world. Day by day Indian children learn not only to appreciate and feel at home in that world, but to consider its rhythms and demands as of the highest consequence. A child falls and stumbles, for instance; the mother naturally reassures him or her, but the mother also smooths out the earth or some leaves. A child asks for something. The mother responds affirmatively — but quickly observes how good the day is or, if the day is not good, how full the river has become or, if that is not the case, how impressively strong and forceful the wind has turned out to be in recent hours: anything to show the child that generosity is not only something a parent demonstrates toward a boy or a girl but rather, one of many "signs" that the universe can be generous too.

Pueblo and Hopi mothers are especially inclined, on many occasions, to make mention of those "signs"; to turn everyday, apparently insignificant, events into meditative occasions — embarked upon gently, however, and without the intrusion of self-important didactic sermons. If a boy feels petulant, the mother tells herself as well as the child that there are dark clouds above, or that there may soon be those clouds — and so it goes, the threatening sky that alternates with the warm, open sky. If a girl feels troubled or confused, the mother points to the turbulence in a stream; to the shifting direction of a weathervane; to a path that suddenly divides. Such moments may strike a white outsider as "symbolic," as perhaps overly portentous. Are not the children being reminded that their various states of mind resemble the fluctuations, some quite threatening, of the natural world? But for Indian children such connections are themselves quite natural and part of what one expects and needs from life. In time, those children become the apparently imperturbable and strangely, wonderfully (or unnervingly) detached philosophical Indian youths whom whites remark upon, speculate about, and, not rarely, dismiss as hopelessly "primitive" in their "thinking," or given to "superstitions," or possessed of a "magical," and "illogical" outlook.

Without question Indian parents hold on to assumptions and values that white parents, a few miles away in Albuquerque, for instance, would find strange, absurd, wrongheaded, if spelled out and discussed. But Indians have no interest in doing that; they are not given to wordy analyses of their "child-rearing practices." Perhaps it can be said, as a fairly safe generalization, that Indian parents encourage their children to be sensitive to their kin, their tribe, and to their land, but not to themselves as individuals possessed of a discrete mind, a discrete "personality," a discrete bundle of assets and liabilities, gifts and conflicts.

Of course many white people, especially out West, love the world around them and try to establish in their children a similar high regard for and responsiveness to that world — the "environment," as it is called. But Indian parents aren't trying to inculcate a particular "attitude" in their children. There is a seemingly impersonal quality to the words and gestures a Pueblo or Hopi parent uses when pointing at some element in the surrounding landscape. There is a pantheistic side to Indian life — an emphasis by parents upon the sacred quality of *both* the living and the inanimate world. And, too, there is a subdued but persistent eroticism that is expressed in the contemplative wonder and awe that Indian children learn to feel when they stare at the sky, the horizon, the land both near and far. A thunderstorm, a windstorm, or simply a bright, clear day — and the Pueblo or Hopi child is happy, is ready (if it were possible) to reach out and touch with great satisfaction the sun, the dark clouds, the air rushing by so noisily. Mothers extend their arms, sing the praises of what is to be seen from the door of the house. Children watch and feel impelled to do likewise. The figurative language Indian parents and children use when talking, the frequent resort to metaphors and similes, the vivid, animistic thinking that a white observer cannot help noticing, the protectiveness toward land that others consider mere desert at best — all of those characteristics are of a piece: expressions of a continuing willingness, passionate at that, to invest the mind's imagination in the world around it.

Do Indian children, or for that matter their parents, actually believe that the clouds seek one another, or feel themselves called away by the wind, or importuned by the sun? Do they believe that horses talk to one another — that whinnying is quite the same as using words? Do they believe in the sun's capacity to have ideas, to express itself, to do things for one or another purpose? Such questions prompt an enigmatic but gracious smile from those Indians who hear them — that is, those Indians who feel comfortable enough with white people to talk with them at any length, with any candor. And almost always, such questions puzzle thoughtful, tactful Indians; they can't for the life of them understand why the white man always has to pin down a person's ideas or convictions. The white man's questions are surprising, amusing — and an occasion for sadness; how to share words and beliefs with people who see "another sky, another sun"?

No wonder Pueblo and Hopi children are carefully controlled and restrained when in the company of white people. It is not only a matter of suspicion, skepticism, outright fear; the boy or girl is also likely to have a sense of futility: what is the point of trying to make ourselves known to "them," when they only seem to want to know us as they know themselves? Of course, Indians realize that the white man is also a part of the world, so a Pueblo boy or girl is taught to be quite respectful of white people — but for reasons the latter often don't comprehend. If a child learns to show concern and care for the earth, even the ungenerous desert earth, and for the sky, even the threatening and dangerous sky of severe lightning storms, then the same holds for individual whites (a teacher, an official from the Bureau of Indian Affairs) or for the mass of them (thousands of strangers who live in a city like Albuquerque).

Nothing is more tempting for a psychologically "oriented" observer than to uncover the "origins" of the politeness and deference of Indian children. Have the Pueblos or Hopis taught their young ones to conceal the anger and contempt they feel toward the white people? Is it a matter of unconscious "denial" or of various "reaction-formations"? Conscious (and deliberate) suppression? Pretense, if not outright lying? Pueblo and Hopi boys and girls seem to regard white people as part of Nature's scheme of things for New Mexico and Arizona, even as the sun comes to those places, and the moon, and the wind. If there are bad times as a result of what whites do, there is no cause to become excessively alarmed, unremittingly hateful; the world, as a whole, deserves too much respect for any segment of that world to be granted the ultimate authority that goes with fear or hate — or indeed efforts to conceal those emotions. Indian parents manage without many words to let their children know that "the Anglos of Albuquerque," as the expression goes in some Pueblo reservations, are "neither the beginning nor the end."

On the other hand, the white man long ago conquered America's Indians and still very much dominates them. Pueblos and Hopis are not unaware of that historical fact, that contemporary state of affairs. Again: children who learn to regard a dangerous lightning storm or a devastating windstorm as part of their fate as human beings may learn to accept in a similar vein the white man and his various habits. But to "accept" is not to be fooled by; nor are Indians able or inclined to forget what they have seen and continue to see — arrogance, exploitation, cruelty, trickery, dozens of deceptions, all in the name of a "democracy." Indian children share with

Chicano children an abiding distrust of the social myths and political pieties that teachers try to impose in the classroom. And some Indian children do indeed share with Chicano children an inclination to pretend compliance, play at being cooperative, while reserving the expression of quite other attitudes for "later." But Chicano children are much more outspoken than Indians when off by themselves, much more inclined to use their own Spanish language forcefully, critically, self-protectively. Pueblo and Hopi children have been warned repeatedly that a consuming hate for the white man is evidence of the final subjection of the Indian.

Indian parents want their children to be different from the white man; to resist him in many ways; but to do so without becoming defined in their own minds as, above all, resisters. A last-ditch survivor who hates the enemy passionately and fights him without letup is to be, finally, trapped and destroyed. The respect that Indian children learn to show various white people is not only a measure of fear and intimidation. Those children are often shrewdly observant of white people — even as those same children keep their eyes on coyotes or mountain lions.

A people prepared anyway to use vivid imagery as a means of making intelligible a mysterious world has not in that regard been deterred by the conquering white man. A people capable of terse, aphoristic descriptions of everything visible under the sun is not going to be deterred by bragging, strutting, brilliantly technological men and women who do, after all, walk as Indians do, and even upon occasion smile as Indians do. Whites are *people,* Indian children are told, perhaps upon occasion with condescension or a sense of the irony involved in the declaration. The point is to give those children, likely as not headed for no college, and maybe not a high school, a reminder that will prove unforgettable and helpful.

Social scientists use words like "context" or "frame of reference"; Indian mothers are the last ones to want their children denied such. A people who look at the sun, the moon, the stars, the sky, the clouds, the distances of the prairie, the desert, the mountains, are not a people unable to manage for themselves what others would call a "perspective" or two about the "Anglos of Albuquerque" or the "white man down in Phoenix."

Indian children are watchful of white men and have been told that watchfulness is a virtue. The white man is greedy, demanding, shrewd, but sees only what he wants to see and accordingly misses rather a lot. Such knowledge (and self-knowledge) gets constantly, if indirectly or slyly expressed — in drawings done, remarks spoken, cryptic references or comparisons made. Indian children who are gentle, tender, cautious, may suddenly start making bold and fierce analogies, or self-deprecating ones that are susceptible to several (and possibly, contradictory) interpretations. Children who seem vulnerable and submissive to white political and educational authority can call upon "spirits" and "ancestors" whose stories, allegories are full of pointed thrusts, startling assertions, and haughty self-confidence — as if to say to themselves, "Who are these pathetic, driven, nervously insecure white people? When will they learn to relax and feel at ease with the world?"

Many Pueblo or Hopi children regard white people as noisy, truculent, full of braggadocio. What would they do without their ever-working mouths and their greedy eyes and their long, grasping arms? And what would they do without their endless road signs, telling how fast to drive, or how far it is from here to there, or what is coming ahead in the way of twists and turns, ups and downs? If preoccupation with time is "the white man's madness," then it is only one form of madness that afflicts him. Indian children are brought up to love the land, feel close to it, respect it, but not own it, or survey it to boast of the extent of ownership. Space for whites means measured land, in the possession of so-and-so; space for a Hopi child or a Pueblo child means land right here, that is familiar and a constant companion, friendly land as far as the eye can reach.

Needless to say it was the white man who came up with the notion of reservations, and Indians have had no choice but to learn to accept someone else's (a strange person's, an alien person's, a conquering nation's) notion of land — something set aside and defined by markers, maps, gates, and legal documents. But sometimes a Pueblo or Hopi child becomes playful yet quite serious, too, and begins to construct fantasies about the land. The white man will pick up and leave, will be called back by his God, and the Indians will have the land to themselves again. What then? It will be a rather strange time, the boys and girls know. No one will worry about town lines, city limits, state boundaries. The word "reservation" will disappear from usage. Fences will vanish from sight, as will a lot of roads. At a certain point, however (variable, depending upon the whim of a particular child), such a return to the past is abandoned, even ridiculed. Indian children have been told (in school as well as at home) what it was like a hundred or two hundred years ago, but they find it hard to go back that far even in their minds.

They retain from their ancestors an awe of the land, a constant regard for it, an inclination to find in it a kind of ultimate reassurance that others might describe as "religious." But they also feel a shyness and even a certain awe of those who don't share such attitudes. If the white people are resented and feared for their power and their history of plunder, they are also regarded as weirdly successful, able to defy spirits and powers that Indians listen carefully to, revere, worry about, and try to placate. The white man is the one who dares affront or take control of Nature's various "spirits," and seemingly without being ruined! Of course, not all whites are so sure of themselves and their future. But the doubters, or those who go further and turn to the Indians with admiration for their values and beliefs, are not the people who run America, New Mexico or Arizona, Albuquerque or Phoenix, and, very important, the Bureau of Indian Affairs. If America's white people express any self-doubt, any open self-criticism, Indian children have, by and large, not yet learned of it.

Nor do those children expect to live a life thoroughly different from the ones their parents have lived. They have few dreams of glory. Sometimes an Indian child does indeed imagine himself flying a jet airplane, or imagine herself an actress on television or a stewardess flying all over the world for virtually nothing. Those daydreams don't last long, however; and they are often followed by a sense of shame and an awareness of how absurd it is for a Pueblo child of eight or nine to have such ideas. The childhood fantasy lacks one of its most important elements: the capacity to be convincing and satisfying. Pueblo children under ten laugh at themselves when they speak of "becoming white," behaving as white people do when grown up. Hopi children tell one another what they think white boys and girls of their age might want to be like when older, but make a clear distinction between "them" and "us." And running through the comments one hears from Indian parents and their children is a very special fear (even children of seven or eight have it): the white man as a terribly dangerous person, a *child*, a *possessed* child, actually. Some Indian children will speak of whites as children who are captured by coyotes, made to become coyotes "inside," then let loose to prey upon Indians, who are sheep or goats or chickens. Such stories are not literally believed by a child who has heard them; rather, they are fables that help express a boy's, a girl's (or a parent's) confusions, apprehensions, judgments.

Nevertheless, Indian children are not without envy of and admiration for the white world. Even the Hopis, relatively more removed both physically and culturally from the white world than the Pueblos are, cannot find it in themselves completely to scorn white people and the way they live. There is the unavoidable matter of wealth and power. People who want nothing more than to be left alone with their land, their traditions, their memories of the past and their unashamedly limited hopes for the future are not able to protect themselves, as they may want to, from the appetites of those who lord it over them. An Indian boy of ten or eleven may one time repeat his father's words, talk about how strange it is that the white man is always worried that someone is going to attack him and take his money away, and so is always building and expanding military bases; but another time the same boy acknowledges the invincible strengths of the United States Air Force. And even speaks with admiration of the jet fighters that crisscross the sky, or the helicopters that appear out of nowhere and quickly move over the reservation.

Unlike Chicano children, Eskimo children, or for that matter black or Appalachian children, Indian children don't regard the pilots of those jets or helicopters as privileged men, whose careers might with great luck be emulated. In fact Indian boys (the girls almost never speak about planes, and even when they are roaring overhead, try to ignore them) aren't interested in who flies those planes. Pueblo or Hopi boys talk as if the planes were automatically piloted. They compare the planes to giant birds, to eagles or hawks. They endow the plane, as they do many other inanimate objects in the world, with a variety of emotions — the pride that goes with the achievement of speed, the shame that a noisy person ought to feel as the invader of a quiet neighborhood. Moreover, those Indian children are uniquely curious about the origins of military hardware — where is it made, out of what, by whom? They do not, like others, simply take for granted the presence of an air force base with all its equipment. They are ever on the lookout for a symbolic event.

Beauty is what Indian children of the Southwest immediately see in those fast-flying planes — but also ugliness, even the grotesque. The children are entranced by the fast-moving white against the blue sky. The children dislike and fear the noise. As for helicopters, they are "a plane born too soon," or "a spider who became a giant," or "a bad spirit who won't be happy until we're scared." And no point trying to talk about motors or miles per hour or firing range or bombing range; those are issues that prompt the interest of different children but do not intrigue Indian children. They are likely to wonder about other matters: what their ancestors are thinking, out there on the distant mesa, as the white man's newest toy howls and screams, pierces the clouds, rises above them, heads seemingly toward the sun itself, makes a reversal and shows every intention of plunging nonstop into the sacred earth of a reservation, the last hope of a people.

The white man is due a certain respect. He manages tricks no Indian would ever dream up. And there is a certain excitement in the various technological outbursts New Mexico and Arizona have witnessed: explosions and implosions; faster-than-sound missiles; dams that make mesas seem like anthills; highways that seem to girdle the world; buildings that don't know when to stop growing taller; speedy elevators that move so fast they don't seem to move at all; chairlifts that grab people, carry them up mountains higher and higher, smaller and smaller to the eye. What is the matter with the white man, though: will he ever stop and bow his head, or must he always be looking over his shoulder, or around the next corner, the next bend?

Some white Southerners, at least the more traditional ones, abhor the new South, with all its rush, hurry, and bustle, and defiantly consider themselves relaxed, contented, if not lazy as can be — compared to the nervous, industrious Yankees, who never seem to sit still. Indian children have learned to make a similar distinction. For Pueblo children, and more so for Hopi children, there is a substantial difference between themselves and white people. The latter are variously described as "strong," "ambitious," "greedy," "not people to trust"; the Indians are "slow," "happy," and, yes, "fools," the last because they have been all too trustworthy, all too lacking in greed. And yet no Indian child wants to be greedy like the white man, or a liar or a thief, as the white man was, historically, in connection with Indians — even as no white Southerner of a certain kind is ready to acknowledge an interest in Yankee commercial virtues. At least publicly and formally; at moments, when caught off guard, a plantation owner will speak his envy of a Yankee industrialist, and an Indian child can say that he wouldn't mind "owning a few fast planes." Then he would be able to "beat" the white man; and if that were to happen, the Indian would be "on top," and the white man's children would be going to a Bureau of the White Man's Affairs school, and wouldn't that be a day, *the* day!

Fantasies do indeed run wild in young Indians — fantasies of conquest but, strangely, not of sustained glory. The Indian child soon stops himself short: why bother stealing the white man's jets, the white man's "thunder"? Without it, the white man would be nothing. Indians can enjoy their own thunder (nature's kind), or hide from it, but certainly they have no desire to call it *theirs*. The white man is obsessed with ownership — *his* planes, *his* speed and power, *his* thunder. The white man himself has referred to his cars and planes as "thunderbirds," and confirmed what the Indians have known all along.

The reputed anthropomorphism of Indians is more than matched by their ability, in a second, to show how concrete, logical, pragmatically materialistic they can also be — a touch cynical about themselves as well as others. There are other ambiguities or apparent inconsistencies. Pueblo Indian children can abandon their gracefully maintained composure, their unnerving capacity for silence, their "impenetrable" psychological armor, and acknowledge outspokenly the grim future they see ahead — poverty, social exclusion, political impotence. That is particularly true of those children whose parents have tried to keep a foot in the white world. One day the child is a Pueblo, and glad of it, proud of it. The next day the child has in several respects stopped sounding like an Indian — and instead emphasizes what others would refer to as economic "variables," or the social and political problems that all poor people, of whatever background, have to struggle with. And does so with no restraint, with anger and sadness.

At times like these children abandon even the inclination to call upon Nature as an ally. The vivid, metaphoric, historically conscious attitudes of the Indian give way to the grim, sociological line of reasoning that poor children all over the United States have had to learn, whenever they accompany their parents to county officials, to welfare workers, to protest meetings, or as they hear their lives discussed even by sympathetic teachers, let alone the crude and callous ones. Hopi children, less involved with white people than Pueblos are, go in and out of moods: at times quite oblivious of the white world, or slyly contemptuous of its values; at other times almost brutally willing to recognize that, as life in America goes, they are weak, poor, curbed, and not exactly possessed of a promising future.

Both Pueblo and Hopi children have a rather special notion of the future. The tribe *has* a future. Even extinction would be a future, a prelude to survival of another kind. Children who misunderstand or dislike the white man's obsession with time have an ease with the concept of eternity that escapes many white children, including even those brought up in strictly religious homes (Appalachian fundamentalist, for example). Eight- or nine-year-old Indian children speak of "the seasons that never end," or the ancestors who are there, waiting for everyone alive to join them. Indian children are certain that in eternity there will be a delicious freedom from the constraints of this world: having to put clothes on and off, having to worry about washing hands or cleaning teeth, having to do the chores around the house. What else happens when one has joined the ancestors? The children know: involvement in Nature, the experience of being part of the land, the sky, the sun, the moon. Much of the seeming aloofness or detachment of Indian children is an ironic consequence of an effort to "be with" the natural world, respond attentively to it, contemplate its character, nuances, subtleties.

All of that may well be unnecessarily complicated, metaphysical, metapsychological. For Indian children there are daily experiences with parents who evoke spirits or ancestors, and speak to the wind, and call upon the sky, and hand down stories or legends meant to teach a child not only how to behave "in the present time of this life," as one Hopi mother put it, but "in the future time, when all life joins the world and stays with the world — no more moving around." If that is confusing, then perhaps Dante might be called upon for help — the notion of this life as a part of a journey, with a destination in mind, a final place of "being," of "rest," in the sense of a continuing state, as opposed to a temporary or changing one. Words and more words don't quite clarify the mother's meaning; nor, altogether, do cross-cultural references. Various theological comparisons, however interesting, come across at best as suggestive. The more one tries to talk about "ideas" that have their origin (according to Hopi mothers) in the ripples of a lake, no less, or in the gusts of wind, or in the moon's sudden, intense, probing light, the more one is inclined to remember a Hopi child's distinction between his people and the white man: "We look and dream; they look and want to get."

It can be argued that Indians are ignorant, are badly educated, are cursed by a culturally sanctioned kind of "primitive thinking," are thereby prevented from making "progress" — utilizing and contributing to scientific knowledge. Certainly many Indian children do not much respond to science lessons, engineering projects, or ordinary technological efforts — a bulldozer at work on a road, a helicopter surveying the approach of a storm. Maybe it is best to say that the children do indeed respond, but in their own way. They have acquired a sense of proportion about man and his prowess that distinguishes them from other American children. An Indian child at work drawing is like a Chinese or Japanese artist of several centuries ago — less impressed by man and his artifacts than bound by the spell of trees, shrubs, waterfalls, hills, terraces, mountains. For Indian children, as for Oriental artists, there are always dragons in the world, fearsome objects who threaten the ordinary shape of things, but their power, to a degree, has to do with one's willingness to yield to them through fear or an exaggerated notion of one's own inadequacies or inabilities. The white man and his artifacts are, perhaps, dragons that Indian children must learn to subdue psychologically. One ought to stay skeptical of those who, though they have prevailed in many ways, may get destined to failure on the grandest scale.

Such generalizations are made concrete to Indian boys and

girls. They are made to live close to history, made to reflect upon history. They are reminded that guns won over bows and arrows, that no matter how fast an Indian runs, he cannot keep up with a car, a truck, a plane. They are told, further, as other American children are told, that America is a strong nation, the strongest in the world, perhaps. If other nations, even whole continents, dare not take on this nation, what are a few thousand Hopis or Pueblos to do? It is possible to achieve what social scientists call a "perspective," and with it to hold on for dear life. For that to happen, however, one must take stock not only of oneself but the white man. Indians have long given themselves their limited due in relationship to the surrounding world. But the white man, they know, can't simply be treated like an ill wind, or a passing psychological scrutiny that, ironically, the Indian parent denies himself or herself and doesn't extend to his or her children. Mothers and fathers who avoid analysis of their own and their children's motives talk at great length (and were doing so long before "psychology" became as American as apple pie) about the white man's "insecurity," his fear that he will be found inadequate, wanting, someone's inferior.

The word "insecurity" seems so much a part of white sensibility that its use among Indians, even their children of elementary school age, can strike an outsider as yet additional evidence of the influence a so-called dominant (certainly domineering) culture can exert on even those remote physically and spiritually from its heart. But elderly Indians, great-grandparents, often tell small Indian boys and girls that the white man has always been "insecure" and will be "until he leaves us." Why is he like that — and, not incidentally, where will he be going when he "leaves"? The answers vary yet also have a strange consistency. In sum, the white man's insecurity is an irreducible aspect of his temperament, his character; and in turn, the phenomenon of white men is an aspect of the world's nature. One might just as well ask why a perfect day yields to a stormy, threatening day. In the long reach of history, however, the bad can turn to good — the white man's crazy assaults on people, places, things, his triumphs that have cost him and the world so much, will dissolve when he, somehow, sometime disappears. The point is not to elevate the Indian in some persisting struggle, give him the desperate reassurance of an eventual upset "victory." The point is to understand the rhythms of Nature, its cyclical twists and turns.

The idea of winning (and its obverse, of losing) has not come easily to the Pueblos, the Hopis. They have, of course, experienced loss, have known defeat; they have taken on the white man, and other Indians, in particular battles or prolonged struggles over land and water. But they have not dreamed of *winning*, of *conquering*, of becoming *strongest*, most *powerful*. The Apaches and the Navahos, nomadic and strong-minded, have in the past wanted Hopi or Pueblo territory, but even they, often called warlike, are not exactly obsessed with *winning*. They want to get their own way; they want to have more land for their sheep; but they do not visualize the struggle as one entered into by a potential winner and a potential loser. Indian children often talk of having fights and enjoying them, or having fights and not liking them one bit, or having fights and getting their way, or having fights and yielding to someone. But they aren't inclined to say: I won or I lost. They know the words, have learned the meaning of "win" or "lose" in school. But they seem to crave no victories — at least over opponents. They want to feel strong, or feel able to handle themselves well in an ordinary child's game (or contest). They even want their *way* and are willing (some more than others, naturally) to fight to get that privilege. But they stop short of regarding themselves as winners and losers, as ones who have overcome another person and, by virtue of doing so have acquired a certain psychological distinction — self-approval and the admiration of others.

The psychology of the ancient Romans that Simone Weil has, better than anyone else, exposed in all its raw horror — a form of totalitarianism become incarnate in family life as well as an empire's politics — is the extreme opposite of the psychology of certain Indian children. Hopi boys and girls even have trouble staking out a territorial position for themselves in a backyard and defending it, calling it *theirs.* They are also known to ask their teachers with incredulity why there are so many countries in the world, and why so many wars between those countries. Yes, struggles between Indian tribes have been a relatively constant part of their history, and took place long before the white man arrived in America. But Pueblo and Hopi children, at least, have never been taught that they belong to tribes that *won,* or *lost,* certain battles or wars. They learn, unquestionably, that the white man is the one who rules America; and they have heard about other tribes — enemies for a while, or longtime allies, or at different times both. But it is not a Pueblo or Hopi child's inclination to characterize others as winners or losers. Even the white man's military successes aren't viewed by the Pueblos or Hopis as decisive judgments on their own worth, or for that matter, the worth of the conqueror. A conqueror is not necessarily a winner, anyway — not for people quite comfortable with irony and ambiguity. Conquerors can get into a great deal of trouble, however powerful they are. Those beaten back by force of arms can sit and watch and live and *be* — a line of "existential" thinking that comes quite naturally to Indians, but may strike many white people, including social scientists, as all too "passive."

Many Pueblo or Hopi boys and girls are quite aware of the

temperamental difference between themselves and white children of their age. A Pueblo boy wonders why white children want so many toys when there is a tree to climb, a canyon to explore, a hill to scramble up, a slingshot to be made. A Pueblo girl wonders why white girls don't learn how to make dishes or collect firewood or take care of animals. Such generalizations about white children are based on what is seen on television or read in books or heard from parents or relatives. The same boy or girl can make a more pointed summary of the differences between themselves and white children: the latter are eager to buy, to own, to win; whereas the Indian is eager to look, to enjoy what is seen, to be worthy of his people, their land, their world, and not least, their future. It is not a future of specific years; it is a vague time ahead when the world will somehow right itself, become less at the mercy of various plunderers. It is an ahistorical time, really, a notion of transcendence: human beings as predecessors of a higher state — glimpsed but not realized in this life. And that being the case, the Indian child learns to regard himself or herself with a certain skeptical aloofness that borders on indifference and contrasts with the intense self-centeredness that characterizes most white middle-class American children.

In their drawings those Indian children show, at six or seven, an astonishing lack of interest in representing themselves or others they know. Often other American children get great satisfaction in putting adults down by means of drawing what amounts to caricatures. The children also may try to give themselves a boost — make self-portraits that banish fears, doubts, inadequacies by means of larger-than-life representation. But among the Pueblos or Hopis there is no great interest in self-representation on the part of adults *or* children. Boys and girls aren't even drawn to making pictures of dogs or horses, both of which may be constant and adored companions. A hill, a sky, an expanse of land, a brooding, lonely mesa — these command the crayons of Indian children, who demonstrate endless patience and solicitude as they do their artistic work. The very suggestion that a particular child draw someone may be greeted by a polite demurrer or a sharp look: "Why?" the outsider is silently asked. Actually Indian children know why. They know out of their experience in schools, or with television, how concerned white people are with themselves, how important they believe they are, how dedicated they are to their own advancement. That realization does indeed get impressed in drawings, but indirectly.

A Hopi child draws a moon that seems to be sagging, weighted down by a burden; or one that is protected from the earth by clouds. The child explains that it is sad for the moon to be visited by men and their machines, and that the moon may well, one day, try to hide and stay hidden from the ever more mobile and grasping white man. So with the sun; Hopi children have in recent years, for obvious reasons, been wondering when it will be the sun's turn for one of those astronaut landings. The sun may well be less willing to endure quietly such an affront, or so the children believe. And what if the sun turned its back, so to speak, on the earth? What if the sun did just the opposite, decided (out of anger) to pay all the more attention to the earth? Such questions are not academic ones to Indian children of the Southwest, for whom the sun and the moon are such important and constant friends. That is to say, they are not questions asked in response to an outsider's questions of his own, or in response to a schoolteacher's request for information or the exercise of imagination. Rather, the children themselves struggle to make sense of what they know is happening and what they believe to be the impact of those events upon the natural world.

When Indian boys and girls, in school or elsewhere, are

confronted with a white person of authority and influence, they do not usually lower their heads as Chicano children do — a sign of deference and fear, however qualified through unspoken fantasies and daydreams of vengeance. Pueblo children are apt to become impassive: if offended, they turn away directly, without hesitation. They gaze out the window. They look at someone else. They ask if they may be excused. They change the subject quickly, forcefully. Hopi children are somewhat more taciturn and tactful, but no less impatient, with the white outsider. For a Hopi child a white person's question or request may be an occasion for a responsive observation that seems, on its face, utterly irrelevant — as if the boy or girl has not simply changed the subject but has not really heard or understood what the subject was in the first place.

A teacher, for instance, asks a child what she might want to be doing in five or ten years, or what he'd like to do when school is over. The child replies that she or he has no idea, but someone, somewhere does, and maybe in time the answer will be forthcoming. The teacher suspects coyness, intransigence, rebelliousness, secretiveness, a failure of "communication," cultural "deprivation," or, more self-critically, a "problem in cross-cultural perspective." The child has no such series of speculations to mull over. The child has, in fact, tried to let the teacher have a very appropriate answer to the question — namely, that it is not for her or him to have on the tip of the tongue a statement for the teacher, because the future can never be anticipated by anyone living, though an ancestor now "gone," but very much present in the universe, may have some knowledge of what is to come, and in time, may reveal that knowledge.

Rather difficult, that, for a child to have in mind and try to convey to a white person! Yet Indian children often regard themselves as "waiting" to grow up, by which they mean that an ancestor, long dead, but attentively watching, will eventually "decide" to let it be known what a particular child's life is going to be like — whereupon the child's life will hasten to confirm the prophecy. No wonder such children are taught to look at certain distant mesas with awe. Sometimes boys or girls fall prey to intense curiosity, which prompts wayward if not sacrilegious behavior — attempts to "listen in," hear the secrets of the ancestors, presumably being discussed in councils held on top of a sacred mesa. Soon enough the children are taught that they have been insolent, prying, presumptuous, disrespectful; and that if they continue to be so, they will never live the full life, the nature of which they have been so anxious to ascertain. Often it is a grandparent who reprimands the child, lets the child know that one must wait for a life to reveal itself (be revealed, actually) rather than try to rush things — or gain an advance reading, as the white man might put it.

Consequences of such an attitude toward life, toward the future, are rather apparent in Indian children. They do not constantly try to picture themselves something — doctor, lawyer, Indian chief, as the saying goes. Certainly not the last of those three! If asked what they see ahead for themselves, they become evasive. They also reach a silent conclusion about the questioner: one more white man — or an Indian who has become a white man by leaving the reservation not only physically but spiritually. How dare anyone say that he *will be* this, she *will be* that! It is not only arrogant, the pride or hubris Western man has long known about, though by no means overcome; it is quite literally an incredible request. Indians don't give individual will nearly the status or authority whites do.

Thus, the "child-rearing practices" of Indian parents become a vehicle for a specific psychological, philosophical, and religious view of life's meaning, purpose, rhythm, and momentum. The child learns to regard himself or herself as not only a small part of the universe but as intimately linked to a tribe's history — to the point that growing up itself has to do with decisions made by the dead as well as the living. And, of course, such a child's view of death does not resemble that acquired by white children, starting at the age of five or six. Death is a departure, necessarily; but not to a distant, unimaginable place. Death is a short but significant walk, an important but not total transformation: one goes to the mesa, for instance, or up a canyon, or to the source of a river, and in that new home starts an active life of continued communion with the living. It is not a systematic theology, of course. Much that children learn about their ancestors, about spirits that are part of the natural world, or about the "power" of the sun, the moon, the earth, has an idiosyncratic quality deriving from a particular parent's personal style: imagination, narrative capability, an interest in explaining things at length, as opposed to making a brief and final statement.

There is an awareness on the part of Indian parents (and, eventually, their children) that the craving for consistency of opinion and behavior present in many white communities is not at all desirable. In that regard, a number of better-educated Pueblo and Hopi parents are quick to talk about various anthropological observers and how hard their work must be, because on the one hand they are looking for threads of consistency, for patterns and continuities, and on the other hand Indians are often quite willing to oblige a visitor, once they sense what is being sought — to the point that inconsistencies or discontinuities or the utterly idiosyncratic get set aside, go unmentioned, are somehow overlooked, not only by the observer, but by the "informants," who quickly sense what it may be that they "ought" to say. Indians have learned to be

extraordinarily sensitive to the wishes and hopes of white people, including academic observers. They are also, many of
them, able to hold on to their integrity — go so far but no
further. Many of them take pains to tell their children that
they must "prepare" themselves, slowly, for the white man,
learn how to deal with him, even learn how to go along with
him — but only to a degree.

The Hopis, especially, are aware of the differences between
themselves and white people — differences of philosophy and
psychology as much as money, power, or social position. The
Hopi child is told that he may acquire a lot of information from
whites, may come to appreciate and like certain whites, and
certainly has to learn how to live with whites (who are everywhere, even when not in sight), because their influence has
shaped both the appearance and the reality of America. But
there are places of refuge, and the Hopi child learns them. Not
only the reservation itself: the child comes to realize that the
ultimate sanctuary is within the mind. There is no safer, more
protected way of speaking to others (and oneself) than through
dreams.

The dream is important to Indian children — to Hopis or
Pueblos, certainly. The white outsider must keep in mind constantly the way he or she has, almost without knowing it,
assumed a function for dreams that others might well, and do,
find unfamiliar or even inconceivable. For twentieth-century
white child psychiatrists, obviously, the dream of a child is a
means of knowing that child — knowing about particular, but
also shared, struggles, conflicts, worries, lusts. A dream
remembered is a dream that tells of an especially vexing
"problem" a boy or girl happens at the time to be going
through. White children (and their parents, too, of course)
often forget their dreams promptly on awakening and make
no mention at all of the fact that a dream has taken place. Nor

do white parents (even the upper middle class, psychiatrically sophisticated) ask their children day after day whether (and if so, what) they have dreamed. But for Indian parents and children the dream is quite another kind of event — a means of talking to oneself, a means of hearing the messages of ancestors long dead, a shared way for, say, a mother and child to speak to one another about the values of a particular tribe. All seemingly important, but how does one go about making the correct interpretation of Indian dreams? (How, for that matter, does one do so with respect to the dreams reported by analysands?) Indian parents don't worry about such questions. They simply tell their children that a dream is the mind's way of drawing pictures, and that the result is edifying, because the pictures tell a dreamer's story, *or* are drawn by an ancestor who wants to tell a story through the medium of a person. Some Pueblos or Hopis or Utes are convinced that children's dreams, especially, are the chosen way for ancestors to keep in touch with today's people.

It is astonishing for one who is not an Indian to listen to Indian parents and their children talking about their dreams. The children tell their mothers and fathers what they "saw" and then make a kind of extrapolation (rather than interpretation). That is, they move from a recitation of visual imagery to a narrative account of what an ancestor wants to convey, or what the boy himself or the girl herself wants to say. And it is all done in a casual, matter-of-fact manner — no portentous comments, no comments at all, really. A grandfather, for example, dead a few years, appears in his nine-year-old grandson's dream. The old man is walking on the mesa, then decides to sit down under a tree. He smiles when it rains but does not frown when the rain quickly stops. Instead he gets up and starts walking toward a stream, beyond the mesa. The boy "saw no more"; he tells his father what he did see, though, and the father says "thank you." The father seems pleased. He announces that this is a good day because his old father has sent back word that he is prospering, that he has found out how to manage over there, on the mesa, and so his kin, still alive, need not worry about him. Good tidings are, of course, good tidings; the father and son, not to mention others in the family, rejoice. A Western Union telegram, a phone call, a newspaper report, a television documentary, an article in a magazine, a whole book — none of them would be given any greater "credibility" by the child who had the dream, or by his parents.

At breakfast especially, children in many Indian families refer to the dreams of the night before — with pleasure, with concern, with confusion or apprehension. They don't talk *about* their dreams. The "pictures" are reported — as if a factual account of an event. Then there is silence, and soon enough, a change of subject: someone else's "pictures" offered, or a return to the more tangible business of the day. At times mothers or fathers consider dreams to be evidence; a child who "saw" a storm in his or her sleep is the equivalent of a weatherman — and maybe as accurate. A dream is a strongly held vision — the dreamer's, or through him or her, someone else's. When the dream is put into words, it is that person's assertion, conviction, prophecy, statement of regret, concern, intent.

At times Indians sound as if they had been reading some of Carl Jung's more speculative writings on dreams; especially when children are told by their parents that their "people" have just come to life through a certain "picture" or series of "pictures." There is an acknowledgment of what white psychoanalysts would regard as the unconscious, if not the collective unconscious. At other moments, listening to children in a Pueblo or Hopi village, one is reminded of the transcendentalism of Ralph Waldo Emerson, with its emphasis on the importance of the spiritual and the supraindividual as against the material and the empirical; or the romantic idealism espoused in England by Coleridge and Thomas Carlyle. Those writers had tired of the Enlightenment, were interested in something beyond the rational and mechanistic point of view that, in the name of a certain kind of science, was dominating the intellectual world and making serious inroads on the religious and ethical convictions of the nineteenth century. How ironic then, that in 1836, when the Transcendental Club was founded in Boston, there were about twenty-five hundred miles away so-called savages whose way of regarding spiritual and religious matters, as well as the tangible, visible surrounding world of things and people, was quite similar to the tenets upheld by Ralph Waldo Emerson!

The "poor white man" whom one hears Indian children refer to, the "crazy white man" whom one hears Indian parents refer to, is the white man those children and parents know as fiercely devoted to the acquisition of goods and land, the white man obsessed by machines, who has a manipulative relationship to the universe. In contrast, Indians teach their children to treasure the enigmatic, to celebrate the world rather than try to change it, to enjoy the various confusions that present themselves, to equate (sometimes, at least) what is baffling, cryptic, or inscrutable with the "transcendent" — in the white man's philosophical language. Kant's willingness to acknowledge the mind's serious and continuing limits is not unlike the Indian's insistence on the difference between "the white man's thinking" (full of theories, formulations, schemes for doing things, for winning control over the natural world, for understanding it fully and "definitively") and the Indian's thinking, which challenges (in its own quiet, meditative, pastoral manner) just about all the assumptions that white people hold dear.

Time for an Indian child is not something measured, spent, consumed, or wasted; it is, rather, a characteristic of living experience — a gift to us by the life around us, of which we are a part. Such a notion may seem hazy and annoyingly mystical to the white people who visit Indians and "study" them for a while and sit down to write books; or the white people who read such books to learn what the Indians are "like," what "motivates" them, what they think, and why they have the opinions they do. But many Indians don't think of themselves as *having* opinions; they don't think of themselves as having a certain amount of money, or as having a certain number of years in which to do something or achieve something; they don't think of themselves as proprietors, or as the ones who discovered something, or invented something. Even the "roles" (as others would put it) of parent and child are not regarded as altogether time-bound — determined by age. Parents will arbitrarily, it seems, decide that one child *is* an elderly ancestor who has "come back on a visit." A mother will tell her children that she is one of them — and maybe that one of them is her own senior in wisdom or good judgment because he or she "carries" a particular ancestor "inside." Such talk doesn't prevent a parent from also being a parent. And many Indians have, by their own acknowledgment, become white men — taken up white points of view. Many other Indians try to have it both ways — go to church *and* take part in their own tribe's dances, rites, sacred or religious practices. Still others pretend to talk and think like white people when with them, and express quite different ideas when off by themselves. Often Indians tell their children that their chief task in life is somehow to learn how to live an Indian life in a white world. But in general, Indian children of New Mexico and Arizona are not told precisely how to achieve this, because to do so would be a white man's way of approaching the matter. Those children are sent home from school with lists, enumerations, definitions, causal explanations, chronologies — only to be reminded that the white man is always trying to talk his way through life and out of its inherent and ineradicable mysteries, paradoxes, ironies, all of which for many Pueblo or Hopi parents are simply part of life, and best left alone, even affirmed, rather than "explained."

Over and over again children of one or another pueblo connect the white man as a plunderer of land and resources to the white man as a big talker, a smooth talker, a fast talker addicted to words. For a Hopi or Pueblo child, the *world* is God, as compared to the white man's interest in *words* as a means of reaching and understanding God — not to mention "the Word became flesh." Indian children don't have to *learn* silence; they *are* silent. They can stare a long time at a cloud and feel as if they have left themselves, joined it. It is a shift in perspective that many white children would find hard, even frightening, to contemplate. And when Indian children are finally persuaded in school to draw a person, they prefer the white man to themselves as "subject." He is the one, after all, who loves mirrors, cultivates his "image," dwells on himself constantly. A picture of him seems to be a favor to him. Indian children know how to extend charity to others.

The white man is pitied as much as feared or regarded as someone necessarily obeyed. A Hopi child says that yes, she knows the white man is dangerous and untrustworthy, but that is because he is not only a coyote or mountain lion, but a mouse, a rabbit, a snake. A white man used to words and anxious to interpret what he sees and hears can only comment on the psychological use to which such a child puts animals — objects of attribution, projection, displacement, and so on. Through those animals the Hopis express fears and hates and worries they don't know themselves to possess, or do indeed sense in themselves, but shun expressing directly because of a discerning appraisal of the risks involved (the white man's anger and retaliatory vengeance). And again, there is the matter of pity. Would it do any good at all for the Hopis, say, to tell the white people a few things about themselves that they may not know or care to know? This kind of reflective mixture of skepticism, detachment, and compassion is strikingly evident in the Pueblos and Hopis.

Even eight- and nine-year-old Indian children can sometimes speak about white people with astonishing concern — as if a mighty nation like the United States is, ironically, in great jeopardy, whereas the Indian reservations of Arizona or New Mexico are in no danger at all. It does not quite work to dismiss such an attitude as psychopathological — a child's "denial" of reality, or a projection of vulnerability upon the "aggressor," and maybe, a little "identification" with that aggressor. The children who regard the white world with a certain worried and even sympathetic foreboding have learned from their parents to connect the way human beings act to the natural world and its various dangers. As a matter of fact, Indians regard the white man as an extraordinarily strange animal — the very one Konrad Lorenz and others have identified as the only species capable of out-and-out cruelty. Other animals kill for food, but man may kill out of sadism, calculated meanness. The detachment of an ethologist like Lorenz is the detachment of a Hopi child who announces (at nine) that she prays to the spirits who hover over the reservation that somehow they will find a way to change the white man. Then he will stop being so restless and reckless. Then those pilots who streak across the sky, leaving a trail of smoke and noise, will land their planes, walk away from them, find a tree to sit under, a hill on which to stand — and look at the sky rather than desecrate it.

For the Hopis, especially, white people are ravenous because for some reason they have become lost and show no signs of finding their way home. A Hopi boy of eleven can even construct a history of white people from an Indian child's perspective, and in its emphasis tell rather a lot about the ethical values of his own people as well as of the white man. What he stresses, of course, is the waywardness and wantonness of white people; they are driven by spirits, he has been told, that are powerful, demanding, arbitrary. People so driven are slaves, are in prison, he believes. They are blind, too; they don't know what ails them, what urges them on, for all their economic and political prowess. And, very important, they are an example, an object lesson — people who deserve moral scrutiny of a kind rarely accorded the rich and strong by the poor and weak. It is a scrutiny intensely philosophical, ethical, psychological.

While Indian children in Bureau of Indian Affairs schools are taught to read and write (and sometimes made to feel inadequate or members of a backward people), the parents of those children are at work providing another kind of education for their sons and daughters. Often it is done through Socratic questions. What do you think the white man is after, when he speeds at ninety miles an hour across our land? Or when he sends his planes across our skies, roaring and going up and down, crisscrossing each other's paths? Have you seen the cars and trucks and trailers near the canyon? Have you seen the people rushing past each other to get out of the big buses — so that one person can say he saw something first, photographed something first, rather than second, third, or fourth? Why do they talk so much and so fast? Why are they always signing treaties, drawing up truces, pacts, agreements, new laws or "understandings"? Why do they buy so many pills, so many medicines — for everything, from sleeping to waking up to digesting their food to covering their skins under the sun?

Those questions are not original or unique. American social critics have asked them and others like them, on and off, for years. More than any of the other so-called minorities in this country, Indians are anxious to take the measure of the dominant white majority — but not only as persecuted or impoverished people always must do. Indians regard themselves — many of them in the Southwest, at least, do — as an object lesson of sorts to the white man, a means by which he may, in the long run, be brought up short. It is an astonishing historical sense the Hopis especially, but also the Pueblos and Utes, have about themselves and the people who have exerted such overwhelming control over their lives for so long. And an astonishing detachment — of an ultimate sort that philosophers and theologians understand, perhaps, better than psychiatrists. Time and again Indian fathers, especially, tell their children that one reason they are here is to teach others. The self-effacing Indian, the quiet and humble Indian, the Indian utterly preoccupied with the world, is the Indian who also has a fate: to be a witness to the depredations and excesses of others — and, maybe, a source of help, one day, to those others, when and if they ever start coming to their senses.

Put differently, it is a self-conceived task of many Indian parents to teach their sons and daughters a conscious appreciation of the ethical, aesthetic, and psychological differences between their view of the world and the white man's — in the hope that those Indian children will not only stand fast by their own beliefs, but someday, somehow, be in a position to help the white people change their own beliefs, or at the very least, come to appreciate explicitly what they are. Of all people it was Sören Kierkegaard who, in *Fear and Trembling,* best appreciated and described the kind of attitude Indians encourage in their children. It is an attitude of calculated, unremitting, entirely assertive resignation. It is *not* an attitude of passive acquiescence in the face of a vastly superior foe. The Indian child is told that he or she has an important and continuing responsibility — to care passionately for the land, the world near and far, in the hope that others will do likewise. Best to keep quiet in the face of the braggadocio of others; best to acknowledge frankly their seemingly unlimited power; best to take what little they offer by way of remuneration for their many misdeeds. But at no time ought an Indian miss an opportunity, however subtle, to make his or her position known. The white man can kill all Indians and thereby eliminate their collective position. Short of that step, however, the reservations will persist, and on them children will also persist — boys and girls who go to Bureau of Indian Affairs schools and look and listen and constantly teach their teachers. Those teachers have come to know the paradox of bright, sensitive children who are eager to learn from the white man but are unwilling, finally, to think as he does, or abandon a way of life that seems hopelessly "out-of-date," "unproductive," or worse.

I don't think it farfetched, in this regard, to call upon Kierkegaard's Christ, the Man who confused just about everyone by His willingness to be defeated so long as He made clear his beliefs — in the hope that, ultimately, others would come to see their value. Kierkegaard was intrigued with and at times puzzled (as many others have been) by Christ's apparent "passivity," His recognition that there was no hope of changing many people, at least in this world, only the hope of converting some, teaching some by example, winning some over spiritually. Kierkegaard knew that such an attitude required an extraordinary kind of historical detachment — a sense of time quite different from that most people have. And also an ability to resign oneself to defeat, humiliation, renunciation — if need be, death itself — not only out of a belief in one's principles, but out of a passionate conviction that there is no other alternative, because there is indeed a Devil at work in the world. But at the same time one does not give up hope. Kierkegaard's resignation was the prelude to a "leap of faith." The surrender of the weak to God's will makes for a strength that eludes secular approximations or understanding.

The suffering Christ, the fatalistic Christ, the resigned but passionate Christ becomes — over a span of time that defies the tidy burgher's estimation — the triumphant Christ. Kierkegaard's brilliant, compelling psychological scrutiny of Christ and of those who would follow Him applies rather well to Hopi or Pueblo parents and their children, some of whom seem almost crazily determined to let centuries go by, if need be, in the confident assumption that their "right" will prevail over the white man's "might." And even as Christ enraged some who found Him not only a challenge to their power but a strangely unsettling and incomprehensible influence, so some Pueblos, Hopis, and Utes have prompted in various white "principalities and powers" a strange sense of incredulity: what *do* they want, and why are they so "different"? Nor can such a question be answered with a psychological or psychiatric inventory of "traits" or "problems" or "complexes." The transcendentalism of Emerson was meant to put materialism and empiricism in their place — give the spiritual, the supraindividual, a certain philosophical sanction. By the same token, Indian parents every day urge upon their children another kind of transcendence. Emerson's suspicions about messianic industrialism or science as God's wisdom have been more than shared by ordinary Indian "uneducated" parents.

It is a commonplace among those who have met and talked with a number of Indians in the Southwest that they get, or indeed always are, "high." They are high on the land, high on the sky, high on a river, high in response to a view of a mesa. But it is not only a psychological "lift"; it is a religious experience felt by people for whom the so-called natural order is nothing less than a supernatural phenomenon — again, the world as God. In his essays Ralph Waldo Emerson, a different and better white man than many Indians have known for several hundred years, pointed out that the world as a whole escapes anyone's, any age's, any culture's limits of definition. Through their thoughts and words, and with every feeling in their bodies, many Indian parents let their children know that their lives are part of a transcendent spirit; and that such knowledge is the world's only chance, its last, best hope. What eighteenth-century Yankee intellectuals struggled hard to find out for themselves, Indians know as a psychological and spiritual fact of their lives. It is a supremely confident conviction for a much-defeated people to have — and to hold so long, so tenaciously, against such long odds. It is a conviction that gives testimony to the persistence of faith. It is a conviction that continues to frustrate, unnerve, perplex, and enrage the white man — who has not been loath, historically, to denounce or outlaw what gets in his way, or more recently, to analyze it endlessly.

PART SIX

REFERENCES

1. THE WEST

BY THE TIME the reader goes through this section (patience and will permitting) he or she may well wonder why the author indulged his arrogance and egotism with yet another book on Chicanos, Eskimos, and Indians when so many books about one or another of those "groups" have appeared. As I indicated at the very beginning of this volume, the same thought repeatedly crossed my mind before I began to pursue the work that was, of course, a preface to the preceding writing. Rather thoroughly, I believe, I went through the "literature" and also talked or corresponded with a number of scholars in the field, as well as with the political activists or community organizers I met among Chicano migrants in Florida and in the Rio Grande Valley of Texas. It turned out that there hadn't yet been an effort such as the one I wanted to undertake — a look by a child psychiatrist at how Chicano, Indian, and Eskimo children manage to come to terms with themselves and the world around them, year after year of their lives. With that ascertained, and driven by my interest in how various children respond to the particular social, cultural, economic, and historical circumstances of their lives, I went ahead with the "fieldwork," as it is called — getting to know, spending time with, learning from, a number of boys and girls. I also did some reading, some studying. The point of this part of the book is to make available and at times discuss three bodies of knowledge, so to speak — or more broadly, a literature of the West.

And it is best to start at that level because in a very real sense the children whose lives I have tried to evoke, in the limited way possible for one like me, have constantly had to come to terms with the West's social history — the same history that a number of gifted historians and essayists, not to mention novelists, have given us. Like the South, the frontier West has generated some brilliant analytical studies from scholars who have been able to walk gracefully and intelligently (but unostentatiously) across those boundaries that mark off one discipline from another. Especially in the last quarter of a century, we have been graced with enormously suggestive books: Henry Nash Smith's *Virgin Land: The American West as Symbol and Myth* (Harvard University Press, 1950 and 1970); Richard Slotkin's *Regeneration Through Violence: The Mythology of the American Frontier, 1600–1860* (Wesleyan University Press, 1973); Richard A. Bartlett's *The New Country: A Social History of the American Frontier, 1776–1890* (Oxford University Press, 1974); and Kevin Starr's only slightly more restricted, with respect to subject matter, *Americans* and the California Dream, 1850–1915 (Oxford University Press, 1973). Those four books, with respect to the West, have begun a new field of inquiry — a fusion of historical narrative, literary criticism, and social comment. They are indispensable companions for someone wandering through Texas or New Mexico or Arizona or southern California or Alaska — a means, really, of learning what happened "before." (Often one hears Indian children, especially, say — because they have been told so often: "Before us there were others.")

Also of great value is David Lavender's direct and vivid *The American West* (Penguin, 1965). And, in a more emphatically literary vein, Edwin Russell's quite illuminating *Frontier: American Literature and the American West* (Princeton University Press, 1965). In a literary vein, too, is Kenneth Lynn's quite fine *Mark Twain and Southwestern Humor* (Atlantic-Little, Brown, 1960). A fine anthology of writings, incidentally (literary and otherwise), is *The American Frontier: Readings and Documents*, edited by Robert V. Hine and Edwin R. Bingham (Little, Brown, 1972). If one goes back to original sources, the best start, perhaps, is James Fenimore Cooper's Leather-Stocking series, especially *The Prairie* (1827), a recent edition of which, with a fine introduction by Henry Nash Smith, was published in 1963 (Holt, Rinehart & Winston). As for nonfiction, Francis Parkman's *The Oregon Trail* (Grosset & Dunlap, 1927, and more recently, New American Library, 1964) is worth special mention. Also there is General Thomas James's *Three Years Among the Indians and Mexicans*, edited and introduced by Milo Milton Ouaife (Citadel, 1966). Then there are the letter writers: for instance, *The Letters of George Catlin and His Family*, edited by Marjorie Catlin Roehm (University of California Press, 1966), and *The Frederic Remington–Owen Wister Letters*, edited by Ben Merchant Vorpahl, with a lovely introductory note by Wallace Stegner (West Publishing Company, 1972). Quite another viewpoint, a sensitive, intrepid woman's, is the journal entries, and essays based on them, of Isabella L. Bird: *A Lady's Life in the Rocky Mountains*, sensitively introduced by Daniel J. Boorstin (University of Oklahoma Press, 1960). Also from the University of Oklahoma, but from its faculty, not its press, is an excellent account of the development of western agriculture in the important, post–Civil War period: *The Farmers' Frontier, 1865–1900*, by Gilbert C. Fite (Holt, Rinehart & Winston, 1966).

Another way to approach any region is through the artists or photographers who have struggled visually to comprehend and portray it. *The American West: Painters from Catlin to Russell*, with reproductions assembled by Larry Curry, and a foreword by Archibald Hanna (Viking, 1972), provides an excellent sense of what the West has inspired in the way of paintings and sketches. There have been dozens of photographic attempts to capture (as only the camera can) one or another aspect of the West's environment or its social and cultural life. One can respond personally and mention two of special value: *The Western Wilderness of North America*, photographs by H. W. Gleason, text by George Crassette (Barre, 1972), and the extraordinary and compelling *Images, 1923–1974*, of Ansel Adams, with yet another foreword by Wallace Stegner (New York Graphic Society, 1974). That last book challenges, maybe defies, description; for me it evokes dozens of memories: of children; of the land they know and love; of the mountains they look toward and up to; of the rivers they count on and mention often enough — of the West in all its awesome yet immediate and tangible presence. There is, finally, a journal that deserves mention: *Journal of the West,* appropriately enough devoted to Western history and geography. It comes out of Los Angeles, but covers the prairie, mountain, and Pacific states. The issue for July 1971 offers an especially valuable article by Robert L. Munkres — "Indian-White Contact Before 1870: Cultural Factors in Conflict"; but each issue is full of interesting and helpful essays.

Now for a region within a region: the Southwest, which has generated its own special literature and scholarly tradition. One begins with Paul Horgan's *Great River: The Rio Grande in North American History* (Rinehart, 1954), a two-volume chronicle of four civilizations that have been nourished by that river — the Indian, the Spanish, the Mexican, and the Anglo-American. Horgan is a novelist who has lent his intelligence and narrative skill to the telling of regional history. The result is a brilliant and indispensable pair of books. Another book of his, *The Centuries of Santa Fe* (Dutton, 1965), provides a helpful account of an important southwestern cultural center. Horgan has drawn from his *Great River,* added some notes from a journal of his, and given us *The Heroic Triad,* which provides "Backgrounds of Our Three Southwestern Cultures" (Meridian, 1971). His books are, again, indispensable and a joy to read — including his most recent *Lamy of Santa Fe* (Farrar, Straus and Giroux, 1975). Spiritual kin to Horgan, if less elegant — though quite learned and marvelously informative — is J. Frank Dobie, a vivid storyteller and an authority on "the life and literature of the Southwest," of which he offers an important *Guide* (Southern Methodist University Press, 1952). The volume is an outgrowth of a course he taught for years at the University of Texas. His last book, published posthumously, offers finely wrought sketches of certain southwestern personalities — a cowboy preacher, a rancher, a homesteader, some teachers: *Out of the Old Rock* (Little, Brown, 1972). Horgan and Dobie are the giants of southwestern social history and literature — and by any standards remarkable writers and observers. A comprehensive survey of their work, and that of scores of others, is found in *Southwest Heritage: A Literary History with Bibliography* (University of New Mexico Press, 1972).

Others have written wisely or instructively of the region. It was Charles F. Lummis who first referred to the stretch of land that includes Texas, New Mexico, and Arizona as *The Land of Poco Tiempo* (University of New Mexico Press, 1952). The book was initially published in 1893 and is still an excellent way for the reader to begin to get a feel for New Mexico especially — its people, their diverse histories and ways of getting on. A formal history of the region, and very well written, too, is Howard Roberts Loman's *The Far Southwest: A Territorial History, 1846–1912* (Norton, 1970). If one wants to go back even further, there is *A History of the Ancient Southwest,* by Harold Sterling Gladwin (Wheelright, 1957). There is also *Ancient Life in the American Southwest,* by Edgar L. Hewett (Biblo & Tannen, 1968). And the region has generated an interesting kind of travel reportage, mixed with social or historical comment; a good example, from the earlier part of this century, is *Through Our Unknown Southwest,* by Agnes C. Lant (McBride, 1925). In a slightly more specialized vein, there is *This Reckless Breed of Men: The Trappers and Fur Traders of the Southwest,* by Robert Glass Cleland (Knopf, 1950).

R. L. Duffus has a more scholarly approach, though he writes for the general reader in *The Santa Fe Trail* (University of New Mexico Press, 1972). The region as a whole, as with the larger West, can be studied in various ways. There are legends — true stories embellished or become slightly apocryphal; see J. Frank Dobie's *Coronado's Children* (Grosset & Dunlap, 1950), or his *Tales of Old Time Texas* (Little, Brown, 1955). There is popular fiction — Zane Grey's western adventure stories, which, one after the other, my mother, Iowa-born and no stranger to the Far West, used to give me as a child. There are fifty-eight books in all, with titles like *Captives of the Desert, Lost Pueblo, Wild Horse Mesa,* not to mention *The Lone Star Ranger* and *Stranger from the Tonto.* The distortions, the prejudices, the underlying (and rather obvious) social and racial assumptions to be found in those volumes are also part of the Southwest's history and the history of the rest of the country, too — because Zane Grey and others like him have had an enormous and continuing national appeal.

The region has had its photographers; an especially important one, historically, was Adam Clark Vroman, who was born in 1856 and died in 1916. His photographs have been brought together by Ruth Mohood and introduced by Beaumont Newhall in *Photographer of the Southwest* (Ward Ritchie Press, 1961). *The Great Southwest,* by Elna Bakker and Richard G. Lillard (American West, 1972), has, besides a useful text, fine photographs in both black and white and color. Another way to get closer to the Southwest is through its wildlife, its terrain, its flowers. In this regard, a few books (there are others like them) are of help: *Desert Wild Flowers,* by Edmund C. Folger (Stanford, 1969); *Desert Wildlife,* also by Edmund C. Folger (Stanford, 1961); *Wildlife of the Intermountain West,* by Vinson Brown, Charles Yocom, and Aldene Starbuck (Naturegraph, 1958); and *The Desert World: Plant and Animal Life of the American Desert,* by David F. Costello (Crowell, 1972). The reader has presumably noticed how often the children who speak in this volume respond to plants, animals, trees, the land.

One can with each state — Texas, New Mexico, Arizona, California — compile even more specialized lists of books. There is Elroy Bode's *Texas Sketchbook: Impressions of People and Places* (Texas Western Press, 1967). There are, again, J. Frank Dobie's *Texas Stories.* There is Mary Austin's *The Land of Little Rain,* a beautifully constructed series of portraits of the border region of California and Arizona, including the Mojave Desert, the Sierras, and Death Valley (Doubleday, 1961). But I will try to indicate the range of books available for each state by mentioning some devoted to New Mexico, where I lived for several years and had a chance to visit bookstores as well as children and their families. To begin with, there is Willa Cather's *Death Comes for the Archbishop* (Knopf, 1959). I suppose if I were asked to add to Paul Horgan's work, so far as New Mexico goes, I would recommend Willa Cather's novel, followed by a close inspection of Georgia O'Keeffe's painting (see the fine, illustrated catalogue published by the Whitney Museum of American Art in 1970, with Lloyd Goodrich's moving essay on the painter). From the work of those two one moves into specifics: the arts and crafts, with *New Mexico Village Arts*, by Roland F. Dickey (University of New Mexico Press, 1970); the land, and its striking beauty, with *New Mexico*, by David Muench and Tony Hellerman (Belding, 1974); history, with Erna Fergusson's deservedly well-known *New Mexico* (Knopf, 1971), and Richard Ellis's historical reader, *New Mexico: Past and Present* (University of New Mexico Press, 1971); more localized history, with *Echoes of the Past: New Mexico's Ghost Towns*, by Patricia Meleski (University of New Mexico Press, 1972), or *Philmont: A History of New Mexico's Cimarron Country*, by Lawrence R. Murphy (University of New Mexico Press, 1972); politics, with *Politics in New Mexico*, by Jack E. Holmes (University of New Mexico Press, 1967); geography and the natural landscape, with *Historical Atlas of New Mexico*, by Warren Beck and Ynez Haase (University of Oklahoma Press, 1969), and *Mosaic of New Mexico's Scenery, Rocks and History*, edited by Paige Christiansen and Frank Kottlowski (New Mexico State Bureau of Mines & Mineral Resources, 1972); and religious architecture, important in the state, with *The Religious Architecture of New Mexico*, by George Kubler (University of New Mexico Press, 1972). Of great value, finally, with respect to New Mexico and all other southwestern states, indeed every state in the Union, is the "guide" compiled by workers of the Writers' Program of the Works Progress Administration.

2. ESKIMOS

PERHAPS the best way to begin this section is to make mention of the first book of poems by John Haines: *Winter News* (Wesleyan University Press, 1966). Haines is an American who left the East Coast for Fairbanks, Alaska, rather than San Francisco or Los Angeles. And, in turn, he left Fairbanks for his own "primitive," hand-built cabin, sixty-eight miles away — a homesteader with eyes and ears and a large gift for words. In "Listening in October," we are told about the Eskimo's world, the world Haines became so wedded to: "There are silences so deep/you can hear/the journeys of the soul/enormous footsteps/downward in a freezing earth." We are told about the hunters — once every Eskimo, even small boys and girls; and still whole villages of men, women and children, all on the prowl: "Bathed in sweat and tumult/he slakes and kills,/eats meat/and knows blood./His other half/lies in shadow/and longs for stillness,/a corner of the evening/where birds/rest from flight:/cool grass grows at his feet, dark mice feed/from his hands." One can describe easily enough the hunter; to know, even vaguely or at best approximately that "other half," to see it and feel it developing in children, and to try to come back "home" with words for it, a book about it — that may be an observer's vain hope, a writer's futile exercise.

One thing I did learn (too late, maybe) from an old Eskimo woman: "We are here; do not worry so much. So many of your people worry! Just sit with us. Join us. Here: have some tea." No rebuke; no advice about what to say, either. She was remembering others; she was offering her own kind of prayer for me, and for herself, and for her grandchildren whom I was getting to know. She was prepared to accept whatever fate would bring to her, to us. I wonder now, as I compile this strange list, called a bibliography, what she would think of it, of me; even as I've wondered often what she would think of this entire book. I know what she has *said*, in response to a presentation of (and explanation of) the other, earlier books in this series: polite acknowledgment, tactful but evasive expressions of approval. But there is an "other half," and it "longs for stillness," and it has no great interest in words and more words but rather looks excitedly at the cold sun, and the green and blue sky, the tangible beauty of the air, with its momentary silence, to be followed by the wind — which would, perhaps, bring the thousands of familiar worlds, each different, of a snowstorm.

In 1897 Dr. Fridtjof Nansen's *Farthest North* was published (Harper & Brothers): "being the record," one reads, "of a voyage of exploration of the ship *Fram* 1893–96 and of a fifteen months' sleigh journey by Dr. Nansen and Lieutenant Johansen." The record mounted up: two thick volumes, and they are to this day living companions for others, on other voyages — and too, companions of John Haines's *Winter News,* because Nansen was wonderfully open to the world he traveled through and determined to convey its startling, bitter, treacherous, appealing beauty to his readers.

Nansen's books, Haines's book, are part of a genre. Over the decades a number of bold, imaginative, and resourceful people have left the safety of one or another "civilized" nation — or, maybe, one should say, left temperate weather for the Arctic. And found there, often, peace as well as a new kind of war: an end to one set of dissatisfactions, a beginning of a new kind of struggle to live. Before the reader rushes to one or another textbook, plying a certain theory "about" the Eskimos, perhaps he or she might want to read Haines, read Nansen, read other spiritual kin of theirs: Dr. Elisha Kent Kane's two-volume account of his observations and experiences (from 1853 to 1855) in *Arctic Explorations* (Childs & Peterson, 1856), an account recently given a scholarly and appreciative examination by George Corner in *Doctor Kane of the Arctic Seas* (Temple, 1972); Isaac Hayes's narrative — another physician and an associate of Dr. Kane — contained in *An Arctic Boat Journey* (Houghton Mifflin, 1883); May Kellogg Sullivan's *A Woman Who Went to Alaska* (Earle, 1903); Commander Robert E. Peary's narrative of "a polar expedition," from 1905 to 1906, *Nearest the Pole* (Doubleday, 1907); Peter Freuchen's *Arctic Adventure* (Farrar & Rinehart, 1935) and *Book of the Eskimos* (World, 1961); Farley Mowat's *People of the Deer* (Atlantic–Little, Brown, 1952) and *The Desperate People* (Atlantic–Little, Brown, 1960), both intensely personal as well as factual and reportorial; Sheila Burnford's *One Woman's Arctic* (Atlantic–Little, Brown, 1972); Duncan Pryde's *Nunaga: Ten Years of Eskimo Life* (Walker, 1971).

There is a related tradition, kin to the above — a mixture of grandly related autobiographical adventure, factual presentation of relatively brief but strongly experienced Arctic visits, and so-called travel literature of a serious and quite detailed kind: *Son of the Smoky Sea,* by Nutchuk, a half-Norwegian, half-Eskimo lad who speaks through the help of Alden Hatch (Messner, 1941); Robert Marshall's arduous journeys of exploration and personal enjoyment, offered in *Alaska Wilderness* (University of California Press, 1970); Frederick Schwatka's *The Children of the Cold* (Educational, 1895), a lean, straightforward, and compelling account of "where and how they live," and a fine, unprepossessingly "psychological" discussion of "Eskimo patience": *Thrilling Tales of the Frozen North,* by William Wharton (Potter, 1895) — thrilling indeed, and true, and well written; *Alaska: An Empire in the Making,* by John Underwood (Dodd, Mead, 1913); *We Are Alaskans,* by Mary Lee Davis (Wilde, 1931); *The Land of Tomorrow,* by William Stephenson (Doran, 1919); *Alaska and the Canadian Northwest,* by Harold Griffin (Norton, 1944); *Our Summer with the Eskimos,* by Constance and Harmon Helmricks (Little, Brown, 1948); Katharine Scherman's *Spring on an Arctic Island* (Little, Brown, 1956); Edith Iglauer's modest but finely evocative *The New People* (Doubleday, 1966); the anthology *The Alaska Book,* full of interesting articles, among them the late Senator Ernest Gruening's essay "Alaska, The Forty-Ninth State," written originally for the 1959 *Britannica Book of the Year;* and finally, a pamphlet rather than a book, but a fascinating pamphlet, indeed: *In Alaska,* one of a series of "Selections from the *Youth's Companion.*" The last was in the nineteenth century an illustrated weekly family paper, whose aim was to "represent real life." The essays in the pamphlet on Alaska, published in 1897 (Perry Mason, Boston), are clearly and forthrightly written and full of shrewd comments. Perhaps one day we will be lucky enough to have similarly lucid and penetrating narrative essays coming out of the various social science departments of our universities.

To move on — to the best that those departments have given us: a fine report on one Eskimo village I happen to know quite well: *Point Hope,* by James Vanstone (University of Washington Press, 1962). The author conveys sensitively the contemporary pressures that exert themselves on coastal Eskimos. Another such sensitive account, broader in coverage, yet briefer, less detailed, is Norman Chance's *The Eskimo of North Alaska* (Holt, Rinehart & Winston, 1966). Perhaps the most comprehensive and longest ethnographic study of the Eskimo is Robert Spencer's *The North Alaskan Eskimo* (Smithsonian, 1969), an utterly necessary volume for anyone who wants to come to terms with the very best kind of Eskimo-oriented social anthropology. Also necessary, and a model of psychologically sensitive anthropological inquiry, is Jean L. Briggs's *Never in Anger* (Harvard University Press, 1970), a study of a small group of Eskimos who live in the Canadian Northwest Territories. The author is refreshingly candid and forthcoming about her own emotions, as well as those of the Eskimos, whose trust she only slowly earned, as she was shrewd enough to see — however gracious the hospitality she always received. The subtlety of Eskimo behavior is matched by her own delicacy of introspection. Also concerned with Eskimos of the Canadian Northwest Territories is Asen Balikci's *The Netsilik Eskimo* (American Museum of Natural History, 1970) and Diamond Jenness's *The People of the Twilight* (University of Chicago Press, 1959), both unpretentious but effective instruments of mediation between a distant land and the interested reader. And to move from Canada to Greenland, in Finn Gad's *The History of Greenland* (volume I) there is an invaluable discussion of the West Greenland Eskimo culture after 1650 (Hurst, 1970): history become brilliant social narration and cultural portrayal.

The Eskimos can be silent, then tersely, luminously eloquent. They can be silent because they are preoccupied with mental pictures rather than words — and not all such visual images get recorded for anyone, relative, friend, or neighbor, never mind busybody visitor with his secret (or so he thinks) research-minded grandiosity. We are lucky to have a few books that give a glimmer of Eskimo talk, Eskimo thought — connected to Eskimo artistic work. These are not especially well-known books, but they constitute a special kind of cultural documentary — a proud and reticent people's images, given us by publishers prepared to pay deference to the coherence others impose upon the world. One such book, slim and beautifully designed, is *Eskimo*; it is an effort of three outsiders to give many other outsiders a sense of the "space concepts" Eskimos have but, of course, don't talk about as such — their sense of where they live, their sense of place, its extent and bearing upon their lives. Edmund Carpenter has provided a succinct, poetic anthropological text, Frederick Varley a series of sketches, and Robert Flaherty has photographed Eskimo carvings (University of Toronto Press, 1970). Another quite beautifully (simply, even starkly) designed book is *Eskimo Art*, by Cottie Burland (Hamlyn, 1973). A series of prints, with short accompanying texts and a longer introduction, is to be found in *Arts of the Eskimo*, edited by Ernst Roch (Barre, 1975). The same conscientious publisher is responsible for James Houston's *Eskimo Prints* (1967), a less ambitious but no less intelligently arranged book. Edmund Carpenter, an anthropologist who knows the Eskimo quite well, has tried hard to bring alive Eskimo life through a blend of words and photographs of Eskimo "art objects." (The Eskimos would not like that phrase; they do not make things to hold them apart for abstract perusal, but rather create, construct, mold, build as part of being, living, affirming themselves — and hope that what is seen will help others along the same lines.) Carpenter's title, appropriately enough, is *Eskimo Realities* (Holt, Rinehart & Winston, 1973). And finally there is a book whose title is self-explanatory: *Alaskan Eskimo Life in the 1890's as Sketched by Native Artists*, by George Phebus (Smithsonian, 1972). An excellent, succinct text accompanies the gentle, finely wrought drawings. Many of the drawings were done by schoolchildren and are of obvious comparative value to those that appear in this book.

There are three short but immensely revealing books in which Eskimos themselves speak: *I Am Eskimo: Aknik My Name*, by Paul Green and illustrated by George Ahgupuk (Alaska Northwest, 1959), village tales of a kind often heard in Eskimo settlements; *Eskimo Songs and Stories*, translated by Edward Field and illustrated by Kiakshuk and Pudlo (Delacorte, 1973); and *I Breathe a New Song: Poems of the Eskimo*, edited by Richard Lewis and illustrated by Oonark.

There is, besides the Eskimo oral tradition, to a limited degree made "literary" by the above three books, a related fictional genre: poems, novels, and short stories inspired by Alaska and the Canadian Northwest, including the

Eskimos who live there, but written by outsiders, white Americans or Canadians who have trekked north, stayed, returned, set to work writing. Robert Service, for instance, who was born in 1874; he was a Canadian poet and novelist, two of whose volumes of poetry have to do with the Arctic life of Canada: *Songs of a Sourdough* (1907) and *Ballads of a Cheechako* (1909). His novel, *The Trail of '98* (1910), deals with the gold fever of those last years of the nineteenth century. Even today Eskimos pass down, generation to generation, stories about the madly greedy whites, hungry for a mere rock, a piece of "metal." Jack London was born two years after Service, in San Francisco, and he, too, went north to the Arctic. Later he worked what he saw into his novels: *The Son of the Wolf* (1900) and *The Call of the Wild* (1903). Both writers, by the way, were fed stories, factual and otherwise, by a legendary man, a sort of Paul Bunyan or John Henry — "Klondike Mike"; his story has been written up as *Klondike Mike: An Alaskan Odyssey,* by Merrill Denison (Johnson, 1948). More recently there have been James Houston's *The White Dawn,* "an Eskimo Saga," so-called, and certainly an exciting adventure story (Harcourt Brace Jovanovich, 1971); and the social psychiatrist Alexander Leighton's *Come Near* (Norton, 1971). Leighton's work with people from widely different backgrounds is itself a work of art as well as science; his novel is a tender and yet powerful one — an unusual and exemplary way for a psychiatrist to share knowledge gained in the course of "research"! For younger readers there have been, among others, Miriam MacMillan's *Etuk: The Eskimo Hunter* (Dodd, Mead, 1950) and *Julie of the Wolves,* by Jean Craighead George (Harper, 1972).

In a special class is Robert Flaherty's *Nanook of the North* — the great film documentary. A modest but powerful book (of the same title) has been made with footage from that documentary (Windmill, 1971). I think Flaherty would like very much *Dwellers of the Tundra,* an essay joined to photographs of "life in an Alaskan Eskimo village." The author and photographer are anthropologists: Aylette Jenness and Jonathan Jenness (Macmillan, 1970); they are also poets. And the same holds for the Canadian photographer Fred Bruemmer, who has graced us with lyrical and harshly "real" views of Eskimos in two first-rate volumes: *Seasons of the Eskimo: A Vanishing Way of Life* (New York Graphic Society, 1971) and *The Arctic* (Quadrangle, 1974). Other photographic books of help are *Alaska and Its Wildlife,* by Bryan Sage (Viking, 1973), a "subject" Eskimo children have their own, unscholarly way of approaching and coming to terms with, and *High Arctic,* by George Miksch Sutton (Eriksson, 1971), the visual record of an unusual "expedition to the unspoiled North" by a distinguished ornithologist. Eskimo children not only know a thing or two about birds, but about the men who fly single-engine planes — the so-called bush-pilots, whose life is described in *Sourdough Sky,* with pictures as a bonus. The authors are Stephen Mills and James Phillips (Bonanza, 1960). And finally, a splendid splash of color photographs in a large-sized book: *Alaska* by Robert Reynolds (Belding, 1971).

Education, for Eskimo children, is something to contend with, as well as experience. A book that sheds most light on a host of social and psychological problems connected with such education is *Education in the North* (University of Alaska Press, 1972). The editor is Frank Darrell, one of the world's leading authorities on the subject; he has gathered together a number of articles, all with references and bibliographies. The articles deal with "cross-cultural education" in the various "circum-polar nations" and provide an invaluable survey of the educational problems children face in Alaska, Canada, Greenland, the Soviet North, and so on. With respect to the education of Eskimo children, the University of Alaska has published a number of helpful pamphlets: *Teaching English to Alaska Natives*, by Lee Salisbury — a lovely essay; *Bilingual Education in Alaska*, by James Orvik; and various specific reports, such as *Educational Facilities for Aniak, Emmonak and Mountain Village Area High Schools*. I must mention, too, the film documentary work done by my friend Leonard Kamerling among the Eskimos of Alaska. He has tried to make films that the people of certain Arctic villages themselves consider to be honest expressions of what they have to say, what they feel about their particular lives, about "life." The result is work of depth and haunting beauty. Some of his footage and the words of some of the people he has worked with have been put into *Kassigeluremint* (which means "the people of Kasigluk"), a pamphlet issued by the University of Alaska's Rural School Project. (Kasigluk is a village west of Bethel on the Johnson River.)

I would like to mention some work done by psychiatrists, and especially the ongoing, sensitive, and important observations of Joseph Lubart — made among Canadian Eskimos. His paper "Field Study of the Problems of Adaptation of Mackenzie Delta Eskimos to Social & Economic Change" (*Psychiatry*, November 1969) is an example of the help a thoughtful psychiatrist can offer to students of social change. Also helpful is "Notes on Eskimo Patterns of Suicide" (*Southwestern Journal of Anthropology*, 11:24, 1955). Fairbanks harbors urban Eskimos; the city suffers from the constant pressures of a fast-growing state. Some of the results of that "growth" are documented in "Suicide and Culture in Fairbanks," by Michael Parkin (*Psychiatry*, February 1974), and by "Migration and Psychopathology of Eskimo Women," by Joseph Bloom (*American Journal of Psychiatry*, April 1973). An interesting ethnopsychiatric essay is Zachary Gussow's "Pibloktoq (Hysteria) Among the Polar Eskimo," in volume I of *The Psychoanalytic Study of Society* (International University Press, 1960). And finally, I must mention the *Tundra Times*, a weekly newspaper published in Fairbanks, Alaska; for years I have read it and found in it a constant flow of accurate, intelligent comment on the difficulties Eskimos must keep struggling with. But there are lively accounts of the "good news" Eskimos must also know and live by; the proof: their vital, generous selves. If there are moments of "hysteria" (few, actually) and hours of heavy drinking (many in some villages, none in others) there is also endurance, day in, day out — a lifetime of it, against odds I fear one like me can only try to suggest.

3. CHICANOS

BEFORE MOVING into the world of books directly about Chicanos, one ought, perhaps, for obvious historical, social, and cultural reasons, suggest some reading that is concerned with Mexico. Even the Spanish-speaking people of northern New Mexico, here the longest of those whose language is Spanish and who live in the Southwest, came from Mexico, however stubbornly they claim themselves *Spanish.* As for the people of the Rio Grande Valley, they know full well, thousands of them, that the great river both is and is not a barrier between Mexico and the United States. In their minds, in their hearts, and often physically, too, they go back and forth — legally or otherwise. In any event, Oscar Lewis's work is of obvious importance: *Pedro Martínez: A Mexican Peasant and His Family* (Random House, 1964); *The Children of Sánchez* (Random House, 1961); *Life in a Mexican Village: Tepoztlán Restudied* (University of Illinois Press, 1951); *Anthropological Essays* (Random House, 1970). His study of Tepoztlán is particularly interesting, and ought to be compared with Robert Redfield's report based on work done in the 1920s: *Tepoztlán: A Mexican Village* (University of Chicago Press, 1930). Another, more recent, study of Mexican village life is Lola Romanucci-Ross's *Conflict, Violence, and Morality in a Mexican Village* (National, 1973). And of obvious significance to anyone interested in Americans of Mexican ancestry is *Tijuana: Urbanization in a Border Culture,* by John A. Price (University of Notre Dame Press, 1973). Two books that provide a useful historical and sociological glimpse of Mexico are *The Mexicans: The Making of a Nation,* by Victor Alba (Pegasus, 1970) and Martin Needler's *Politics and Society in Mexico* (University of New Mexico Press, 1971). But the best way, perhaps, to approach Mexico is through Octavio Paz — *The Labyrinth of Solitude: Life and Thought in Mexico* (Grove, 1961); or through *The Good Conscience,* by Carlos Fuentes (Noonday, 1961); or through John Womack's extraordinary *Zapata and the Mexican Revolution* (Knopf, 1969); or through Frank Waters's *Mexico Mystique* (Swallow, 1974); or through the young novelist Carter Wilson's *A Green Tree and a Dry Tree* (Macmillan, 1972). An important book that traces the complex relationship between American writers (William Carlos Williams, Archibald MacLeish, Hart Crane, John Steinbeck, among others) and Mexico is Cecil Robinson's *With the Ear of Strangers* (University of Arizona Press, 1969).

I would more generally like to mention the work of several anthropologists who have observed peasant life in a number of countries. One obtains from those writers a sense of what a "field worker" might try better to do — but, more existentially, try to *be.* Starting with the latter: Hortense Powdermaker's quite moving *Stranger and Friend* (Norton, 1966); E. E. Evans-Pritchard's *Essays in Social Anthropology* (Free Press, 1963); Franz Boas's *Race, Language & Culture* (Free Press, 1940); Clifford Geertz's wonderful essay "From the Native's Point of View: On the Nature of Anthropological Understanding," *Bulletin of the American Academy of Arts & Sciences* (October 1974). Then, with respect to peasant life: Robert Redfield's brief but important *Peasant Society & Culture* (University of Chicago Press, 1957), and two anthologies — *Peasants in the Modern World,* edited by Philip Bock (University of New Mexico Press, 1969), and *Peasants in Cities,* edited by William Mongin (Houghton Mifflin, 1970).

There is a growing body of writing *by* Chicanos (novels, poems, essays, autobiographies), as opposed to the literature of the social science kind *about*

Chicanos. *Chicano Literature* provides a good introduction to the former; the editors are Antonia Castañeda Shular, Tomás Ybarra-Frausto, and Joseph Sommers, and they offer the reader a bilingual text (Prentice-Hall, 1972). *Aztlan: An Anthology of Mexican American Literature*, edited by Luis Valdez and Stan Steiner (Knopf, 1972), has a mixed "literary" and sociological content, as does *The Chicanos: Mexican American Voices*, edited by Ed Ludwig and James Santibañez (Penguin, 1971). An important collection of shorter fiction devoted to "the Mexican-American experience" is *The Chicano: From Carica-ture to Self-Portrait*, edited by Edward Simmen (Mentor, 1971). Some novels have been published that are of importance; Rudolfo Anaya's *Bless Me, Ultima* (Quinto Sol, 1972), for example. Anaya is from New Mexico and now lives in Los Angeles. Also, *The Plum Pickers*, by Raymond Barrio (Harper, 1971), which portrays Chicano migrant life in California. Texas migrant life is described faithfully in the novel *Return to Ramos*, by Leo Cardenas (Hill & Wang, 1970). *The Bracero*, a novel by Eugene Nelson (Thorp Springs, 1972), is concerned with migrant life. A very good novel of "acculturation" — a Mexican boy moves north to a barrio of Sacramento — is Ernesto Galarza's *Barrio Boy* (University of Notre Dame Press, 1971). Joseph Krumgold's *And Now, Miguel* (Crowell, 1953), though written for young readers, offers a valuable introduc-tion to the stable, rural life of the Spanish-speaking people of northern New Mexico. So do Sabine R. Ulibbari's fine stories, collected under the title of *Tierra Amarilla* (University of New Mexico Press, 1971); and so do (I hope) the sketches I attempted in *The Old Ones of New Mexico* (University of New Mexico Press, 1973). Of great interest is *I Am Joaquin*, Rodolfo ("Corky") Gonzales's epic poem, privately printed (1967) in Denver. He is an important political organizer of urban Chicanos; the poem is a powerful one.

An excellent bibliography, *The Mexican American*, edited by Luis Nogales, was published in 1971 (Stanford). Even so, one wants to mention a few books published before and after 1971 that are particularly helpful to those who want to learn about the fate of Chicano people. The largest and most comprehen-sive study is *The Mexican American People*, by Leo Grebler, Joan Moore, and Ralph Guzman (Free Press, 1970). The book would be considered "old" by some today. Each year is a century in the life of a political activist, and maybe, the life of a people struggling for a halfway decent life. But the authors offer their readers an enormous amount of information, and also an extensive bibliography. Another valuable book, if a bit "old," is *A Documentary History of the Mexican American*, edited by Wayne Moquin (Praeger, 1971). The book contains moving, instructive personal statements. Stan Steiner's *La Raza: The Mexican Americans* (Harper, 1970) provides a valuable introduction to the history and problems of Chicanos. A passionate and well-written history of the Spanish-speaking people of the Southwest — and by now a historical docu-ment itself — is Carey McWilliams's *North from Mexico*, originally published in 1948 and reissued in 1961 (Lippincott). Another, a more recent and also quite readable history, is *The Chicanos*, by Matt S. Meier and Feliciano Rivera (Hill & Wang, 1972).

Moving to shorter and more specialized volumes — to document one or another aspect of Chicano life in this country — I would especially recommend *Spanish-Speaking Children of the Southwest: Their Education and the Public Welfare,* by Herschel T. Manuel (University of Texas Press, 1965). It is one of the few books primarily concerned with Chicano *children* — from a sociological point of view. In the same tradition is Thomas P. Carter's *Mexican Americans in School: A History of Educational Neglect* (College Entrance Examination Board, 1970). And for those interested in pursuing the matter further, and thereby learning of the extent to which Chicanos have suffered educationally, there is *Materials Relating to the Education of Spanish-Speaking People in the United States,* an annotated bibliography (Greenwood, 1959).

My own work in the Rio Grande Valley of Texas was assisted considerably by a few books, most especially William Madsen's quite sensitive *The Mexican-Americans of South Texas* (Holt, Rinehart & Winston, 1964). An anthropologist, Madsen is wonderfully responsive to the psychological life of the people he writes about and clearly feels close to. Also quite impressive, and unique, too, is Carrol Norquest's *Rio Grande Wetbacks: Mexican Migrant Workers* (University of New Mexico Press, 1972). The author was a farmer for many years in the Valley and has written a series of sketches that tell about people, places, events. More scholarly is Arthur Rubel's *Across the Tracks: Mexican-Americans in a Texas City* (University of Texas Press, 1966). Rubel worked with William Madsen in the Rio Grande Valley. An analysis of the recent political changes taking place in the Valley is found in John Staples Shockley's *Chicano Revolt in a Texas Town* (University of Notre Dame Press, 1974). The town is Crystal City. And though it is not directly concerned with Texas, but rather southern California, Margaret Clark's *Health in the Mexican-American Culture* (University of California Press, 1970) offers a lot of information for a physician who wants to work with Chicano families. Also of considerable worth is Ari Kiev's *Curanderismo: Mexican American Folk Psychiatry* (Free Press, 1968), though now, even among isolated migrants, the value of modern medicine is usually appreciated, its absence regretted. And finally, Frank Kostyu's *Shadows in the Valley* (Doubleday, 1970) gives an unpretentious but strongly rendered account of "life" among migrants in the south of Texas.

In New Mexico my work with Spanish-speaking people was helped substantially by Nancie C. González's very fine *The Spanish-Americans of New Mexico* (University of New Mexico Press, 1967). She has recorded faithfully the pride and dignity of the people she knows so well. George Sanchez's *Forgotten People* (Calvin Horn, 1967) also concerns itself sympathetically with the same people. Peter Nabokov's *Tijerina and the Courthouse Raid* (University of New Mexico Press, 1969) is concerned with a specific moment of history, and with the brief celebrity of a political activist, but in the course of presenting "facts," he manages to convey rather a lot about the social and cultural problems of the people Reies Lopez Tijerina claimed to speak for. Another book that gives a good account of the same episode is *Grito,* by Richard Gardner (Harper, 1971). And finally, Leon Swadesh's *Los Primeros Pobladores: Hispanic Americans of the Ute Frontier* (University of Notre Dame Press, 1974) gives a first-rate historical account of the Spanish-speaking people who ventured north to the New Mexico–Colorado borderland and settled there.

570   REFERENCES

There are a number of relatively short, but all too thoroughly instructive (and saddening and enraging) books about the condition of Chicano migrants of the Southwest: Julian Samora's *Los Mojados: The Wetback Story* (University of Notre Dame Press, 1971); Ernesto Galarza's *Merchants of Labor: The Mexican Bracero Story* (McNally & Loftin, 1964); Ronald Taylor's *Sweatshops in the Sun* (Beacon, 1973), which is devoted to "child labor on the farm" and has a section on Chicano migrant children; *The Ripe Harvest*, an essential collection of essays by educators who have worked with migrant children, edited by Arnold Cheyney (University of Miami Press, 1972). A lovely, sensitive book in a class all its own is Celia S. Heller's *Mexican American Youth: Forgotten Youth at the Crossroads* (Random House, 1966). In a country attentive to the slightest fluctuations in mood of upper-middle-class youth, it is astonishing to come across this book — written in the early 1960s, when eyes were directed elsewhere, with respect to the subject of "youth."

There is a tradition of protest among Spanish-speaking people of the Southwest, even if it is a tradition unknown to Anglos who read books or (for that matter) Chicanos caught up in trying to get through a given day, never mind change their lot. David Weber has brought together a number of essays that evoke that tradition, under the title of *Foreigners in Their Native Land* (University of New Mexico Press, 1973). Another anthology, quite interesting and revealing, is *La Causa Chicana*, edited by Margaret Mongold (Family Service Association, 1972). The articles are grounded in contemporary reality and are less historically conscious than those in Weber's book, but they cover terrain largely ignored elsewhere; for example, the essay of Amado M. Padilla — a devastating critique, "Psychological Research and the Mexican American." He shows how narrow, distorted, and even arrogant such "research" has been — almost all of it done by Anglos, and as he puts it, done "with a laboratory-oriented approach." And he shows that the "results" invariably have been used to "prove" the inferiority, the psychological "backwardness" of Chicanos. One can only hope that he will have a new "literature" to examine in the near future.

Every oppressed people finds its leaders as it struggles for political and economic justice; Cesar Chavez has become one of those leaders, a man of Christian faith and uncompromising determination, a man whose own young life very much resembled the lives of millions of Chicanos, among them the hundreds of thousands of agricultural migrants in the Southwest. There are two biographies of Chavez, each well worth reading: Peter Matthiessen's *Sol Si Puedes: Cesar Chavez and the New American Revolution* (Random House, 1969) and Ronald Taylor's *Chavez and the Farm Workers* (Beacon, 1975). The corruptions and worse of California's agricultural life, as it affects Chicanos, have been documented in Ernesto Galarza's *Spiders in the House and Workers in the Field* (University of Notre Dame Press, 1970). One hopes his book will soon become (with the implementation in 1975 of a new state labor relations law that covers agricultural workers) a historical record rather than an achievement of contemporary social analysis. As long ago as 1920, there were excellent reports on how Chicanos lived (and suffered) in California; see *The Mexican in Los Angeles*, a survey — now reissued by R & E Research,

1970. The brief but strongly worded, affecting documentary essays continue: *Pain and Promise: The Chicano Today*, edited by Edward Simmen (Mentor, 1972); *The Chicanos: Life and Struggles of the Mexican Minority in the United States*, by Gilberto López y Rivas (Monthly Review, 1974); *Somos Chicanos: Strangers in Our Land*, by David Gomez (Beacon, 1973); *Mexican Americans in the Southwest*, by Ernesto Galarza, Herman Gallegos, and Julian Somora (McNally & Loftin, 1970); and not least, a thick report issued by the superintendent of documents at the Printing Office of the United States Government: *Hearings Before the United States Commission of Civil Rights*, held in San Antonio, Texas, December 9–14, 1968. Maybe those hearings are quite enough — all any of us needs to read. For those who were there, the long days of testimony provided lesson after lesson: victims and more victims.

Needless to say, the problems of bilingual education constantly bear down upon Chicano children — though unnecessarily, often enough, because the "problems" commonly are generated by Anglo school authorities rather than Chicano children, who usually have negotiated their way back and forth, between English and Spanish, far more successfully at home, or in the neighborhood, than in school, where until recently they were told to abandon Spanish and speak their schoolteacher's English. Two excellent books devoted to the educational issues of which almost every Chicano child has his or her own quite distinct knowledge are *Educating the Mexican American*, edited by Henry Sioux Johnson and William J. Hernandez (Judson Press, 1970), and *Living and Learning in Two Languages: Bilingual-Bicultural Education in the United States*, by Frances Willard Van Malitz (McGraw-Hill, 1975). And more broadly or conceptually, *Language and Poverty*, edited by Frederick Williams (Markham, 1970).

Finally, there are a number of references that are, perhaps, related by their possible value for someone who wants to approach the lives of Chicanos in a slightly irregular way — not through the obvious introductory or scholarly avenues. A truly exhaustive, and really quite loving, bibliography — yes, one exists! — is the "Selective Bibliography" that Matt S. Meier and Feliciano Rivera have issued "for the study of Mexican American History," published by the Spartan Bookstore of San Jose State College in California. *El Grito* has been a vigorous journal of "contemporary Mexican American thought," and *Voices: Readings from El Grito, 1967–1971* (Quinto Sol, 1971) sheds light in dozens of directions. So has every issue of *Aztlan,* a "Chicano Journal of the Social Sciences and the Arts," published by the Chicano Studies Center at the University of California at Los Angeles. A thin but touching book is Sandra Weiner's *Small Hands, Big Hands* (Pantheon, 1970). The book offers seven short but revealing portraits of Chicano migrants and has in addition some good photographs. In *Minorities and Politics*, edited by Henry Tobias and Charles Woodhouse (University of New Mexico Press, 1969), there is a marvelous chapter by Frances Swadesh: "The Alianza Movement of New Mexico: The Interplay of Social Change and Public Commentary." Another quite sensitive and scholarly article is Ozzie G. Simmons's "Mutual Images and Expectations of Anglo-Americans and Mexican-Americans," to be found in the Spring 1971 issue of *Daedalus*. And in *Psychiatry* (May 1975) is the article "Ego

Modalities in the Manifest Dreams of Male and Female Chicanos," by C. Brooks Brenneis and Samuel Roll, two psychologists who have helped along considerably a body of research that is all too meager.

Often as I went from the ranches of the Rio Grande Valley to San Antonio and took note of the various struggles of urban Chicanos, newly arrived from an agricultural life, I thought of a book I'd read in early 1970, a book about a barrio of Ciudad Guayana, Venezuela — but for all the world, in many respects, about the barrios of San Antonio. I have read and reread the book in recent years and strongly urge it on any reader who has had the patience to follow me this far in the thickets of a bibliographical essay; it is *The View from the Barrio,* by Lisa Redfield Peattie (University of Michigan Press, 1968). And I have also thought, over and over again, about the extraordinary thesis of a Harvard senior I had the privilege of working with: William C. Bryson's "The Social Basis of South Texas Bossism," a brilliant and many-sided examination of one important aspect of the Rio Grande Valley — and an example of what a college student can see and do, given his own determination, not to mention thoughtfulness and idealistic activism.

4. INDIANS

OF THE THREE peoples whose children this book is concerned with, the Indians have been the subject of by far the largest number of books — to the point that Chicanos and Eskimos, themselves not ignored recently, seem by comparison neglected. The University of Oklahoma Press, for instance, has a catalogue of no fewer than 250 books devoted to the American Indian — and from only one publisher! I remember going through that catalogue and wondering why anyone, anywhere, would want to write one word more — especially since the serious grievances of thousands of Indians have yet to be redressed, for all those millions of words. I suppose each writer hopes that one day soon there will be changes; and so his or her words will, finally, be of some use: as background, as data, as ideas or observations to be kept in mind by those working on behalf of, or alongside, Indians — who do not themselves need historical or visual reminders but who don't mind if a few more whites (as I heard one Indian boy put it) "find out about themselves by finding out what they tried to do to us, and how we fought back, and we still do."

In that vein, I mention certain books that have helped me, meant a lot to me, or educated me. I begin with the Indian writer N. Scott Momaday: *The Way to Rainy Mountain* (University of New Mexico Press, 1969) and *House Made of Dawn* (Harper & Row, 1968). The first is a meditation of sorts, a look by a distinguished Indian scholar and writer at the legendary and metaphysical roots of his people, the Kiowa. The second is a sad, piercing novel — an Indian trying to comprehend the white world, which he cannot ignore (no Indian can) and which he has such good reason to fear, distrust, hate. Momaday has managed to evoke the complexity and ambiguity of the Indian experience in this country. He is a marvelous storyteller.

We are, incidentally, lucky to have a comprehensive bibliography whose title tells us what it does indeed offer: *American Indian and Eskimo Authors*, compiled by Arlene Hirschfelder for the Association on American Indian Affairs (the association, 1973). It is interesting to compare the literary tradition of the Indians with that of the Chicanos or the Eskimos. Chicanos have, of course, moved back and forth, speaking Spanish, speaking English. The Indians had their various languages, too — but were militarily subdued and compelled to speak English. Chicanos have wandered across the nation, come to grips more casually with its (Anglo) language and culture. And, of course, Eskimos have been, for a long time, removed from all but the harsh world of Arctic weather and the demands of survival — though not so now. There are many, many times more novels, poems, or essays written by Indians than by Chicanos or Eskimos, and as mentioned earlier, quite literally hundreds more books have been devoted to Indian life. As a result this section of the bibliographical essay will be shorter. Any attempt to be even remotely as comprehensive with regard to books by or about Indians as I try to be with regard to the "literature" on Chicanos and Eskimos would require a book itself. One can hope only to lead the reader to certain points of departure.

To continue with Indian writers: *Come to Power* offers eleven contemporary American Indian poets (Crossing Press, 1974); *The Man to Send Rain Clouds* offers contemporary stories by American Indians (Viking, 1974); *Shaking the Pumpkin* offers the more traditional poetry of American Indians — a wide range of it (Doubleday, 1972); so do *In the Trail of the Wind* (Farrar, Straus & Giroux, 1971) and *The Magic World* (Morrow, 1971). Each of those books offers not only poems or stories but songs, orations, declarations, outcries, and not least, reveries that are highly idiosyncratic and very much connected to tribal customs and traditions. There are, too, larger stories, longer poems: *Four Masterworks of American Indian Literature*, edited and with commentary by John Bierhorst (Farrar, Straus & Giroux, 1974); full-length novels, such as James Welch's highly regarded *Winter in the Blood* (Harper & Row, 1974), or Thomas Fall's *The Ordeal of Running Standing* (McCall, 1970). For children there are *The Trees Stand Shining*, which contains poetry of American Indians, accompanied by the paintings of Robert Parker, who lived as a child at the edge of the Mescelero Apache reservation in New Mexico (Dial, 1971); also, *American Indian Tales & Legends*, nicely illustrated by Miloslav Traup (Hamlyn, 1965); and, quite instructive, Betty Baker's lovely *Big Push*, a strong evocation of Hopi childhood, illustrated by the wife of a Hopi, Bonnie Johnson (Coward, McCann & Geoghegan, 1972). And Nancy Wood's brief and luminous arrangements of Pueblo wisdom, *Many Winters* (Doubleday, 1974), is meant for people of all ages — for anyone who cares to be touched by the old Indian men and women of the Taos Pueblo.

There is, of course, a substantial Indian literature and social history written by white observers, visitors, travelers, friends. The books mentioned at the beginning of this essay are part of that genre — for instance, James Fenimore Cooper's *The Last of the Mohicans*, or the *Indian Sketches* of John Treat Irving, Jr., the nephew of Washington Irving (University of Oklahoma Press, 1955). Irving reported, Cooper used his imagination; so it still goes —

with H. L. Van Brunt's *Indian Territory and Other Poems* (The Smith, 1974), a poet's effort to draw on his Oklahoma origins, or with Conrad Richter's *A Country of Strangers* (Knopf, 1966), a novel that grapples with Indianness, if one may put it that way, and whiteness: how does the Indian get to think of himself as such, as *not* white, as very much and distinctively a member of a particular tribe? Ross Santee's *Apache Land* (University of Nebraska Press, 1971) offers almost exquisitely wrought sketches of one tribe's life. Oliver La Farge's *Laughing Boy* has been justly hailed over the decades (Houghton Mifflin, 1929 and 1957); his many other essays and reports on the Indians of the Southwest also deserve mention, as does Edmund Wilson's *Apologies to the Iroquois* (Farrar, Straus & Giroux, 1960), which (like so much of his writing) stands out as a landmark of shrewd social analysis.

Indian cultural critics and political activists have made their mark increasingly on the American reader's consciousness: Vine Deloria's *We Talk, You Listen* (Macmillan, 1970) and *Custer Died for Your Sins* (Macmillan, 1969); Alvin Josephy's scholarly but forceful *The Indian Heritage of America* (Knopf, 1968) and *Red Powder* (American Heritage, 1971). Certain whites have, in that regard, helped out: Stan Steiner's *The New Indians* (Harper, 1968); Ralph Andrist's *The Long Death* (Macmillan, 1964), a social history of the last days (of self-government and dignity) the Plains Indians knew; Alice Marriott and Carol Rachlin, with their *American Epic: The Story of the American Indian* (Putnam's, 1969); John Terrell, with *Apache Chronicle* (World, 1972) and a number of other books about Indians in general, the Navahos in particular; Dee Brown's *Bury My Heart at Wounded Knee*, with the pointed subtitle *An Indian History of the American West* (Holt, Rinehart & Winston, 1970); an important anthology, edited by Elsie Clews Parsons, *American Indian Life* (University of Nebraska Press, 1923 and 1970) and full of wise, reflective anthropological essays — old but still (and in some instances, unfortunately) up to date; and Angie Debo's *A History of the Indians of the United States* (University of Oklahoma Press, 1970). The list could be doubled, tripled.

The various professions have been brought into contact with Indian life, sometimes to valuable effect: activist lawyers and doctors who have given of themselves above and beyond the call of duty, as defined by the Bureau of Indian Affairs. The relationship of Indian rights to white man's law has been carefully documented in *Red Man's Land, White Man's Law*, by Wilcomb Washburn (Scribner's, 1971), a history of the Indian's legal status in America. And *American Indian Medicine*, by Virgil Vogel (University of Oklahoma Press, 1971), examines the culture of various Indian tribes through a scrutiny of their medical beliefs and practices over the generations.

The anthropological literature on American Indians is substantial, to say the least. Two important volumes of a general, descriptive nature are: *Indians of North America*, by Harold Driver (University of Chicago Press, 1970), and *The North American Indians: A Sourcebook*, edited by Roger Owen, James Deetz, and Anthony Fisher (Macmillan, 1967), a big and helpful book, full of valuable articles by distinguished anthropologists. Two anthologies of importance are *Social Anthropology of North American Tribes*, edited by Fred Eggan (University of Chicago Press, 1955), and *Personalities and Cultures*, edited by

Robert Hunt (Natural History, 1967), which is only partly concerned with the New World, but in a quite special way — for instance, David F. Aberle's "The Psychosocial Analysis of a Hopi Life-History." Murray Wax's *Indian Americans* (Prentice-Hall, 1971) offers an intelligent and psychologically sophisticated anthropological survey of present-day Indian difficulties (personal and educational as well as political and economic).

There is an oral history, it can be called, of American Indians, some of it of the unself-conscious but eloquent kind that preceded by decades the emergence of the "field" called "oral history" — for instance, Charles Eastman's *Indian Boyhood* (McClure, Phillips, 1902). More recently, there is *To Be an Indian* (Holt, Rinehart & Winston, 1971) and *I Have Spoken,* a compilation of Indian voices, edited by Virginia Armstrong (Swallow, 1971), and yes, the voices of Indian scholars too — in *Indian Voices, The First Convocation of American Indian Scholars* (Indian Historian Press, 1970), the essays of which possess an unusually candid and often autobiographical tone. And Herman Grey's *Tales from the Mohaves* (University of Oklahoma Press, 1970) walks a tightrope between personal statement and fictional elaboration or disguise.

The social history of the Indian, as recorded by the white man, tells a lot about the white man as well as the victimized "subject," known as the "red man." The Indian, like the black man, has constantly held up a mirror to America. In this regard, Colonel Richard Irving Dodge's *Our Wild Indians* (Worthington, 1883) offers an instructive account of a military man's thirty-three years' personal experience among, as he put it, "the red men of the Great West." One learns of their social life, their religion, their "habits, traits, customs and exploits." One is provided with "thrilling adventures." One even has the privilege of reading an introduction by General William Tecumseh Sherman, to whom the book is dedicated. But most importantly, one senses struggle within the author: he went West to bring the Indians under "control," but he couldn't help noticing and remarking upon how decent, honorable, and intelligent, by and large, they were — and how unfairly they were treated. And so his large book, by implication, constantly describes the condition of nineteenth-century America's white man. More explicitly, there is *The Reformers and the American Indian* (University of Missouri Press, 1971), by Robert Winston Mardock — a view of the struggle a few generous and kind spirits waged, so often without success, against their government's political, military, and economic policies. Also valuable is *Americanizing the American Indian,* an anthology edited by Francis Paul Prucha (Harvard University Press, 1973); in it one reads the arguments of those in the nineteenth century who wanted to do away with reservations, break up the tribal structure, make the Indian "just like others." In the name of compassion, an assault on a people and their culture was advocated and launched. Also helpful is Helen Hunt Jackson's nineteenth-century eloquent classic of social protest, *A Century of Dishonor* (Harper, 1881 and 1965). She makes it all too clear what was done to the Indian *and why,* as does Wilbur Jacobs in a recent historical work, *Dispossessing the American Indian* (Scribners, 1972); and as did the anthropologist Clark Wissler in his influential books *Red Man Reservations* (Collier, 1971) and *Indians of the United States* (Doubleday, 1945).

In his own quiet, idiosyncratic, and suggestive way Frank Waters, the novel-ist, essayist, social and religious philosopher, has tried to do the same — reveal to us ourselves, our Anglo selves, our white selves, as he went about letting us know how the Spanish-speaking and Indian people of the Southwest live and think and feel. He belongs in the company of Paul Horgan and J. Frank Dobie — a "literary" man as well as a social observer, a man of wisdom and cultivation whose "perspective," as it is put these days, might be de-scribed as broad enough to be transcendent and, maybe, liberating. His *The Man Who Killed the Deer* is a novel about Pueblo Indian life — and more: the values of a people given the life of fiction (Swallow, 1942 and 1970). His book *Pumpkin Seed Point* is an autobiographical account of his experiences with the Hopi; he lived among them for several years (Swallow, 1969). His *Masked Gods* (University of New Mexico Press, 1950) is a detailed and important study of Navaho and Pueblo "ceremonialism" — the Indian view of life. It is a study that offers the general reader what anthropologists like Elsie Clews Parsons have offered social scientists — an understanding of a religious tradition quite different from the prevailing American one. His *Book of the Hopi* (Ballantine, 1963) brings Hopi mythology alive and is utterly indispensable for anyone who goes among that stubbornly peaceful people. His *People of the Valley* (Swal-low, 1941 and 1969) is a novel that reveals how it goes for New Mexico's Spanish-speaking people, caught as they are between their own past and our America's pressing, technological world. Swallow Press has also published an interesting series of *Conversations with Frank Waters* (1971) that deserves a wide readership.

There are other helpful if somewhat less inspired books about the Pueblos and Hopis that readers of this book might find of interest: *The Zunis: Self Portrayals* — the authors, the Zuni people themselves, and the sympathetic publishers, the University of New Mexico Press, 1972; *The Tewa World*: a monograph on the Pueblos of New Mexico by Alfonso Ortiz (University of Chicago Press, 1969); and, edited by the same author, a collection of recent essays by various social scientists, called *New Perspectives on the Pueblos* (University of New Mexico Press, 1972); *The Pueblo Indians of North America*, by Edward Dozier (Holt, Rinehart & Winston, 1970); and, by the same pub-lisher (1966) and same author, *Hano: A Tewa Indian Community in Arizona*; *Cochiti: A New Mexico Pueblo, Past & Present* by Charles H. Lange (Univer-sity of Southern Illinois Press, 1968); *The Hopi Way*, by Laura Thompson and Alice Joseph (Russell & Russell, 1965), originally issued in 1944 under the sponsorship of the United States Indian Service, as the government agency was then called; *The Fourth World of the Hopis*, by Harold Courlander (Crown, 1971); *The Hopi Child*, by Wayne Dennis (Appleton-Century, 1940, and Arno, 1972), a finely done evocation of the social and cultural side of Hopi childhood, with first-rate psychological observations worked into the text gently and helpfully; *Culture in Crisis: A Study of the Hopi Indians*, by Laura Thompson (Russell & Russell, 1950); Erna Fergusson's delightful *Dancing Gods: Indian Ceremonials of New Mexico and Arizona* (University of New Mexico Press, 1931 and 1970); and, on the same subject, Elsie Clews Parsons's monograph *Hopi and Zuni Ceremonialism*, available as a reprint (Kraus,

1964). Two other monographs of hers, *The Social Organization of the Tewa of New Mexico* and *A Pueblo Indian Journal: 1920–1921,* are also available and worth getting to know (Kraus, 1974). And finally, a gentle book, lovely to behold, with extraordinary photographs and Indian testimonies: *Mother Earth, Father Sky,* with photographs by Marcia Keegan (Grossman, 1974).

There are other books about Indians with photographs — scores of them. One has a hard time knowing which to mention. For historical reasons, as well as on their own merit, Edward Curtis's early twentieth-century photographs are of enormous significance: *Portraits from North American Indian Life* (Promontory, 1972) and *In a Sacred Manner We Live* (Barre, 1972) and *The North American Indians* (Aperture, 1972). Also of great historical value are A. C. Vroman's Southwestern Indian photographs, published as *Dwellers at the Source* (Grossman, 1973). Norman Feder's thick, comprehensive *American Indian Art* (Abrams, 1965) provides the reader with a sense of the attachment Indians feel to their own history and indicates the way they use their artistic impulses to say so. George Catlin, the nineteenth-century artist who regarded the Indian so carefully, emphasized at every turn how intimately Indians live with their aesthetic and cultural values — not the lip service some of the rest of us all too casually pay. Harold M. Cracken's *George Catlin and the Old Frontier* (Dial, 1959) offers a careful biography and dozens of reproductions, in color and in black and white. Also of significance is a book of photographs from the Wanamaker expedition of 1913, an attempt (one in a continuing series that span decades, centuries even) of concerned white people to learn about (with reform in mind) the "condition" of Indians. The result: extraordinarily direct, thoughtful photographs, many of which are included in *American Indian Portraits,* edited by Charles Reynolds (Stephen Green, 1971). And finally, *The Pottery of San Ildefonso Pueblo,* by Kenneth Chapman (University of New Mexico Press, 1970), an illustrated, scholarly but accessible introduction to and survey of an important aspect of Pueblo life.

Though I spent much less time with Navaho children than with Pueblo or Hopi children, I want to mention a few books that take up Navaho life in different ways — especially because when I was an undergraduate at Harvard I had the privilege of taking one of Clyde Kluckhohn's courses, and was surprised at how many of his ideas and observations had become buried in my mind for two decades, only to emerge as I was wandering from reservation to reservation, and within them, home to home, in the 1970s. So, in gratitude and respect: *Children of the People,* by Dorothea Leighton and Clyde Kluckhohn (Harvard University Press, 1947), and *The Navaho,* published a year earlier by the same authors and the same press. More recently there has been an important collection of essays, dedicated to Clyde Kluckhohn, and edited by Evon Vogt and Ethel Albert: *People of Rimrock: A Study of Values in Five Cultures* (Harvard University Press, 1966). The Navahos figure prominently in the essays, but so do the Zuni, the Spanish-speaking people of New Mexico, Mormons, and Texas homesteaders, all of whom live near one another in northern and western New Mexico. Very much worth reading, in addition, are the following: T. D. Allen's *Navahos Have Five Fingers* (University of Oklahoma Press, 1963); *The Fifth World of Foster Bennett,* by Vincent Craponzano (Viking, 1972), an important critique of anthropology and, too, a portrayal of the Navahos, as met and seen by yet another outsider; John Upton Terrell's *The Navahos* (Weybright and Talley, 1970); *The Navaho Mountain Community*, by Mary Shepardson and Blowden Hammond (University of California Press, 1970); and recently reissued (University of Nebraska Press, 1966), the touching *Son of Old Man Hat*, a Navaho autobiography recorded by Walter Dyk.

I cannot even begin to mention dozens of books that concern themselves with the various other American Indian tribes of our Plains, or of the Northwest, or even the East. Yet, because many of Canada's Indians live near its Eskimo people and share their fate, not unlike the fate of Alaska's Eskimos, and because it is important for readers in the United States of America, who may be acquainted with our history, to realize that there is a larger (cultural and geographical) context to that history, I want to mention *The Unjust Society: The Tragedy of Canada's Indians* (Hurtig, 1969). And I also want to mention two especially sensitive and psychologically sophisticated anthropological studies that are of help to the reader interested in America's Indians, even if the immediate concern of the authors is Canada and its problems: *The Ojibwa Woman*, by Ruth Landes (Norton, 1971), an excellent analysis of how men and women grow up (differently) among the Ojibwa Indians of western Ontario; and *Indian and White*, a study of "self-image and interaction" among the people of a Canadian plains community, by Wiels Winther Braroe (Stanford, 1975).

Finally, as with Chicanos, one makes mention of federal efforts at documentation; they have been numerous, extensive, and sadly ineffective in mobilizing political change — no reflection on them, merely a statement about the relationship between the "word," so to speak, and the crude matter of "power." All one need do is read the several volumes of the most recent survey of Indian education — and then go visit the schools run by the Bureau of Indian Affairs in Alaska or New Mexico, to realize the continuing discrepancy between what is known and what *is*. See *Hearings Before the Subcommittee on Indian Education* of the Committee on Labor and Public Welfare, 1969 (Government Printing Office), and *Indian Education: A National Tragedy, A National Challenge*, issued by the same committee in 1969. In Canada there is the two-volume *A Survey of the Contemporary Indians of Canada*, published by the Indian Affairs Branch of the Canadian government in 1967.

So far as my own profession goes, there is a valuable tradition of inquiry: "Acute Culture Conflict in a Hopi Adolescent," by Aaron H. Canter, in *Clinical Studies in Culture Conflict*, edited by Georgene Seward (Ronald, 1958), and, in the same volume, "Search for Identity by a Mexican-American" by Horace Peak — two excellent accounts of how particular human beings have managed psychologically under the stresses of "culture conflict"; Clyde Kluckhohn's "Some Aspects of Navaho Infancy and Early Childhood," published in *Psychoanalysis and the Social Sciences*, edited by Geza Roheim (International University Press, 1947); Bert Kaplan's excellent "Psychological Themes in Zuni Mythology and Zuni TAT's" in volume II of *The Psychoanalytic Study of Society*, edited by Warner Muensterberger and Sidney

Axelrod (International University Press, 1962); in *Psychiatry* (August 1971) a fine essay, "Changes in Mastery Style with Age: A Study of Navaho Dreams," by Alan Krohn and David Gutmann; and in the *American Journal of Psychiatry*, Robert Bergman's important and moving account of his work with the Navahos: "A School for Medicine Men" (June 1973). Also of value, in the same journal, is "A System of Neglect: Indian Boarding Schools," by Eric Dlugokinski and Lyn Kramer (June 1974). These articles, one after the other, tell of efforts by psychiatrists to struggle against alcoholism, apathy, suicide — the accumulated sadness and despair of what has been, alas, a persisting endemic form of American colonialism exerted within our borders.